D1326272

Emigration from North-East Scotland

VOLUME TWO

Beyond the Broad Atlantic

AUP titles of related interest

THE ELGINS 1766-1917
a tale of aristocrats, proconsuls and their wives
Sydney Checkland

PERSPECTIVES IN SCOTTISH SOCIAL HISTORY
essays in honour of Rosalind Mitchison
editor Leah Leneman

PORTABLE UTOPIA
Glasgow and the United States 1820-1920
Bernard Aspinwall

ABERDEENSHIRE TO AFRICA
Northeast Scots and British Overseas Expansion
John D Hargreaves

THE LIFE OF LORD MOUNT STEPHEN
Heather Gilbert
Vol One: Awakening Continent
Vol Two: The End of the Road

Emigration from North-East Scotland

VOLUME TWO

Beyond the Broad Atlantic

MARJORY HARPER

ABERDEEN UNIVERSITY PRESS

First published 1988
Aberdeen University Press
A member of the Pergamon Group

© Marjory Harper 1988

British Library Cataloguing in Publication Data

Harper, Marjory
Emigration from north-east Scotland
1. Scotland. North-east Scotland
Emigration 1800-1900
I. Title
304.8′09412

ISBN 0 08 036415 2 V.1
ISBN 0 08 036393 8 V.2

180014

MORAY DISTRICT
LIBRARY SERVICE

325·2

PRINTED IN GREAT BRITAIN
THE UNIVERSITY PRESS
ABERDEEN

CONTENTS

List of Illustrations   vi
Preface   ix
Abbreviations   xi

1 STIMULATING THE EMIGRANT   1
2 'THE GOLDEN WEST—GRANARY OF THE WORLD'   51
3 'NATURE'S GENTLEMEN'   102
4 THE RELUCTANT EMIGRANT   147
5 PHILANTHROPY AND EMIGRATION   183
6 THE FEMALE EMIGRANT   231
EPILOGUE   288

Bibliography   293
Index   303

ILLUSTRATIONS

1   Canadian advertising for immigrants from Great Britain, c.1900-1910. Public Archives of Canada, C9671   22

2   Scottish immigrants waiting to go ashore at Quebec, c.1911. Public Archives of Canada, 10225   24

3   Scottish immigrants, Quebec, c.1911. Public Archives of Canada, 10268   25

4   A typical new town on the prairies, c.1900. Public Archives of Canada, C30143   85

5   Coutts Marjoribanks. Courtesy of the Earl of Haddo   124

6   First passenger train to Vernon, 14 October 1891. Courtesy of the Earl of Haddo   125

7   Guisachan Ranch. Courtesy of the Earl of Haddo   126

8   The Jam Factory, Vernon. Courtesy of the Earl of Haddo   126

9   Coldstream Ranch. Courtesy of the Earl of Haddo   129

10   Lord Aberdeen and Edward Kelly at Coldstream. Courtesy of the Earl of Haddo   131

11   After a hunting trip, Guisachan. Courtesy of the Earl of Haddo   133

12   Walhachin today   137

13   Herring boats, Fraserburgh Harbour. George Washington Wilson Collection, Aberdeen University Library, C2618   154

14   William Quarrier. Courtesy of Quarrier's Homes   190

15   Quarrier's Orphan Homes of Scotland. Courtesy of Quarrier's Homes   191

16   Fairknowe Receiving Home, Brockville, Ontario. Courtesy of Quarrier's Homes   194

17   William Booth   211

18   Immigrants for domestic service, Quebec, c.1911. Public Archives of Canada, C9652   238

19   The Countess of Aberdeen in her going-away dress, 1877. (Presentation engraving for Haddo tenantry)   248

20   Haddo House, Tarves, Aberdeenshire   249

MAPS

1	Canada	33
2	Territory covered by John McBean, 1902-1906	82
3	British Columbia	114
4	The Okanagan Valley, British Columbia	115

Preface

During most of the nineteenth century British—and Scottish—emigration statistics were dominated by the massive exodus to the USA. Yet from the earliest days of the movement emigrants from the North-East corner of Scotland showed a distinct preference for settlement in Canada. This preference became even more marked towards the end of the nineteenth century, and in the three decades preceding the First World War the history of emigration from the North-East region became virtually the history of emigration to the Dominion of Canada alone.

This study analyses the reasons for Canada's continuing—and increasing—popularity with emigrants from the counties of Kincardine, Aberdeen, Banff, Elgin (Moray) and Nairn. It discusses how the Dominion's attributes were consistently promoted in the region, sometimes, it seems, to the virtual exclusion of other destinations, and it assesses the crucial part played by agents in encouraging and organising emigration. Different categories of emigrants clearly had different needs and ambitions. Farmers and farm labourers continued to crave personal independence and better prospects for their families; business and professional people sought improved outlets for their capital and energies; tradesmen were attracted by the offer of high wages, often as temporary contract workers; a significant number of women responded to the insatiable Canadian demand for domestic servants, often going out in organised emigrant parties; and contingents of destitute children were despatched by a variety of philanthropic agencies to make a fresh start on the other side of the Atlantic. The factors which stimulated and sustained these different aspects of the emigration movement are examined, with reference to the ways in which the emigrants' expectations were fulfilled or disappointed by their subsequent experiences.

It would be impossible to acknowledge all the assistance I have received in researching and writing this book. My colleagues at Aberdeen University have, through formal and informal discussions, helped me to clarify my ideas and encouraged me to investigate new avenues of enquiry. The conferences and seminars organised by the Centre of Canadian Studies in Edinburgh not only broadened my knowledge of Canadian affairs, past and present, but also gave me the opportunity to discuss my own work; I am grateful to Ged Martin for inviting me to these meetings and for introducing me to scholars from both sides of the Atlantic who have themselves subsequently provided me with help and advice. Numerous librarians and archivists greatly eased the task of locating sources of information; and I am especially grateful to the staff of the inter-library loan department of Aberdeen University Library, and to Myrtle Anderson-Smith and Mary Williamson of the Department of Special Collections for their help over the last four years.

I owe a particular debt of thanks to the individuals who allowed me to make use of their private collections of papers. The late John McBean of Inverness gave me completely free access to the extensive correspondence of his uncle, and subsequently deposited these papers in Aberdeen University Archives. The Earl of Haddo permitted me not only to make use of unpublished papers in the Haddo House Archive but also to reproduce Canadian photographs from the private albums of the Aberdeen family. Gilbert Buchan and Annie Noble of Inverallochy provided me with some fascinating insights into emigration from fishing communities, and I received further help in researching this topic from Malcolm Gray and James Coull, as well as from numerous Canadian correspondents. It is always a pleasure to visit Quarrier's Homes at Bridge of Weir; not only are the records a mine of information, but I am always made welcome by Willam Dunbar and his staff, who suffer uncomplainingly my intrusion into their working day. Similarly, it was a pleasure to spend time in the Archives of the Salvation Army International Headquarters in London, and I am grateful to Major Jenty Fairbank for her help in identifying relevant sources of information. Major W. L. Brown of the Salvation Army in Toronto also went to a great deal of trouble on my behalf in compiling lists of Scottish settlers who emigrated to Canada under the Salvation Army's auspices.

Part of the research for this book was undertaken during a six-week trip to North America, which would not have been possible without financial support from the Canadian High Commission and the Carnegie Trust, in the form of a Canada Research Award and a Carnegie Travel Grant. I am indebted to many individuals whose assistance and hospitality enabled me to make best use of that research visit, in particular Professor Edward Cowan of the University of Guelph and Dr Hugh MacMillan, Ontario Archives Liaison Officer. The courteous and efficient staff of the Public Archives of Canada—especially Pat Kennedy, Marianne McLean, Bennett McCardle and Tom Nesmith—were always on hand to offer help and information, as were the staff of the Provincial Archives of Ontario and British Columbia and the local museums in Vernon and Kelowna, British Columbia. Professor Margaret Ormsby welcomed me to her home in the Okanagan Valley, where we discussed the merits of Lord Aberdeen's fruit-farming ventures in that most beautiful part of British Columbia; and Robert Middleton too spared time to share with me the fruit of his own researches into the Aberdeen family's British Columbian adventures.

Once again, I am grateful to the University of Aberdeen Development Trust for financial support in the form of a Research Fellowship in Northern Scottish History, which has allowed me to undertake this work, and also for generous assistance with publication costs.

Abbreviations

AFP   *Aberdeen Free Press*
AJ   *Aberdeen Journal*
ALU   *Aberdeen Ladies' Union*
APL   *Aberdeen Public Library*
AUA   *Aberdeen University Archives*
Blackwood's   *Blackwood's Edinburgh Magazine*
BWEA   British Women's Emigration Association
Chambers'   *Chambers' Edinburgh Journal*
CIL   Colonial Intelligence League
CPR   Canadian Pacific Railway
DNB   *Dictionary of National Biography*
EE   *Evening Express*
EG   *Evening Gazette*
EIO   Emigrants' Information Office
FH   *Fraserburgh Herald*
FMCES   Female Middle Class Emigration Society
GCJ   *Granite Cutters' Journal*
GFS   Girls' Friendly Society
GRA   Grampian Region Archives
NCW   National Council of Women
NRA   National Register of Archives
NUWW   National Union of Women Workers
PAC   Public Archives of Canada
PP   Parliamentary Paper
SACS   South Africa Colonisation Society
SAX   South Africa Expansion Committee
SOSBW   Society for the Overseas Settlement of British Women
VON   Victorian Order of Nurses
West. Rev.   *Westminster Review*

CHAPTER I

Stimulating the Emigrant

For several centuries before 1763 emigration, although an ever-present feature of Scottish life, had been a sporadic, localised and unco-ordinated movement of individuals or small groups. It remained of little numerical significance until the late eighteenth century, when considerable numbers of Highlanders began to respond to rising rents and successive bad harvests by leaving for America, not now as individuals, but in organised emigrant parties. Then in the nineteenth century emigration became an established national—indeed international—phenomenon, involving participants of various classes and occupations from all over Britain and Europe. The exodus gathered momentum as the century progressed; for whereas 9,242,039 people left the British Isles in the sixty-six years between 1815 and 1880, a total of 12,691,620 emigrants was to leave in the next thirty-three years before 1914. While the United States continued to account for the majority of these emigrants, its predominance came to depend more and more on the large numbers of foreigners who sailed from British ports, rather than on emigrants of British origin.[1] The development of enthusiastic agency work, combined with the growth of imperialist sentiment in the late nineteenth century, increasingly diverted the attention of British emigrants to Britain's overseas territories, particularly across the Atlantic. Canada absorbed twenty per cent of the exodus from the British Isles in the period 1881-1913, and in 1913 it accounted for the majority of such departures for the first time since 1834. Twenty-nine per cent of the 1,150,927 Scottish emigrants in this period went to Canada, and it was the favourite destination of the Scots in six of the seven years 1907-13.[2] Meanwhile Canada's particular popularity with emigrants from North-East Scotland, which had been evident since the early nineteenth century, became even more pronounced after 1880. In this area Canadian settlement was consistently advocated by a variety of local, as well as national, promoters, at times to the virtual exclusion of other destinations. As a result, the history of emigration from North-East Scotland increasingly seems to have become—with a few exceptions—the history of the exodus to Canada, and the different aspects of this transatlantic movement will be examined in detail in the following study.

But such a local emigrant movement should first be set in a wider context. For instance, what were the prevailing attitudes towards emigration *per se* and towards different destinations in late nineteenth and early twentieth

1

century Britain, and how did changing attitudes and policies affect the volume and direction of the movement? What were the main needs and ambitions of the 12,691,620 emigrants who sailed from the British Isles between 1881 and 1913? How were they informed and persuaded of better opportunities abroad, and by what means might indigent emigrants be sponsored?

State-aided emigration: the pros and cons

The agricultural and commercial depression which afflicted the British Isles in the late nineteenth century gave rise to renewed arguments in favour of state-aided emigration. More than a decade after the short-lived National Emigration League had failed to persuade the government to endorse state-aided emigration, the cause was revived through the formation in July 1883 of the National Association for Promoting State-Directed Emigration and Colonisation. This pressure group put forward more coherent arguments than its predecessor, whose diverse membership had been unable to agree on the precise meaning and application of 'state-aided' emigration.[3] The National Association claimed that the twin problems of overpopulation at home and under-population in Britain's overseas territories (particularly Canada) could be solved if the State would provide financial aid to assist the 'natural flow' of people across the Atlantic. It suggested that the British and Canadian authorities co-operate in devising a colonisation scheme whereby able-bodied men who could not afford to emigrate unaided should, after basic agricultural training at home, be taken out to Canada in government ships, along with their families. It anticipated that 200,000 individuals a year could be removed in this way and settled on free grants of prairie land, which they would be required to clear and cultivate; and it expected that all the emigrants should ultimately repay their passage money in full, with interest. The Association stressed that it did not advocate the removal of destitute or 'idle' emigrants as an alternative to social reform at home, and it cited recent schemes of privately-assisted colonisation—particularly that of Lady Gordon Cathcart[4]—in support of the feasibility of a similar project under government direction.

But when it approached the Colonial Office with its proposals in 1883, the National Association was told that the government would not consider state-aided colonisation unless an intermediary body (such as a railway or land company) would guarantee the repayment of settlers' loans. Thus rebuffed by the government, the National Association, under Lord Brabazon, its energetic Irish president, now mounted a sustained publicity campaign, organising conferences and arguing its case in pamphlets and in the newspaper and periodical press.[5] It harnessed to its cause the growing imperialist sentiment in Britain, pointing out that state-aided colonisation would not only relieve overpopulation and hardship at home, but would advance the unity of the Empire, by building up the colonies and creating new markets for the manufactures of the home country.[6] The Association's resolve was further strengthened when the Napier Commission of Enquiry into the Condition of Scottish Crofters and Cottars reported in 1884 that state-directed emigration was the only solution to overpopulation in the Highlands—although attempts to implement such a scheme foundered for four years because of the government's continuing refusal to assume responsibility for recovering the emigrants' advances.[7]

Then when rising unemployment and distress in 1886-7 provoked violent demonstrations in London and renewed petitions from charitable societies for state-aided emigration, the National Association resumed its lobbying of the Colonial Office and Parliament. Around 160 of its most influential supporters in both Houses of Parliament formed a colonisation committee to prepare a bill in favour of state aid, and in November 1888 they secured the appointment of a select committee; it was to enquire into past and present proposals for and experiments in publicly-assisted emigration, and advise on future policy. Between 1882 and 1884 over nine thousand emigrants had left Ireland for Canada and the USA thanks to a combination of private aid (£10,000) and two government grants totalling £150,000; then in 1888 the Napier Commission's recommendation had at last taken partial effect when the government set aside £10,000 to help establish a small colony of Highlanders in Canada. In Spring 1888 thirty Highland families were given loans of £120 each and settled on 60-acre homesteads at Killarney, Manitoba, followed in 1889 by forty-nine families who were settled at Saltcoats, 200 miles further north-west. The scheme was administered by an Emigration Board representing the various interested parties, which was made responsible for collecting the settlers' repayments over an eight-year period from 1892.[8]

The select committee was not convinced either by these examples or by previous experiments that government funding should be provided on a larger or more permanent basis. In March 1891 it reported that it could find 'no grounds for thinking that the present condition of the United Kingdom generally calls for any general scheme of state-organised colonisation or emigration'.[9] This statement effectively silenced the state emigrationists, and the government continued to evade any large-scale financial responsibility for emigration until after the First World War. The select committee had argued that since previous schemes had foundered on financial problems, particularly difficulties in securing the repayment of loans, so the expense of any major new experiment would greatly outweigh its advantages. But the National Association and its supporters were not defeated simply by the government's refusal to spend money on emigration or colonisation. On practical grounds, it was claimed that recruits selected from urban areas would be unlikely to succeed as pioneer colonial agriculturists,[10] although probably more serious was the ideological opposition encountered by the National Association throughout its campaign. Adherents of *laissez faire* doctrine disliked any prospect of centralisation or the extension of state responsibility, and condemned government aid to the able-bodied as indiscriminate charity which would corrupt the recipients and burden ratepayers. It was feared not only that state aid would erode the work of the many private societies and individuals who were assisting the needy to emigrate, but also that those who were perfectly capable of emigrating unaided would cease to act for themselves and expect the state to finance their removal. Meanwhile socialist opposition centred on the claim that state-aided emigration was a discreditable attempt to evade social reform at home by removing a potentially troublesome labour force to the colonies, where it would form artificially concentrated—and unwanted—pools of labour.[11]

But at the root of the demise of the National Association for Promoting State-Directed Emigration and Colonisation was simply the fact that it had outlived its usefulness. The campaign for state-funded emigration had thrived on economic depression and lost credibility with the return of better conditions in the early 1890s. A certain proportion of emigrants always required financial assistance, but on the whole they were now adequately served by a variety of charitable societies, without recourse to state subsidies. And whereas much British emigration in the earlier period had been a flight of paupers or potential paupers, in the quarter-century before the First World War probably a larger proportion of emigrants than ever before left with the positive intention of capitalising on better opportunities abroad. This, of course, had always been the priority of most emigrants from North-East Scotland, but in the late nineteenth and early twentieth centuries the national exodus began to take on a more confident and prosperous appearance;[12] and this was matched by the increasing determination of Britain's colonies not to accept the dregs of the home country's surplus population.

Dissemination of information: the Emigrants' Information Office

But the promotion of officially funded emigration by the National Association and charitable societies and individuals was not entirely fruitless. It served not only to focus public attention once more on the pros and cons of emigration in general and state-aided emigration in particular; it also resulted in the creation of the Emigrants' Information Office, which for thirty-two years offered an extremely useful information and advisory service to intending emigrants. The Office, which was under the control of the Colonial Secretary and was staffed by a voluntary committee, was opened to the public on 11 October 1886, and was given a government grant of £650[13] to cover the cost of collecting and disseminating impartial information about Britain's overseas possessions. But although it was created in response to pressure from the emigration lobby, the Colonial Secretary was determined that the Office should not actively promote emigration or be given such wide powers as its predecessor, the Colonial Land and Emigration Commission. Its function was 'solely to collect and marshal information about the colonies which will enable emigrants to make up their own minds on the subject';[14] and Charles Lucas was appointed as its head mainly because he could be relied on to ensure that the Office would not exceed its authority or press for further government intervention in emigration.

Despite these limitations, the Emigrants' Information Office fulfilled an important function, assembling and relaying much-needed information and advice to prospective emigrants for over a quarter of a century. It was enthusiastically patronised from the day it opened—between 11 October and 31 December 1886 it received 4,272 letters, and subsequently dealt with an average of 9,500 letters and 3,600 personal enquiries a year.[15] Using information obtained from colonial newspapers, agents and correspondents, it gave advice on such issues as the availability of free or assisted passages, land grants, land prices, wages and living costs, and the nature and extent of openings for emigrants in a variety of destinations. Much of this material was made available in an ever-increasing volume of literature; quarterly general circulars (issued free) offered up-to-date information in a condensed form, while more detailed quarterly circulars were available to those who wanted to know more about conditions and prospects in specific locations. Handbooks (costing one penny) covering these individual destinations were also published annually, and although the Emigrants' Information Office initially confined its publications to Canada and the Australasian and South African colonies, it soon responded to public demand for more information on tropical colonies and foreign countries, including the United States.[16] Its professedly impartial publications were intended to provide a corrective to the more biased and subjective articles, pamphlets and guidebooks which were regularly published by colonial agents, railway companies and other such interested parties.

From its detailed records the Emigrants' Information Office was also able to construct a general picture of the occupational and age structure and economic circumstances of its clients, as well as their preferred destinations. Its annual reports therefore reflected to some extent changing attitudes to emigration itself and to different destinations. For instance, initially it was besieged mainly by impoverished enquirers—within a week of opening it had dealt with 1,000 personal enquiries and over 4,000 letters, from distressed applicants who expected to be given financial aid to emigrate.[17] By 1890, however, its workload had eased considerably as a result of better economic conditions in Britain, and in 1893 it noted that most clients could now pay their own passages, less than ten per cent being totally indigent. Retrospective observations on emigrant departures in its annual reports complemented the statistics and commentary in the Board of Trade returns; they reiterated and enlarged upon the reasons for fluctuations in the figures, such as the sudden rise in South African emigration in 1889 (due to the opening up of the Transvaal goldfields) or the steady decline in the popularity of the Australian colonies (due to the termination of assisted passages and the opposition of the labour movement). But the Emigrants' Information Office did not simply reflect attitudes to emigration; it also played a part in moulding them, in particular fostering the growing imperialist sympathy and gradually steering emigrants' attention towards Britain's overseas territories through its published recommendations. Whereas between 1891 and 1900 only twenty-eight per cent of emigrants chose destinations within the British Empire, in the following decade this figure increased to sixty-three per cent and in 1913 stood at seventy-eight per cent; and one commentator is in no doubt that this trend 'was at least partly due to the work of the Emigrants' Information Office'.[18]

The EIO's influence was not limited to London. Many thousand copies of its various publications were regularly mailed to individuals and institutions such as charitable societies and workmen's clubs, as well as to provincial newspapers all over the country. The Office made maximum use of its meagre grant, enlisting the co-operation of libraries and labour exchanges to display its information and distribute its literature. Initially small paid branches of the Office were established in a number of provincial centres if demand warranted it, usually under the auspices of the local public library. One such branch was opened in Aberdeen in January 1896, following the success of the only other Scottish office, in Glasgow; after a year this most northerly outpost was commended as one of the five most successful branch offices in the country, but two years later financial considerations forced its closure, along with six other branches, and the EIO reverted to its policy of simply displaying its material in the libraries and relying on librarians to supply circulars to interested parties.[19]

Information was thus made available to potential emigrants all over the country. On 11 October 1886, the day the EIO commenced business, the *Aberdeen Journal* reported that its circulars were to be sent to the Aberdeen Association for Improving the Condition of the Poor, which two months earlier had formed an emigration committee to collect and disseminate material on colonial opportunities for working people.[20] The EIO literature was also available at the local Post Office, and on 12 October the *Aberdeen Journal* published a summary of its first circulars, as it was to do regularly thereafter. But the local press did far more to promote emigration than merely reproduce government circulars; as in the earlier nineteenth century, it continued to be a mine of information on all aspects of emigration. As well as reporting the extent and direction of the national and local movement, it advertised railway and shipping facilities, and opportunities for land acquisition or employment; it drew attention to the services provided by local agents, intimated and reported their lectures, published a considerable volume of emigrant correspondence, and reviewed the numerous pamphlets, emigrant guidebooks and travelogues which were published in the late nineteenth and early twentieth centuries.

Rival destinations

Although settlement in Canada was clearly the recurring theme of all this material, it was not the exclusive focus of attention. Other destinations were represented from time to time in advertisements, lectures, correspondence and reports. There were occasional advertisements for land or employment in the United States, occasional lectures by American emigration agents, and occasional indications of a positive response in North-East Scotland to these opportunities.[21] On 16 June 1888, for instance, the *Aberdeen Journal* reported that a large number of emigrants had left the city the previous day, bound for Santa Barbara, California; and on 8 March 1905 it noted that fourteen agriculturists from Huntly had been persuaded by a former emigrant, then on a visit home, that they could improve their prospects by becoming farmers and ranchers in Montana and Oregon. But these were isolated examples; the United States continued to appeal more to tradesmen than to farmers, and from the 1860s until the First World War the bulk of emigrants from North-East Scotland to the USA were granite tradesmen, often crossing the Atlantic seasonally in order to take advantage of the demand for skilled (and highly paid) labour in the American quarries and stoneyards.[22] But the lure of the United States even for tradesmen was fading, for in the wake of recurring economic crises in the late nineteenth century, the country began to impose stricter controls on immigration, and fewer employment opportunities became available.[23]

Emigration to South Africa also fluctuated according to economic and political conditions. The discovery of gold on the Witwatersrand in the Transvaal in 1886 led to a steady growth in settlement during the following decade, and from 1895 to 1897 South Africa was second only to the United States in its popularity with British—and Scottish—emigrants. Immediately after the Boer War there was a dramatic increase in emigration to the newly acquired British territories, and 1903 brought a record number of arrivals from both Scotland (8,158) and Britain as a whole (62,824). But the euphoria was short-lived, for the deceptive post-war prosperity was followed by a lengthy depression from 1904 to 1910: South Africa's undeveloped economy could absorb only limited numbers of skilled tradesmen and domestic servants, and the hordes of unskilled labourers who flocked to Johannesburg and the surrounding goldfields in the hope of making a quick fortune generally faced the twin problems of unemployment and a very high cost of living.

Intending emigrants from North-East Scotland were warned about these drawbacks. On 12 May 1881, for instance, the *Aberdeen Journal* published a letter from a former railway clerk in Aberdeen, writing from Cape Colony, who drew attention to the restricted labour market and high living costs there. Then on 25 February 1889, quoting from an EIO circular, it qualified a report of the good demand for artisans at Johannesburg with a reminder of the cost of living in the Transvaal; and on 27 December 1893 the *Journal* reprinted a recent article from the *Cape Times*, which spoke of a glut of labour in the towns of the Rand, not just among the unskilled and those of sedentary occupations, but also among trained artisans. Up to five hundred settlers were pouring in each week from Europe, persuaded by 'extravagent' propaganda in the British press, and undeterred by warnings that the supply of labour at the Rand greatly exceeded demand.

Most of those who emigrated from Aberdeen to South Africa fell into two distinct categories: skilled artisans and certain types of women, who were generally responding to specific offers of employment. The most consistent encouragement was given to the women, particularly to domestic servants and to the relatives of soldier-settlers after the Boer War. Several Aberdeen employment agencies advertised situations for nursemaids, housekeepers, cooks and general servants, who were always in demand;[24] then from 1901 to 1903 persistent—and successful—efforts were made to persuade suitable women to emigrate under the auspices of the Scottish Women's Emigration Committee and its Aberdeen representative, Caroline Phillips.[25]

The *Aberdeen Journal* also periodically carried advertisements (inserted by local agents) for various kinds of tradesmen, often for employment in public building works, the gold mines or the granite industry.[26] The development of gold mining greatly stimulated railway construction, and on 16 January 1889 Walter Peace, the Natal government emigration agent, advertised in the *Aberdeen Journal* for fifty experienced stone masons to work on the Natal government railways. Successful applicants would be given a free third-class passage from London to Natal and could obtain passages for their families at a rate of £12 per adult. A fortnight later Peace visited Aberdeen to select applicants, and his meeting in a local granite yard was attended by over 100 masons; the following month the *Aberdeen Journal* reported the departure of fifty of these men for Natal, followed in June by fourteen masons who were also going out to fulfil specific government contracts.[27] On 10 February 1890 Peace again advertised for joiners to take up a one-year contract on public works in Natal, and—perhaps in response to this appeal—the *Aberdeen Journal* of 14 March reported that about forty joiners from various parts of the county had just left Aberdeen for Natal, where they were to be employed in constructing the new railway to Johannesburg. But employment opportunities for tradesmen fluctuated according to economic circumstances, and perhaps press warnings and conflicting accounts of conditions did discourage the exodus to some extent. The Aberdeen *Granite Cutters' Journal*, for instance, frequently warned masons to keep away from South Africa when trade was slack and the labour market overstocked, or at least urged them to exercise caution in the face of conflicting reports of the demand for labour.[28] Certainly North-East interest in South Africa was confined to the same periods as national interest in the region, and after a flurry of advertisements and articles in the 1890s and early 1900s,[29] the local press rarely referred to South African settlement after 1903.

More consistent attention was paid to Australasia and indeed, given the tradition of settlement in these colonies, it might have been expected that the area would remain an important emigrant destination in the late nineteenth century. But although it was the second most popular destination with Scottish emigrants in the years 1882-7 and 1891-2, interest in Australasia fluctuated according to the amount of financial assistance offered to settlers, the degree of opposition mounted by the Antipodean labour unions, and the enthusiasm with which the various provinces were promoted by emigration agents. The Canadian Immigration Department was well aware of the threat posed by those Australasian colonies which periodically offered free and assisted passages to emigrants. In at least three annual reports to Ottawa—in 1881, 1882 and 1883—the Canadian High Commissioner in London complained that the New Zealand government's offer of free passages to domestic servants and the availability of £2 and £5 passages to New South Wales, were thwarting

Canadian efforts to attract settlers (who had to pay their own fares of at least £8).[30] But more serious still were the activities of the Queensland government, which in the 1880s offered free passages to farm labourers and domestic servants, and assisted passages to selected tradesmen. Then after being suspended during the early 1890s, Queensland reintroduced free passages by the end of the decade. As a result, according to the Carnoustie-based Canadian agent, Thomas Duncan, emigrants' attention was once more diverted from Canada by booking agents who were interested only in securing their commission along with the Queensland government's bonus of 10s. 6d. per adult.[31] There was a heated debate at this time among Canadian emigration officials, with many of the British-based agents claiming that the decline of interest in Canada was due to competition from other colonies, particularly Queensland. They therefore advocated the introduction of a limited system of assisted emigration to Canada, under which selected settlers would have their passages paid in advance, and would also receive financial help in taking up a homestead, the loans to be repaid in annual instalments.[32] Their suggestions were not taken up by the Canadian government, however, which confined itself to extending its bonus payments on selected settlers from the prairie provinces to the whole of the Dominion in 1903 and raising this payment from seven shillings to £1 per adult three years later.[33] But from 1909 the offer of free passages to Queensland for agricultural settlers and their families who could put down a (refundable) deposit of £50 ensured further emigrant interest in that colony, especially after the deposit was reduced to £5 in 1911.[34] According to the *Aberdeen Journal* of 25 February 1911, the announcement of this reduction had immediately resulted in over 100 applications for passage to Queensland being made in Aberdeen, and it forecast a significant boom in departures to that part of Australia.

From time to time Queensland's case was actively promoted by a variety of agents in North-East Scotland. On 22 October 1881, for instance, Peter Fleming, the Queensland government agent based in Dundee, intimated in the *Aberdeen Journal* that he was about to visit the North-East to meet and select applicants for free passages at Aberdeen, Kintore, Inverurie, Turriff, Macduff, Keith, Fochabers, Rothes, Dufftown and Huntly. And in October 1910 J. N. Campbell, the Director of Emigration for the Queensland government, spent some time at W. T. Moffatt's booking office in Aberdeen interviewing intending settlers and trying to persuade agriculturists and domestic servants in particular of the attractions of Queensland.[35] The work of these selecting agents was complemented by official itinerant lecturers such as George Russell, who addressed meetings in Aberdeen and Buckie in 1882 and 1883 respectively, and M. H. Black (a former emigrant himself and member of the Queensland Legislature) who spoke at a large gathering in Aberdeen in 1894.[36] Their efforts were not entirely fruitless, despite the complaint of one emigrant correspondent in 1910 that Queensland's agents were not so numerous or assertive as their Canadian counterparts, and failed to redirect the attention of Scottish agricultural emigrants from North America to Australia.[37] As far as North-East Scotland was concerned, the publicity campaign of the 1880s paid off, in that the *Aberdeen Journal* of 11

June 1888 could report the departure of up to fifty emigrants from Aberdeen en route to Queensland, followed on 16 July by another contingent of farm servants and on 30 July by a further twenty-five agriculturists, all having been selected under the free passage scheme.

Other parts of Australasia were also promoted from time to time in the North-East, through lectures, emigrant correspondence, specific job advertisements and recruitment visits by agents.[38] On 25 January 1910 the *Aberdeen Journal* noted that 'from the more than usual interest that is being taken in the visit to Aberdeen of Mr H. S. Ranford, the Western Australian Government emigration agent ... it is evident that there is going to be a considerable exodus of people from the city and county to Western Australia'. During his short visit Ranford addressed two crowded meetings in the YMCA in Aberdeen and attended several local booking agents' offices, where he was 'besieged' with people, over 200 of whom intimated their intention to emigrate. In the earlier part of the nineteenth century New Zealand's popularity had rested largely on the tireless campaigns of a variety of provincial agents, and agents and lecturers continued to visit North-East Scotland from time to time towards the end of the century. In April 1885, for instance, Arthur Clayden addressed a number of meetings in Aberdeenshire, Kincardineshire and Angus,[39] after which he returned to New Zealand and persuaded the government there to give financial assistance to agricultural settlers with some capital; in a letter to the *Aberdeen Journal* on 2 April 1886 he announced that *bona fide* farmers who had capital of £100, and £50 for each child over twelve, could obtain passage discounts to the value of £10 per adult, and he intimated his own intention of forming a Scottish settlement (similar to that at Otago) on 100,000 acres of government land at Raglan County, Auckland. Further particulars could be had from his associate, James Strachan, an advocate in Aberdeen, who concurred with Clayden's optimistic belief that the current agricultural depression in New Zealand merely offered a golden opportunity to farmers to invest in land and stock at bargain prices.[40] Another associate of Strachan, William Courtney, also visited Aberdeen from time to time to promote agricultural emigration to Taranaki,[41] and the islands were further recommended by a visitor to New Zealand, writing to the *Aberdeen Journal* in 1890, who declared that the country was 'just filled with Aberdonians ... [who] have proved themselves ... to be men of energy and pluck, well fitted to become the best class of colonists'.[42]

Yet despite these recommendations, Australia and New Zealand were only sporadically popular with emigrants from North-East Scotland, and could never compete with the consistent appeal of Canada. In 1909 ticket agents in the North of Scotland warned of the dangers of Antipodean competition, particularly after Canada had suffered a temporary setback because of a commercial depression; yet the head of the Canadian emigration service in Britain remained confident that, with a little effort, the Dominion could easily overcome this threat. The Canadian government agent in Aberdeen, he reported, 'does not find in his district that the emigrating public are seriously considering the competition of Australia and other Colonies with Canada'; and, he continued, 'with Canada's obvious natural advantages, and the shortness of the journey there, it is quite apparent that a little more expenditure, and the relaxation of restrictions, incident upon improved commercial prosperity in Canada would very quickly off-set any temporary advantage which other Colonies may have secured owing to last year's restrictions, and trade depression across the Atlantic'.[43] But while Canada's appeal was largely due to the fact that equally attractive—and better—opportunities across the Atlantic were repeatedly and convincingly presented to potential emigrants, political conditions in Australasia also hampered their efforts to mount a consistent and positive immigration policy. The vociferous and powerful Labour opposition to immigration succeeded in putting a stop to schemes of assistance from around 1891 until the early twentieth century, a policy which coincided with several years of drought in Australia. Eventually the Antipodean colonies saw the advantages of promoting British settlement—partly because of the example of Canadian success and partly because it would ensure that the Antipodes remained white; they therefore renewed their schemes of assistance, but although arrivals from Britain increased markedly from 1908, the new movement had barely become established before it was interrupted by the outbreak of the First World War.

Linked with ambivalent official attitudes to emigration was the fact that encouragement to settle at the Antipodes was often qualified by warnings from dissatisfied settlers. For instance, the *Aberdeen Journal* on 12 March 1891 published a lengthy indictment of both Australia and New Zealand by a local emigrant who declared that he had been misled by persuasive propaganda and who wanted his grievances publicised as a caution to other intending emigrants. He had gone initially to New South Wales, on the invitation of a relative already settled there, but on arriving at Newcastle, he found he had been deceived in his impression that there was a ready demand for all kinds of labour. He subsequently encountered similar depression and unemployment at Sydney and Melbourne, so that after only three months his savings were almost exhausted and he was forced to take employment as a farm worker at wages and conditions inferior to those in many parts of Scotland. After fifteen months he had moved to Canterbury, New Zealand, on the suggestion of another relative, but had fared no better there. Unemployment was rife in New Zealand, as in Australia, although the intending emigrant was not told of the glut of labour; and even landowning did not pay, he declared, unless it was conducted on a very extensive scale by large capitalists. A block of government land which he had been allocated near Canterbury had been utterly worthless, and after less than two years at the Antipodes he was preparing to return to Scotland to take up farm work there.

Similar sentiments were expressed in 1906 by William Cruden, who had emigrated to New Zealand the previous year, with savings of £1,000.[44] Originally from Aberdeenshire, he had spent seven years farming at Winnipeg before selling out at a profit and returning to Scotland. Almost immediately he had been persuaded by the 'seductive' literature of the High Commissioner's office to re-emigrate to New Zealand with his family, on the assurance that land was cheap and easily obtainable. But he had been disappointed, finding that the intending farmer required at least £1,400 capital in order to obtain decent land, and he had been forced to take up work as a gardener. Up to 300 of his 500 fellow-passengers, having been similarly deceived, had already left in disgust, and he himself intended to return to Scotland to publicise his experiences if he did not secure land within a year. He compared the attitude of the New Zealand government unfavourably with that of Canada, which treated its settlers as national assets and took great care of them on arrival, rather than abrogating all their responsibilities once the fare had been paid.

Canada: reservations, warnings and complaints

So the spotlight was turned on Canada partly because encouragement to emigrate elsewhere was often muted and qualified by complaints and warnings in the press. That is not to say Canada totally escaped criticism, but on the whole the warnings were constructive and intending emigrants from North-East Scotland were offered much more positive—and repeated—encouragement to go there than anywhere else. Of course, at local as well as national level there were always those who opposed emigration *per se*, wherever it was directed. The *Aberdeen Journal* on 11 March 1904 referred to a recent meeting of the Garioch presbytery, at which complaints had been raised about depopulation in the parishes of Rayne and Culsalmond, and attributed partly to 'the tendency ... for young men to go to foreign countries, fostered by all the agencies at work promoting emigration to South Africa and Canada'. Some time later, on 6 April 1910, the *Aberdeen Journal* complained about a recent extensive exodus from Morayshire to Canada, which was imposing 'a very serious drain on the young manhood and womanhood of the country'; and later that year John MacLennan, the Canadian government agent for the North of Scotland, reported to his superiors in Ottawa that he was encountering increasing opposition to his work on this old, much-used argument:

> In meeting and speaking with the large farmers throughout the district, I find the feeling growing against our work. I am told everywhere that we are taking the best men and leaving only second and third class. I am confining my lectures this year to the purely rural districts and trying as far as possible to meet the objections and opposition raised. It is indispensable to our success that we do not antagonise too much the large farmers, as they are still a powerful force in the community.[45]

In his lectures he tried to neutralise their opposition by pointing out that his aim was not to depopulate Scotland but to redirect the existing emigrant tide towards Canada. But six months later MacLennan predicted that since the recent census results had shown a large decrease in the population of rural districts, he would have to contend with the antagonism of 'public bodies, the Press and ... influential men'.[46] He was right. During Spring 1911 the *Aberdeen Journal* made frequent references to rural depopulation revealed by the census in a variety of parishes in the region, a major cause of which was said to be large-scale emigration.[47] Then in May the General Assemblies of both the Free and United Free Churches complained about the 'menace' of an 'exceedingly onerous' tide of emigration, the Free Church, for example, claiming that it posed a threat to national stability and was particularly ominous for the future of Protestantism in Scotland.[48] At the same time concern was being expressed in Parliament about the recent large exodus from rural areas when questions were raised about the activities of Canadian government emigration agents stationed in Britain and Ireland.[49] And at the Church of Scotland General Assembly the following year there were renewed complaints about extensive emigration and in particular the insufficient care taken by booking agents in ensuring supervised passages and employment for the emigrants on arrival.[50] On 10 May 1912 the *Aberdeen Journal* quoted a *Daily Mail* report on 'The flight from Scotland' which asserted that there was insufficient recognition of the threat posed by the monthly departure of up to 1,000 emigrants from Aberdeenshire, Banffshire and Kincardineshire alone:

> The astonishing thing about this serious and persistent ebb of the best section of Scotland's population is that no one outside the districts actually affected appears to realise that it is going on. Here in Aberdeen all sorts and conditions of men tell you that "emigration is draining the best blood of the country" with sufficient repetition of the same phrase to make it sound like a melancholy proverb of the place. Yet nowhere is there sign of any measure planned to stop the rot that is eating into the prosperity of Scotland.

And in an editorial of its own on 17 June the *Aberdeen Journal* reiterated the complaint that little was being done to stem the continuing flood of emigration.

But most of the specific complaints about Canada in fact came from tradesmen and non-agricultural labourers who had been unable to find remunerative work in the Dominion during economic depressions, and who blamed their misfortune on the false promises of agents.[51] On 15 December 1894, for instance, the *Aberdeen Journal* published a letter from an Aberdonian in Montreal to a friend at home, in which he complained that too much emigrant literature told only one side of the story. Although wages were high, so was the cost of living, and he claimed that a man would be better off in Aberdeen earning fifteen shillings a week than in Montreal earning thirty shillings. Furthermore, the much vaunted 'free land' in the west was often miles from the railway, and even if farmers did manage to improve a few acres, raise a crop and get it to market, the low prices for grain would not repay their efforts. Such press warnings did not go unheeded in North-East Scotland, as John MacLennan acknowledged, initially on 15 February 1908, when he reported that he was finding it 'uphill work' to recruit emigrants from his district. Business was slack both at his own office and at the booking agencies, and even the 'farm delegate' attached to his office was attracting only small audiences to his meetings. On 22 February MacLennan complained further in his weekly report to Ottawa:

> It is a difficult matter to create any enthusiasm this year for Canada. In spite of our statements that there are ample opportunities and abundance of work for the agriculturist and Railroad laborer, yet the Press has poisoned the public mind respecting the terrible suffering claimed to exist in Canada that our work this year is going to be greatly hampered and will show a big falling off. The same condition obtains everywhere through my district. Mr Bredin our delegate did not have a single caller in some of the offices visited.

He reiterated these complaints in his annual report at the end of the year:

> The year opened in the midst of the great commercial and industrial depression which has prevailed everywhere for the past eighteen months. This stringency had the effect of largely stopping the movement from this district; even the classes for which we had openings were sceptical, and it was difficult to convince them that there was any work to be had, in view of the many conflicting reports and the requirements of the department. It made it often disagreeable for myself and other government representatives on account of the wide publicity given by newspapers to these reports, and no matter how strenuously we might deny the statements, the public were disposed to accept the press news in preference to our denials.[52]

From time to time the booking agents came in for particular criticism, not only from dissatisfied settlers but from the Canadian immigration authorities. They did not only receive the shipping companies' commission of six shillings per passenger and the railway companies' commission of five per cent on rail fares; since January 1893 these ticket agents had also been entitled to a bonus of seven shillings from the Dominion government on each farm labourer and domestic servant they sent to Western Canada. In 1903 the system was extended to provinces east of Manitoba and in 1906 the bonus was raised to £1.[53] So it was clearly in the agents' interests to promote Canada, and the Dominion immigration authorities kept them well supplied with posters, maps and pamphlets to assist them in their task. But over-enthusiastic agents, in their eagerness to recruit as many eligible settlers as possible, did not always impose sufficiently high standards of selection or supervision:

> Interested in their own reward in the shape of a commission, and subject to only nominal control by the shipping companies and the government agents, they were often not the best persons to advise and assist the intending immigrant, especially as they seldom had personal knowledge of Canada or other countries of settlement.[54]

On a number of occasions agents' bonuses were revoked when emigrants were found to be unsuitable or did not take up the stipulated occupations; and much of the correspondence between booking agents and the Department of Immigration was concerned with disputed bonus claims.[55] The Dominion government agents based in Aberdeen sometimes expressed reservations about the activities of some of the local booking agents. In 1911, for instance, W. B. Cumming, while admitting that the Aberdeen agents MacKay Brothers were 'very active and energetic', added that 'in their anxiety to do business they are sometimes inclined to overstep the mark in advertising, when I have to restrain them'.[56] And on 12 January 1914 G. G. Archibald sent a memorandum to the Department of Immigration in Ottawa concerning William Maitland, an agent based in Longside, near Peterhead:

> I meet Mr. Maitland frequently at lectures. He is a peripatetic sort of agent, and while he does a large business, it is not always of a satisfactory character. A great many complaints are made about his failure to implement his promises with regard to looking after the baggage etc., of settlers.[57]

Maitland, who was a tailor to trade and (like many agents) ran his ticket business as a sideline, often fell foul of the Canadian immigration authorities in Ottawa, mainly for carelessness in making passage arrangements and neglecting to submit his claims for bonus payments on emigrants until several months after they had sailed.[58] He was also the only North-East agent in this period to be involved in a court case, when in April 1912 he appeared in Aberdeen Sheriff Court charged with failing to supply contract tickets to two farm servants whom he had booked to sail to Canada. Two months earlier Peter Simpson and William Walker, both from Echt, had paid a deposit of £1 each to Maitland in return for securing assisted passages to Ontario on 23 March and subsequent employment as farm labourers. In return for this payment Maitland was legally required to hand over contract tickets bearing the vessel's name and date of sailing, but he failed to do so, with the result that Simpson and Walker were prevented from sailing on the appointed date. After they had complained to the Board of Trade emigration officer in Aberdeen, charges were brought against Maitland for contravening the Board of Trade's passage booking regulations, and he was fined £2 and told to improve his business practice.[59]

The agency network

But warnings and complaints were greatly outweighed by positive publicity about Canada. Most of the derogatory comments were confined to the years 1907-8 and 1913 and were directed specifically against tradesmen and unskilled labourers who intended to settle in the cities. Nearly all the warnings mentioned in the letters quoted above gave corresponding encouragement to emigrants to settle on the land,[60] the main exception being the Manitoba correspondent of 15 April 1908, who pointed out that demand for farm servants dropped sharply during the long winter, when unemployed labourers generally had to spend their summer wages on board and lodging. Most of the disputes involving booking agents were relatively minor administrative problems and on the whole they were a great asset to the Canadian government. They formed part of a much bigger network of agents who by various means ensured that Canada was repeatedly brought to the notice of potential emigrants from North-East Scotland. Indeed, if any one factor were to be held responsible for generating and sustaining the area's remarkable interest in Canada in the quarter-century before the First World War, it would surely be the part played by this network of agents. If the limited and sporadic agency work on behalf of places like Queensland brought a temporary rise in emigration in the 1880s,[61] then clearly much more could be expected from the intensive, unremitting publicity given to Canada. The value of enthusiastic, competent agents was recognised by contemporaries, such as the correspondent of the *Aberdeen Journal* who in 1910 lamented Queensland's continuing lack of population;[62] he claimed that most of the emigrants who were flocking from Scotland to Canada had never even heard of Queensland, and he urged that agents of the Canadian calibre should be sent to Scotland by the Queensland government to redirect the emigrant tide to the Antipodes.

Newspaper editors sometimes acted as unofficial emigration agents, in particular John Bruce of the *Aberdeen Free Press*. In the early twentieth century he gave regular and extensive coverage to Canadian affairs and from time to time published special illustrated supplements advocating emigration. In 1911 J. Obed Smith, the Canadian government's Assistant Superintendent of Emigration in London, wrote to W. D. Scott, his superior in Ottawa, recommending that Bruce be given financial help with the publication of these special issues; for 'there is no better friend to Canada than this newspaper, and it has an enormous circulation throughout not only the North, but extending to the Southern parts of Scotland'.[63] The request was granted and Scott himself admitted some time later that 'I do not think there is a single paper in the British Isles which has been more friendly towards Canada than the Aberdeen Free Press and there is no doubt but that the publicity already secured through this paper has been highly advantageous to Canada'.[64]

But probably the major secret of the agents' success was the way in which they established personal contact with potential emigrants. Their lectures—too numerous to list individually—were delivered not only in Aberdeen city but throughout the region, and were widely intimated and reported in the local press. In this way the lecturers' message reached a wider audience, and supplemented the emigrant correspondence, advertisements, EIO circulars, book reviews and general information on Canada with which the newspaper-reading public was inundated. Not all the lecturers were officially-appointed emigration agents; valuable work continued to be done by local people who spoke about their experiences of Canada at meetings in village halls, by representatives of societies which had conducted experiments in emigration, by politicians or other public figures who thought they had something useful to say on the subject, or by visiting Canadians who promoted their country in an unofficial capacity. Many lectures were given by schoolmasters and clergymen, with the aid of lantern slides and literature made available by the Dominion government agents.[65] In November 1905, for instance, the Rev A. J. Vining of Winnipeg lectured to a large audience in Crown Terrace Baptist Church, Aberdeen, dealing with opportunities in Western Canada, and two months later W. Stark, President of the Canadian Colonisation Society, delivered a similar lecture in another church in the city. In November 1906 D. C. Cruickshank, relating his experiences of twenty years in Alberta, advised the young among his Rothienorman audience to emigrate to that province; and at the same time the Rev G. C. Milne of Woodside Congregational Church was promoting Canada in general to a large audience in Aberdeen.[66]

Several lectures on Canada were delivered under the auspices of the Royal Scottish Geographical Society, including one in Aberdeen in 1899 by Colonel Bailey, the Society's secretary, another in 1903 by W. A. Hickman and two in 1911, in Aberdeen and Ballater, by Hennessey Cook, a Fellow of the Society.[67] After completing his five-year term of office as Governor-General of Canada, Lord Aberdeen addressed a number of meetings in North-East Scotland on the subject of emigration, including one in the Music Hall, Aberdeen, in November 1899, at which he gave advice on the kind of settlers Canada required.[68] The Aberdeen YMCA and YWCA also hosted several lectures on Canadian emigration: in March 1885 J. E. Cracknell from Manitoba spoke in the YWCA on Manitoba and the Rocky Mountains, and in October 1905 Beecher Smith from Lancashire, in the context of a talk on the prairies, explained the function of an Emigration Advice Department established by the Lancashire branch of the YMCA. After Smith had spoken, a number of intending emigrants in the large audience had private interviews with him, and he repeated the public lecture at Bucksburn the following evening.[69] Mutual Improvement Associations provided another forum for the promotion of emigration to Canada,[70] then after the Salvation Army had established a separate Emigration Department in 1903, its resident and itinerant agents joined the ranks of those who advocated settlement in Canada.[71]

Official representatives of Canadian business and farming interests, the various Canadian provinces and the transcontinental railway companies also appeared in North-East Scotland from time to time.[72] Their itineraries were usually arranged by the booking agents throughout the region, who also gave these visitors the use of their premises to conduct interviews and select recruits. On 7 February 1912, for instance, the *Aberdeen Journal* intimated that W. Hadden, a Canadian farmer and businessman, was to be available at Paton's Aberdeen agency to give advice and information to intending emigrants. In February 1913 Mrs H. Niblett of Winnipeg attended Paton's to offer a similar service to women emigrants. She also gave eight lectures during this visit and a further nine lectures during a second visit to the North-East a year later.[73] The Ontario government agent, a Captain Thomson, was based at W. T. Moffatt's quayside office in 1910 and at Paton's in 1913, two occasions on which he visited Aberdeen to promote his province and select applicants for specific situations.[74] In November 1912 MacKay Brothers of Aberdeen arranged for Malcolm McIntyre, an agent of the Canadian Pacific Railway based in Glasgow, to speak about the Company's emigration policy to an audience at Alford; in 1913 and 1914 two employment agents from Wooler, Ontario, based themselves at MacKays' office when they came to Aberdeen to recruit emigrants; and in May 1914 MacKays' invited a representative of the New Brunswick government to use their office to conduct interviews and select emigrants.[75]

By the early twentieth century the practical organisation of local emigration was largely in the hands of ticket agents. Of 190 such agents in North-East Scotland who were on the Dominion government's books in 1909, almost 100 were active,[76] the most important being MacKay, Paton, Moffatt and R. & J. Davidson in Aberdeen, supplemented by regional offices such as that of William Maitland in Longside and John Sinclair in Elgin. Sinclair, for instance, was described by G. G. Archibald, the Canadian government agent in Aberdeen in 1914, as one of the most active and reliable agents in the region, and he added, 'I know of few, if any, others who get so much new business as a direct result of careful attention to former clients'.[77] Although the agents offered passages to and employment in a number of destinations, and played host to visiting lecturers from the Antipodes as well as North America, the bulk of their work was concerned with Canada. They clearly had a vital rôle, not only in making the emigrants' travelling arrangements but also in actively encouraging their departure, through their own advertisements and the lectures and interviews they organised. They sent their own representatives across the Atlantic to seek out employment opportunities and also liaised with government employment agents in Canada in order to secure situations for their clients. On 6 July 1914, for instance, the *Aberdeen Journal* reported that MacKays' representative, John Campbell, had just returned from Canada with a large number of posts for farm and domestic servants, who were offered fully advanced and assisted passages; and some time earlier, in January 1910, Paton had asked the Department of Immigration in Ottawa to give him the names of government agents in Ontario to whom he could send a number of agricultural clients.[78] Paton, who was acknowledged as 'one of the most reliable agents ... most enterprising in his efforts to do business',[79] worked in conjunction with Mrs Isabella Stewart, who ran a servants' registry in Aberdeen and selected domestic servants for his employment bureau in Toronto. He—and other agents—also visited outlying parts of the region to advise and select emigrants for the posts they advertised. On 11 February 1911, for example, the *Aberdeen Journal* reported Paton's intention of attending the post office and hotel in Tarland to select farm hands and domestic servants for guaranteed posts in Canada, part fares to be advanced to successful applicants. Later, on 28 February, it intimated he was to visit Huntly for a similar purpose, and on 10 February 1914 it was announced that MacKay Brothers were to send a representative to Tarland to meet intending emigrants.

The booking agents also arranged for special emigrant parties to travel to Canada under their personal supervision, and the experiences of these parties were often mentioned in the local press. Alexander Longmuir, an agent in Stonehaven, regularly accompanied parties to Canada, where he himself had lived for sixteen years. On 25 July 1907 the *Aberdeen Journal* published an interview with Longmuir recorded just after he had returned from taking a party of 200 emigrants—including 100 from Aberdeen—to Manitoba. Having accompanied the party as far as Winnipeg and supervised their distribution to situations which he had secured for them in advance, Longmuir then travelled further west to Moose Jaw, before returning to Regina and Winnipeg by a different route. During this trip he visited a number of friends and acquaintances from the North of Scotland, several of whom he himself had persuaded to emigrate. They included a Stonehaven couple who had gone out early in 1906 and who, in addition to their quarter-section of land, ran a temperance hotel in Regina; and another couple who, having left Aberdeen on one of Longmuir's conducted parties in 1906, were successfully running a boarding house in Winnipeg.[80] On 1 April 1911 the *Aberdeen Journal* reported that 400 emigrants had left by train from Aberdeen, 100 of them having been recruited by Paton. They were travelling to Glasgow in specially reserved carriages, accompanied by a Paton's representative, and at least half of them were said to be going out to situations secured for them in advance by the booking agents. Paton commonly despatched such parties throughout the emigration season, from March or April to November, according to demand; in September 1913, for instance, a contingent of 100 emigrants (a large number for the time of year) was sent out to various parts of Canada in a conducted party at the request of several of Paton's Spring recruits who had done well in Canada and wanted their friends and relatives to join them.[81] On 2 June 1913 there was a similar report of a special train which had been chartered by MacKay Brothers to carry 300 emigrants from Aberdeen to Glasgow en route for various ports on the St Lawrence River. The party was to be personally conducted to Canada by Edward MacKay and three of his staff also travelled with the train, which stopped at Stonehaven, Montrose, Arbroath, Dundee and Kircaldy to pick up other emigrants who had booked through the Aberdeen agents. According to the *Aberdeen Journal*:

> The Messrs Mackay Bros. supplied the fullest possible information to all. The emigrants knew exactly what part of Canada they were going to, and how to get there after leaving the steamer. Many had letters of introduction to employers, while most of the tradesmen were going out on "spec." Several had booked right through to Vancouver.

A week later there were similar scenes at Aberdeen railway station when a conducted party organised by Davidson's agency left the city to embark for Canada on the Donaldson liner *Letitia* at Glasgow. Most of the emigrants had been provided with employment in advance, and the *Aberdeen Journal* particularly commended Davidson's arrangements for finding good private situations for domestic servants.

Dominion government agencies and Scottish emigration

The activities of these booking agents, along with the representatives of the Canadian provinces, the transcontinental railway companies and others involved in promoting emigration to Canada, were increasingly underpinned and directed by the Dominion government itself. The Province of Canada had first recognised in the early 1850s that the private exchange of information between friends and relatives ought to be supplemented by a more official means of bringing Canada's attractions to the notice of prospective settlers. In 1852 it created a Bureau of Agriculture, whose head was made responsible for the publication of information to encourage immigration, and two years later the Legislature granted funds for that purpose. In 1859, perhaps in imitation of the assertive campaigns of some of the American states and territories, a Canadian information office was opened in Liverpool under the management of William Dixon and A. B. Hawkes.[82] In 1867 the Federal and Provincial Departments of Agriculture were given concurrent responsibility for immigration, although in practice most of the promotional work was done by the Federal Department, which retained its responsibility for immigration until 1893. The bulk of its budget was spent on encouraging settlement, and it began to station resident agents in various ports and towns in the British Isles to inspect passengers embarking for Canada and to promote the Dominion as an emigrant destination. From 1872 a supervisory officer was stationed in London to co-ordinate these local agencies, the first occupant of this post being William Dixon. For a brief period in the early 1870s some of the provinces, feeling their interests were not being adequately represented by the Dominion agents, began to send rival agents to Britain, usually as temporary, seasonal appointments. But following a Dominion-Provincial conference in 1874 it was agreed that the practice was wasteful and counter-productive; it was therefore discontinued on an assurance that federal officials would co-operate with provincial governments, distribute the literature they provided and give equal treatment to each province when encouraging emigration.

This system of co-operation was eroded by administrative changes the following decade, after the appointment in 1880 of the first High Commissioner for Canada in Great Britain, the Dominion's first official diplomatic representative abroad. His terms of reference specifically included the 'charge, supervision and control' of Canadian emigration offices in the British Isles, under instructions from the responsible Ministry in Ottawa; and for almost a quarter of a century the High Commissioner was to remain at the head of the emigration service in both Britain and Europe.[83] But although both Sir Alexander Galt, the first High Commissioner, and Sir Charles Tupper, his successor, were enthusiastic proponents of emigration, some of the older provinces felt that disproportionate encouragement was being given to settlement on the prairies, and, led by Ontario, they therefore began to reinstate a few separate offices staffed by resident provincial agents.

In 1893 responsibility for immigration was transferred from the Department of Agriculture to the Department of the Interior, where it remained until 1917.[84] Then in 1899 Lord Strathcona, the High Commissioner, recommended that the day-to-day control of European emigration should be given to someone with no other duties, who would conduct it on business lines, rather than on a semi-diplomatic basis. W. T. R. Preston was therefore appointed, under the High Commissioner, Inspector of Emigration Agencies in Europe. But friction soon arose between Strathcona's office and Preston over the latter's determination, supported by his superiors in Ottawa, to wage a much more active publicity campaign. As a result, in 1903 Preston was given the title of Canadian Commissioner of Emigration in Great Britain and Europe, along with separate offices at Charing Cross, London, and an enlarged staff; and he and his successors became increasingly independent of the High Commissioner's control.[85]

Throughout the period under review the number of Dominion government emigration agencies located throughout the British Isles varied according to economic conditions and demand, although the Liverpool, Bristol and Glasgow offices always remained operative and several special agents were appointed from year to year for temporary work in a wide range of locations. The Department of Agriculture and subsequently the Department of the Interior in Ottawa monitored the activities of their territorial agents through the weekly and annual reports submitted by these agents. The responsible departments then compiled their own annual review of the state of immigration on the basis of these reports, supplemented from 1880 by general reports from the High Commissioner and from 1899 by the reports of Preston and his successors, also submitted annually.[86]

The territorial agents were clearly the linchpins in the system. The Ottawa authorities decided policy largely on the basis of their reports, in conjunction with those of their counterparts at the Canadian end. They then relied on the agents to implement that policy, both through their own work and by overseeing and directing the army of ticket agents, visiting delegates and others who represented various Canadian interests throughout Britain and Europe. The agents were charged with the duty of persuading eligible emigrants to settle in Canada and also with discouraging—and eventually prohibiting—the emigration of undesirable settlers. When William Dixon went to Liverpool in 1866, he announced his arrival in 114 British newspapers,[87] setting a precedent for the extensive and varied publicity campaign which was to be waged by his successors during the next half-century. The agents exploited every available promotional tool. In addition to advertising regularly in newspapers they also displayed posters and handbills in libraries, post offices, railway stations, hotels and farmers' and working men's clubs. Government-sponsored pamphlets were also sent to many of these institutions, as well as to individual agriculturists, teachers and clergymen, and atlases, wall maps and other literature were distributed free to schools. Displays of Canadian produce were mounted at agricultural shows and markets, and also in the windows of the agents' offices, which were usually located prominently in the city centres. In later years two travelling horse-drawn exhibition wagons visited the rural districts of Scotland and Ireland during the season, while two motor cars performed a similar function in England, stopping wherever a crowd could be attracted. Delegations of journalists and tenant farmers were invited to undertake Canadian tours at the expense of the Dominion government, in the hope that they would report favourably and deliver promotional lectures on their return; and successful settlers were also brought back at government expense to lecture on their experiences. The agents were particularly anxious to establish personal contact with potential emigrants, both through the regular illustrated lectures delivered by them-

1   Canadian advertising for immigrants from Great Britain, c. 1900–1910.

selves or their helpers, and through informal meetings at weekly markets, hiring fairs, agricultural shows or in the agents' own offices.

What were the effects on North-East Scotland of the Dominion government's ever-increasing involvement in emigration agency work? Although there was no resident government agent in Aberdeen until 1907, the region was not neglected. The whole of Scotland, along with the North of England, came under the responsibility of the long-established Glasgow-based agency,[88] headed for twenty-five years by Thomas Grahame. In July 1897 he was succeeded by H. M. Murray, after Murray had spent the Spring in Canada familiarising himself with current conditions. Through his previous occupation as a purser with the Henderson Line, Murray had several years' experience of emigration work, and he continued to set great store by visiting and encouraging ticket agents, particularly in rural areas. When Murray moved to the Welsh office in 1903 he was replaced by J. Bruce Walker, who later became Assistant Superintendent of Emigration, based in London, and ultimately Director of Emigration for Canada in Europe in the 1920s.

From 1880 to 1892 and again from 1903 to 1907 the Glasgow agents shouldered alone the immense task of representing Canadian interests throughout the whole of Scotland and Northern England. In addition to liaising with booking agents, distributing literature and conducting an extensive correspondence with enquirers, they tried to ensure that visiting lecturers attached to their office covered as much of the country as possible, and also travelled widely themselves. In 1885, for instance, while attending the Highland Society's Show in Aberdeen, Thomas Grahame had long conversations with several farmers seeking information on a variety of provinces, and distributed large quantities of pamphlets. He was also careful to maintain links with former tenant farmer delegates, sending them up-to-date promotional literature so that they could continue to act as unofficial emigration agents in their home areas.[89] In 1892, however, the Canadian government appointed two sub-agents under Grahame, W. G. Stuart and Peter Fleming, to represent Canadian interests in the North and the Lowlands respectively.[90] Stuart, based first in Nethy Bridge and later in Elgin, was a member of Inverness town council and a fluent Gaelic speaker, who was convinced that emigration was the only solution to continuing poverty in the Highlands. He came to the Canadian government's notice during a six-month visit to the Dominion in winter 1891-2, as a result of which he was first appointed a temporary agent at the Highland and Agricultural Society Show in summer 1892, and then a supplementary agent for the North of Scotland in December. Fleming was a seasoned emigration agent, having represented the Queensland government's interests in Scotland in the 1880s[91] and having also worked as a travelling selecting agent for Western Australia at an earlier date. When his work ended with the cessation of assisted passages to Queensland in 1891 he turned his attention to Canada and spent two months touring the Dominion in summer 1892. He then offered his services as an agent for the Scottish Lowlands, and having received a glowing testimonial as to his abilities from the Queensland government, the Canadian immigration authorities duly appointed him to this post.

2   Scottish immigrants waiting to go ashore at Quebec, c. 1911.

3 Scottish immigrants, Quebec, c. 1911.

Stuart and Fleming's territories overlapped, in that they both had responsibility for Aberdeenshire. They followed the pattern set by Thomas Grahame, of concentrating on lecturing during the winter and visiting markets, fairs and shows during the summer. Grahame himself continued to visit the North of Scotland; in 1893, for instance, by public demand he delivered several magic lantern lectures to large audiences in Aberdeenshire, and in 1894, along with Stuart and Fleming, he mounted an exhibition at the Highland Society Show in Aberdeen. Between them, Stuart and Fleming delivered an average of 320 lectures per year, including seventy or eighty in North-East Scotland. Stuart intimated his meetings in advance in the press and, where appropriate, delivered his message in Gaelic. In his 1894 report, having explained that he had lectured in rural areas under the auspices of farming societies and church guilds and in towns to literary and scientific associations, he highly recommended this means of promoting emigration to Canada:

> The meetings held were successful in some cases in convicting those who were half inclined to emigrate, and in all cases they were successful in stimulating an interest in those who otherwise would not take the trouble of reading about the country, while at the same time they have been the means of bringing thousands into touch and sympathy with my work who before were cold and indifferent.

But unless specially invited, he preferred to avoid large towns and concentrated instead on the rural areas, where meetings were cheaper to organise and usually attracted a more desirable class of potential emigrants. In a subsequent report Stuart again emphasised the considerable value of illustrated lectures and personal persuasion in arousing and maintaining interest in Canada:

> The people like to see, as well as hear, and in country districts, by far the most profitable field for emigration work, an illustrated lecture is a never failing attraction; and a crowded meeting means enthusiasm, rivetted attention, eager inquiry, and sometimes public discussion. After the lecture is over pamphlets are distributed which are carried home and read. People talk about Canada at their own firesides, and often write for further and fuller information. If at all practicable a personal visit is arranged and a decided impetus is given to emigration from that district, for the experience of the past four years has clearly demonstrated that it is only by earnest concentration of effort that a desirable class of emigrants can be secured. The Scotch are proverbially cautious; and they will not leave their homes nor change their mode of life until they have looked at the matter carefully in all its bearings, and come to the conscientious conviction that it is to their advantage to do so.[92]

Fleming held similar views, although until 1897 he preferred not to advertise indiscriminately in the press, but targeted his attention exclusively on certain categories of agriculturists. He obtained from the valuation rolls the names and addresses of all farmers paying rents of less than £70 per annum and then sent to each household a selection of attractive literature on Canada, along with a handbill listing the places and times when he was to hold meetings. He too valued the informal personal contact achieved at these gatherings:

> I invariably adopt the conversational style of lecture, and at the outset invite my audience to put any question to me even during the course of my address, and in this way get facts driven home to them and give information and advice on points they are specially desirous of being enlightened upon, in a way which is not possible in a formal lecture with the usual paraphernalia of chairman and other accompaniments. The people are quite at their ease, feel quite at home, and judging from the intelligent questions which are put to me, they are as eager for information and as interested as if I were sitting vis a vis with each individual in my own office. At the conclusion of each meeting numbers of my audience invariably remain behind and an interesting and effective chat with them is the result. This method, after many years' experience in dealing with this class, I have found to be the most effective.[93]

In summer 1896 both Fleming and Stuart accompanied parties of emigrants from Liverpool to Canada, where they then secured situations for them. While in the Dominion they collected fresh information to be used in their winter campaigns and also met several Scottish settlers whom they had first encountered at lectures in Scotland and whom they had helped to persuade to emigrate. In 1897 they were assisted in their itinerant work by Thomas Duncan, a farmer and a Member of the Provincial Parliament of Manitoba, who had been appointed to the Glasgow office as a special agent. It was Duncan who persuaded Peter Fleming that he ought to broaden his approach by advertising in the press, in order to attract larger and more varied audiences to his meetings, since Canada was capable of absorbing more categories of settlers than agriculturists alone.[94] After Fleming retired in 1898 Stuart extended his jurisdiction further south and east, with continuing help from Duncan and the use of a portable tent (supplied by the Glasgow office) which housed an exhibition of Canadian produce. Under instructions from H. M. Murray, Duncan in 1898 visited a number of people in Aberdeen whose friends had emigrated the previous year and who, without exception, had sent home good reports of their situation and prospects. He also gave a helping hand to John Grant, based in Dumfries, who had been appointed agent for the South of Scotland in 1897. After W. G. Stuart's death in April 1899, however, Duncan (now based in Carnoustie) devoted most of his time to the North of Scotland until 1902, when he was transferred to London; and the withdrawal of Grant from agency activity in the same year meant that Canadian emigration work in Scotland was once again confined to the Glasgow office.

The reports of the various agents and their superiors in Ottawa indicate that their work was not without effect. Even in 1881 the Department of Agriculture noted that since Canada's claims had been brought more prominently before the 'emigrating classes' across the Atlantic, there had been a rise not only in the numbers but also in the quality of those arriving; and they attributed this to the enthusiastic reports of recent tenant farmer delegations.[95] It was later argued that the appointment of Stuart and Fleming had helped to prevent the decline in Canada's popularity which affected other parts of the British Isles in the mid-1890s.[96] Then the intensified campaign mounted from 1903 by W. T. R. Preston and the London office provoked increased emigration from Scotland, as elsewhere, an increase which J. Bruce Walker in Glasgow ascribed to excellent newspaper advertising, an abundant supply of literature and the introduction of the touring exhibition wagon.[97] But this higher profile campaign, coupled with the extension of the bonus system to the non-prairie provinces, generated a constant stream of enquiries which the Glasgow office found it ever harder to cope with unaided. In 1907, shortly after J. Bruce Walker had moved from Glasgow to become Assistant Superintendent of Emigration in London, he successfully argued the case for an additional agent to be sent from Canada to cover the North of Scotland. John MacLennan, a Gaelic-speaking Canadian of Highland descent, was duly sent to Aberdeen with his wife and two children, arriving on 4 February to open a new regional office at 26 Guild Street. On 26 January 1907 the *Aberdeen Journal*, reporting MacLennan's imminent arrival, noted that the office, which would service the whole of Scotland north of Perth,[98] was meeting a 'long felt want'; and it attributed its establishment to the Canadian government's recognition of the superior calibre of settlers from the North of Scotland. Within a month of arriving MacLennan observed that 'Aberdeen is a fruitful field', a comment which he reiterated in his annual report at the end of the year, when he declared that 'the future outlook is exceedingly hopeful, and the class who are leaving here are very desirable'.[99]

MacLennan followed the usual procedures of distributing literature to individuals and institutions, liaising with booking agents and lecturing and interviewing throughout his area. His surviving weekly reports to the Department of the Interior supplement his more general annual reports; they give a detailed insight into the nature and scope of his activities, and in particular reveal the daunting and unremitting workload which was imposed on him. Most of his time at the Aberdeen office was spent in initiating or answering correspondence, with the help of a typist, or in interviewing ticket agents and prospective emigrants. In his first annual report MacLennan noted that the office, which was open to the public from 8.15 am to 9.30 or even 10.30 pm six days a week,[100] had received an average of twenty-five to thirty visitors daily, although his weekly reports indicate that the number of daily visitors was sometimes very large indeed. During the first week of opening, for instance, MacLennan conducted 258 interviews, 114 of these in one day, and during the following week he interviewed 345 visitors.[101] He also received an average of 100 letters per week, though in winter 1909-10 his incoming mail increased dramatically, and during one week in January 1910 he received as many as 1,299 letters.[102] When MacLennan arrived in Aberdeen, he was faced with a backlog of mail to answer, and he continued to send out about 100 items of correspondence a week, not only letters but also maps, atlases and parcels of promotional literature. During 1908, for instance, the Aberdeen office despatched a total of 7,500 school atlases and 150 wall maps,[103] and several of the letters received were from teachers who used the Canadian government publications as textbooks. MacLennan was also responsible for ensuring that the booking agents were kept well supplied with pamphlets; after J. Obed Smith had inspected the Aberdeen office in February 1909, he reported to Ottawa that MacLennan had distributed about 45,000 general and specialist (provincial) pamphlets during the preceding year, but since the supply of his booking agents was almost exhausted, he would require at least 40,000 copies of general promotional publications, such as *Canada, the Land of Opportunity* or *Canada in a Nutshell.*[104]

It was also part of MacLennan's duties to inspect all the booking agencies within his territory, as well as to receive their bonus claims on eligible emigrants and forward these to Ottawa. By February 1909 he had visited— sometimes more than once—149 of the 190 booking offices in his area, which sometimes involved making week-long trips to the Northern or Western Isles. He often took the opportunity, during visits to outlying areas, to interview individuals who were interested in emigrating, but who could not readily attend his office in Aberdeen; on one occasion in February 1911 he spent six hours one evening at Sinclair's agency in Elgin, interviewing twenty-three people, nearly all of whom he persuaded to book passages to Canada.[105]

But probably more important than the formal interviews—whether at the Aberdeen office or arranged by the booking agents themselves at their premises—were the spontaneous discussions that arose in the course of MacLennan's attendance at markets, shows and hiring fairs all over his area. In May and November, for instance, his weekly reports contained many references to visits he had made to feeing markets, and throughout the summer he was kept busy attending agricultural shows throughout the North. In July 1908 he was given the use of the Department's motor car to assist him in his advertising, and it duly appeared at shows in Aberdeen, Stonehaven, Elgin, Cawdor, Nairn, Inverness and Keith, the latter being attended by over 20,000 people.[106] In a four-week period in July and August 1909 MacLennan travelled widely, attending shows at Elgin, Tain, Monquhitter, Banchory, Turriff, Wick, Huntly, Insch, Fortrose, Keith, Aberchirder, Nairn, Grantown and Pitlochry;[107] and he also made periodic appearances at such diverse events as the weekly farmers' market in Aberdeen and the annual Highland Gathering at Braemar.[108]

MacLennan also undertook an extensive lecture campaign throughout his district, sometimes arranging his lecture trips to coincide with visits to shows or hiring fairs. He was a popular speaker, who often drew capacity audiences. In October 1907, for instance, he reported that he had delivered an illustrated lecture to a 'large and very appreciative audience' at Huntly, many of whom had been unable to gain entry to the hall;[109] on 28 January 1909 the *Aberdeen Journal* similarly reported that hundreds of people had failed to gain admittance to a lecture he had delivered in Fraserburgh, and on 25 March 1909, following a meeting in Dingwall, he was described by a local newspaper, *The North Star and Farmers' Chronicle*, as 'a taking and forcible speaker [who] knows how to speak to an audience'. Four hundred attended a lecture he gave at Insch in January 1909, while 1,800 heard him speak in Elgin two months later;[110] and J. Obed Smith, in his report of March 1909, noted that during the preceding season MacLennan had delivered eighteen lectures to over 6,000 people.

MacLennan did not work entirely unaided. From time to time special agents were attached to his office, mainly to assist with the lecturing campaign. Their visits were not always a complete success, sometimes because booking agents failed to publicise their meetings in advance, and sometimes because of the calibre of the visiting lecturers themselves. In Spring 1908, for instance, Donald Grant, a farm delegate from Souris, Manitoba, was sent to Aberdeen and told to hold meetings throughout the district. But although MacLennan asked the local booking agents to publicise these meetings, only four even replied to his letter. Grant's success was further limited by bad weather and, as MacLennan later reported, while he had 'considerable ability in getting in touch with the people and impressing them with his mission, ... his indifference to his apparel and personal appearance ... was somewhat against him'.[111] MacLennan was critical of another farmer delegate, A. R. Bredin from Manitoba, who was also attached to the Aberdeen office for a few days in Spring 1908:

> Mr Bredin is very agreeable and approachable and thoroughly competent to answer questions, but he lacks an important element in a successful delegate, in that he is not aggressive enough. A successful delegate must take the initiative as many of the interviewers are totally lost in the presence of a stranger. Our men must therefore anticipate the questions and answer them without waiting.[112]

And among other reasons why MacLennan and the booking agents did not welcome the appointment of farm delegates was the fact that many of them promoted their own area of settlement at the expense of other regions and did not therefore present a balanced assessment of the claims of the Dominion as a whole.[113] MacLennan was also expected to co-operate with visiting agents representing Canadian provincial and business interests, but he did not have a very high regard for some of these visitors either. On 24 October 1908 he commented that a recent lecture in Aberdeen by A. Moore of Calgary, representing the Canadian Pacific Railway, had failed because 'he is not a good speaker and has not a sufficient knowledge of general conditions to enable him to answer enquirers readily and satisfactorily'; and he was even more critical of Ontario's provincial agent who, he declared, was out to sabotage the work of the Dominion government agents:

> Had interview with Mr Thomson the Ontario Government representative who found general fault with everything we are doing. He goes among the agents discrediting the work of our Government in Ontario in matters of finding situations etc.[114]

But MacLennan and his superiors were well pleased with Hugh McKerracher of Paisley, Ontario, who was appointed in May 1907 to take charge of the travelling exhibition wagon in the North of Scotland. McKerracher's wife came from Aberdeenshire, and he travelled widely with his exhibition, not only in that county, but throughout the remotest parts of the Highlands, and assisted MacLennan at agricultural shows with what the latter regarded as one of his Department's most effective means of advertising. McKerracher's work was also warmly commended by J. Bruce Walker, Assistant Superintendent of Emigration, in a letter to W. D. Scott, his superior in Ottawa, on 26 November 1907:

> The Highland exhibition democrat, in charge of Mr McKerracher, and which has been attached to Mr MacLennan's division at Aberdeen, has been doing splendid work since it was placed upon the road. The appointment of Mr McKerracher for such work was a singularly fortunate one, and he has been able to accomplish the duty of advertising Canada in a way that commands my warmest approval. He has been confined exclusively to the Highland districts never coming south of Aberdeen, but has penetrated as far north as Caithness, Ross, Sutherland and Inverness, as well as along the Moray Firth to the Counties of Elgin and Moray.[115]

The *Aberdeen Journal* too, in reporting McKerracher's visit to a cattle show at Maud on 8 September 1908, noted his skill in convincing his audience of Canada's attributes:

> Mr McKerracher has a frank, hail-fellow-well-met sort of manner, with a good gift of speech, and an unbounded enthusiasm for Canada. He has the knack of interesting those whom he meets by the glowing accounts he gives of the great field awaiting agriculturists in Canada. He shows how Scotsmen have developed the resources, and increased the land values of the country districts, and he has been adding his quota to the number of emigrants who have elected to make the Dominion their home.

And J. Obed Smith, in his report of March 1909 on the work of the Aberdeen office, felt that the choice of travelling agent had been vindicated, in that 'no better service could be accomplished than that which is being attained through Mr McKerracher and under Mr MacLennan's guidance. This is an illustration of my idea, that to get more of the class of people we require we must get away from the larger towns into the smaller places, just as Mr McKerracher does among the Highlands of Scotland'.

Apart from a two-month visit to Canada in summer 1910, MacLennan was based at Aberdeen from February 1907 until April 1911. He was then transferred to the Liverpool agency, being succeeded by W. B. Cumming, whose grandfather had emigrated from Elgin to Canada around 1830. Cumming continued MacLennan's policy of visiting agricultural fairs and feeing markets, and conducted interviews which had been arranged by the booking agents throughout his region. He was faithfully assisted by Hugh McKerracher, who not only mounted the travelling exhibition, but also gave over fifty lectures during the winter of 1911-12. Indeed, under Cumming and his successors the winter lecturing campaign was stepped up, seventy-seven lectures being delivered by Cumming or his assistants between October 1911 and March 1912, entirely in rural areas, and often in country schoolhouses.[116]

When Cumming resigned from his post over a pay dispute in August 1912,[117] he was replaced temporarily by Frederick Campbell, who had originally been appointed a delegate from Nova Scotia to Britain two years earlier. Then in February 1913 G. G. Archibald was appointed government emigration agent for the North of Scotland, retaining this post until the outbreak of the First World War brought an end to that era of emigration agency activity.

Under both Campbell and Archibald the lecturing campaign continued unabated; in the winter of 1912-13 103 lectures were delivered in Northern Scotland under the Dominion government's auspices; by Campbell (32), McKerracher (47), by Mrs H. Niblett, visiting from Winnipeg (8), by James Murray, the clerk at the Aberdeen office (7) and ultimately by Archibald (9). The lectures were generally followed by personal interviews, and in addition, 4,290 casual callers were interviewed at the Aberdeen office, which was now located in a more prominent position, on the city's main street. During the following year 122 lectures were delivered in Archibald's territory, forty-three by the agent himself, fifty by McKerracher, twenty by James Murray and nine by Mrs Niblett. The lecturers concentrated on rural districts remote from the railway, where they generally attracted enthusiastic capacity audiences, and even though the big farmers in these areas were unsympathetic to their cause, they generally gave them a respectful hearing.[118] The regular agents were assisted by a number of farm delegates, including three Scottish emigrants who had been in Canada for a total of ninety-eight years; and they also had unofficial help from successful settlers who were visiting their homeland. Archibald attached particular importance to the value of precedent and to the quiet way in which these emigrants encouraged their friends and acquaintances to follow their example. In his first annual report in 1913 he noted that 'When a bright young man or woman returns home from Canada with the marks of success those who have not yet decided about emigration have placed before them a concrete fact that convinces much more surely than lectures or pamphlets'; and in 1914, after reporting a great rush to Canada between January and March, he added that 'in nearly all cases the emigration was influenced to a large extent by the Canadian success of some friend or relative'.

The evidence for emigration

The reports of the various agents indicate not only the ways in which they tried to stimulate interest in emigration, but also reflect something of the (sometimes fluctuating) response to their endeavours. In 1907 business was brisk, and in his very first weekly report, on 2 March, MacLennan noted that 150 people had left Aberdeen for Canada in two recent sailings (presumably from Liverpool). The following week he reported:

A large number are leaving here for Canada by every Boat. The total since Jan. 1st leaving this city is 561—250 of them having left in the last ten days and a large number more would have gone except that they cannot get booking this

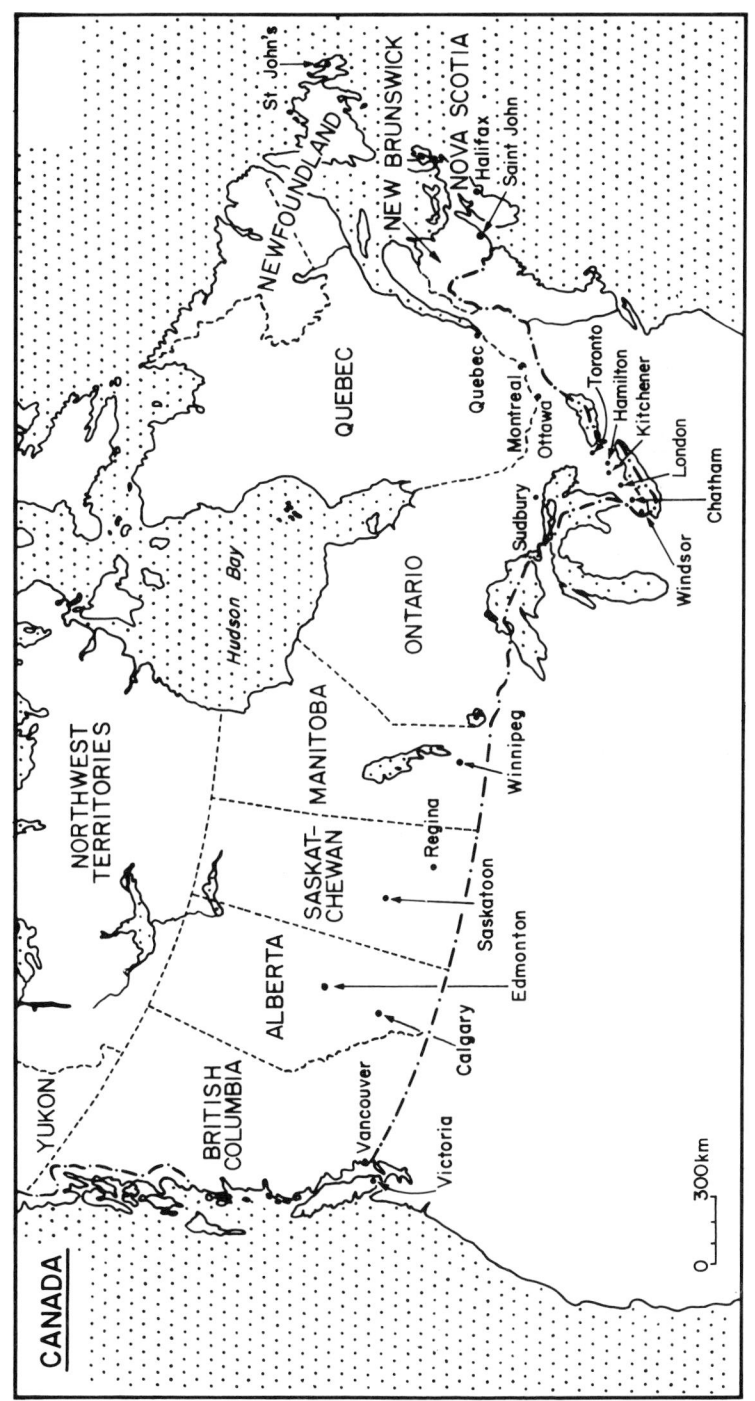

month. There are some splendid men going from the surrounding country. The outlook is good.

Two weeks later, on 23 March, the exodus had not abated:

> The rush still continues from here. 70 of the number who were to go out 10 days ago for Mr Smart will leave on the 30th inst. Booking Agents cannot fill the demands for April and first of May consequently I presume that some of those who are ready to go now, will not go out later. There will be a big rush after the 28th of May when the time of service of a large number expires. Everything looks favourable.

And on 1 June MacLennan duly reported that 'the crowds leaving on trains for every boat sailing shows that the good work is still going on'. In his later review of the year's work he reckoned that over 1,200 emigrants had left Aberdeen for Canada in 1907. But this estimate was more than doubled by J. Obed Smith, who subsequently claimed that 3,000 emigrants—practically one per cent of the county's population—had gone from Aberdeenshire to Canada in 1907; and Smith noted that the entire county of Inverness, with a population of 90,000 and 'any number' of booking agents, had not sent away as many emigrants as some individual villages in Aberdeenshire.[119]

In 1908-9 however, a reaction set in, caused partly by unfavourable press reports of the effects of a trade depression in Canada. As Obed Smith observed:

> It was found that a number of intending emigrants were somewhat discouraged by the news of lack of employment in large centres like Montreal, Toronto, Winnipeg and Vancouver, and our Agent finds it extremely difficult to get them to see any distinction between idle men in Toronto or Winnipeg, and the farmer forty or fifty miles away in want of a servant.[120]

But even agriculturists were being discouraged from emigrating at this time by the imposition of the £5 landing money charge, levied on emigrants after 1907.[121] As a result, noted MacLennan on 2 May 1908:

> A very quiet week in this district. Booking agents are hoping for better results at Term time after May 28th but I do not anticipate much movement as a large number of the farm hands have not the necessary £5 after paying their fares.

In 1909 however, the number of farm and domestic servants leaving the North of Scotland was twenty per cent up on similar departures the previous year, and by 1910 confidence was clearly returning. On 19 February MacLennan predicted that the exodus from his area was likely to double that of 1909 and a month later he reported:

> We are having splendid results. Hundreds of the very best classes are leaving every week. I have continual calls from booking agents to come to the various

towns to meet groups of men and women who are desirous of getting information.[122]

During the first three months of 1910 three times as many farm servants emigrated from his region as during the same period the previous year.[123] This momentum was maintained throughout the rest of the year and into 1911, which MacLennan anticipated was likely to be another record year. 'Canada is the chief topic of conversation in the North of Scotland', he asserted on 4 February, and the week ending 1 April 'was the largest week in the history of Emigration from this section. Over 450 left Aberdeen for Saturday's sailing from Glasgow, and 150 left by the Liverpool boats during the week'. Unfortunately however, many of those leaving were tradesmen or men of sedentary occupations, classes of settler not then wanted in Canada; so when adverse reports of the experiences of some of these emigrants began to filter back to Scotland by late 1913, the exodus received another check. But this too was regarded as a temporary setback by G. G. Archibald, who predicted in his annual report for 1913-14 (submitted five months before the outbreak of war brought an abrupt end to emigration) that 'Many are but marking time in the land of the heather until they answer that insistent call which bids them wrest from Canada that future which is denied their best efforts in the home of their fathers'.

The government agents' comments were based largely on statistics submitted by the booking agents, who dealt with the actual removal of emigrants. MacLennan's prediction of intensified interest in his report of 19 February 1910, for instance, was based on the fact that two ticket agents, in Fraserburgh and Arbroath, had already submitted more bonus claims that year than in the whole preceding three-year period. And since some Aberdeen ticket offices had received over 100 Spring bookings by November 1910, MacLennan anticipated a continuing large exodus in 1911.[124] From the volume of bonus claims made by their booking agents, the Aberdeen office was able to chart local interest in emigration, at least in terms of those categories of emigrants eligible for bonus payments. In 1910, MacLennan reported, 3,042 bonus applications were submitted by agents in his region, this being nearly two-and-a-half times the number made during 1909. In 1911 the number of claims rose to 3,804, but fell in 1912 and 1913 to 3,773 and 2,864 respectively.[125]

There is no complete statistical record of the number of emigrants who left North-East Scotland for Canada—or probably any other destination—during the period under review. Yet it is still possible to make a general assessment of the extent and nature of the movement by piecing together occasional statistical references from a variety of sources on both sides of the Atlantic. These include the bonus claims recorded by John MacLennan and his successors and mentioned, as above, in their annual reports of 1910-14, and the Department of the Interior's temporary record of the counties of origin of all British settlers; this states that together, the counties of Banff, Kincardine, Moray or Elgin, Nairn, and particularly Aberdeen, sent a total of 361, 894 and 1,669 settlers to Canada in the years 1902, 1903 and 1904 respectively.[126] There are also periodic indications in the correspondence of some booking agents of the number of emigrants who passed through their hands. In 1911, for instance, H. W. J. Paton in Aberdeen declared that his firm normally gave advances to up to 300 emigrants per year to assist them to go to Canada. His business subsequently increased steadily with the escalating interest in emigration; for in reviewing his achievements in 1919, Paton noted that in the five years after he opened his agency in 1908, business had increased tenfold, until in 1913 he was handling 2,000 passengers a year, nearly half of whom went to Canada.[127] Then the Aberdeen County Medical Officer, Dr Watt, in his annual report for 1913, alleged that emigration and migration were largely responsible for a decrease of 7,673 in the county's population since the 1910 census; and on the basis of figures supplied by G. G. Archibald, he reckoned that almost 4,000 of these people had gone abroad, primarily to Canada.[128]

These occasional statistics can be supplemented by the more frequent— though still unsystematic—references to the departure of emigrants for Canada made by the *Aberdeen Journal*, which cover not only the period when alternative Canadian sources are intermittently available, but also the years before 1900, when the Canadian immigration authorities never specifically recorded departures from North-East Scotland. On at least 429 occasions between 1881 and 1914 the *Aberdeen Journal* made reference to contingents of emigrants leaving Aberdeen railway station en route for a variety of destinations. Seventy-seven of these entries did not enumerate the emigrants in the party, but if the figures in the remaining 352 entries are added together, a total of 13,919 emigrants is obtained. Canada was the destination most frequently mentioned, appearing in 315 of the 429 press references, and a total of 11,264 emigrants is obtained by adding together the figures given in 288 of these entries.

But clearly this figure cannot be taken as a reliable indication of the extent of emigration from North-East Scotland to Canada. In the first place, the *Aberdeen Journal* did not systematically record every single departure of emigrant parties from the locality; and of those which it did record, in some cases no statistics at all were given, the party being described simply as 'large' or 'small'; in other cases the figures given were only approximate; and in many instances it is impossible to isolate the Canadian element in a mixed contingent which was ultimately bound for a number of foreign destinations.[129] Indeed, the dangers of relying on the local press for statistical information are readily seen by comparing the *Aberdeen Journal*'s records with those of the Canadian immigration authorities; for example, whereas in the three years 1902-4 the Department of the Interior recorded the arrival of a total of 2,924 settlers from North-East Scotland, the *Aberdeen Journal* enumerated the departure of only 157 individuals for the Dominion in the same period. J. Obed Smith declared that 3,000 people emigrated from Aberdeenshire alone to Canada in 1907, but the *Aberdeen Journal* noted only 1,741 at the most.[130] And the total of 14,700 bonus claims alone submitted by ticket agents to the Dominion government office in Aberdeen between 1909 and 1913 greatly exceeds the entire exodus enumerated by the *Aberdeen Journal* throughout the period 1881-1914.[131]

The inadequacy of the various sources of information therefore makes it impossible to obtain an accurate statistical record of emigration from North-East Scotland to Canada during the three decades preceding the First World War. But by making use of some of the scanty Canadian records which have survived, it is possible to give a rough estimate of the extent of this movement. Between 1902 and 1904 the counties of North-East Scotland provided an average each year of just over ten per cent of Scotland's emigrants to Canada; and if this percentage is applied to Scottish emigration statistics for the remaining years when no individual county figures are available, it appears that the North-East region may have sent a total of around 35,440 emigrants to Canada during the period 1881-1914.

Despite the limitations of the local press as a source of statistical information, it nevertheless gives an insight into the conduct and effects of the emigrant movement, supplying valuable non-quantitative evidence which complements and expands the reports of the Canadian government agents. While these agents viewed their work in Northern Scotland as part of a national and international campaign to promote settlement in Canada, the local press considered the exodus more in the light of its impact on the North-East region, and often highlighted particular communities and institutions which were affected by the loss of population. At the simplest level, of course, the newspapers provided corroborative proof that emigration was indeed taking place; and their descriptions of scenes that occurred at local railway stations when emigrant parties took their leave reflect continuing contemporary interest in the movement to Canada. On 4 June 1910, for instance, the *Aberdeen Journal* noted a revival of interest after a period when the departure of large emigrant parties had become so commonplace that it had ceased to be a novelty and had attracted less public attention than the departure of much smaller contingents in earlier periods. That week, however, an extra-heavy exodus had led to renewed public interest, when a large crowd had gathered to watch the departure of a special train taking a mixed party of around 250 emigrants to Liverpool to embark for Canada on the SS *Empress of Ireland*:

> There were artisans, with their families, going out to start life afresh; in other carriages, here and there in the long train, were wives and children going out to join husbands and fathers, who had preceded them; there were reserved compartments, in which were companies of girls, who, having clubbed together, were going out as servants and seamstresses; but young men of the farming and labouring classes composed the greater proportion of the special's living freight.

And the departure of a total of 270 emigrants on various trains for Liverpool and Glasgow the following day had brought another huge crowd to Aberdeen Joint Station.

On 5 June 1911, after noting that there were still 'no signs of any abatement in the large numbers who are weekly leaving these shores for Canada', the *Aberdeen Journal* went on to report that 'On Saturday morning two large parties said good-bye to the Granite City, and, notwithstanding the early hour, a large number of friends and relatives of the emigrants found their way to the Joint Station for the purpose of saying farewell'. By 1913 public interest was even more intense. On 8 March the *Aberdeen Journal* reported the scenes that had taken place at the Joint Station when fifty emigrants had left the previous evening:

> A crowd, numbering several hundreds, assembled to witness the departure of the last train. The relatives of the emigrants were admitted to the platform, but others were not allowed to enter the barriers. There was much handshaking in the neighbourhood of the reserved carriages in which the emigrants travelled, and not a few mothers, wives, and sisters were in tears. Punctually to the minute the train steamed out of the station. A vigorous cheer was raised by the crowd, and was re-echoed from the carriages. For a moment there was a flutter of waving kerchiefs, but the last carriage speedily passed beyond the circle of light, and the station soon resumed its normal appearance.

The scene was re-enacted a fortnight later, when almost 300 emigrants, bound for Canada and the USA, were seen off to Glasgow by a crowd of several hundred, posing a considerable threat to public order:

> The railway officials were ready for all emergencies. The barricade gates were closed, and a posse of police ... was on the spot. About half-past 7 o'clock the station area was crowded, there being a sea of faces from one end to the other. None but ticket-holders were allowed through the gates. The crowd became denser every minute, and it required all the skill of the police officers to keep order. As the time for the departure of the train came on the situation became somewhat alarming. A rush was made at one of the gates, but police reinforcements were at hand, and, along with the railway porters, drove the intruders back. In other quarters things were kept lively by a number of young men attempting to jump the railings, and those who did get over were speedily turned back by the police. Crowds came trooping in from the Denburn direction. These, however, were led through the gateways, and when the gong for the departure of the train sounded order prevailed.[132]

These public demonstrations extended even to provincial stations, as when twelve emigrants left Fraserburgh on 4 April, the *Aberdeen Journal* reported the following day that they had been seen off by a crowd of almost 1,000.

Fraserburgh was one of the regional centres regularly singled out by the *Aberdeen Journal* in its selective reports of significant emigrant departures. On 20 March 1888, for instance, it noted that a large number of people had left the district in the previous fortnight, mainly for central Canada, and in reporting the departure of another large party from the area on 19 April 1889, it drew particular attention to the favourable reports that had been sent home by recent settlers. On a number of occasions the newspaper named the individual emigrants, including fourteen who were seen off by several hundred well-wishers in April 1910, and those who made up another large party from Fraserburgh later that year.[133] In the six months from April to September 1910, the *Aberdeen Journal* noted, around 100 Fraserburgh people had sought new homes across the Atlantic. This trend was stepped up the following year, for on 9 January 1911 the *Aberdeen Journal* reported that the 300 people who were to leave that year would form the biggest annual emigration in the town's history. Over 100 passages had already been booked, with British Columbia the most popular destination, and by the end of the year (as the newspaper noted on 26 December) 350 people had indeed emigrated from Fraserburgh, almost all bound for Canada. In fact, the numerical significance of Fraserburgh people in Manitoba was such that in April 1911 they formed a Fraserburgh Society in Winnipeg; expatriates from other parts of the North-East were subsequently admitted and by the end of the year the Society had been transformed into the Aberdeenshire, Kincardineshire and Banffshire Association, with a membership of 220.[134]

Detailed press reporting of local emigration is particularly useful for periods in which no alternative sources of information—such as the Dominion government agents' reports—are available. In Spring 1882, for instance, when there was a significant upsurge in emigration from North-East Scotland, the *Aberdeen Journal*, having sought information from several booking agents on the character and extent of the exodus, published a detailed analysis of their reports in an article on 26 May. It stressed that its estimates of local emigration were only an approximation, which seriously understated the true volume of the movement, since it had taken into account only those emigrants who had dealt with local ticket agencies and excluded the many who had made their bookings direct from Glasgow. Even so, almost 1,000 people were reckoned to have emigrated from Aberdeen city alone since January, primarily to Canada and particularly to Manitoba, where about 400 had settled; and many more were booked to leave in June. Emigrants from other parts of the region had settled in a variety of locations in North America, Australasia and Africa, and among the places highlighted as having experienced a significant exodus were Ellon, New Deer, Fraserburgh, Peterhead, Maud, Oldmeldrum, Inverurie, Huntly, Alford, Fyvie, Keith, Banff, Turriff, Elgin and Inverness. Some of the emigrants from Peterhead had been persuaded to leave by the success of earlier emigrants, mainly in America, while one emigrant from Ellon (Charles Marr) had induced around twenty of his fellow-townsmen to accompany him to Canada. Inverness had despatched well over 200 emigrants during the Spring, including sixty to Canada, and even the village and district of Maud in Aberdeenshire had lost thirty-eight inhabitants in this way between January and April 1882.

Another upsurge in emigration from Aberdeenshire in 1888 was discussed in detail by the *Aberdeen Journal* in a report on 14 April. On this occasion the local interest coincided with an increased exodus of working people from all over the British Isles, a 'steady, continuous stream' which the newspaper likened to 'the great depletion of the country' which had occurred after the Australian gold discoveries in the 1850s and which it predicted would continue until the end of the year. Demand had not slackened even when shipowners had raised their fares, and indeed many people, in order to secure a passage, had been willing and able to pay higher rates for superior accommodation. It was reckoned that over 1,000 emigrants had left Aberdeen city alone in the previous eight weeks, with one single local agent, Robert Davidson, having sent out 400 clients in that period.

Even when alternative sources of information do become available, the *Aberdeen Journal* continues to provide corroborative evidence of emigration, often in a form which also reveals some of the social effects of the exodus on the local community. On 29 May 1907, for instance, it claimed that recent emigration to Canada and the USA had seriously affected the letting of property in Aberdeen, particularly in the Torry district; and later that year, on 22 October, it reported the annual meeting of the Aberdeen YMCA, which had lost many of its most vigorous members during the year, partly as a result of an 'unprecedented rush of emigration'. On another occasion, on 27 March 1911, it was noted that Crown Terrace Baptist Church in the city was about to lose fifteen members to Canada, most of whom were emigrating for the sake of giving their children a better start in life. The annual report for 1911 made to the Trustees and Managers of the Aberdeen Savings Bank, and published in the *Aberdeen Journal* on 28 June 1912, shows the effects of emigration on the bank's deposits. During the year ended 20 November 1911 850 depositors who had uplifted their credit balances, amounting to a total of around £25,000, had specified that they were closing their accounts in order to emigrate; and in the period from 20 November 1911 to 20 June 1912 a further 570 depositors had withdrawn £14,866 for the same purpose. Far from their emigration being a reaction to poverty, the working people who made up most of the Savings Bank's depositors clearly regarded their removal as an investment for themselves and their families. The majority, according to the Bank's report, were emigrating to Canada, with the rest settling either in the USA or Australia; and, it concluded, 'there can be no doubt that the exodus from Scotland, but particularly from the northern portion of it, is, in relation to its population, very great indeed'.[135]

Although North-East Scotland supplied only a small fraction of the twelve-and-a-half million emigrants who left the British Isles between 1881 and 1914, within the area the steady drain of population abroad remained a significant feature of social and economic life, which provoked regular contemporary comment. During the earlier part of the nineteenth century prospective emigrants in this region, as in the rest of the country, were bombarded with information and advice from a variety of countries, inviting them to take advantage of their offers of employment or land in abundance. Even at this stage Canada was clearly the destination which aroused most interest in North-East Scotland, particularly when its attractions were publicised by earlier emigrants from the region, whose advice was felt to have a greater seal of authenticity. Then after Confederation the Canadian government launched an aggressive international recruitment campaign in Britain and Europe, attempting, through various promotional tools, to divert emigrants away from the USA to its own territories, especially the newly-opened western prairies. In North-East Scotland, where this campaign was built on a solid foundation of enthusiasm for Canada, the Dominion government's endeavours were particularly successful. It rapidly cornered the main part of the emigration market in this area, overcoming the periodic challenges of rival destinations in the USA, the Antipodes and South Africa and adding its official voice to the many private campaigners who continued to advocate settlement in Canada.

It has been demonstrated that probably the most crucial element in this official recruitment campaign was the systematic use of an army of agents, whose task it was to inform, persuade and assist intending emigrants. Dominion government emigration agents, stationed at strategic locations all over Britain and Europe, ensured that the areas for which they were responsible were saturated with promotional material, communicated verbally, visually and through the distribution of literature. They were supported in this task by visiting farm delegates, provincial agents and representatives of the transcontinental railway companies, as well as by a vast number of ticket agents, who made the practical arrangements for the emigrants' removal.

Having established that North-East Scotland was consistently bombarded with propaganda encouraging emigration to Canada, the following chapters will examine the nature of this encouragement in some detail. The Canadian campaign was clearly targeted at certain specific categories of settler; so were they satisfied with the recruits they obtained from North-East Scotland, or did they have to cope with an influx of unsuitable emigrants? As for the emigrants themselves, local press evidence indicates that they preferred Canada to any other destination; but what were the particular incentives that persuaded them to flock to the Dominion in increasing numbers, and did their subsequent experiences confirm or deny their high expectations?

NOTES

1) A total of 4,042,070 foreign emigrants sailed from British ports in the years 1881-1913. Eighty per cent of these emigrants were bound for the USA, and they also accounted for 42 per cent of total departures from the British Isles to the USA. (See *Board of Trade annual returns: papers relating to emigration, 1881-1913*, abstract reproduced in table I). Emigration statistics should be treated with caution, however, for they were never collected primarily in order to record emigration as such, and they can distort the true nature of the movement. For instance, 'emigration' was calculated by subtracting arrivals in Britain from non-European countries from departures to these regions, but the balance clearly did not reflect true emigration, for the two movements were not directly related. It was not until 1912 that emigrants were distinguished from temporary passengers in the returns.

2) *Ibid.* Canada accounted for 26 per cent of English emigrants between 1881 and 1913, and a numerical majority in each year from 1905 to 1913. (Seven per cent of Irish emigrants, 15 per cent of foreign emigrants, 1 per cent of those of indeterminate nationality, and 41 per cent of emigrants of British colonial origin (after 1908) also went to Canada).

3) The National Emigration League had been made up of a coalition of private societies which had aimed to aid emigration from distressed areas, but it was unable to formulate any clear policy through which to achieve its aims. (See

Howard Malchow, *Population pressures: emigration and government in late nineteenth-century Britain* (Palo Alto, Calif.), 1979, pp. 13-53).

4) In 1883 and 1884 Lady Gordon Cathcart settled 66 distressed families from her Hebridean estates on land in western Canada under the provisions of the 1872 Dominion Land Act. The scheme succeeded, although the settlers were unwilling to repay their advances.

5) See, for instance, Lord Brabazon, 'State-directed emigration: its necessity' in *Nineteenth Century*, vol. 16 (Nov. 1884) pp. 764-87; 'State-directed colonisation' in *West. Rev.*, vol. 128 (Apr. 1887) pp. 71-82; and 'Colonies and colonisation' in *ibid*, vol. 131 (Jan. 1889) pp. 13-25.

6) See, for instance, 'The economy of emigration' in *West. Rev.*, vol. 125 (Apr. 1886) pp. 515-27; and 'Work for willing hands: a practical plan for state-aided emigration' in *Blackwood's*, vol. 143 (Feb. 1888) pp. 273-8.

7) Following the Napier Commission's report, both New Zealand and Canada offered free grants of land to crofter emigrants. In New Zealand 10,000 acres were set apart for 1,000 crofters, who could each then purchase a further 20 acres at £1 per acre; while the Canadian government agreed to grant 160 acres to settlers in Manitoba and the North-West Territories. Neither Canada nor New Zealand, however, would accept responsibility for recovering the loans which were to be advanced to the settlers by the British government.

8) For details of the Irish and Highland emigration schemes, see W. A. Carrothers, *Emigration from the British Isles*, pp. 230-5; and Stuart MacDonald, 'Crofter colonisation in Canada, 1886-1902: the Scottish political background' in *Northern Scotland*, vol. 7, no. 1 (1986) pp. 47-59.

9) *Report from the Select Committee on Colonisation* (PP 1890-91 (152) XI, p. 586)

10) See, for instance, J. H. Tuke, 'State aid to emigrants, a reply to Lord Brabazon' in *Nineteenth Century*, vol. 17 (Feb. 1885) pp. 280-96.

11) See, for instance, John Martineau, 'Natural emigration' in *Blackwood's*, vol. 146 (July 1889) pp. 36-48; and Malchow, *Population pressures*, pp. 188-9. See also 'Justitia', *Emigration and the Malthusian craze in relation to the labourers' position* (1886) in British Library Tracts, 1867-87 (8282. de. 24. 1-18 (5)).

12) Note, in respect of the better economic circumstances of emigrants, the marked decline in Irish emigration in the late nineteenth century (partly for lack of population on which to draw).

13) The report of the Colonisation Committee in 1891 recommended that this grant be increased to £1,000 so that branch offices could be opened in Ireland, Scotland and some of the main provincial towns in England. (PP 1892 [C.6573] LVI, p. 3.

14) *Report on the Emigrants' Information Office for the half year ended 31 March 1887* (PP 1887 [C.5078] vol. LVII, p. 673).

15) *Ibid*, p. 670; and subsequent annual reports of the EIO.

16) See, for instance, annual reports for year ended 1890—information on tropical colonies included; and 1893—information on USA included. (PP 1890-91 [C.6277] LVI, p. 149; and PP 1893-94 [C.7269] LX, p. 535).

17) *AJ*, 20 Oct. 1886. Only three applications were said to have come from people with capital.

18) W. A. Carrothers, *Emigration from the British Isles*, pp. 241, 242.

19) See *AJ*, 14 Dec. 1895, 18 Jan. 1898.

20) *Ibid*, 17 Sept. 1886.

21) E.g., *ibid*, 12 May 1883, 26 June 1885, 7 Sept. 1886, 21 Mar. 1889.

22) See vol. I, pp. 254-9.

23) See, for instance, United States Statutes at Large, 48th Congress, 1883-5, vol. 23, p. 332: An Act to prohibit the importation and migration of foreigners and aliens under contract or agreement to perform labour in the United States, its territories and the District of Columbia.

24) E.g., *AJ*, 7 Feb. 1888, 24 June 1891, 29 Oct. 1892, 4 Oct. 1895, 1 Jan. 1910, 26 Feb. 1913.

25) E.g., *ibid*, 26, 28 May, 7 June, 22, 23 Oct., 25 Nov. 1902; 15 Jan., 7 Mar. 1903. See also below, pp. 234-5.

26) See, for instance, 6 June 1891, 7 Dec. 1895, 8 May, 11, 24 July 1896, 28 Apr. 1897. See also *Granite Cutters' Journal*, vol. I, no. 3 (July 1901), p. 6; no. 11 (Mar. 1902) (AUA, MSS 2655/2/1/1-9).

27) *AJ*, 26, 30 Jan., 22 Feb., 6 June 1889.

28) See, for instance, *GCJ*, vol. I, no. 6 (Oct. 1901), p. 6.

29) For instance, the only interviews with returned emigrants or travellers to South Africa which were published in the *Aberdeen Journal* appeared in 1896 (9 June and 29 December) as did the only report of a (well-attended) lecture on the Transvaal (16 October) and on 25 December 1897 it was reported that 'a considerable number of masons' had left for South Africa that year. In both 1896 and 1897 South Africa was the second most popular destination with Scottish and British emigrants.

30) Dept of Agriculture, *annual reports on immigration, 1881, 1882, 1883* (in National Library of Canada, Official Publications Division).

31) Dept of the Interior, *annual report on immigration, 1900*. See also Lord Strathcona to James Smart, Deputy Minister of the Interior, letter dated 23 Mar. 1899 (PAC, microfilm reel no. C-4728, vol. 60, file 2634, part 2).

32) See, for instance, reports of H. M. Murray (Glasgow agent) in Dept of the Interior, *annual reports on immigration, 1899 and 1900*; see also W. T. R. Preston, Asst Supt of Emigration, London to James Smart, Deputy Minister of the Interior, Ottawa, letter dated 9 June 1899 (PAC, C-4741, vol. 74, file 4995).

33) See below, p. 14.

34) *AJ*, 11 Nov. 1909.

35) *Ibid*, 17 Oct. 1910.

36) *Ibid*, 14 Apr. 1882, 12 June 1883, 30 Jan. 1894.

37) *Ibid*, 23 June 1910.

38) See, for instance, *ibid*, 16 May 1884 (lecture to the Aberdeen Chamber of Commerce by Sir Henry Parkes, former Prime Minister of New South Wales); 20 Jan. 1886 (advertisement for a children's nurse to go to Australia); 3 Mar. 1887 (report of the experiences of a local emigrant in Western Australia); 22 Oct. 1908 (intimation of visit to MacKay Brothers' agency by Mrs Thomas Menzies, lady superintendent, to recruit female emigrants); 23 Dec. 1908 (advertisement by R. B. Arthur's agency in Aberdeen for 15 agriculturists for farms in New South Wales, at £6 assisted passages); 16 July 1910 (lecture by a Melbourne settler of 25 years' standing, visiting Britain as a representative of the Victoria government).

39) *Ibid*, 10 Apr. (Aberdeen); 13, 15, 16 Apr. (Laurencekirk, Banchory, Aboyne, Ballater).

40) *Ibid*, 30 July 1886.

41) *Ibid*, 4 Mar. 1891, 18, 21 Mar. 1893, 26 Mar. 1894.

42) *Ibid*, 12 Nov. 1890.

43) J. Obed Smith, Asst Supt of Emigration, London, to W. D. Scott, Supt of Immigration, Ottawa: report on British agencies, 15 Mar. 1909 (in PAC, RG

76, C-10294, vol. 405, file 590687, part 1: reports and correspondence of John MacLennan, immigration agent in Scotland).

44) *AJ*, 21 June 1906, taken from a New Zealand newspaper.

45) Report for week ending 16 Oct. 1910 (PAC, RG 76, C-10294, vol. 405, file 590687, part 1).

46) *Ibid*, week ending 15 Apr. 1911.

47) See, for instance, 6, 7, 10 Apr. 1911.

48) *AJ*, 25, 27 May 1911. For the past decade, it pointed out, Scottish (Presbyterian) emigration had largely surpassed the Irish (Roman Catholic) exodus.

49) *Ibid*, 2 June 1911. See also *Hansard: official reports, first series*, vol. xxvi (22 May—16 June 1911), pp. 864, 1054.

50) *Ibid*, 24 May 1912.

51) See also below, pp. 170-8.

52) MacLennan's Report, incorporated in Dept of the Interior, *annual report on immigration, 1908-9*.

53) The bonus payments were introduced five years after the ending of a passenger warrant system which had operated between 1872 and 1888. Steamship companies, led by the Beaver Line, had negotiated with the Dominion government to offer assisted passages to Canadian ports in order to counteract competition from American shipping lines on the transatlantic route.

54) H. Gordon Skilling, *Canadian representation abroad: from agency to embassy* (Toronto, 1945), p. 19.

55) See, for instance, W. D. Scott, Ottawa, to MacKay, Aberdeen, 3 Oct. 1913, and *ibid*, 22 Sept. 1914. On the latter occasion, after complaining that MacKay had sent out a girl who had no intention of entering domestic service, Scott went on: 'While this matter is under discussion I would point out that the above is only one out of several cases which have lately come to our attention where girls booked by you to Canada have not made good and I would like you to understand that if this state of affairs is going to continue the Department will, much to our regret, be obliged to report unfavourably upon the cases of immigrants selected by your officials. (PAC, RG 76, C-10644, vol. 564, file 809010, MacKay Brothers, Aberdeen, lists, 1910-19).

56) *Ibid*.

57) PAC, RG 76, C-10621, vol. 530, file 803485, part 1: W. G. Maitland, Longside, Aberdeenshire, booking agent, lists, 1910-19.

58) *Ibid*. See, for instance, letters dated 9 Apr., 15, 28 May, 3 July 1912. See also W. D. Scott to Maitland, 7 Aug. 1913, returning eleven bonus applications for Spring sailings which had not been received until July: 'I do not see any reason why bonus claims should be kept in the office four or five months before mailing and as you have been repeatedly warned that claims for bonus should be sent to our office prior to the sailing of the immigrant, it has been decided that we would not consider any belated claims received from your firm'.

59) *AJ*, 5 Apr. 1912. Maitland said in his defence that he had withheld the tickets because of uncertainty over the vessel's sailing date, owing to a dockers' strike, but the sheriff ruled that the payment of a deposit constituted the making of a definite contract, and that Maitland was bound to issue the tickets in return.

60) See, for instance, letters of 2 Apr., 26 Dec. 1907, 24 Jan., 13 Apr. 1908, 8 Sept. 1913.

61) See above, pp. 9-10.

62) *AJ*, 23 June 1910; see also above, p. 9.

63) Smith to Scott, 28 Nov. 1911 (PAC, RG 76, C-10291-2, vol. 401, file 572933:

J. Fraser, Auditor-General, Ottawa, re. advertising in the *Aberdeen Free Press*, 1906, 1909-14).

64) *Ibid*, memo. by Scott, 9 Jan. 1919.

65) See, for instance, report by H. M. Murray, Glasgow agent, 1901, in which he noted that the Glasgow office's three sets of slides had been in daily use for a period of over four months; and *ibid*, 1902, when, apart from the official agents' work, he reported that nearly 200 meetings had been held by voluntary lecturers who used these slides and distributed pamphlets supplied by the office. (Murray's reports incorporated in Dept of the Interior, *annual reports on immigration, 1901 and 1902*).

66) *AJ*, 7 Nov. 1905, 27 Jan., 28, 29 Nov. 1906.

67) *Ibid*, 12 May 1899, 29 Jan. 1903, 22 Dec. 1911.

68) *Ibid*, 24 Nov. 1899. See also 27 Feb. 1899 for a lecture by Lord Aberdeen to the Haddo House Club, and 18 Apr. 1898 for a similar lecture to the Haddo House Club by his secretary in Canada, Captain John Sinclair.

69) *Ibid*, 6 Mar. 1885, 24, 25 Oct. 1905. See also 22 Apr. 1898, 20 June 1906 and 10 Jan. 1912 for other lectures on Canada organised under the auspices of the Aberdeen YMCA.

70) For instance, *ibid*, 21 Jan. 1909, when a 'farmer delegate' addressed a meeting at Aberlour; Strachan Mutual Improvement Association in 1907 also debated the pros and cons of emigration itself (*AJ*, 18 Jan. 1907) and came down in its favour by sixteen votes to eight.

71) See below, pp. 209-19.

72) See also below, pp. 67-74.

73) *AJ*, 4 Feb. 1913; see also G. G. Archibald's report, incorporated in Dept of the Interior, *annual report on immigration, 1913*.

74) *AJ*, 12 Feb. 1910, 28 Jan. 1913.

75) *Ibid*, 6 Nov. 1912, 22 Feb. 1913, 12 Jan., 2 May 1914.

76) J. Obed Smith's report on British agencies, 15 Mar. 1909.

77) Memo. from Archibald to Ottawa, 6 Apr. 1914 (PAC, RG 76, C-10315, vol. 435, file 652801).

78) Paton to W. D. Scott, 27 Jan. 1910 (PAC, RG 76, C-10627, vol. 538, file 803839).

79) *Ibid* (undated, probably 1911).

80) See also *AJ*, 1 Mar. 1912; and MacLennan's report for week ending 30 May 1908, in which he noted that Longmuir had sailed on 3 May with 113 farm and domestic servants for Manitoba and the North-West.

81) *AJ*, 1 Sept. 1913. See also 28 Feb. 1912, 7 Apr., 1 June 1914.

82) See vol. I, p. 197.

83) Canada Statutes, 43 Vic., 1880, c. 11, sec. 2(2). For more detailed information on the organisation of agency work in Britain and Europe, see H. G. Skilling, *Canadian representation abroad*, ch. 1.

84) After 1917 responsibility for immigration fell to the new Ministry of Immigration and Colonisation. Two years later it took over the quarantine service, which had remained with the Department of Agriculture in 1893.

85) Preston's successor, J. Bruce Walker, was made Assistant Superintendent of Immigration (under the Superintendent of Immigration at the Department of the Interior in Ottawa) and his successor, J. Obed Smith, was ultimately made Superintendent of Emigration for Canada in Europe. It was not until 1938, however, that the High Commissioner's titular responsibility for emigration activities was removed from the statute book.

86) Between 1880 and 1899 the territorial agents submitted their annual reports to

the High Commissioner, who then forwarded them to Ottawa, along with his own summary report, which he had compiled from information in the territorial agents' submissions. After 1899 the territorial agents reported to Preston, who then drew up an annual summary report, in addition to that which continued to be sent to Ottawa by the High Commissioner. Between 1904 and 1906 this somewhat cumbersome procedure was bypassed when the High Commissioner did not report to Ottawa on emigration matters and the territorial agents communicated directly with the Department of the Interior.

87) Skilling, *Canadian representation abroad*, p. 15.
88) This office, which functioned from 1869-76 and again from 1880, was first located at Carlisle but was moved to Glasgow because of the latter's importance as a shipping port for Canada. It was reckoned to be the most important regional office after Liverpool. (See report of 10 Aug. 1892 from Sir Charles Tupper to the Hon. E. Dewdney, Minister of the Interior, in PAC, C-4660, vol. 5, file 41, part 1: emigration from Britain 1892-1914).
89) See Grahame's reports in Dept of Agriculture, *annual reports on immigration, 1885 and 1887*; and Dept of the Interior, *annual report on immigration, 1894*.
90) Emigration Staff, GB, 1893-6 (PAC, C-10680, vol. 679, file 41, part 1).
91) See above, pp. 9-10.
92) Dept of the Interior, *annual report on immigration, 1896*
93) *Ibid*, Fleming's report.
94) In the course of his work as an Australian emigration agent, Fleming had found it a mistake to send out non-agricultural settlers, and he had subsequently applied the same principle to Canada.
95) *Annual report on immigration.*
96) Emigration Staff, GB, 1893-6 (PAC, C-10680, vol. 679, file 41, part 1).
97) Dept of the Interior, *annual report on immigration, 1904*.
98) It covered the Northern and Western Isles, and the counties of Caithness, Sutherland, Ross and Cromarty, Inverness, Nairn, Moray, Banff, Aberdeen, Kincardine, Angus and parts of Perth and Argyll.
99) See MacLennan's report for week ending 2 Mar. 1907; and his annual report in Dept of the Interior, *annual report on immigration, 1907*.
100) But closed on Wednesday and Saturday afternoons
101) MacLennan's report in Dept of the Interior, *annual report on immigration, 1907*; and MacLennan's weekly reports for weeks ending 2 & 9 Mar. 1907.
102) Week ending 22 Jan. 1910.
103) J. Obed Smith's report on British agencies, 15 Mar. 1909.
104) *Ibid.*
105) Report for week ending 18 Feb. 1911.
106) Reports for weeks ending 18, 25 July, 1, 8, 15 Aug. 1908.
107) Reports for weeks ending 31 July, 7, 14, 21 Aug. 1909.
108) For instance, weeks ending 18 Apr., 5 Sept. 1908.
109) Week ending 26 Oct. 1907.
110) Weeks ending 16 Jan., 20 Mar. 1909.
111) MacLennan's report on Grant's visit to Scotland (PAC, C-10425, vol. 191, file 760771). See also MacLennan's weekly reports, weeks ending 13 Apr. & 9 Nov. 1907 for complaints about lethargic agents. In April a visiting farm delegate had gone to Ballater with little success because the agent had not announced his visit; and in November MacLennan commented of Banchory, that 'not much can be done at that point as agent takes no interest in the matter'.
112) MacLennan's report on Bredin (PAC, C-10414, vol. 479, file 742357).
113) J. Obed Smith's report on British agencies, 15 Mar. 1909.

114) MacLennan's report for week ending 4 May 1907. In April 1913 T. A. Myles arrived in Aberdeen to open an emigration office for the Manitoba government. Until separate premises were made ready at the end of May he had to conduct his business from the Dominion government office, but there is no record of what the then agent, G. G. Archibald, thought of him. (See *AFP*, 10 Apr. 1913).

115) PAC, C-10318, vol. 440, file 662655.

116) Cumming's report in Dept of the Interior, *annual report on immigration, 1911-12*. See also reports of Cumming's lectures in *AJ*, 14, 27 Feb. 1912 (Alvah and Torphins).

117) Cumming resigned along with John MacLennan after they had both complained that their salaries of $1,800 per annum, in Aberdeen and Liverpool respectively, were less than those of their counterparts in Glasgow, Belfast and Dublin. Hugh McIntyre, the Glasgow agent, also resigned from his post for personal reasons at the same time, and went back to his former agency in Birmingham.

118) Archibald's reports in Dept of the Interior, *annual reports on immigration, 1912-13 and 1913-14*. For intimation and reports of lectures delivered by the agents in North-East Scotland, see *AJ*, 27 Nov. 1912 (Murray at Alford), 29 Nov., 7 Dec. 1912 (Campbell at Maud and Oldmeldrum), 11 Dec. 1912 (Murray at Fyvie), 3, 14 Nov., 5, 13, 19 Dec. 1913 (Archibald at Kemnay, Ballater, Rothienorman, Forgue, Tarland), 10 Jan. 1914 (Archibald at Pitmedden).

119) Obed Smith's report on British agencies, 15 Mar. 1909. See also MacLennan's report in Dept of the Interior, *annual report on immigration, 1907*.

120) J. Obed Smith's report on British agencies, 15 Mar. 1909.

121) Agriculturists and domestic servants were later exempted from this charge.

122) MacLennan's report for week ending 26 Mar. 1910.

123) MacLennan's report in Dept of the Interior, *annual report on immigration, 1909-10*.

124) MacLennan's report for week ending 19 Nov. 1910.

125) See Cumming's and Archibald's reports in Dept of the Interior, *annual reports on immigration, 1912-13 and 1913-14*.

126) PAC, C-4763, vol. 99, file 12681-C: counties from which British immigrants came, 1902-8. The exact returns were as follows: *1902* Aberdeen (255), Banff (35), Kincardine (28), Moray/Elgin (39), Nairn (4); *1903* Aberdeen (601), Banff (146), Kincardine (44), Moray/Elgin (87), Nairn (16); *1904* Aberdeen (1,210), Banff (191), Kincardine (116), Moray/Elgin (124), Nairn (28).

127) PAC, RG 76, C-10627, vol. 538, file 803839: letter from Richard Tew & Co. to Paton, 30 Nov. 1911; and Paton to W. D. Scott, 1 Mar. 1919. This second letter contained an application from Paton for a post with the Canadian Immigration Department, in the context of which he reviewed his business achievements in Aberdeen.

128) Report quoted in *AJ*, 11 July 1914.

129) The newspaper rarely differentiated between the destinations. See, for instance, 18 Feb. 1911, when it reported that 78 emigrants were going to 'Canada, the USA and South Africa'.

130) That is, where the newspaper enumerated contingents which were going to 'Canada and the USA', the figure has been taken to represent Canada alone.

131) Although bonus claims came from agents throughout the North of Scotland, it seems that most were submitted by ticket agents in the North-East (see, for instance, J. Obed Smith's report on British agencies, quoted above, pp. 29, 31).

132) *AJ*, 22 Mar. 1913.

133) *Ibid*, 30 Apr., 24 Sept. 1910.
134) *Ibid*, 19 Apr., 27 Dec. 1911.
135) See also report of the Savings Bank's next annual meeting in *AJ*, 25 Dec. 1913. Sir John Sinclair, one of the trustees, reported to this meeting that although continuing emigration had prevented an increase in deposits during the year, in fact a considerable return tide was beginning to set in of emigrants who had been unable to find work in Canada.

TABLE I
SCOTTISH EMIGRATION, 1881–1913

YEAR	CANADA	USA	AUSTRALIA	NEW ZEALAND	CAPE & NATAL	ELSE- WHERE	TOTAL
1881	3,182	18,238	2,433			2,973	26,826
TOTAL	34,561	307,973	24,093			25,887	392,514
1882	4,630	19,004	6,240		1,428	940	32,242
TOTAL	53,475	295,539	38,604		13,614	12,056	413,288
1883	3,871	15,332	10,975		278	683	31,139
TOTAL	53,566	252,226	73,017		6,713	11,635	397,157
1884	3,163	12,752	4,952		191	895	21,953
TOTAL	37,043	203,519	45,944		4,699	12,696	303,901
1885	2,345	13,241	4,731		275	775	21,367
TOTAL	22,928	184,470	40,689		3,960	12,338	264,385
1886	2,971	16,786	4,240		461	865	25,323
TOTAL	30,121	238,386	44,055		4,659	13,580	330,801
1887	3,612	25,373	3,847		463	1,070	34,365
TOTAL	44,406	296,901	35,198		5,658	14,331	396,494
1888	5,351	26,006	2,799		606	1,111	35,873
TOTAL	49,107	293,087	31,725		7,705	16,870	398,494
1889	3,649	17,567	2,374		979	785	25,354
TOTAL	38,056	240,395	28,834		15,671	19,685	342,641
1890	2,421	13,861	2,396		765	1,210	20,653
TOTAL	31,897	233,522	21,570		12,083	16,908	315,980
1891	2,370	15,376	2,459		448	1,537	22,190
TOTAL	33,752	252,016	19,957		10,686	18,132	334,543
1892	1,938	16,406	2,030		1,281	1,670	23,325
TOTAL	41,866	235,221	16,183		11,641	16,486	321,397
1893	1,958	16,534	1,246		985	1,914	22,637
TOTAL	50,381	213,212	11,412		16,158	16,470	307,633
1894	914	10,151	941		1,148	1,278	14,432
TOTAL	23,633	159,431	11,151		16,760	15,852	226,827
1895	1,404	13,244	623		2,073	950	18,294
TOTAL	22,357	195,632	10,809		25,988	16,996	271,772
1896	1,563	10,535	677		3,093	998	16,866
TOTAL	22,590	154,496	10,710		35,840	18,316	241,952
1897	1,281	9,121	1,032		3,516	1,174	16,124
TOTAL	22,669	132,048	12,396		28,801	17,366	213,280
1898	1,717	7,372	1,142		3,623	1,716	15,570
TOTAL	27,487	123,703	11,020		25,635	17,326	205,171
1899	1,703	8,128	1,328		2,973	1,940	16,072
TOTAL	33,669	159,143	12,268		18,863	16,753	240,696
1900	1,733	11,504	1,557		4,114	1,564	20,472
TOTAL	50,007	189,391	15,723		25,518	17,922	298,561
1901	2,235	11,414	1,801		4,128	1,342	20,920
TOTAL	42,898	194,941	15,754		28,553	20,429	302,575
1902	3,811	12,225	1,791		7,091	1,367	26,285
TOTAL	67,600	232,099	14,675		51,886	20,519	386,779
1903	10,296	15,318	1,660		8,158	1,369	36,801
TOTAL	99,582	251,941	12,573		62,824	22,086	449,006
1904	12,715	17,111	1,751		4,554	1,314	37,445
TOTAL	91,684	291,945	14,210		32,278	23,760	453,877
1905	14,214	19,785	1,872		4,487	1,152	41,510
TOTAL	108,118	276,636	15,488		31,166	28,254	459,662

TABLE I—*continued*

YEAR	CANADA	USA	AUSTRALIA	NEW ZEALAND	CAPE & NATAL	ELSE-WHERE	TOTAL
1906	22,278	23,221	1,027	1,207	3,170	2,259	53,162
TOTAL	141,786	338,612	11,039	8,550	26,323	31,427	557,737
1907	33,393	24,365	1,916	1,238	2,844	2,599	66,355
TOTAL	185,831	366,396	16,445	8,622	23,264	34,391	634,949
1908	16,705	14,720	2,886	1,920	2,780	3,262	42,273
TOTAL	95,428	198,321	22,161	11,739	21,944	36,818	386,411
1909	18,423	21,486	3,208	1,943	3,436	4,388	52,884
TOTAL	113,318	259,933	27,727	10,623	24,649	38,128	474,378
1910	35,570	27,918	5,149	1,721	4,660	4,766	79,784
TOTAL	196,305	303,364	36,289	9,957	30,838	42,106	618,859
1911	41,218	23,441	11,616	1,761	5,389	5,427	88,852
TOTAL	213,361	250,969	69,055	12,239	34,528	43,273	623,425
1912*	37,154	18,203	9,348	1,915	2,840	3,955	73,415
TOTAL	219,136	262,066	83,742	13,722	31,888	46,281	656,835
1913	39,697	17,295	6,114	2,170	1,671	3,217	70,164
TOTAL	196,278	129,169	64,219	13,715	25,855	40,404	469,640

'TOTAL' = total emigration from the British Isles.

* Particulars as to the nationality of British passengers were not returned after 31 March 1912. The last country in which a passenger had resided for at least 12 months was taken as the country of residence.

CHAPTER II

'The Golden West—Granary of the World'

As in the earlier part of the nineteenth century, the vast majority of emigrants from North-East Scotland in the period 1880-1914 were involved in agriculture. Small farmers and farm workers continued to constitute the area's main exodus to all destinations, but particularly to Canada, whose intensive publicity campaigns were aimed particularly at attracting energetic farming settlers to the prairies as well as to the more settled eastern provinces. North-East Scotland's agricultural emigrants had always been characterised by a positive determination to improve their situation and prospects,[1] and this determination became even more evident in the face of the severe agricultural depression which afflicted Britain in the late nineteenth century. The North-East corner, by virtue of its emphasis on mixed farming, was spared the worst effects of this crisis, but the prospects for small agriculturists who wanted to secure an independent future on the land were bleak. Several chose to emigrate in order to take advantage of the better opportunities which they felt were afforded to farmers in Canada, opportunities brought to their notice almost incessantly in the press and through the activities of itinerant emigration agents.

But while considerable attention was paid to the grievances and incentives which stimulated farming emigrants to leave Scotland, little unbiased information survives concerning their new settlements. This often makes it difficult to compare their expectations with their subsequent experiences of the realities of pioneer farming. The emigrant letters which appeared intermittently in the local press were often written with a view to publication. A few unsuccessful correspondents warned readers of the pitfalls of emigrating but the letters were more commonly intended to persuade others to follow the writer's example in coming to Canada. Similarly the 'representative' emigrant letters which appeared in Canadian government publications were carefully selected to emphasise only the attributes of Canadian farming. Any examples of private emigrant correspondence are therefore invaluable, particularly if they describe the writer's experiences over a prolonged period. The seventy-four letters written by John McBean, who emigrated from the county of Nairn to Manitoba in July 1902, provide a detailed insight into the advantages and drawbacks of pioneering in Western Canada in the four years before his death in 1906. His largely unvarnished comments form an integral part of

51

this survey of the expectations and experiences of Scottish farming emigrants in Canada in the late nineteenth and early twentieth centuries.

Agricultural depression and emigration

The arguments in favour of state-aided emigration from Britain which re-emerged in the late nineteenth century arose largely as a result of the severe national agricultural and commercial depression. Farmers and farm workers were particularly badly affected by the crisis, which followed a period of prosperity and high land values. As foreign competition in the form of cheap cereals from the American mid-west flooded the British market, prices fell dramatically; and this blow was coupled with an acute decline in home output as the result of a series of bad seasons. Farmers tried to reduce their expenditure by economising on labour; they were helped in this by the increasing use of labour-saving machinery, but farming methods were also altered to some extent, with vast amounts of land across Britain being laid down to grass. J. Bruce of Collithie, Gartly, for instance, told a Royal Commission in 1906 that he had reduced his labour force from eleven to six after turning 100 cultivated acres into permanent sheep pasture.[2]

The great wheat-growing areas, such as East Anglia and Berwickshire, suffered most from the importation of grain from the prairies. North-East Scotland, which produced virtually no wheat, therefore escaped the worst effects of the agricultural crisis, and its cattle pasturing industry even bene-fitted to some extent from the reduced price of imported feedstuffs. Small farmers, who ran mixed units and relied mainly on family labour, did not have to contend with huge labour bills and some landlords, notably Lord Aberdeen, gave repeated rent remissions to tenants to compensate for bad harvests.[3] Proprietors had little difficulty in letting farms and there were relatively few changes of tenancy when leases expired. But North-East Scot-land was not entirely immune from the effects of the depression. In 1894, for instance, Assistant Commissioner James Hope, reporting to the Royal Commission of Agriculture (Scotland) on the situation in the counties of Perth, Fife, Forfar and Aberdeen, remarked that:

> On all hands, and in all quarters, I have ascertained that depression of a very acute kind has prevailed during the past ten years ... all agree that the struggles of the farmers in fighting against adverse circumstances have never been keener than they are at present.[4]

There were frequent comments in the local press about the hardships suffered by tenant farmers as a result of foreign competition, bad seasons and unjust land laws, and the *Aberdeen Journal* in autumn 1881 reported well-attended meetings held throughout the region, at which these men discussed their grievances and suggested possible solutions.[5] Local committees were formed to press for changes; that at Kemnay, for instance, suggested reforms along the lines of the Irish Land Act, including the fair adjustment of rents, security of tenure and ample compensation for permanent improvements.[6] Following a meeting in Aberdeen on 1 December attended by 6,000 people, the Scottish Farmers' Alliance was established to articulate the farmers' demands. The local agitation committees formed themselves into branches of this organisation, which throughout its five-year existence remained strongly based in North-East Scotland.

One correspondent of the *Aberdeen Journal*, however,[7] argued that legislative reforms would not solve the problems of farming in Aberdeenshire, particularly in the hilly inland areas, where the land had been improved to its maximum productivity, but still could not yield satisfactory returns. No amount of legislation could improve the fertility of such land, and he advised tenants in these circumstances to cut their losses and emigrate to Canada. Manitoba and the North-West Territories, he claimed, offered good openings for men with limited capital who were prepared to work hard, while he recommended farmers with more extensive means to settle in the older, more settled provinces, particularly Ontario.

Lord Aberdeen later added his support to the proposal that unemployed farmers and farm workers should emigrate. In a speech at Methlick in December 1886 he expressed his regret at the loss of the flower of the rural population, yet still recommended emigration as being 'worthy of the consideration of those who have saved a little money and who do not want to lose their savings by being out of employment for a winter or more'. His views were brought to wider public attention and strongly supported by James Strachan of Aberdeen in letters to the *Aberdeen Journal* on 13 and 16 December 1886. Strachan cited evidence to support his claim that, despite statements to the contrary by opponents of emigration, there was plenty work for good agricultural labourers in Canada, and also in Australia (of which he had made a particular study). He pointed out that since farmers were economising on labour by all means possible, demand for workers was likely to remain slack for some considerable time, and it was ludicrous that redundant farm labourers should prefer to remain at home in idleness rather than take advantage of openings in the colonies. The simultaneous commercial and industrial depression meant that unemployed farm workers could no longer be readily absorbed into alternative urban employment, and Strachan maintained that urban distress was unquestionably being aggravated by the migration of needy rural labourers to the towns in search of often nonexistent work. Strachan's views were supported and taken further by another correspondent of the *Aberdeen Journal*, 'J.P.'. In a letter published on 14 December, he said that emigration should be considered not only by those who had not secured winter engagements, but also by those who were in employment, since 'emigration to our colonies is the most likely step to give them the chance of getting on in the world; in fact the first step on the ladder by which they may attain independence'. He also suggested that the issue should be debated at meetings of farmers, at which members who had read the latest handbooks and pamphlets should present the case for emigration.

So there was clearly some public support for the emigration of hard-pressed agriculturists, and it seems that such advice did not fall on deaf ears in farming communities. On 17 April 1882, for instance, the *Aberdeen Journal* reported a significant exodus of labourers from the parish of New Deer. Fourteen people had already secured passages, and many more were due to leave at the Whitsunday term, along with several farmers who had also decided to try their fortunes on the other side of the Atlantic. In fact, in a report of the Whitsunday feeing market in Aberdeen on 20 May 1882, the *Aberdeen Journal* noted that recent extensive emigration from Aberdeenshire had significantly reduced the farm labour force and aroused expectations that agricultural wages might be increased.[8] On 25 May it reported the departure from the city the previous day of thirty-five people for Manitoba, mainly agriculturists, 'of whom a large proportion have gone out this year to Canada'; and the following day it confirmed this statement with a more detailed report on the extent and nature of recent emigration:

> Not for many years has there been such a rapid and extensive emigration from this country as has taken place in the course of the present spring; and the northern counties have been depleted to a considerable extent of many skilled workmen, farm labourers, and farmers. Scarcely a week has passed in the course of the past two or three months in which parties of emigrants have not passed through Aberdeen *en route* for the land of their adoption.

The lack of prospects resulting from the agricultural depression was high-lighted as the major cause of the exodus, and the report cited evidence from a number of locations in North-East Scotland to emphasise the widespread interest in emigration. Well over 200 people, half of whom were farm labourers, had left the Inverness district already that season; about sixty of them had gone to Canada, and thirty of that number had settled in Manitoba. There had also been a 'very extensive' departure of small farmers and farm servants from New Maud, where the emigrants claimed that the land was 'worked done'. They believed that by emigrating they would not only be able to earn a better living but also improve their social position. A similar 'desire amongst young people to take a step upward in social circumstances' was apparent among the twelve farm labourers who had left Oldmeldrum for Canada and the USA. Despite the depression, some of these emigrants had accumulated as much as £100 in savings, which they intended to invest in the purchase of land abroad. Most emigrants in fact contrasted their restricted prospects at home with enticing accounts of colonial opportunities. Per-suasive propaganda from Manitoba had influenced a 'considerable number' of emigrants from Peterhead, particularly 'farm servants who are anxious to improve their condition'. The main factor behind the emigration of fifty people from New Deer was the reputedly high colonial wage rate; and the *Aberdeen Journal*'s correspondent in Alford pointed out that since agricultural wages at home were so low, and colonial opportunities so well publicised, 'it was not to be wondered at that young men of spirit should wish to make an effort to raise themselves in the scale of existence'.

Agriculturists continued to respond to the depression by leaving the country. In reporting the winter feeing market held in the city on 12 December

1885, the *Aberdeen Journal* noted that the supply of labour continued to exceed demand, and that the lack of prospects caused many farm servants to emigrate. The newspaper did not always mention the occupations or destinations of emigrants whose departure from Aberdeen railway station it recorded, but from time to time it specifically mentioned the departure of farm servants and farmers. On 20 March 1888, for instance, it reported significant emigration from the Fraserburgh district in the previous fortnight, most of the emigrants being farm servants who were going to the Canadian mid-west. On 16 May 1888 it noted that J. F. Grant, the emigration agent at Cullen, had booked forty emigrants already that season, most of whom were farm servants going to the Toronto area; and on 25 May it mentioned the departure from Aberdeen station of thirty emigrants who had decided to go to Canada instead of seeking new engagements at the Whitsunday term. In December 1901 over forty agricultural labourers from Aberdeenshire and Kincardineshire left Aberdeen en route for various parts of Canada, and a year later the *Aberdeen Journal* reported the departure for Canada of two parties of farm servants 'who have great inducements to settle in the Dominion'.[9] In 1903 'several families' from Aberdeenshire were reported to be among the 2,000 pioneers of the Barr Colony in Saskatchewan, an attempt to create an all-British agricultural settlement at Lloydminster in response to recent heavy American immigration into the North-West Territories.[10] On 13 March 1906 the *Aberdeen Journal* noted that most of the seventy emigrants who had left the city for Canada the previous evening were 'farm servants from the north'; while in reporting the departure of a train-load of 190 emigrants on 4 June 1909, it added that most of the male passengers were farm labourers, 'amongst which class the local emigration agents have been busy since the Whitsunday term'. In May 1911 Francis Godsman, the local agent for the Canadian Pacific and Donaldson Lines, organised the emigration of a party of over forty farm workers, including families from Udny, Newburgh and Garmouth; and the following year the *Aberdeen Journal* noted the departure of a special party of farm hands which had been recruited by local booking agents R. & J. Davidson for distribution to farmers in Western Canada.[11] Among the farmers who emigrated were four from Stonehaven in June 1891, two of whom went to Canada and John Park, who gave up his twenty-five year tenancy of a farm at Lonmay in May 1910 to start farming afresh at Vancouver.[12]

In a review in 1906 of the reasons for the decline in Britain's agricultural population, the Board of Agriculture singled out the importance of emigration, particularly from Scotland. Alongside factors such as redundancies brought about by the mechanisation of farming, the absorption of small holdings, inadequate accommodation and the attractions of town life, it noted that

Many correspondents refer to the absence of an incentive to remain on the land and of any reasonable prospect of advancement in life, and it is mentioned that in some districts, particularly in Scotland, many of the best men have been attracted to the Colonies, where their energies may find wider scope and where the road to independence and a competency is broader and more easy of access.[13]

This statement was corroborated in 1912 by the observations of A. D. Hall,[14] when he toured the agricultural districts of Britain on behalf of *The Times* newspaper, and noted the 'great emigration to Canada' that was still taking place from Aberdeenshire. He blamed the exodus primarily on the onerous and often unrewarding nature of smallholding in the region, but also on the inferior accommodation available for farm workers; in particular, the structure of farming in North-East Scotland made little provision for housing married labourers, who—as in the nineteenth century—often emigrated when they married rather than face the problem of finding accommodation at home.

Further confirmation that farmers and farm servants made up the majority of emigrants from North-East Scotland is found in the records of John MacLennan and his successors, and in the correspondence between booking agents and the Canadian Ministry of the Interior. In his weekly reports MacLennan frequently mentioned the particular interest in emigration evident in farming communities, an interest which he himself stimulated by his visits to cattle sales, agricultural fairs and feeing markets, where he publicised the advantages of settling in Canada. In his report for the week ending 30 March 1907 he noted that the Aberdeen booking agents could not find sufficient accommodation on the emigrant ships to meet the great demand for passages. As a result

> There will be some disappointment at term time when a number of engagements will end at the inability of some [to] secure passages as they hope to ... and a number will be lost to us owing to their engaging for another year by failure to get out at the end of term service.[15]

On two occasions in 1907 MacLennan noted the effect of a bad harvest on emigration. On 1 November he remarked on the continuing steady departure of emigrants with each sailing and the prospect of a big exodus in 1908, and continued: 'The bad harvest weather is having its effect in deciding the matter. The farm servants while out working hard have had to contend with bad weather and the farmer with poor results from his summer's work.' Three weeks later, on 22 November, he reported his visit to a feeing market at Alford, 'where I met a large number of Farm labourers and the bad harvest has the effect of cutting down wages which is not very acceptable to the men, hence a desire to go to Canada and what is true of Alford is true of every section'. Most movement in fact took place around the time of the biannual feeing markets; on 6 June 1908 MacLennan noted a significant exodus of farm servants during the previous fortnight, and on 3 December 1910 he reported that since many good men had failed to secure engagements at the recent feeing markets, 'farmers offering low wages, which they refused ... we are [therefore] going to get some splendid men for Canada'. MacLennan re-emphasised the departure of agriculturists in his annual reports. In 1908-9, for instance, 'a large number of desirable farmers and farm servants' had been encouraged to emigrate following reports of a good harvest and general prosperity in Canada, which they contrasted favourably with conditions at home; and this trend was continued the following year:

> In addition to the large increase of farm servants, this year is specially noted for the number of practical farmers with means who are leaving here for Canada. This is the most hopeful sign of our work in the north and I am confident that the success of the pioneers will mean an addition of many more. High rents and wet seasons for the past three years are doing much to discourage the Scottish farmer, and the splendid reports from our western country are attracting his attention.[16]

Agriculturists who were interested in emigrating to Canada generally made their arrangements to leave through a local booking agent. Since the agents could claim a bonus of £1 per head from the Canadian government on each domestic servant or farm hand whom they sent out, they were obviously primarily concerned with recruiting these most eligible clients. Sometimes they collected together special parties of farm hands, as in 1909, when William Maitland of Longside booked around fifty agricultural labourers to sail on 4 June and wrote to the Department of the Interior in advance to request that government agents should find suitable situations for his recruits.[17] In a letter on 13 July 1910 he pointed out that he had already established a few hundred emigrants in the west through A. E. G. Mutch, a contact in Saskatchewan. Further situations were readily available for a large number of farm hands whom he had booked to leave the following Spring, and Maitland wanted the Department of the Interior to confirm that these recruits would be exempt from the requirement that immigrants should possess at least £5 landing money, in addition to their fare.[18]

Most disputed claims between booking agents and the Department of the Interior were over bonus payments, particularly on farm servants. On several occasions when the Department refused bonuses on immigrants who apparently did not meet the requirements, the booking agents appealed against the decision. Paton's agency in Aberdeen, for instance, complained in February 1910 that they had been refused a bonus on William Buchan who had gone straight from a lifetime of farm service at home to a specific situation on a farm near Morden, Manitoba, for which he had been engaged by Paton's agent in Morden at wages of $225 per year.[19] Later that year the bonus was refused on William and Alex Smith from Dufftown, who had claimed to be miners, but Paton's pointed out that in Dufftown 'nothing but farm work is carried on' and that the Smith brothers had gone out to specific situations at Tantallon, Saskatchewan.[20] In 1912 Paton's claim for a bonus on Alexander Davidson was refused on the grounds that he had previously been employed as an insurance agent, but Paton assured the Department of the Interior that his client had earlier spent twenty-five years in farm service and had gone to Saskatoon with his family to take up a homestead. This statement was later confirmed by Davidson himself in response to a letter from W. D. Scott at the Department of the Interior, asking him to explain his circumstances:[21]

I was much surprised to learn from Mr. Paton ... that my experience in farming had been questioned. I was brought up on a farm & was for many years a farm servant although I was at insurance latterly. I have a thorough practical knowledge of farming and the first thing I did within a month of landing here was to file a homestead ... as did also my son George—aged 18 years who came out here with us ... & my son Alex—aged nearly 20 yrs—who came to Canada last Sept.

Paton's also argued that a bonus claim should be allowed on Donald Ewen who, although a carpenter to trade, had some experience of farm service. He went out on the SS *Parisian* in March 1913 with William Donald, a returning Canadian with whom Ewen intended to enter into a homesteading partnership. And two months later, when a bonus claim on Arthur Cummings was refused because he had been working as a railway porter before leaving, Paton's pointed out that Cummings, like most railway porters, had been recruited from the ranks of farm service and intended to take up farm work in Canada.[22]

MacKay Brothers in Aberdeen also appealed on several occasions against the decision to rescind their bonus on farm servants. For instance, they argued that they should have been paid bonuses on James Low and Alex Sim who went out to Canada in 1911. Although Low had worked as a baker for eleven years prior to emigrating, he had previously spent five years as a farm hand in Aberdeenshire, and intended to take up farm work near Toronto. Likewise Sim, who had not been employed in agriculture immediately prior to his emigration, had worked on a farm in Aberdeenshire from 1903 to 1905 and was also going to take up farm work near Toronto.[23] William Maitland in Longside encountered similar problems when, for instance, his claim for bonus on John Tait and George Sangster was refused on the grounds that they were, respectively, a mason and a dairy produce merchant. Maitland, however, pointed out that both men had prior farming experience, Sangster in particular having worked as a farm servant for thirty years.[24]

On a number of occasions the booking agent in Elgin, John Sinclair, had his appeal against disallowed bonus claims on farming emigrants upheld after the Department of the Interior admitted there had been misunderstandings. Two sons of the Lawrie family from Elgin, who emigrated from the family croft to take up holdings of 320 acres each in Saskatchewan, subsequently lodged a homestead entry of 160 acres for their father, whom Sinclair had persuaded to emigrate with the rest of his family. When the father died shortly before the removal was due to take place, his widow and three remaining children decided they would still take up the homestead, but Sinclair's bonus payment was initially refused on the assumption that the emigrants were going to Canada without any intention of farming.[25]

Persuading the farmer

So there is clear evidence from a number of sources that farmers and farm workers were emigrating from North-East Scotland to Canada in significant numbers in the late nineteenth and early twentieth centuries. But although the exodus was connected to some extent with the fluctuating fortunes of agriculture, even at the height of the depression these emigrants were not driven away simply by negative factors such as bad seasons, low prices and poor wages. Contemporary comments have already indicated that they fully expected to improve their social and economic prospects by going to Canada. They contrasted the poor outlook for agriculture in Scotland with the great incentives apparently available to farmers in Canada, and many emigrants methodically accumulated sufficient savings to cover the costs of passage and of establishing a farming settlement in the Dominion. How did these emigrants become convinced of the advantages of farming in Canada? How do we account for a continuing loss of rural population which, although perhaps most pronounced when times were bad, outlasted the agricultural depression and sometimes seemed to take place almost irrespective of agricultural conditions in North-East Scotland? The answer lies largely in the intensive and prolonged campaign that was launched in the late nineteenth century to attract farming settlers to Canada, particularly to the recently-opened western prairies. The campaign was spearheaded by the government through its Department of the Interior but also involved other parties with a vested interest in populating the Dominion, most notably the transcontinental railway companies. As has been seen already, North-East Scotland, like the rest of Britain, was bombarded with written and verbal propaganda which extolled the advantages of emigrating to Canada, and most of this encouragement was clearly directed at agriculturists. Numerous publications appeared offering specific advice to emigrant farmers, and the agents who descended on the North-East were particularly interested in this category of emigrant. Their pattern of organised, intensive and sustained encouragement to emigrate was superimposed on the more indirect, traditional means by which the North-East public had for long been informed about opportunities to emigrate—that is, through personal, often family connections, private and published emigrant correspondence, occasional press advertisements for employment abroad and factual reports in the local press covering local and national instances of emigration.

There was certainly no lack of information available about the opportunities for agriculturists to emigrate to Canada, particularly to Western Canada. By the Rupert's Land Act of 1868 the Hudson's Bay Company relinquished control over most of the territory which had constituted its fur-trading empire since 1670.[26] A major argument in favour of the acquisition of Rupert's Land by the new Dominion of Canada was the disquiet expressed at the number of people who were leaving the country to take up land in the mid-western states of the USA. Furthermore, surveys and expeditions in the late 1850s had suggested that the region's agricultural potential was too great to warrant its continuing preservation for the benefit of fur traders alone.[27] Government and public attention in Canada turned to the vast, little known prairies, and in 1870 Manitoba was surveyed and united to the three-year-old Dominion. Much further west, British Columbia was added to the Dominion the following year, but the other prairie provinces of Saskatchewan and Alberta were not created out of the North-West Territories until 1905. European settlement on the prairies dated from the Red River colony of the early nineteenth century, and in 1870 was made up of the descendants of the 1812 settlers, ex-Hudson's Bay Company employees, and the half-breed Métis.[28] At this time only 213 people lived in the main settlement of Winnipeg,[29] so determined efforts were made to attract to the region agricultural settlers who would clear the land and engage in the production of wheat. The Dominion Lands Act of 1872 regulated the sale of land in Manitoba and the North-West Territories. Free 160-acre grants (quarter sections) were made to heads of families, or to anyone over twenty-one on payment of a $10 registration fee. Full legal title was given after three years' actual occupancy and on proof of a certain amount of cultivation, and from 1874 settlers were allowed to pre-empt an extra 160 acres adjacent to their homesteads.

But settlement advanced only slowly until the mid-1890s. A speculative land boom from 1881 to 1883, provoked by the construction of the Canadian Pacific Railway, was followed by a period of crop failures and a lengthy depression, and even the completion of the transcontinental rail link in 1885 did not lead to a significant increase in settlement. Several early settlers who were unfitted for prairie farming deserted their homesteads in this period, when economic problems were compounded by frequent changes in Dominion land regulations, and political uncertainty in the wake of the Riel Rebellion of 1885. On a visit to Manitoba in 1894 the Countess of Aberdeen noted that as a result of the depression farmers could not always afford to pay their labourers' wages. She noted a common consensus

> that the present is a bad time & that it will be all that they can do to pull through & the price for wheat is so low that the best crops only increase their grower's difficulties by imposing on him additional expenses for the harvesting & then the large majority of farmers are in the hands of money-lenders because of the purchase of expensive machinery etc. & they are charged 16 & 17 p. cent & even 24 p. cent interest ... Altogether the lot of the Manitoban farmer is not a roseate one, quite apart from the hardships of the climate & the monotony of the prairie.[30]

After 1896, however, conditions began to favour settlement in Western Canada, when the end of the worldwide depression coincided with new developments on the prairies. Improved transportation and irrigation and the adoption of the early-maturing Red Fife wheat (suitable for the short prairie growing season) all helped to focus attention once more on the agricultural potential of Manitoba and the North-West Territories.

The Dominion government made strenuous efforts to promote prairie settlement through publicity campaigns in Eastern Canada, the USA and Europe. The distribution of promotional literature was integral to its campaign and it sponsored the publication of numerous pamphlets and handbooks covering all aspects of farming settlement throughout Canada, but particularly in the mid-west.[31] Other organisations followed suit, such as the

Canadian Pacific Railway Company, which supplied libraries and reading rooms with its publications on farming in Western Canada, and disseminated up-to-date information to newspapers and journals.[32] The British periodical press also reflected—and stimulated—the growing public interest in emigration and the flood of Canadian propaganda was supplemented by regular articles on prairie agriculture in such popular British periodicals as *Chambers' Journal*. One contributor in 1881—an emigrant of twenty years' standing—claimed that Canada was a land of 'peace and plenty', where wages were high and all who were willing to work could be prosperous and independent.[33] His views in fact typified the confident and uncritical approach adopted by most articles and guidebooks which discussed farming settlement in Canada.[34] A standard package of information and advice was generally offered in handbooks, with modifications according to the particular area under consideration. The package usually included a comparison of the emigrant's rosy economic and social outlook in Canada with the limited prospects available to him at home; this would be followed by a general description of farming in Canada, incorporating some discussion of climate, crops, farm labourers' wages and current homestead regulations. Practical advice would then be offered on such issues as the amount of capital required for the various types of farming, how and when to emigrate, what to bring, and how to proceed on arrival, and maps of the Dominion and/or the particular area concerned were often supplied for the use of emigrants.

Provincial newspapers such as the *Aberdeen Journal* also contained regular items of advice and information on farming in Canada. Sometimes these were reproduced from the Canadian handbooks or the quarterly bulletins of advice to emigrants issued by the Emigrants' Information Office, but sometimes they bore particular reference to the experiences of local emigrants. An article on 27 January 1881, for instance, which dealt with the advantages of land ownership in Canada, declared that emigrants from Aberdeenshire and the North of Scotland deserved 'much credit' for their skill in adapting to Canadian methods of farming. And on 21 October 1892 it reported that William McDonald, who farmed 2,720 acres with his sons at Virden, Manitoba, had just won a gold medal in an exhibition of prairie wheat in London. McDonald belonged to the Highlands but had lived in Aberdeenshire and Banffshire before emigrating to Ontario in 1873, moving west to Manitoba nine years later. Two other articles in 1892 highlighted the shortage of farm workers in many parts of Canada and the high wages that they could therefore command, and reported on the favourable prospects for farming in Canada after another bumper harvest.[35] On 11 November 1903 the *Aberdeen Journal* reviewed a recently-published book by the Banffshire journalist James Lumsden, *Through Canada at harvest time: life and labour in the golden west*. The author, who had visited Canada with a party of journalists in autumn 1902, had used his knowledge of agriculture in Northern Scotland to make comparisons between farming practices in the two countries, with the aim of encouraging farming emigrants to settle in Western Canada. In 1907 John Murray Gibbon's impressions of Canada, which had originally appeared in the *Aberdeen Journal*, were published as a book, *The Scot in Canada: a run through the Dominion.* Gibbon concentrated on farming settlement, and recounted a visit to a former blacksmith from Banchory-Devenick, who in 1904 had purchased a 640-acre farm at Indian Head, Saskatchewan, for $13 per acre. By 1907 the value of his property had increased to $30 per acre, and he advised even farm labourers with minimal capital to come to Canada, provided they were willing to work hard and save their wages in order ultimately to purchase farms of their own. The experiences of one such farm labourer who emigrated to Indian Head were subsequently recorded in a special issue of the Toronto-based newspaper, the *Canada Scotsman*, on 15 March 1909.[36] Five thousand copies of this special issue were circulated throughout Scotland in the hope of attracting farming emigrants to the West, and included among several settlers' letters was one from John Potts, a former farm servant from Auchenblae, Kincardineshire, who had emigrated in June 1905. After spending a year working on a threshing rig at Indian Head, he had moved on to a farm at Zealandia, Saskatchewan, and had also persuaded three brothers, a sister, a brother-in-law and a sister-in-law to follow his example in coming to Saskatchewan to take up prairie farming.[37]

The emigrant letter, of course, had for long been a favourite device employed by the newspapers to transmit information about life in the colonies. By the late nineteenth century the vast majority of these letters which appeared in the Northern Scottish newspapers dealt with farming settlement in Canada; and because they described the actual experiences of known people who had emigrated from the region, the information they contained had a much more immediate impact than the impersonal advice quoted from Canadian handbooks or the publications of the Emigrants' Information Office. Emigrant letters which appeared in the *Aberdeen Journal* dealt with settlement in all parts of Canada, but particularly in the West. On 15 April 1881 William Small, a Banffshire farmer, declared in the *Aberdeen Journal* that he was 'perfectly satisfied' that farmers could do better in that part of Canada than they could in Scotland. He was about to return home in order to make arrangements for his final emigration, and hoped that during this time he would be 'able to represent the prospects in this country in such a manner that a number of his acquaintances will determine also to leave Scotland and come out to Canada'. Duncan Smith, who was asked by his friends to write home describing his experiences in Morris, Manitoba, sent his correspondence to the *Aberdeen Journal* on the grounds that public interest in Manitoba warranted its publication. In a letter which was published on 9 March 1885 he described his journey from Quebec to Morris and his experiences of farming in that area, forty-two miles south of Winnipeg. An Aberdonian in Calgary in 1880 recommended emigrants to go in for stock-raising in Alberta, which already had 'a good many Aberdonians around, and room for lots more'. And another correspondent spoke of the 'unequalled' agricultural potential of the North-West Territories, although he would not recommend any except farmers to emigrate.[38] Another emigrant farmer in Manitoba, part of whose letter was quoted in the *Aberdeen Journal* on 21 March 1899, similarly believed that farming was the only occupation worth following in Canada. But even farmers should not expect to make fortunes and he reminded his correspondent, who was thinking of coming to Canada, of the need to work hard in order to succeed. By now the best homesteads had been taken up, although railway land was still available for sale, and he offered to accommodate his friend on one of his own farms until he had found a suitable property, warning him against rushing into an ill-thought-out purchase.

A more encouraging letter appeared in the *Aberdeen Journal* on 8 March 1902 when John Mitchell, an emigrant from Ellon, recounted his experiences of prairie farming during a visit home. Having emigrated initially to Toronto, he had moved to Eastern Assiniboia, 220 miles west of Winnipeg, in 1884, in response to the glowing reports of opportunities in the North-West. He had taken up a homestead grant, purchased the adjoining quarter-section, and by 1902 owned 480 acres and grazed a further 640 acres of government land at a rental of only four cents per acre. In his view, the North-West was suffering from a serious shortage of labour, despite the high wages paid by farmers, and he stressed that Britain could send out any number of farm workers. He himself could place 100 such hands, of either sex, within ten miles of his farm, and he, like others, pointed out the great inducement to agricultural labourers to emigrate, since the high wage rates meant that they could soon save enough money to buy land for themselves.

Further recommendation of Canadian agriculture was contained in a letter from Lord Strathcona, published in the *Aberdeen Journal* on 17 March 1902, in which he brought to the attention of potential emigrants a specific opportunity to settle on western farms. He believed that the thousands of people who wished to better their condition, but who were unable to do so in Britain, would take up homesteads if only they were made more aware of the facilities for doing so. He therefore intimated that specially conducted parties of emigrants, under the charge of Canadian government representatives, were to leave Liverpool for Canada in March and April. On arrival, agents would assist the settlers in reaching their farms, while those who did not want to settle immediately on their own land would be helped to find situations with farmers. The success of Lord Strathcona's appeal can be seen from a subsequent report in the same paper on 22 April, which spoke of a remarkable response in Scotland and estimated that before the end of the season the already large Scottish colony in Canada would have been substantially augmented.[39]

Encouraging personal accounts of Canadian farming continued to appear in the *Aberdeen Journal* right up to the First World War. Stewart Thomson, who left Aberdeen in March 1913 to spend the summer as a student missionary in Saskatchewan, believed that potential emigrants would be interested in his impressions of 'the golden west—granary of the world' and a letter bearing that title appeared in the *Aberdeen Journal* on 23 August. Thomson described the voyage and subsequent journey by 'colonist train' to his destination of Sprattsville, a typical farming settlement where 'wheat was everything'. Although he criticised the tendency of many farmers to take on more land than they could manage, he was convinced of the great potential of the West and urged emigrants to come out while land was still available. He reiterated the advice invariably given to new settlers, that before taking up land of their own, they should first seek labouring employment in order to gain practical experience of prairie farming; and he also reminded them of the need to make maximum use of the ample employment opportunities and high wages available in Spring, summer and autumn, in order to save enough money to see them through the slack winter period. Aberdonians were well represented in the Sprattsville area, and Thomson singled out for comment two former pupils of Gordon's College in Aberdeen who had abandoned academic careers in order to take up prairie farming.

In 1906 W. T. R. Preston, the Commissioner of Emigration for Canada, cited letters from successful emigrant farmers in his evidence to a par-liamentary enquiry into agricultural settlements in the British colonies.[40] Two of these emigrants, James Perrie and James McDiarmid, had come from Northern Scotland. Each had arrived in Canada with capital of only £1, but by 1904 they considered themselves to be worth £3,000 and £4,000 respec-tively. Perrie had worked as a herd boy and ploughman at Enzie, Banffshire, before he emigrated to Ontario in 1872. Six years later he moved west to Manitoba to work on the CPR and in 1880 he took up a homestead and pre-emption at Treherne. When a branch line of the CPR was opened in the area five years later the village of Treherne was located on his property, boosting further immigration, and in 1904 Perrie reckoned that his farm was worth at least $30 per acre. James McDiarmid, who emigrated to the North-West Territories with a large family in 1891, also worked initially on the railway, at the same time as he took up a homestead at Poplar Lake, north of Edmonton. By 1904 he had added a further 800 acres to his property, now valued at $20,000, and his four eldest sons had each taken up a homestead of their own. Both correspondents were convinced that Canada offered good incentives to hard-working farmers, and McDiarmid argued that much more should be done to encourage Scottish emigration in particular:

> When I think of the thousands of small tenants and crofters who are trying to eke out a subsistence in the north of Scotland ... I think something more than has as yet been done should be done to induce these people to come out to this country, where there are still millions of acres to be taken up as free holdings and where they would have every opportunity of bettering their condition ... I do not claim that Scotchmen should have a preference over either English or Irish, as all make good settlers, but I do claim that Scotchmen sooner adapt themselves to the conditions of the country than either of the other two. I do not know a Scotchman who has not bettered his condition by coming to this country, or one who would wish to return to Scotland to earn his living. In fact, I know of no one who has been two or three years in the country who would wish to leave it.[41]

The reproduction of letters from successful farming emigrants was a favourite means used by the Canadian Department of the Interior to lend authenticity to its promotional pamphlets. Some publications in fact consisted entirely of settlers' letters, drawing on the correspondence of men who had come from all over Britain, not least from North-East Scotland. *Letters from successful Scottish ploughmen* was published in 1909 in reply to criticisms made by William Bruce, a member of a recent Scottish farmers' delegation to Canada. He had complained that Scottish farm servants who emigrated were unlikely to improve their position because of their lack of capital,[42] so the pamphlet was intended to disprove these allegations, using illustrations from the correspondence of Scottish settlers who had succeeded from small beginnings. Among the letters quoted were five from men with North-East origins: William Farquhar from Lochlee (Glenesk), George Morrison from Tarves, James Hardie from Forres, David Hunter from Peterculter and George Lute from Aberdeen. All were convinced that their situation and prospects were infinitely better than they could ever have been in Scotland. Hunter, for instance, had come out to Manitoba in 1904 with capital of only $9 and had promptly found a situation at wages of $325 per annum. In 1905 he had lodged a homestead claim at Wadena, Saskatchewan, and in 1909 he considered that his improved property, together with stock and implements, was worth about £4,000. George Morrison too had come out to Hartney, Manitoba in 1884 with very little money, but by 1909 he owned 800 acres, worth from $25,000 to $30,000, as well as some property in the town. He reminded emigrants of the need to work hard to overcome initial difficulties, but he encouraged them to persevere towards the goal of ultimate independence:

> Young men are apt to get discouraged when landing here. Not finding everything as expected, they at first resolve to go back home. Don't do that. Make up your mind to stay. The climate is perhaps a little more extreme than in the north of Scotland, but you can become independent here, something you never can do at home working as a farm hand.[43]

He recommended that emigrants intending to homestead should have initial capital of from £100 to £150 (much more than that possessed by David Hunter on his arrival). George Lute too advised men with 'gumption, grit, ginger, and £100 to start' to come to Canada, where they should first gain experience as farm labourers before purchasing land. He himself had come out in 1907 because he wanted 'health and freedom' and by 1909 he was profitably engaged in mixed farming at Kaiser, Saskatchewan, his only regret being that he had not emigrated earlier.[44]

Similar sentiments and experiences were recorded by eight North-East emigrants in another official pamphlet, *Prosperity follows settlement*, published in 1911. On this occasion the Department of the Interior asked men who had emigrated from all parts of Britain to supply information about their experiences as agricultural labourers and subsequently as independent farmers in the West. This information was then collated and published, along with a number of settlers' letters.[45] The Scottish contributors included Thomas Graham and Frank Birse from Kincardineshire, Alex Thompson, William Gerrard, Alex Wilson, Alex Cumming and Alex McRobb, all from Aberdeenshire and R. G. Brown from Troup, Banffshire. On their arrival all of these men had worked on farms for wages averaging $250 to $300 per annum, before entering homestead claims or renting or buying land of their own. All had done well, sometimes from very modest beginnings. Graham, for instance, had arrived in Winnipeg with only $2.25 in his pocket but within three years he had saved enough money to return to Scotland for a visit; he contrasted this with the nine years he had spent in farm service in Kincardineshire, during which time he had managed to save only half his fare to Canada. After serving their 'apprenticeship' as farm labourers, Thompson and Wilson had bought quarter sections, while Gerrard, Brown, Birse and Cumming had bought half sections. In addition to the three years they had spent working for wages, Birse and Cumming had gained an extra three years' experience on rented farms before deciding to purchase for themselves. All were making substantial profits and strongly recommended emigration, provided the emigrants were willing to work and adapt to Canadian methods of farming. Gerrard, who claimed that he was making a profit of $1,000 a year on his half section at Manitou, Manitoba, said it was immaterial whether or not emigrants possessed any capital on arrival; R. G. Brown, on the other hand, discouraged the absolutely penniless from emigrating but maintained that agriculturists with £100 or more would be foolish to remain in Scotland. Brown had recently sold his half section at Baldour, Manitoba at a profit of $2,500 in order to take up another 320-acre half section in Saskatchewan.

The Canadian government did not only solicit and publish the opinions of successful emigrant farmers. From time to time it also invited official delegations of tenant farmers drawn from all over Britain to tour Canada at the government's expense. The (invariably favourable) reports of these delegates were published by the Department of Agriculture and distributed by Canadian government agents in Britain, while the British provincial press often took up the comments of those representatives who belonged to their region.[46] Thus on 10 March 1894 the *Aberdeen Journal* quoted from the recently published reports of Alexander Fraser of Culloden and John Steven of Fife, members of the 1893 farming delegation, who had been greatly impressed by the extent and success of Scottish farming settlement in Canada. Similar views were expressed by James Spence and John Rae, the two Aberdeen members of another delegation which visited Western Canada in summer 1903.[47] Rae remarked on the 'eminently favourable' conditions for agriculture, the prosperous appearance of towns such as Winnipeg, Brandon and Calgary, and the 'hopefulness and elasticity among the people' that was not evident in Scotland. There were four representatives from North-East Scotland among the twenty-two members of the Scottish Agricultural Commission which toured Canada in autumn 1908—farmers George A. Ferguson of Elgin and James Keith of Pitmedden, along with R. B. Greig, lecturer in agriculture in Marischal College at the University of Aberdeen and Dr R. S. Gibb, proprietor of the estate of Cults, Aberdeen, and a director of the Highland and Agricultural Society. The Commission's report, which discussed the conditions and opportunities for farming in various parts of Canada, was published by the Department of Agriculture along with a selection of letters from successful Scottish settlers. Included in these twenty-five letters was an account by a former farm servant from Auchenblae, J. G.

Lindsay, who after emigrating in June 1905 had initially worked on a thre-shing rig at Indian Head for $1.75 per day until he had accumulated sufficient capital to begin farming on his own account. He had then taken up a home-stead at Zealandia, Saskatchewan, and by 1908 he owned five horses and all the implements necessary to work the farm. He had prepared 100 acres for a crop in 1909 while his brother, who had also emigrated from Kincar-dineshire, had broken and sown 130 acres of ground.[48]

The Canadian government clearly hoped that the favourable reports of emigrants and farming delegations, disseminated in agricultural circles in Britain, would encourage further emigration. But it was not content to confine itself to such indirect means of promoting settlement, and on 19 January 1903 the *Aberdeen Journal* reported that, in pursuit of its campaign to attract emigrants, the Canadian government was about to send a delegation of forty farming experts to Britain. They were to spend several months touring the rural districts in order to give information and advice to prospective emigrants and would also open offices in a number of locations, from where interested parties could obtain precise details about Canadian lands. On 21 March the *Aberdeen Journal* intimated that one of these delegates, C. J. Thomson, was currently in the city and could be consulted at John Cook's shipping and emigration office in Marischal Street. Similarly on 10 November it reported that another delegate, Andrew Grieve—who had emigrated from Fife in 1882 to take up land near Winnipeg—was in Aberdeen and could be consulted either at Cook's office or at his hotel.

From time to time the Canadian government also sent individual farmers to various parts of Britain for short periods in order to stimulate interest in emigration. In December 1904 Alexander McOwan, a farmer in Virden, Manitoba, was sent on a four-month visit to Scotland, and on 29 March 1905 the *Aberdeen Journal* reported that he had extended his period in Aberdeen, where he was interviewing prospective farming emigrants at Sheed's booking office in the city. In February 1907 Hugh McIntosh, who farmed at McLeod, Alberta, was sent to Scotland for three months at a salary of $100 per month. After spending a few days in Glasgow and a week in Edinburgh he came to Aberdeen, where he was based for the remainder of his visit, working under John MacLennan's jurisdiction. Since McIntosh himself had emigrated from Scotland in 1897, MacLennan believed 'he was a good object lesson as to what can be achieved in the Dominion'[49] and he made maximum use of his services. As well as meeting prospective emigrants in Aberdeen, McIntosh was sent to booking agents in Inverurie, Huntly, Turriff, Buckie, Nairn, Invergordon, Tain, Bonar Bridge, Lairg, Golspie and Dornoch, and spent a week visiting country schools in Easter Ross. In the subsequent report of his trip submitted to the Department of the Interior McIntosh spoke of a gen-erally encouraging response where people had been adequately informed in advance about his visit:

> I ... visited several points in Aberdeenshire, Banffshire, Morayshire, Nairnshire, Ross-shire and Sutherlandshire in all about 25 different places. I was very suc-cessful in having a good number of interviews at all points but in one or two

cases the Booking Agents failed to advertise my coming early enough for the country people to know anything about it ... When I had the occasion of going to a country point it was always the most successful of any. The interest in Canada was most intensive. In fact all over Scotland it is nothing but Canada.[50]

The sending of successful farmers to Scotland to recruit emigrants was strongly recommended in 1909 by Charles Ritchie, who had emigrated from Orkney to Saltcoats, Saskatchewan, in 1888 and who had brought out many farm hands from Scotland over the years. In his opinion

> There is a large number of good farm hands in Orkney and Aberdeen that are anxious to come to Canada at the present time. The only way Canada can get the men that will make good farm hands and become good settlers ... is by sending farmers from here that the people know and can trust to tell them the truth and instruct them how to prepare for the passage.[51]

But this kind of direct recruitment through itinerant agents was not restricted to a few farmers who were sent over to Scotland from time to time under the auspices of the Dominion government. The key part played by resident Canadian government agents in encouraging emigration, particularly of agriculturists, has already been emphasised. Peter Fleming in the 1890s, for instance, initially confined his recruitment campaign exclusively to the agricultural classes, sending personal invitations and promotional literature to all the small farmers in districts where he proposed to hold meetings. He believed that these men, although usually interested in hearing about Canada, had to be sensitively persuaded to relinquish their attachment to their home-land and convincingly assured of the advantages of farming in Canada. In his annual report for 1894 he noted that, after a partially failed harvest and a fall in stock and crop prices, large numbers of working farmers had attended his meetings in November and December, some of whom would have emigrated if they had been able to get clear of their leases.[52] Many farmers and farm servants, however, were reluctant to take this momentous step, as Fleming pointed out in his report the following year:

> The chief difficulty is in getting farm servants in this country to realize the possibility of their being in a position within a few years of their arrival in Canada to acquire a homestead of their own, 160 acres in extent, with sufficient capital to start farming on their own account. A condition of things which renders this possible is scarcely conceivable by the ordinary ploughman of this country. Those of that class who have been exceptionally saving and industrious, and who have tried the experiment of farming on their own account, have not as a rule improved their condition to any great extent. When small farms or mod-erately sized crofts come to be let the rents obtained for them are so high that it requires the hardest work combined with the strictest economy to make a bare living out of them. The thought of occupying a homestead of their own does not therefore possess the charm for our ordinary agriculturist that it ought to have. They know that to stock a farm of 160 acres in this country necessitates a capital of from £1,200 to £1,500, and it is difficult for them to grasp the idea that in Canada one tenth of that sum is sufficient to make a fair start.[53]

Fleming's view that agents had to make a special effort to persuade con-servative North-East farmers to emigrate was confirmed eighteen years later when G. G. Archibald, in his annual report for 1913-14, noted an increased interest in emigration in the local farming community, but warned that 'this class of men are rather difficult to approach'. In fact, Archibald and his predecessors did a great deal to encourage farming emigration from the North of Scotland. John MacLennan's weekly reports, for instance, contain not only actual evidence of the farming exodus from his area, but also show the crucial part he himself played in bringing about that movement over a five-year period. Most of his lectures were delivered to audiences of farmers and farm servants. In December 1907 he reported that he had taken a very successful meeting in Rothiemay, attended by over 250 country people. In October 1908 over half of the 500 people who had come to his lecture in Banff were farmers or farm servants, and in one week in January 1909 he spoke to audiences of 700 and 500 in Fraserburgh and Rathen respectively, the latter gathering consisting entirely of agriculturists.[54] On 13 November 1909, after delivering lectures at Duffus, Garmouth, Fochabers, Lhanbryde and Rothes, MacLennan reported optimistically that 'I had a very successful week lecturing in Elgin County to farmers and farm servants, and I look for good results next year'. When in May 1911 he was transferred to the Liverpool office he delivered a farewell lecture in the Music Hall in Aberdeen, in which he advised his large audience, whatever their original occupations, to take up farming in Canada.[55]

The government emigration office in Aberdeen regularly sent circulars and pamphlets to farmers in the hope of arousing their interest in emigration. But MacLennan was acutely aware of the importance of the personal touch, and he and his assistants were assiduous in their attendance at weekly markets, biannual hiring fairs, summer shows and generally at all those events where farming people gathered in large numbers. They discussed emigration with interested individuals, distributed promotional literature and mounted dis-plays of Canadian produce, in their 'travelling exhibition van' or in the Department's motor car. In May 1907 MacLennan reported that he had attended a feeing market at Elgin, where he 'met a large number and did excellent work', and later that year he attended the winter feeing markets at Inverurie, Keith, Dufftown, Elgin, Nairn and Inverness, having previously asked the booking agents in Elgin and Inverness to publicise his forthcoming visits and distribute relevant literature.[56] On 14 September 1907 he reported that as a result of a conversation at a cattle sale in Aberdeen two men subsequently visited the office in search of further information about Canada. A few months later he reported that he had persuaded two farm servants attending the Aberdeen stock market to book passages to Canada,[57] and during the week ending 25 April 1908 he attended four cattle and stock sales—at Ballater, Banchory, Nairn and Peterhead—at which he had the opportunity to meet and converse with a large number of people.

But MacLennan and his helpers were busiest during the summer, when representatives were sent to all the agricultural shows held in the North of Scotland. In one 'red letter' day at the Aberdeen Agricultural Show in July

1907 MacLennan held over 300 personal interviews and distributed 4,000 pamphlets.[58] Then the following month, after he and his assistant had distributed 600 pamphlets and conducted 230 interviews at the Huntly Show, he wrote in his report for the week ending 3 August that 'This is one of the best districts in my territory, the people being all farmers, over 100 having gone to Canada this year'. The following summer MacLennan reported that either he or his assistant Hugh McKerracher had attended shows at Aboyne, Banff, Turriff, Aberchirder, Keith, Elgin, Nairn, Cawdor, Grantown on Spey, Inverness, Invergordon, Tain and Golspie, as well as the four-day Highland Show in Aberdeen.[59] And in July and August 1910, while MacLennan was visiting Canada, another assistant, a Mr Wingate, took his place at shows in Ellon, Fyvie, Mintlaw, Maud, Huntly, Keith, Elgin, Nairn and Dingwall. At Maud he conducted 250 interviews and at Mintlaw, where approximately 15,000 people attended the Show, he interviewed about 100 individuals, a good number of whom subsequently booked passages to Canada. Wingate distributed over 1,000 pamphlets at Huntly, and a further 1,000 at Keith, and in each place he interviewed approximately forty farmers and farm labourers, many of whom were contemplating emigrating to Canada the following Spring.[60]

In 1926, in giving advice to the Department of the Interior on the best way to attract suitable farmers over from the United States, MacLennan drew on his experiences in Scotland to illustrate the importance of getting out into the rural districts and forging links with the farmers, frequenting their meeting-places and getting alongside them. He wrote:

> My office in Aberdeen ... from 1907 to 1911 was within one block of the city market where farmers gathered and could be seen by every passenger coming in by rail and yet if one depended on the Aberdeen office my effort during these 5 years would have been nil. My success there was on hiring day held twice a year in every trading center where all the farm servants, men and women and all farmers that done their trading [sic] in that center met on these days. Then we had a tent at every Fair in every town in that District, besides giving lectures about 60 every year in every community in the North of Scotland and the Islands. Then Mr. McKerracher travelled continuously with a team throughout the country talking to men at the road side. When he saw a farmer he stopped until he came up and opened conversation.[61]

It has been pointed out that MacLennan and his colleagues relied heavily on the co-operation of ticket agents scattered across the region to attend fairs, distribute literature and organise their lectures and interviews, as well as to deal with the actual booking of emigrants' passages. When going to outlying areas these agents of the Dominion government, the different provinces and the transcontinental railway companies addressed gatherings arranged by the booking agents and made use of their premises to conduct personal interviews. Canadian farming delegates visiting Northern Scotland were sent not only to booking offices in the city of Aberdeen, but also to the rural areas, to meet prospective emigrants who were advised of their visits through advertisements in the local press. Similarly on 12 February 1910 the

Aberdeen Journal intimated that the Ontario agent, Captain Thomson, was to be available at W. T. Moffatt's office to give information about the special inducements offered to emigrants to take up farming in that province. And on a number of occasions the representatives of the transcontinental railway companies publicised their emigration schemes by courtesy of the various booking agents. On 15 February 1913, for instance, the *Aberdeen Journal* reported a large attendance at an illustrated lecture in the YWCA in the city, given by a representative of the Grand Trunk Railway and organised by four local booking agents—Paton, MacKay, R. & J. Davidson and W. T. Moffatt.

The Canadian Pacific Railway Company waged a particularly enthusiastic and consistent publicity campaign to attract farming settlers to its lands in Western Canada. As part of its agreement with the Canadian government in 1880, the Company was allocated 25,000,000 acres of land between Winnipeg and the Rocky Mountains, along the proposed line of the track; and it was as a result of this substantial grant that it became, along with the Dominion government, the major coloniser of the prairie provinces. It was particularly anxious to promote immigration, since its success depended both on the sale and development of these otherwise worthless lands and on the growth in railway traffic that would come from increased settlement. Using methods similar to those employed by the Dominion government, agents of the Canadian Pacific Company toured Britain giving illustrated lectures, answering queries and organising displays of prairie produce at agricultural fairs and exhibitions. Soil samples and prairie products were also prominently displayed at the Company's main offices, and a 'Travelling Exhibition Van' similar to that used by MacLennan and McKerracher was used to reach people in remote areas.[62] Prospective emigrants were told about the advantages of buying land from the Company at prices ranging from $2.50 per acre in the 1880s to $20 per acre in the period just before the First World War. By that time emigrants were being urged to take up the CPR's ready-made farms in Southern Alberta, units of 160 or 320 acres suitable for mixed farming. Under the scheme, inaugurated in 1909, the Company agreed to clear and plant fifty or 100 acres, according to the size of the farm, and supply fencing, wells, barns, and a four-roomed house in preparation for the settler's arrival. Emigrants were thus spared some of the hardships of pioneering and were allowed to pay for their farms in instalments over a ten-year period at six per cent interest, the cost of the improvements being added to the initial cost of the land. Emigrants who did not want to go to ready-made farms could select their land on arrival and obtain loans of up to £600 from the Company to cover the cost of clearing, cultivating, fencing and stocking their property, as well as erecting the necessary buildings.

Advertisements for Canadian Pacific lands pointed out that emigrants could acquire a farm of their own for the equivalent of three years' rent at home, and contrasted the ease with which they could become their own masters with the improbability of attaining independence in Britain. One of the advertisements for ready-made farms which appeared in the *Aberdeen Journal* noted this major incentive, and tried to dispel the belief that Western

Canada was primitive, virtually uninhabited and isolated from the rest of the country:[63]

> In the pioneering days in Western Canada the settler endured many hardships. He was far from a railway, separated by many miles from his nearest neighbour, school, and church—a market for his produce almost non-existent, and apparently with no hope of matters bettering themselves. All this is changed now, and under the 'Ready-made' farm scheme, inaugurated by the Canadian Pacific Railway, a farmer with moderate capital can leave this country by a CONDUCTED PARTY, and on his arrival he finds a well-settled and prosperous country, a house and stables erected, about 50 acres of his homestead is broken and sown, a well sunk and pump installed. He is also close to a railway station, markets, schools, and amongst neighbours of his own class and nationality. It must be borne in mind that these farms are not RENTED, but SOLD on the instalment plan ... so that all the settler's work and energy on his farm is for the benefit of himself and his family.

The Canadian Pacific's interests in North-East Scotland were represented by both resident and visiting agents. In November 1910 the manager of the CPR Lands Department visited MacKay Brothers' agency in Aberdeen to explain the advantages of ready-made farms, and the following year a local representative, Captain Gordon, lectured on the same theme at rural venues in the North-East, including Huntly and King Edward.[64] Gordon, who himself farmed in the county of Nairn, had represented the interests of the CPR Land Department in North-East Scotland for the previous twenty-three years, and had extensive knowledge of farming in Western Canada. In November 1912 Malcolm McIntyre came up from Glasgow to speak about Canadian Pacific lands in two lectures; at Alford (organised by MacKay's agency) and in Ellon (at the invitation of Francis Godsman, the local agent of the CPR). And in January 1913 Hector McKenzie, who had taken up one of the ready-made farms in 1911, spoke about his experiences to an audience of prospective emigrants in Oldmeldrum, in a meeting organised by Paton's agency.[65]

Farming emigration from North-East Scotland was promoted not only by official, paid agents of the Canadian government or the railway companies. Most of the church and village hall lectures on Canada given by returned travellers or visiting emigrants dealt primarily with aspects of farming settlement. In March 1885, for instance, J. E. Cracknell, recently returned from a trip to Canada, attracted a large audience to a lecture he delivered in Aberdeen, in which he spoke particularly about the good opportunities afforded to industrious farmers and farm servants in the Dominion. This theme was taken up again the following week in lectures in Aberdeen and Fordyce by the Rev Gavin Lang of Inverness (formerly of Fyvie), who had just returned from a trip across Canada on the Canadian Pacific Railway.[66] Early in 1886 Alexander Begg, a former pupil of Aberdeen Grammar School and a fur trader who had spent seventeen years in the North-West Territories, came to Aberdeen in charge of an exhibition of Canadian farming produce under the auspices of the Canada North West Land Company; and the same month James Burgess, who had lived in Canada for over thirty years, lectured at Rothiemay on the opportunities for farmers and the procedure for acquiring land.[67]

A. J. MacMillan, who had settled in Brandon, Manitoba, in 1882, also gave advice on current Canadian land regulations at lectures in Aberdeen, Strichen, Inverurie, Alford, Tarland, Ellon, Slains, Laurencekirk and Turriff in 1888.[68] He had first returned home the previous year to deliver a series of lectures about his emigrant experiences, as a result of which several people had decided to accompany him back to Canada. Their successful settlement encouraged him to return to Aberdeenshire in winter 1888 to publicise Canadian farming opportunities even more extensively, and his lectures throughout the region attracted large audiences. He reminded them that in Manitoba they could either take up homestead grants or purchase farms at reasonable prices, while men without capital could easily find well-paid farm work and soon save enough money to begin farming on their own account. Among the many other 'unofficial' lectures reported in the *Aberdeen Journal* which encouraged farming people to emigrate was a talk at Nairn in 1889 by Duncan Macarthur of Winnipeg, two lectures by Baillie Stuart of Inverness, at Kincardine O'Neil in 1893 and at Fochabers in 1894, an address at Slains in 1901 by a Mr Taylor from Ontario and a lecture on Manitoba delivered under the auspices of the Lonmay Mutual Improvement Association in 1903.[69] A 'large audience' attended an illustrated lecture in Skene Street Congregational Church in Aberdeen in January 1910, delivered by former Scottish Agricultural Commission delegate R. B. Greig; and a talk at Durris the following month by a Mr Michie who had spent several years in Canada also aroused considerable public interest.[70]

Agriculturists were perhaps most likely to emigrate when this kind of general encouragement was accompanied by a specific offer of employment in Canada. Such posts for farm workers were frequently advertised in the *Aberdeen Journal*. On 25 February 1889, for instance, Ben Reid and Company, seedsmen and nurserymen in Aberdeen, appealed for thirty agricultural labourers, whose transatlantic passages would be paid and who would each receive free board and lodging and wages of £47 per annum. On 21 October 1890 George Bruce of Aberdeen, also a seed merchant and nurseryman, advertised for a cattleman to take charge of an Aberdeen Angus herd in Canada, and on 27 January 1903 the Canadian Land and Ranch Company required two experienced shepherds to take up work at Swift Current, Saskatchewan, at wages of $30 a month. And among the employees for a Manitoba farm requested in an advertisement by George Christie of Great Northern Road, Aberdeen on 12 February 1903 were a married couple and a single male laboourer.

Local booking agents were aware that they were more likely to attract clients if they could combine personal persuasion about the attributes of Canada with the concrete offer of work on arrival. Many of them therefore used their Canadian contacts to try to secure specific farming situations for clients in advance. Booking agents who could offer specific situations to recruits commonly advertised these posts in the local press. Among the city agencies which advertised particular Canadian farming jobs in the *Aberdeen*

Journal were MacKay's, Paton's, Davidson's, Moffatt's, Mrs Stewart's, Swanson's and the Northern Ocean Ticket Office, along with Alexander Longmuir in nearby Stonehaven. Sometimes the need was for an individual, as with the cattleman for Ontario sought by MacKay's in January 1910, the ranch hand for British Columbia sought by Davidson's in May 1912 or the farm labourer for Manitoba, also sought by Davidson's, in February 1913.[71] On other occasions the need was for a married couple, seen in MacKay's advertisement in 1910 for two couples to take up farm service in New Brunswick and Ontario, each post offering a wage of $20 a month and a free cottage.[72] And sometimes the booking agents tried to recruit agriculturists en bloc, often in order to make up their personally conducted parties. On 23 March 1910, for instance, the Northern Ocean Ticket Office appealed for twenty farm hands; and on 4 April MacKay Brothers announced that they required ten experienced farm hands to leave with a conducted party on 30 April, the recruits being promised 'first class situations with good farmers' at wages of up to $25 a month. On several occasions Alexander Longmuir advertised for agriculturists to join his conducted parties,[73] and on 10 February 1913 T. Joss of King Street, Aberdeen, appealed for fifty youths to join his specially-conducted parties, which were to leave on 27 February and 8 March under the auspices of the Boys' Farmer League of Canada.

Individual employers in Canada sometimes dealt directly with the Scottish booking agents in order to secure the labour force they required. Thus in 1912 Paton's despatched a Mr and Mrs Argo to a farm at Lorne Park, Ontario, in response to a request from the farmer, a Mr Albertson, to recruit 'several couples' who would go out to work for himself and neighbouring farmers.[74] And on another occasion a farmer from Brandon, Manitoba who was visiting Aberdeen chose, during his visit, two employees to accompany him back to Canada, the passage arrangements of Thomas Walker and James Pittendreigh being made through MacKay's agency.[75] Some of the Canadian employers were former emigrants from North-East Scotland who, when they required labour for their farms, wished to engage recruits from their home region, and advertised their requirements in the *Aberdeen Journal* under the auspices of local booking agents. Thus on 27 July 1910 MacKay's intimated that an Aberdeenshire farmer in Manitoba required six threshers at $60 a month; on 29 March 1911 the same agency advertised for several farm hands to go out to a former Turriff farmer, also now in Manitoba; and on 27 May 1912 Davidson's agency appealed for three experienced farm hands to engage with an Aberdeenshire farmer, once more in Manitoba, at wages of £7 a month.

It is clear that agriculturists in North-East Scotland were given widespread encouragement to settle in Canada, through a combination of promotional literature, the personal persuasion of numerous agents and lecturers, and the specific offer of employment on Canadian farms. Only very occasionally were they warned of the drawbacks involved in emigrating, usually in the published correspondence of disillusioned emigrants who had a particular axe to grind. One correspondent of the *Aberdeen Journal* on 4 January 1884 warned readers 'not to put too much faith in the representations of land and steamship agents, whose only care is to reap the profit of passing emigrants through their hands'. He advised them to settle in Ontario rather than further west, where he claimed the climate was severe, the rail freight charges exorbitant and the general cost of establishing a settlement far greater than was suggested in the promotional literature. On 11 August 1903 another correspondent of the *Aberdeen Journal*, who had recently emigrated to Red Deer, Alberta, complained bitterly about the misleading information given to emigrants before they left home. Expressing opinions very different from those normally voiced in published correspondence, he warned men without capital to avoid the West, where the work was onerous and the wages poor:

> After a lapse of nearly four months in this wild country, I am very much discouraged. My mind is so full that I can hardly write as I would like ... We left Toronto on the 31st March, and after over four days' travelling in cars, which at home would be called box waggons, we arrived at Calgary ... This train was a special, with about 400 on board, from Toronto and district, going out West to make their fortunes. Fortunes, did I say? Well, if the truth were told, many of them come out to eke out a miserable existence ... This is a little place with a little over 1000 inhabitants, and is just like many another little Western town. The people are sleepy, with no "go" in them, and, so far as I personally am concerned, it is the last place on God's earth that I would care to remain in; but what is a fellow to do? The other places are no better, and many of them much worse. Edmonton, the only town of importance north of here, is overdone, and property is up to famine price.

The writer and his family had intended to take up a homestead, which he had been told could be obtained for $10 within a mile of the railway. But on arrival they had found the nearest homesteads were thirty-five miles distant from the railway, and the nearest decent land even further afield—up to eighty miles away from the railway. He complained about the high cost of living, and alleged that hundreds of disillusioned emigrants were leaving the area.

These complaints were reiterated by another Aberdeenshire settler in Alberta, in a letter published in the *Aberdeen Journal* on 8 September 1910. This correspondent too reminded emigrants that they should not believe implicitly the glowing accounts presented in promotional pamphlets, and warned them that they must be prepared to overcome many hardships associated with pioneer farming. Although he himself did not regret his decision to take up a prairie homestead, he pointed out to those who were contemplating this step that they would have to spend much time and effort and considerably more money than their $10 registration fee on their quarter-section in order to make it profitable. He had spent $1,000 on clearing and cultivating his own 'free land', on digging a well and on purchasing essential implements. And he suggested that emigrants should possess at least a little initial capital, since farm labourers could not make such substantial savings from their wages as the pamphlets often led them to believe.[76] This warning was reiterated in an article in the *Aberdeen Free Press* on 22 May 1913, which noted that several Aberdeenshire farmers had received letters from ploughmen, formerly in their employment, who had recently emigrated to Canada:

> Some of the letters contain tidings of success, but others sound the note of blighted hopes and empty purses. Several farmers have been asked by former servants to forward their homeward passage money, in return for which free service will be given on arriving in this country.

Some contributors to periodicals such as *Chambers' Journal* claimed to present a more balanced account of emigrants' prospects than was evident in the one-sided, eulogistic official publications, which tended to highlight all the advantages and none of the drawbacks of Canadian farming. On at least three occasions articles on emigration in *Chambers' Journal* were justified on the grounds that readers deserved to know the whole truth about life in the colonies, preferably from the pens of those who had personal experience of its virtues and defects. G. J. Webster, in an article in 1905 on 'Ranching in the Canadian North-West',[77] drew on his own experience in giving advice and information, primarily to wealthier emigrants. He believed that the existing literature, useful and extensive though it was, did not cover some major issues; and although he welcomed the ease with which emigrants could become independent through the purchase of their own land, he also pointed out some of the hazards of pioneer ranching in the North-West. In 1910 an article by W. S. Ferguson warned emigrants against believing agents who claimed that they could enjoy the 'amenities and comforts' of Canadian life without first encountering and overcoming the difficulties of pioneering. Such misleading claims had brought about the return of a number of disillusioned settlers, and Ferguson particularly advised inexperienced emigrants against taking up the much-vaunted ready made farms until they had been in the country long enough to make a wise investment.[78]

Then the following year *Chambers' Journal* appealed to readers who had emigrated, particularly women, to submit short articles for publication describing their experiences and outlining the daily routine of colonial life.[79] *Chambers'* argued that there was a clear need for such basic 'domestic' information, since most existing literature was too vague and superficial to be of practical use to intending emigrants, as well as being totally biased in favour of emigration. Married men in particular, who were anxious to know whether the colonial life would suit their wives and families, might be deterred by the lack of honest practical information in many handbooks; and *Chambers'* thought that such information, supplied by ordinary emigrants, would assist readers in making up their minds about the pros and cons of emigration. There was a good response to the appeal, and in February 1912 some of the replies were published. Three women in Alberta, one in British Columbia and one in Manitoba described their experiences as emigrants, mentioning not only the advantages of colonial life but also the problems of loneliness and unrelenting toil, which they noted were rarely mentioned in official guidebooks.

Indeed, apart from these few instances of qualified encouragement—and occasionally outright discouragement—to farming emigrants, most of the advice offered to farmers at this time was wholeheartedly in favour of their moving to Canada. Since most published correspondence was carefully written or selected to convey a particular point of view, it is difficult to obtain an unbiased account of the real feelings and experiences of settlers involved in pioneer farming. Any examples of private correspondence are therefore invaluable. The seventy-four letters of an early twentieth-century Nairnshire emigrant, John McBean, fall into this category, and merit special attention because of the detailed—and largely unvarnished—information they provide about many aspects of pioneering on the Canadian prairies. McBean was the eldest of a family of six children brought up on the farm of Keppernach in the parish of Ardclach. His father had spent thirty-six years as head game-keeper on the nearby estate of Lord Cawdor before he took up this farm in 1868, and when he died eleven years later the tenancy was carried on by his widow. When she died in 1901 John, as the eldest son, was expected to take over the farm, but after only a year he relinquished this right to his brother Andrew in order to emigrate to Manitoba. From then until his death in 1906 at the age of forty-four, McBean worked first as a farm labourer and then as a journalist for two leading agricultural periodicals, travelling widely throughout the province in the course of his journalistic employment. He was a prolific letter-writer, and details of his experiences and ambitions, along with his impressions of Manitoba, its inhabitants and prospects, were contained in his correspondence with his brother and sister in Scotland between July 1902 and February 1906.[80]

Pioneering in Manitoba: the letters of John McBean

McBean emigrated in 1902, at a time when the Department of the Interior and the Canadian Pacific Railway Company were making a determined effort to boost British emigration. This was in response to the large influx of Americans and Europeans to the prairies the previous year, which had provoked a clamour for more British settlers for the West.[81] But McBean objected to what he regarded as the deceptive methods of promoting settlement, particularly the practice of inviting influential individuals from Scotland to tour the Dominion, with the intention that they should then use their influence to bring about emigration. Shortly after arriving in Canada he wrote to his sister:

> This country is being boomed at a fearful rate at present. The emigration department have brought over about one hundred school teachers and as many editors free of charge, and all expenses paid. The object is to bring the advantages of the country before the people of Scotland. Mr Barron of the *Inverness Courier* is among the crowd. The whole business is looked upon here as a huge swindle. It is entirely the work of Lord Strathcona and the Canadian Pacific Railway, which dominates the Government of this country in every conceivable way.[82]

In his letters McBean did not discuss the reasons for his emigration, or whether he felt he had been misled by this kind of propaganda. But he later admitted in a newspaper article that his curiosity had been aroused by the conflicting accounts of Canada emanating on the one hand from Canadian agents in Britain, and on the other from disillusioned emigrant farmers; and so, 'with the object of ascertaining profitably the real state of matters, and with the matured conviction that here were opportunities quite outside the reach of the farmer at home, I resolved to emigrate'.[83] Clearly he was not driven solely by curiosity and the desire to discover who was telling the truth about Canada; like many of his contemporaries, it seems that he too was seeking greater independence and an opportunity for advancement. His horizons had never been limited just to the affairs of the family farm, but had been broadened by the education he had received at Nairn Academy and by his subsequent involvement with the Mutual Improvement Association in Nairn. He had developed an aptitude for journalism, and contributed occasional articles on agricultural topics to the *Banffshire Journal*, the *Highland News* and *The Scotsman*.[84] Perhaps his academic interests encouraged his restlessness, for he sometimes referred disparagingly to the monotony and predictability of life in Ardclach, and the impossibility of improving his situation there. In 1905, for instance, replying to his sister's comment on the poverty at Keppernach, he remembered his own 'utter helplessness' to improve conditions when he had been in charge of the farm, and his superstitious belief that the place lay under a 'demonaical curse'.[85] McBean certainly exhibited great personal pride and a dogged determination to succeed through his own efforts, even if this meant starting on the lowest rung of the ladder. Writing to his brother on 21 September 1902 he said of the factor at Ardclach:

> I do not believe but he could get me a place here if he tried. However I prefer depending entirely upon my own exertions, and I am pretty confident that I shall get on although I am about as far down the rope in the meantime as I can be.

And early in 1903 he chided his sister for sending him money, asserting that he could support himself on the remainder of his savings.[86]

John McBean sailed from Glasgow on the SS *Sardinian* of the Allan Line on 7 June 1902, arriving at Quebec ten days later. After applying unsuccessfully for a place on a ship taking horses from Montreal to South Africa,[87] he travelled west to Winnipeg with a party of over 200 emigrants, and from July until November he was employed by a Dutch farmer at the township of Lintrathen, about thirty miles from the border between Manitoba and the United States. His career as a farm labourer was terminated by accident and illness before the end of 1902, and McBean was obliged to turn (not unwillingly) to less strenuous pursuits. He gave up his first intention of seeking a teaching post in favour of commercial work, which would require less training and which was probably more readily available.[88] Turning his attention to journalism again, he submitted articles to a number of papers in Winnipeg, which, he alleged, were eager to publish his material, but not to pay him for it.[89] In January 1903 he was offered the chance of employment on the *Farmers' Advocate and Home Magazine*, a fortnightly agricultural journal which was published both in Winnipeg and in London, Ontario. In mid-February, when he thought there was no likelihood of a better job,[90] he accepted this offer, and was subsequently sent on a 'trial trip' through Manitoba, to collect subscriptions and advertisement fees, find new subscribers and write articles on the districts visited. Success on this trip was to guarantee him regular summer field work of the same nature, and editorial employment in the office during the following winter. He was given the use of a horse and buggy and was paid $1.25 per day, his expenses, and $4 a column for every article he wrote, being expected to produce an article for each issue of the paper.[91]

Having earned the approval of his employers on his probationary trip, McBean was immediately sent out again, to Northern Manitoba, and then to the North-West Territories in April and May 1903 to canvass new settlers on behalf of the *Farmers' Advocate*. Despite earlier promises of a permanent post he was only employed on a month-to-month basis, and after a renewed bout of illness during a visit to the Barr Colony in late April, he became pessimistic about his chances of continuing employment. Most of the canvassing work was now being conducted in the new territories, and he was not fit enough for the rough life on horseback which that entailed.[92] Nevertheless, he was re-engaged for a month in June 1903, to cover the season of agricultural fairs, and again in July, on the Winnipeg editor's own responsibility. In August 1903 the paper's publishers in London, Ontario finally approved his appointment to a permanent post as Associate Editor and Livestock Representative.[93] In the next nine months McBean undertook a number of trips in Manitoba, canvassing for subscriptions and advertisements, and reporting on agricultural fairs, and particularly on stockbreeding. He became—by his own account—an acknowledged expert in the latter field, and was expected to visit and report on every herd in Manitoba and as far west as Regina in the North-West Territories at least once a year.[94]

But although he enjoyed his writing assignments, McBean disliked the canvassing, likening it to pedlar's work,[95] yet he was expected to raise enough subscriptions during a trip to cover his expenses and salary. Even a remunerative trip, such as that among Southern Manitoba stockbreeders in November 1903, he saw in terms of bolstering his reputation with his employers in order to convince them that they should retain his services.[96] During this trip he had secured more advertisements than had ever been achieved by an *Advocate* field representative, as each farmer he had visited had taken out advertising with him. But when the paper was published weekly from January 1904, McBean's work became increasingly difficult and disheartening, since the stockmen were unwilling to pay the doubled rates now demanded for advertising.[97] He was convinced that his employers were seeking his dismissal on the excuse that stock advertising did not pay, and that the department should therefore be axed. Changes in the office management heightened his suspicions, particularly the appointment of an eminent agricultural editor (a former professor of the Iowa Agricultural College) who assumed many of McBean's duties.[98]

McBean resigned from the *Farmers' Advocate* in April 1904, and by August he was working for a rival, larger agricultural periodical, the *Nor' West Farmer*. This paper, which covered Manitoba, Assiniboia, Saskatchewan, Alberta and British Columbia, claimed that its circulation was larger than the combined circulation of all other agricultural papers taken in Western Canada.[99] McBean's duties were similar to those on the *Farmers' Advocate*, a combination of field work in order to increase subscriptions and advertising, with the preparation of descriptive articles, and general office-based editorial work. But he was again employed only in a temporary capacity, and seems to have had no greater measure of job security than in his previous post; indeed, he was apparently under even more pressure to succeed. He thought his services would be retained only for as long as he was successful in canvassing, and complained that he was given no independence or freedom to write.[100] When working for the *Advocate*, he knew that he had given satisfaction when he had improved business to an extent to which his employers were unaccustomed, but the *Nor' West Farmer* was a much more popular paper with a much wider circulation, and accepted good business as a matter of course.[101] When a new employee was appointed to the office staff in November 1904, McBean was not dismissed, as he had at first expected, but put back on to field work, at a most uncongenial time of year. He vowed then that he would not spend another winter in such employment, driving over the prairie in sub-zero temperatures, waiting in small towns for farmers who never appeared, and suffering the 'lonely monotony of a new town every day and a new bed every night'.[102] Yet when early in 1905 he was offered the post of editor-in-chief of a new agricultural paper to be launched in Brandon, he declined the post, even though the $1,200 a year salary offered was nearly double his earnings with the *Nor' West Farmer*. But as he wrote to his brother, he believed that any such new farming paper would founder, and as even the *Farmers' Advocate* was struggling at the time, he could not realistically expect to make a new paper a viable concern single-handedly.[103]

McBean in fact continued to travel for the *Nor' West Farmer* throughout most of 1905, until his health finally gave way. But by this time he had become engaged to Agnes Lumb of Glen Stewart, Cartwright, Manitoba, one of eight children of a pioneer farming family.[104] Perhaps it was her encouragement, reinforced by the feeling of a lack of personal success with the *Nor' West Farmer*, which led him to put down a $200 deposit on a farm in April 1905.[105] McBean hoped to work this 640-acre farm near Killarney, close to the American border, in partnership with his brother Andrew, whom he expected to emigrate in summer 1906.[106] These plans were thwarted by John McBean's recurring illness and then his death in Brandon General Hospital on 23 March 1906,[107] following which his brother abandoned his plans to emigrate and remained on the farm at Keppernach.

The pressures of John McBean's lifestyle, particularly during the time he was employed as a travelling representative of the *Farmers' Advocate* and the *Nor' West Farmer*, probably contributed to his frequent illnesses and early death. In addition to the persistent fear of dismissal from his employment. which put him under constant pressure to prove himself, he also had to live on a salary which he regarded as inadequate,[108] and savings which were increasingly eroded by medical expenses. On 14 May 1903, for instance, he told his brother that he had just spent over $40 on doctors' bills. The following month he told him that, owing to the expense of board and laundry, he could only just live on his wages of $40 a month,[109] and on 11 July 1903 he thanked him for a remittance of £4. This had arrived at an opportune moment, just after the expenses of his attendance at the Winnipeg Exhibition had drained him of all his resources. He regularly changed his Winnipeg lodgings in an attempt to secure the most favourable terms, which made allowance for his frequent absences, and he ultimately rented a furnished room in the city, buying his meals in an hotel.[110]

Although John McBean's career in Canada was brief, he had a splendid opportunity to observe prairie life, not only during his extensive travels, but also through his work as a farm labourer. Like so many newly-arrived immigrants, McBean first worked for a farmer, at Lintrathen in Southern Manitoba, and his letters from July to December 1902 contained information on the physical layout of the area, aspects of local government, the climate and farming operations.[111] His dislike of the drudgery and monotony of the work, and his determination to change his occupation as soon as possible, come through strongly in the correspondence. Like many of his contemporaries,[112] he was struck by the isolation of prairie life, although he was too busy to be homesick. He wrote to his brother on 6 July 1902 that 'This is the most lonely place I was ever in, but the work is so hard and continuous that one has no time for reflection'. By the time he wrote to his sister on 20 August, he had ploughed thirty acres of previously unbroken prairie, and, with the assistance of a youth (a 'lazy loafer') had also mown, raked, coiled and stacked 120 tons of hay. All farming operations were performed very roughly, the only redeeming feature being that the work was done quickly. He had originally been engaged at the maximum wage for a 'greenhorn', $20 a month, until the threshing had been completed. But he had asked for the maximum wage rate for the province, $25 a month, and was granted the increase once he had proved he could perform the work as well as an experienced settler. He subsequently described how farming operations accelerated all over the province in August, when a bumper harvest was gathered in the face of uncertain weather, with the help of a large number of extra hands, many of whom came from Eastern Canada, but about 5,000 of whom came over from Scotland.[113]

McBean was to be paid once the threshing was over and his employer had sold his wheat. After that, he assured his sister, he would be £15 better off than when he arrived, and would leave Lintrathen to seek work either in Winnipeg or in the far west, on the Pacific coast. Although four neighbouring farmers asked him to consider a winter engagement when his first job ended, he was determined to escape from the 'awful den of drudgery' and the never-ending routine of eating, sleeping and working, which sapped the strength and spirit of all who persisted in such monotonous employment for any

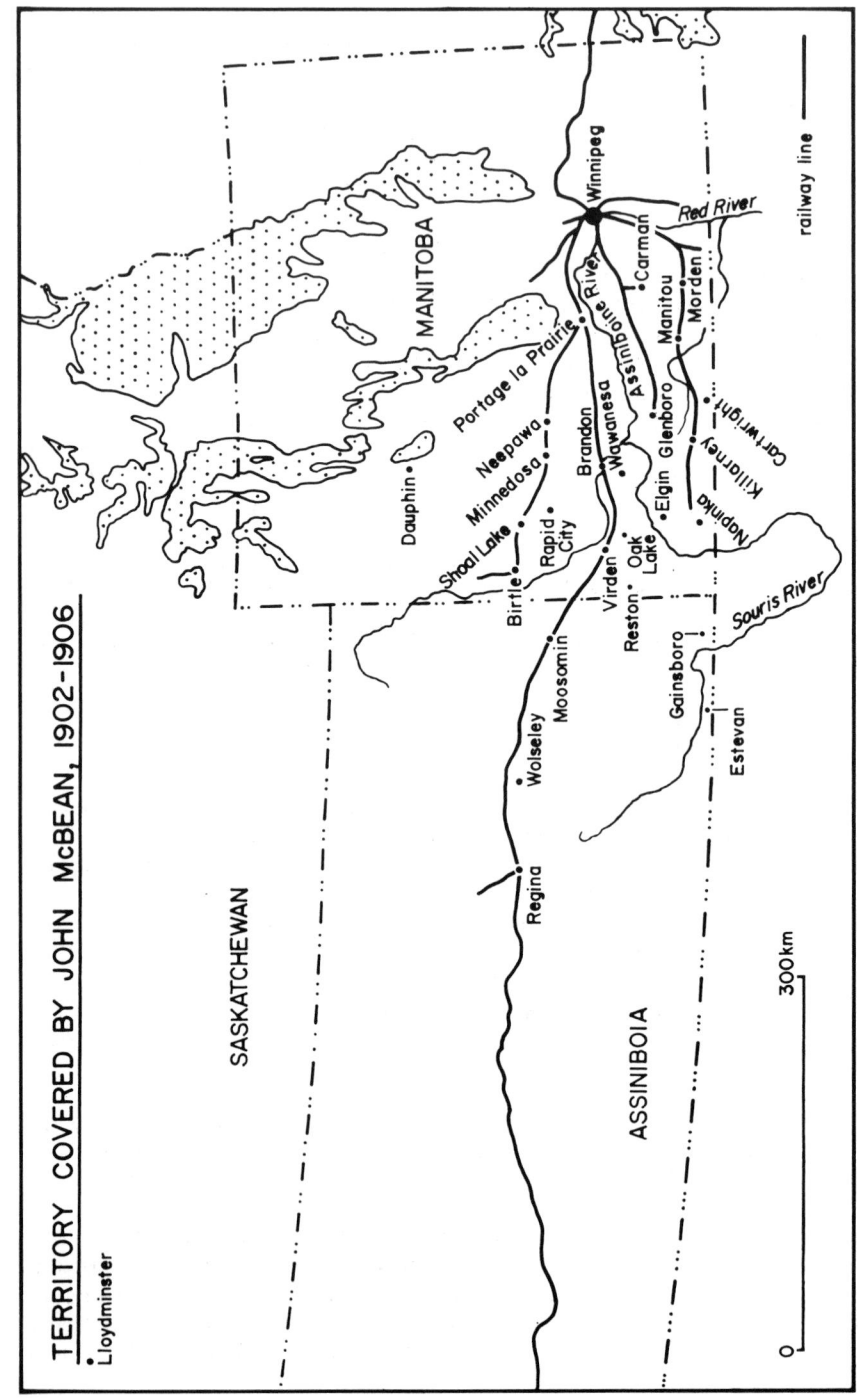

TERRITORY COVERED BY JOHN McBEAN, 1902-1906

length of time. He hoped to be accepted into the Mounted Police or into some other occupation which would allow him spare time to study to improve his prospects further.[114] When injury (a broken rib) and illness (pneumonia) upset his plans at the end of 1902, his employer offered to maintain him during his convalescence and then re-engage him for the Spring work at a wage of $280 a year.[115] But McBean told his brother that he would 'work for bare existence at any occupation under the sun before I will accept any wages to slave on a Canadian farm again'.[116] He admitted he was in a minority in his denunciation of farm life; agriculture was the main concern of everyone in the province and 'it is considered rank heresy to breath [sic] a word against farming here, and everyone talks farms, wheat and stock.'[117] In later correspondence McBean periodically re-emphasised his determination not to go back to farm work, even though it would have been more remunerative than his earnings as a journalist.[118]

McBean's dislike of farm work seems to have arisen partly out of contempt for his first employer, who was a 'disagreeable tyrant'. His observations of prairie farming society quickly led him to the rather patronising conclusion that the settlers were on the whole ill-bred and precocious:

> The people have sprung up in a short decade from labourers, farm servants, and incapable mechanics, with a mixture of well educated pennieless ne'er do weels, to farmers owning from a quarter to a mile and a half of land, with stock, implements, and a buggy; and they feel that the position requires an assumption of dignity in accordance with the circumstances. The assumed dignity is foreign to their natures, is aggressively ostentatious, and its effect is disagreeable. Etiquette is studied from books, and a display of its most objectionable phrases go bandied about the table at every meal.[119]

Yet McBean's opinions were not entirely consistent, for he praised the social equality practised in Western Canada and indeed regarded this as a redeeming feature of life in Manitoba. Although hired labourers were required to work like slaves, in all other respects they were treated as equals, an attitude which pervaded not only farming circles, but also business life in Winnipeg.[120] McBean's overall impressions of Canadian life seemed to improve after he took up his more interesting journalistic employment, although his opinions fluctuated in accordance with his own circumstances. On 29 June 1903, when things were going well for him, he wrote enthusiastically to his sister:

> What an education I am getting here! My pulse throbs continuously with the pleasurable excitement of work of a very high calling. I feel that I have a very large share in the making of Western Canada.

Two years later, when trying to persuade his brother to emigrate, he stressed that Canada was a land of liberty and patriotism, and the most law-abiding country in the world,[121] although some comments in earlier letters tended to refute the latter claim. On 17 September 1903, for instance, he told his brother how he had been interrupted in the composition of his letter by the arrival of a fellow-traveller at his hotel in Napinka, who showed him a revolver given him by a woman who wished him to shoot her husband:

> I know all the parties well, and I should not be the least surprised if the shooting does come off. The traveller has been in a shooting scrape before over a woman and the husband is a man who fears no man living even if he were armed with all the weapons of hell. This is rather a wild country. There was a fellow I knew very well, also a traveller, got his head shot off by a halfbreed last Friday, the breed committing suicide immediately after.

From time to time McBean made observations on the towns and districts he visited, but perhaps his most interesting comments concerned the disproportionate rôle which he felt was played by Scottish settlers in Manitoba. Soon after arriving at Lintrathen, he noticed the predominance of Scots among the mixture of nationalities in the area, and after moving to Winnipeg he further commented that all men in Canada claimed to be Scots first and Canadians second. All the *Farmers' Advocate* staff were of Scottish extraction, with the exception of its Irish manager. The father of one Scottish employee was a native of Aberdeen, and Scots were also employed in the office of the *Nor' West Farmer*.[122] Two of the doctors who treated McBean in hospitals in Winnipeg and Brandon in 1902 and 1906 respectively were natives of Northern Scotland.[123]

McBean encountered more Scots on his travels, several of them from the Highlands. Visiting Brandon in March 1903 he met three emigrants from Harris and two Scottish ex-policemen.[124] He also had letters of introduction from a George Bain of Nairn to friends in that area, while an acquaintance of the McBean family, John Macqueen, formerly of Knockando, Morayshire, successfully farmed 480 acres near Brandon.[125] His brother, Alick Macqueen, subsequently asked McBean to help him find employment as the manager of a stock farm.[126] Writing to his sister from Dauphin, Northern Manitoba, on 21 March 1903, McBean spoke—not altogether favourably—of the extent of Scottish influence in the province:

> I meet lots of Scotsmen everywhere I go. They are the predominating nationality all over the province. They are hard to deal with however and I would as soon meet any other race for business reasons.

Several of these Scottish businessmen were cattle farmers, and McBean noted that well-to-do Scots formed the majority of successful stockbreeders in Manitoba.[127] In fact, most of the Scots he encountered seemed to be prospering, including the several Invernesians he met in Winnipeg in 1903, a Black Isle man whose thriving farm and herd of shorthorn cattle he visited in 1904, and the Glaswegian immigrant, an acquaintance of his sister, who owned a general store and a well-stocked 620-acre farm at Oak Lake, Manitoba.[128] He took particular notice of settlers who had come from his home area, such as the grieve's son from the farm of Easter Delnies, near Nairn, who worked as a travelling representative for a Montreal firm, and the Bowie family, who

4   A typical new town on the prairies, c. 1900.

had emigrated from Nairn and who were prospering in the shoemaking trade in Manitoba.[129] On two occasions he visited cousins of the Free Church minister in Ardclach, one of whom was a former chief factor of the Hudson's Bay Company, and the other town clerk of Portage la Prairie.[130] Although the latter had emigrated over forty years earlier, and had never been out of Canada since, he retained a lively interest in Scottish affairs. He subscribed to the *Highland News*, and remembered when the agricultural column of that paper had been edited by John McBean.[131] On another occasion McBean asked his brother at home to discover the whereabouts of a Dr Craik, a well-known stockbreeder from Craigellachie, Morayshire, on behalf of Craik's niece in Canada, who was anxious to revive links after a twenty-year loss of communication. This niece, whom McBean had met in his travels, was, he said, one of the leading women in Canada, at whose home Lord Aberdeen and his family had stayed when Lord Aberdeen had been Governor-General.[132]

McBean was required to comment on various aspects of immigration at the very outset of his journalistic career, as part of his probationary work for the *Farmers' Advocate*. The manager asked on 9 January 1903 that he

> furnish us with an article in about thirty days, giving your ideas of Canada before you left home; what influenced you to immigrate; what reliance you placed on newspaper reports of the country circulated in Scotland; what you thought of the government information furnished through the Immigration Department; how the reality corresponded with your preconceived ideas and your previous information; your impressions of the country as a scene for immigration; and what class or classes of men would you recommend to immigrate.

This article appeared in a special Immigration Issue of the *Farmers' Advocate*, published on 20 March and distributed in Britain. After explaining that he had been led to emigrate partly by curiosity at the conflicting accounts of Canada circulating in Britain, and partly by a feeling that there must be some truth in the agents' claims, McBean compared his expectations with his experiences and on that basis offered advice to intending emigrants. He warned that success would not come easily—the new settler had to be hard-working, adaptable and willing to accept instruction from others better versed in prairie farming:

> The life of a farm servant is not in any respect a paradise, and under prevailing conditions, in the busy season of "work, eat and sleep," there is little time for amusement, recreation or self improvement. For that reason, a farmer or farm servant should not come out here with a view to remaining more than a short time as a hired man. On the other hand, a couple of years' working for a capable farmer is a training which will afterwards be found to have been indispensable. Not that there is much to learn in farming here which requires art in its performance. A Scotchman's chief trouble will be to "unlearn" that high finish and general tidiness to which he had been accustomed.

The settler should not entertain unrealistic expectations of immediate success:

I believe a man cannot change his country without experiencing a period of disappointment. There are many causes for such a feeling, and all combined make it rather a cold and a trying time for the young immigrant. He has generally formed in his imagination a picture, topographical, commercial and social, of the country before his arrival, and finds by experience that his picture has been but a "painted ship upon a painted ocean." He has little to talk of in common with his new associates, and that in which they are interested does not for some time appeal to his sympathies. The modes of working are new to him, and his bungling of a job causes him humiliating annoyance. It need not do so, however, for there are few in the country who have not had similar experiences in the past, and if he be not of that conceited type that refuses to receive instruction, he will generally find correction considerately and kindly administered.

He offered the following guidelines to intending emigrants:

> the man with actual experience in farming starts far ahead of the man without it. A farm servant or working farmer from the Old Country commands the full pay for his services as a hired man to begin with, and should he be possessed of some capital realized or saved beforehand, only a comparatively short time of service is necessary before establishing himself as a farmer. The man with capital and experience has nothing to fear if he begin cautiously; and the man with capital, without experience, will be equally safe if he leave his capital in the bank till his experience catches up to it. There are certainly opportunities in this country undreamt of at home for the persevering, energetic young man, and if he be a small capitalist, so much the easier and quicker will he arrive at independence. To the farm servant who has saved money and is thinking of joining the police force or the railway service to better his position, I would say with all confidence, and with the crude force of Canadian slang—Don't be a blamed fool! Come out here and in a few years you will have attained a position of comfort, security and independence for yourself and posterity, such as is not possessed by the highest official on any police force or railway service in the world. To the small farmer or crofter who struggles to pay the landlord, and who finds after doing so that someone else must want, this country appeals strongly, and with the efforts futilly put forth there, he would be sure to succeed here.[133]

Copies of this special issue of the *Farmers' Advocate* were mailed to all McBean's acquaintances, as well as to public figures, and he encouraged his brother and sister to direct intending emigrants to the *Advocate* office in Winnipeg, in the hope that these new settlers would subscribe to the paper in return for assistance given. On 1 June 1903, following a week in which he had been visited by fifty new settlers, he urged his brother:

> All you meet coming to Canada, send them the "Farmers Advocate" ... and give them my name. There is no place in Canada where respectable immigrants will receive as good advice or meet with such a hearty welcome as in the Advocate office.[134]

At this time McBean had just recruited his brother as a Scottish agent for the *Farmers' Advocate*, Andrew receiving forty per cent of the money collected in subscriptions. John McBean hoped that through this agency sales of and interest in the *Advocate* would be stimulated to an extent that would warrant his being sent over to Britain to establish multiple agencies.[135]

McBean did not only discuss immigration and immigrants in the context of his work, but also in general correspondence with his brother and sister. He believed that prospects were better and wages higher in Manitoba than in Eastern Canada, and noted that he constantly met new settlers who were all employed at good wages. Once they had been out for a year or two they often went further west to take up homesteads.[136] Despite his emphatic denunciation of farm life after his experience at Lintrathen, McBean still had great faith in Canada's potential for farming settlement. A year after his arrival he held out the incentive of independence to all who could take up land of their own and who were prepared to work hard on it. As he wrote to his brother on 18 June 1903:

> I think it is the duty of every British subject to take up land in Canada just now. It is a duty he owes to himself to take the opportunity now offered of becoming independent. There is no doubt about the facts of the case. A man can buy the best land in Western Canada for thirty dollars an acre and each acre will yield about half that value annually. But land can be got far cheaper than that—for five to seven dollars unimproved, and it can be broken with little expense but with lots of hard work. Then a man can homestead on 160 acres for ten dollars, perform his homestead duties which involves 6 months a year's residence, and in three years he can sell the farm for $1,600.00. These are facts which should appeal to all the struggling small farmers and crofters who grind out their lives working for a landlord, but on the road I used to meet men every day who came here without any means and who are now in splendid positions. Some of them knew nothing of farming before coming here.

One man to whom these incentives did appeal was Bill Forbes, an acquaintance of the McBeans, who in 1903 was managing a large cattle ranch in Colorado. Having been fired with enthusiasm by McBean's articles on immigration in the *Farmers' Advocate*, he wrote directly to ask his advice about coming to Canada in order to secure independence for himself and good prospects for his sons. McBean advised him to come north, in the expectation that he would be able to find him a situation somewhere in the area through which he had travelled on behalf of the *Advocate*.[137] The following year he helped another acquaintance and recent immigrant, George Black, by finding him a job with a farmer near Portage la Prairie, describing Black as 'strong and willing ... made by nature for Manitoba farming and ... not so green as he looks'.[138]

McBean's belief in the advantages of farming in Canada was confirmed as he met an increasing number of successful farmers in his travels.[139] He sometimes suggested that former neighbours might consider emigrating to Canada, particularly if they were experiencing hard times at home. On three occasions he mentioned James Davidson in the context of his possible emigration. He offered to help him establish himself on a farm, instructing Andrew on 10 January 1904:

If Jamie Davidson intends coming out here tell him to let me know at once and also let me know how much money he can invest when he arrives, and I shall be on the outlook for a farm to suit him.[140]

He was also strongly in favour of another neighbour, 'Lawtie', coming to Canada in 1905, and asked his brother to encourage him at least to come out and inspect the country if he had not settled the lease of his farm of Coulmony by the Whitsunday term. In Canada, McBean stressed, he could buy and stock a farm of 320 acres for less money than he could rent a 100-acre holding at home, while he would make at least four times the returns out of such a farm, with no rental or manure bills to pay and less than half the number of servants.[141]

It was some time before McBean put his principles into practice in terms of recommending his own brother to emigrate to Manitoba. He first spoke of this possibility in a letter to Margaret on 10 March 1903, when his attitude was decidedly negative, based on his belief that Andrew was not of a sufficiently resilient character to overcome the hardships of the pioneering life:

I would never think of advising Andy to sell out and come here, for I know he would hate the country, and the people he would never get along with. He is not made of that material which takes the best side of a question, and I believe did he come here he would die of homesickness. Any man who comes here has to allow his very nature to change with the change of circumstances and I am certain Andy would never submit to the process. He would never cease to blame me for misleading him, into a barrenness of social life such as he would find here for a long time after arriving.

McBean readily admitted that Canada offered great opportunities to farming immigrants who were patient and persevering, able to withstand hardships during the first decade of their settlement, until the continuing development of Manitoba had brought about increased land values and increased wealth. Yet he questioned whether his brother had the patience and perseverance required for ultimate success, despite apparently having sufficient capital to undertake prairie farming. As he wrote to Margaret on 2 April 1903:

With the money Keppernach would realise however a good start could be made and in about ten years with ordinary industry he would certainly have attained independence and a degree of wealth far ahead of anything possible in Keppernach ... after that ten year period he would undoubtedly be in a position to make money. That is supposing no misfortunes or calamities had interfered with his progress during that period.

No doubt John McBean's own experiences at Lintrathen were fresh in his mind as he reiterated his grounds for opposing Andrew's emigration, emphasising the dreary, hard life of prairie farming communities, and suggesting that his brother should choose an easier, if less eventful, career on the family farm in Scotland. He continued:

But, what a period of hard dreary monotonous drudgery those ten years would be to him! He is in many ways unconstituted for such a life. He has none of that philosophical temperament which is adapatable to change of scene, and, far less, conditions of life. He would no sooner commence life here than he would conclude that he had made a mistake and he would chaff the heart out of himself with vain regrets and magnified disappointments. Besides he is pretty sanguine of more prosperous times in Keppernach and should his hopes be realised he will most certainly lead an easy if uneventful life there compared with the unqualified hardness of life here.

Should Andrew decide on his own initiative to emigrate to Manitoba, however, his brother would put no obstacle in his way; on the contrary, he would give him all possible encouragement, and the same kind of assistance he offered to neighbours who came out to Manitoba:

> maybe by the time he may do so, I shall be in a position to find a location for him where he shall have every advantage of my experience, for if I continue to travel about I am almost certain to come across something in which it would be an advantage to invest.[142]

Perhaps Margaret McBean was instrumental in gradually persuading John that their brother would make a successful emigrant. She had evidently discussed the subject further with him by the time he wrote on 16 August 1903, more positively, but still warning her:

> If you do advise Andy to come out here, do not use anything in the way of strong persuasion. It would be far better if the initiative came from himself. Praise Canada as much as you like. It is really worthy of it all, but I would let him find out for himself that it would be to his advantage to come here.

Although he was now more favourably disposed to the idea of Andrew emigrating, he believed, like many emigrants who refused to cajole their relatives into joining them, that 'conviction brought about by persuasive measures ... is never lasting, nor does it have the solid foundation of confidence. There is always a doubt in it, and when trials come, the doubt becomes the conviction'. He was still sceptical as to whether his brother would actually come to Manitoba, telling Margaret the following month that Andrew had spoken of going to South America because he would not be able to stand the cold in Canada, but he added that 'there is little or no chance of his doing either however and I shall not bother trying to change his intention'.[143]

The issue was then dropped until August 1904 when John McBean broached it in a letter to his brother, apparently for the first time. As he had predicted in 1903, he had now come across a farm in which he thought it would be profitable to invest. The property was located near Killarney in Southern Manitoba, close to the American border and near to both the Canadian Pacific and Canadian National Railways. It consisted of 640 acres of open prairie, all good, easily cultivable and well-watered land, which was on offer at a price of $10,000, payable in easy instalments at six per cent interest after making a deposit of $200. John McBean suggested that Andrew should consider coming out to join him in this venture, reiterating his plea two months later, when he told him that the farm would yield at least four times the required annual outlay of £100.[144] By early 1905 he was strongly advocating that his brother should come to Canada, and he restated his own faith in the country where he said he had made so many friends, and which he now regarded as his permanent home. But despite his enthusiasm, he still admitted that Andrew would face initial difficulties. As he wrote to Margaret on 5 January 1905:

> Do you think Andy will come to Canada? I hope he will! He will never get any further ahead in Keppernach; and here he has every chance to prosper. I am certain he will not like it at first. It is hard to part with one's home and with ones household gods, and harder still to part with the old associations of ones country.

He later warned Andrew of the likelihood of early disappointment experienced by most emigrants, whatever their destination, but pointed out that, being his own master, Andrew would not suffer the 'abject drudgery' endured by John McBean in 1902.[145]

What had brought about John McBean's change of heart in regard to his brother's emigration? The offer of a prairie farm was the major catalyst, for it seems that the only way he could afford to take advantage of this offer was by going into partnership with Andrew.[146] But what had turned McBean's attention from journalism back to farming? The insecurity of his position with the *Nor' West Farmer* probably led him to consider an alternative career, but it is likely that the influence of his fianceé's family was a more persuasive factor. Early in 1905 he became engaged to Agnes Lumb, whose family owned 1,280 acres of land near Killarney. One of the early pioneering families in the area, they had overcome severe hardships and by this time possessed large quantities of stock and had won prizes for the best wheat grown in Manitoba.[147] They were firmly in favour of John McBean returning to a farming career, which they believed was the haven of the poor man in Canada. Mrs Lumb in particular did much to reverse McBean's poor opinion of Canadian farmers, formed during his early employment at Lintrathen.[148] Her rôle is evident through correspondence she had with John and Margaret McBean, which was later forwarded to Andrew at Keppernach, and which may have influenced him in his decision to emigrate.

In this correspondence[149] Mrs Lumb discussed the financial implications for the McBeans if they purchased the property near Killarney to which she had drawn John McBean's attention. She emphasised her family's opinion that they were unlikely to have the offer of a better property in the future, and she stressed the importance of a quick decision. Since settlers had begun to appreciate the superior quality of the territory around Cartwright, land prices, which had remained surprisingly static while rising disproportionately elsewhere, had started to escalate, and land was becoming scarce near good markets. The section in question, which had previously been bought by speculators at $8 an acre, was now offered at $12. It was virtually the only parcel of land available near Cartwright, and she predicted that if it were subdivided, it would not long remain on the market. Although the McBeans would require capital of $5,000 to $8,000 (£1,000 to £1,500) in order to make the purchase, she recommended that they buy the whole section, since any surrounding land would be taken up so quickly that there would be no possibility of adding to the holding in the future, and in any case, if the brothers were in partnership, they would ultimately require a whole section between them. She thought the holding could be secured by payment of the $200 deposit, with the remainder of the first payment of $1,000 being made by May 1906. The latter sum could be raised more easily if John McBean had 100 acres broken up in 1905, ready to produce a profitable crop when his brother arrived in 1906. One of Mrs Lumb's sons, who had bought a half section in 1903 at $6.50 an acre, had paid the first of eight annual instalments of his purchase price by this method; the fifty-seven acres which he had broken during his first year of occupation had produced a crop yielding $965 in 1904, and there was no reason why the McBeans' section should not be equally profitable.

Although John McBean told Mrs Lumb that neither he nor his brother could afford to have the land prepared to produce a harvest in 1906, he still put down the $200 deposit on the holding in April 1905, in the hope of taking possession of it with Andrew in 1906.[150] If Andrew decided not to emigrate John would then lose the $200, but he maintained that was preferable to losing the chance of such a 'rare bargain'. He claimed that inferior land was selling at $20 per acre, and was confident that he and his brother would be able to pay off their debt within ten years. His proposition, he felt, should appeal to Andrew far more than a renewed lease of Keppernach at an increased rental.[151] John McBean was probably influenced in his decision not only by the Lumb family's persuasion and his own dissatisfaction with his work, but also by his brother's unfavourable position at home. He periodically reminded Andrew of the opportunity to become independent by coming to Canada, echoing the most common encouragement given to farmers to emigrate. On 9 October 1904, for instance, he urged his brother that he had nothing to lose by giving up his lease and that he should 'give the matter every consideration. It is simply slavery to work for landlords in that country. Here if you have hard work it all goes to benefit yourself and no landlord to be considered'.[152]

Writing to Margaret shortly afterwards, on 18 November, John McBean remarked that Andrew should come to Manitoba to escape the numbing effects of the 'continued and prolonged adversity' which he was experiencing at home. And by 7 April 1905 he had

no hesitation in advising you [Andrew] to sell off next May and come out here with all the money the sale will bring. If you remain there you will never, if you live a million years, be able to pay the lawful shares to the other members of the family. Out here I give you my guarantee that you can do so, with the same amount of exertion you would spend there merely to exist, in ten years or probably less. No man alive knows this country, its possibilities or its drawbacks better than I do ... I am amongst farmers on their own farms every day. I hear all their tales of success and failure, and I have never come across an absolute failure yet that was not attributable to the faults or mismanagement of the victim. Hundreds of successful men I have met, in fact I meet some of them every day who have borrowed the ten dollars or part of it that paid their Homestead entry fee and the great majority of them are now worth thousands of dollars. There is no doubt about this country. It has possibilites that no other country can offer, and possibilities that no other in the world's history has ever had to offer.[153]

He again expressed the hope that Andrew would seriously consider the wisdom of emigrating, and inform him of his decision in his next letter. His views were echoed by Mrs Lumb in her letter to Margaret McBean on 27 May 1905. If Andrew were only just keeping his head above water at home, she declared, and if he had the means to begin prairie farming, or the will to succeed from small beginnings, then he should join his brother in Manitoba immediately. She acknowledged, however, that only Andrew himself understood his own situation and prospects; only he would know whether the picture she painted of prospects at Killarney compared favourably or not with renting a farm in Scotland, and if he were making ends meet and living free of debt there, she hesitated to advise him to break up his home in order to become a pioneer prairie farmer.

By late autumn 1905 it was clear that Andrew McBean did indeed intend to emigrate to Canada, having apparently intimated his intention to the factor of Keppernach. When his plans were upset by John's death in March 1906, he did not immediately abandon the idea of emigrating, but wrote to his brother's former colleague, A. P. Ketchen of the *Nor' West Farmer*, for advice on the matter. On 8 July 1906 Ketchen replied, mainly in connection with the winding up of John McBean's affairs, but he also enclosed a number of pamphlets and circulars regarding settlement in Western Canada, and noted cautiously:

In reply to your questions as to whether or not I would advise you to come to Canada at 40 with L600 or L700 capital, I scarcely know what to say. One hesitates to offer advice on such an important business matter involving a complete change of all ones plan of life. It is possible that if you were to come to Canada you might be disappointed with conditions here and might regret your move; but if your health is good and you do not mind putting up with some deprivations and other vicissitudes incidental to pioneer life you can scarcely fail to better your position in this country. With the capital you mention you could make a very nice start in Canada, especially in Western Canada. Before selling out your effects in Scotland however, I would advise you to come out and see the country for yourself. Perhaps you could arrange to have some one else dispose of your effects there if you would be satisfied to remain in Canada. In any event the expense would not be very heavy to go back again.

Despite Ketchen's qualified recommendation—or perhaps because of it— Andrew McBean did not subsequently go to Manitoba, either for a trial visit, or as a permanent emigrant, choosing instead to remain on the family farm in Northern Scotland.

When he first went to Canada, John McBean wrote more frequently and at greater length to his sister, describing his activities and his impressions of the country. Through his different occupations, and particularly through his widespread travelling, he had a unique opportunity to observe the growth and development of Western Canada, and his first-hand accounts shed valuable light on the nature of Manitoba society at this crucial period in its development. But his comments were not entirely consistent, often fluctuating in accordance with his own circumstances. Shortly after he arrived in Manitoba, for instance, he criticised the 'deceptive' methods of encouraging settlement employed by the Department of the Interior and the CPR, yet within a year he himself was producing promotional literature under the auspices of the *Farmers' Advocate*. He had bitter memories of his own initial experiences of prairie farm work, and remained firmly opposed to his brother emigrating until an opportunity arose for him to acquire a prairie farm of his own. Since he was financially incapable of seizing this opportunity by himself, John McBean then began to correspond more regularly with his brother, in an attempt to persuade Andrew to put up the required capital and join him in the venture. In these letters he glossed over his earlier opinion that his brother would rebel against the 'monotonous drudgery' of farm work. He emphasised instead the poor prospects at Keppernach and pointed out that any amount of hard farm labour was tolerable when the land was one's own. John McBean's correspondence with his brother from August 1904 until his death also highlights once again the part played by personal persuasion in encouraging secondary emigration; for it is clear that, if his elder brother had not died, Andrew McBean would almost certainly have joined him in partnership on a prairie farm.

John McBean's letters, like all emigrant correspondence, were not completely unbiased. At times he clearly tailored his comments to fit his own interests, particularly when he realised the financial advantage of persuading his brother to join him in Canada. But the letters were not intended for publication, and in the sometimes ambivalent and contradictory views expressed, they reflect the mixed fortunes of many pioneer emigrants in this period. Despite his faith in the future of Western Canada, John McBean did not have an easy life or enjoy great personal success. Probably the restlessness and discontent which are evident in many of his letters sprang largely from the fact that he never achieved the independence he desired; his whole career in Manitoba was spent in the service of others, often performing what he considered to be menial or degrading duties, generally without any security of employment. Frequently burdened by ill-health, he always hoped for an improvement in his fortunes, but his death in 1906, as he was on the threshhold of an independent farming career, denied him the opportunity to prove whether in becoming his own master he would have achieved the contentment, security and success he craved.

NOTES

1) See M. D. Harper, 'Emigration from the North-East of Scotland, 1830-1880' (unpub. Ph.D., Aberd., 1984), ch. VIII.
2) PP 1906 [Cd. 3273], XCVI, 583. *Board of Agriculture. Report on the decline of the agricultural population of Britain, 1881-1906*, p. 108.
3) PP 1894 [C 7400], XVI, Pts I to III. *Royal Commission on Agricultural Depression. First General Report 1894*. Evidence and appendices, p. 489: evidence of George Muirhead, land agent of Lord Aberdeen (qu. 30,356—30,612). Lord Aberdeen gave rent remissions to his tenants in 1880, 1886 and 1892. The 1880 abatement amounted to £19,791, equivalent to about half the annual rental; that in 1886 amounted to £5,068 on a rental of £43,030 and that in 1892 to £2,039 on a rental of £40,728. In 1886 Lord Aberdeen also allowed a revaluation of farms to all tenants who applied for it, which resulted in a fall of around twenty-three per cent on a rental of about £11,000. And he contradicted the general tendency of landlords at that time to consolidate their properties. In 1926 he announced that in his fifty years as laird, the holdings on his estates had increased from 935 to 957 and that 588 houses had also been built. (*'We Twa': reminiscences of Lord and Lady Aberdeen* (London, 1926), p. 313).
4) Report by James Hope in *ibid*, [C 7342], XVI, Part I, 805.
5) See *AJ*, 6 Sept. 1881 (Ellon); 7 Sept. (Oldmeldrum); 8 Sept. (Huntly); 14 Sept. (Alford); 16 Sept. (Rhynie and New Deer); 19 Sept. (Lonmay); 20 Sept. (Ellon); 21 Sept. (Inverurie); 22 Sept. (Old Deer). See also *ibid*, 8 Nov., 22, 28 Dec. 1888.
6) *Ibid*, 9 Sept. 1881.
7) *Ibid*, 7 Oct. 1881.
8) See also *ibid*, 28 May 1889. Wages at the Insch feeing market in May 1889 were said to have risen as a result of the extensive emigration which had been going on for some time.
9) *AJ*, 5 Dec. 1901, 5 Dec. 1902.
10) See *AJ*, 21 Feb. 1903. Although 378 homesteads were taken up, considerably fewer than the 15,000 settlers anticipated by the colony's founders (Archdeacon Lloyd of Saskatchewan and the Rev I. M. Barr of London) actually went out. Many of them came from urban backgrounds, knew little of agriculture and soon became discontented. The attempt to found an exclusive settlement of inexperienced British agriculturists did not succeed and it was only with the introduction of American and Canadian farmers, and the coming of the railway in 1905, that the settlement began to become more prosperous. (See also W. A. Carrothers, *Emigration from the British Isles*, p. 247).
11) *AJ*, 31 May 1911, 11 June 1912.
12) *Ibid*, 2 June 1891, 23 May 1910.
13) PP 1906 [Cd. 3273], XCVI, 583, pp. 15-6.
14) A. D. Hall, *A Pilgrimage of British Farming 1910-1912* (London, 1913, reprinted from *The Times*, pp. 383-4).
15) PAC, RG 76, C-10294-5, vol. 405, file 590687: correspondence and weekly reports of John MacLennan.
16) MacLennan's annual reports, in Dept of the Interior, *annual reports on immigration, 1908-9 and 1909-10*.
17) PAC, RG 76, C-10621, vol. 530, file 803485. Correspondence of W. G. Maitland, booking agent, Longside, Aberdeenshire. Maitland to W. D. Scott, Supt of Immigration, Dept of the Interior, 1 May 1909.

18) Maitland did not expect that his recruits would be in a position to provide £5 landing money, and in a letter of 9 August 1910 W. D. Scott confirmed that farm labourers and domestic servants were indeed exempt from the requirement to provide this sum.

19) PAC, RG 76, C-10627, vol. 538, file 803839. Correspondence of H. W. J. Paton, booking agent, Aberdeen. Paton to J. Obed Smith, Canadian Emigration Commissioner in London, 24 Feb. 1910. The bonus was later allowed.

20) *Ibid*, Paton to Smith, 4 Oct. 1910.

21) *Ibid*, undated letter from A. Davidson to W. D. Scott. See also Paton to Scott, 12 & 30 July 1912.

22) *Ibid*, 23 June, 8 Aug. 1913.

23) PAC, RG 76, C-10644, vol. 564, file 809010. Correspondence of MacKay Brothers, Aberdeen, booking agents. MacKay to J. Obed Smith, 12 June 1911.

24) Maitland to J. Obed Smith, 16 June 1913.

25) PAC, RG 76, C-10315, vol. 435, file 652801. Correspondence of John Sinclair, booking agent, Elgin. Sinclair to W. D. Scott, 13 June 1911.

26) Rupert's Land had been granted to the Company under its charter in 1670, and it held exclusive trading rights in the remaining western regions. See W. Kaye Lamb, *History of the Canadian Pacific Railway* (New York, 1977), p. 4.

27) *Ibid*, pp. 5-7. See also W. A. Mackintosh, *Prairie settlement, the geographical setting* (Toronto, 1934), pp. 27-43.

28) The Métis were of mixed French and Indian blood.

29) A. G. Bradley, *Canada in the twentieth century* (London, 1905), p. 248.

30) *The Canadian Journal of Lady Aberdeen, 1893-1898*, ed. by John T. Saywell (Toronto, 1960), p. 127.

31) See, for instance: *What Canada produces. Information for intending emigrants* (1874); *The province of Manitoba and N. West Territory. Information for intending immigrants* (1881); *Western Canada and its great resources: the testimony of settlers, farmer delegates and high authorities* (1893); *A guide to homesteaders in Manitoba and the Territories of Western Canada* (1900); *Homes for millions in Canada's vast agricultural domain of virgin opportunity and infinite resources* (1904). All the above handbooks were published by the Department of the Interior. Among the publications of the Canadian Department of Agriculture were: *What farmers say of their personal experience in the Canadian North-West* (1881, 1883, 1884); *The agricultural resources of Canada. Reports of tenant farmers' delegates and other informations on Manitoba, the North-West Territories and other parts of the Dominion of Canada as a field for the settlement of agriculturists etc* (1881); and *The visit of the tenant farmer delegates to Canada in 1890* (1891).

32) See, for instance, Canadian Pacific Railway Company: *Practical hints from farmers in the Canadian North-West* (London, 188-?); *Successful farming in Manitoba. 100 farmers testify* (Winnipeg, 1889); *Everyday questions answered in regard to the Canadian West and its opportunities and rewards for farmers* (Montreal, 1889); and *Western Canada: Manitoba, Assiniboia, Alberta, Saskatchewan and Northern Ontario. How to get there, how to select lands, how to make a home* (Montreal? 1896). See also James Hedges, *Building the Canadian West: the land and colonisation policies of the Canadian Pacific Railway* (New York, 1939), pp. 94-125.

33) 'Life in Canada' in *Chambers'*, (1881), pp. 9-11, 288 & 649-52. The un-named author gave some information on land prices but advised readers who were interested in farming in Canada to consult the reports of the various tenant

farmers' delegations which had visited Canada and whose observations had been published by the Department of the Interior.

34) See, for instance, P. B. Gregson, 'Farming in Alberta' in *ibid* (2 Oct. 1909), pp. 702-3; 'Canada as a home' in *West. Rev.* n.s. 62 (July 1882), pp. 1-28; and *Emigration to North-Western Canada: information for intending settlers* (Ottawa, Dept of the Interior, 1893).

35) *AJ*, 23 July, 28 Nov. 1892. Farm workers in Winnipeg could command $35-50 a month.

36) This newspaper was founded in October 1908 with the main aim of persuading Scottish immigrants who had settled in the cities to move into prairie farming. (See PAC, RG 76, C-10638, vol. 557, file 806656).

37) See also below, p. 67 and n. 48.

38) *AJ*, 1 Jan. 1890, 30 Mar. 1891.

39) A party of 300 Scots settlers had sailed from the Clyde three weeks earlier, followed by a second contingent that week. Further parties were to leave in the following weeks. Most of the emigrants in fact came from Lanarkshire, although some were said to be from the North and the Lothians.

40) PP 1906 [Cd. 2978], LXXXVI, 533. *Report of the departmental committee appointed to consider Mr Rider Haggard's report on agricultural settlements in the British colonies.* Appendix I: Papers handed in by W. T. R. Preston. (A) Letters from emigrants. Letters dated 18, 15 Feb. 1904.

41) *Ibid*, p. 274. (Letter dated 15 Feb. 1904). See also *AJ*, 23 Aug. 1905.

42) PAC, RG 76, C-10633, vol. 548, file 805711. W. D. Scott, Supt of Immigration, to J. Bruce Walker, Commissioner of Immigration, Winnipeg, 20 Nov. 1908.

43) *Ibid*, undated letter.

44) *Ibid*, undated letter.

45) PAC, RG 76, C-10638, vol. 556, file 806960.

46) See, for instance, Dept of Agriculture, *Report of the tenant farmers' delegates on the Dominion of Canada as a field for settlement* (1880); *ibid*, *The agricultural resources of Canada. Reports of tenant farmers' delegates* (1881); *The visit of the tenant farmer delegates to Canada in 1890. The report of Arthur Daniel etc* (1891); and *AJ*, 27 Nov. 1894— reports of the tenant farmers' visits could be obtained from the Canadian government emigration agent, W. G. Stuart, at Nethy Bridge.

47) *AJ*, 14 Dec. 1903. These views too had recently been published in pamphlet form.

48) PAC, RG 76, C-10638, vol. 557, file 807080, part 1 *Canada as seen through Scottish eyes*, p. 44. See also above, p. 62 & n. 37 for the letter of John Potts, who presumably accompanied Lindsay from Auchenblae to Indian Head in June 1905. The 25 letters from emigrants quoted in the pamphlet were followed by nine shorter accounts from settlers, consisting of answers to specific questions about farming, and included the responses of North-East emigrants George Morrison and David Hunter, which also appeared in the publication *Letters from successful Scottish ploughmen.* For further details of the 1908 Agricultural Commission, and lectures subsequently delivered by the delegates in North-East Scotland, see *AJ*, 27 July, 4 Aug. 1908; 11, 12 Feb, 5 Mar., 26 Apr. 1909.

49) PAC, RG 76, C-10296, vol. 406, file 593269 (Hugh McIntosh nominated as a farm delegate to the Old Country): letter from J. Bruce Walker, Asst Supt of Emigration, London, to W. D. Scott, Supt of Immigration, Ottawa, 7 June 1907. See also John MacLennan's report for week ending 6 Apr. 1907.

50) *Ibid.* McIntosh's (undated) report.

51)   Letter dated 8 Jan. 1909 in *Prosperity follows settlement*, p. 34.
52)   If they relinquished their leases at other than the stipulated times, these tenant farmers could lose the right to compensation for any improvements they had made during their tenancy.
53)   Fleming's report, in Dept of the Interior, *annual report on immigration, 1895*.
54)   See MacLennan's reports for weeks ending 7 Dec. 1907, 31 Oct. 1908, 30 Jan. 1909.
55)   *AJ*, 10 May 1911.
56)   See MacLennan's reports for weeks ending 25 May, 23 Nov. 1907.
57)   *Ibid*, week ending 21 Mar. 1908.
58)   *Ibid*, week ending 27 July 1907.
59)   *Ibid*, weeks ending 25 July, 1, 8, 15, 22, 29 Aug., 5 Sept. 1908.
60)   *Ibid*, weeks ending 23, 30 July, 6, 13, 20 Aug. 1910.
61)   *Ibid*, 22 Apr. 1926.
62)   For details see Hedges, *Building the Canadian West*, pp. 94-125.
63)   *AJ*, 3 Jan. 1913.
64)   *Ibid*, 4 Nov. 1910, 20, 25, 31 Jan. 1911.
65)   *Ibid*, 6, 8 Nov. 1912, 7, 9 Jan. 1913.
66)   *Ibid*, 11, 17, 21 Mar. 1885.
67)   *Ibid*, 1, 14 Jan. 1886.
68)   *Ibid*, 22, 25, 28, 29 Feb., 1, 2, 3 Mar. 1888.
69)   *Ibid*, 31 Aug. 1889, 3 Apr. 1893, 1 Feb. 1894, 30 Dec. 1901, 25 Feb. 1903.
70)   *Ibid*, 27 Jan., 21 Feb. 1910. See also above, p. 66.
71)   *AJ*, 27 Jan. 1910, 27 May 1912, 14 Feb. 1913.
72)   *Ibid*, 18 Jan. 1910.
73)   See, for instance, *ibid*, 8 Mar. 1910, 11 Mar. 1911, 28 Jan. 1913.
74)   Letter dated 14 Mar. 1912. Argo, a farmer's son, in fact possessed capital of £600, but according to Paton, 'is going out first to learn Canadian farming for a year before purchasing'.
75)   Letter dated 2 Aug. 1912.
76)   See also *AJ*, 16 July 1910 for J. Obed Smith's reply to this letter.
77)   G. J. Webster, 'Ranching in the Canadian North-West' in *Chambers'*, (17 June 1905), pp. 453-7.
78)   'Ready made Canadian farms by easy payment' in *ibid* (28 May 1910), p. 412. This article appeared in response to an earlier article of the same title, in praise of ready made farms, in *ibid* (26 Feb. 1910), p. 205.
79)   'Daily life on colonial farms (a plea for first hand information)' in *ibid* (12 Aug. 1911), pp. 591-2. See also 'Real experiences on colonial farms' in *ibid* (10 Feb. 1912), pp. 172-6.
80)   AUA, MS 3184. Material gifted by Mr John McBean of Inverness in October 1984. The collection consists of thirty-four letter written by McBean to the donor's father, Andrew McBean, Keppernach, Ardclach, and thirty-nine letters and one postcard written to Margaret McBean, matron of Hawkhead Hospital, Paisley. There are also two letters from McBean's prospective mother-in-law to John/Andrew and Margaret McBean respectively, a postcard from his fianceé to Margaret, and a few items of miscellaneous correspondence dealing with John McBean's affairs after his death.
81)   Fifty thousand people had arrived in Canada in 1901, of whom only 10,000 were British. (Statement made by W. T. R. Preston to *The Scotsman* during his visit to Glasgow in connection with the departure of conducted parties; see *AJ*, 22 Apr. 1902). See also above, p. 55 & n. 11, regarding the reasons for the creation of the Barr Colony.

82) John McBean to Margaret McBean, 2 Sept. 1902. In later letters McBean occasionally expressed the view that Western Canada was being promoted too vociferously. See, for instance, John McBean to Andrew McBean, 16 Feb. 1903; an article written by McBean about the Carman district had appeared in four Canadian papers, while others had quoted from it and commented favourably that, unlike so much other writing, it was not overdrawn in its descriptions.

83) *Farmers' Advocate and Home Magazine*, vol. xxxviii, no. 570 (20 Mar. 1903), pp. 247.

84) See JM to MM, 21 Mar. 1903.

85) JM to MM, 12 Feb. 1905: views expressed in the context of a recommendation that Andrew McBean should emigrate to Canada—see below, pp. 89-93. See also JM to MM, 29 June, 15 Nov. 1903, JM to AM, 5 Aug. 1904.

86) JM to MM, 28 Jan. 1903: he had been frugal since arriving in Canada and still had $100 in savings.

87) JM to MM, 20 Aug. 1902.

88) *Ibid*, 9 Jan., 7 Feb. 1903. He was being coached in shorthand by a fellow-lodger in Winnipeg, a Western Canadian who had abandoned farm work after ten years to attend Business College with the intention of taking up office work (JM to MM, 3 Feb. 1903).

89) *Ibid*, 28 Jan., 7 Feb. 1903.

90) *Ibid*, 3, 7, 23 Feb. 1903.

91) JM to AM, 16 Feb. 1903; JM to MM, 23 Feb. 1903.

92) JM to MM, 15 May 1903.

93) JM to AM, 31 July 1903; JM to MM, 16 Aug., 27 Sept. 1903. See also JM to MM, 29 May 1903; JM to AM, 5 July 1903.

94) JM to MM, 29 May, 27 Sept., 4 Nov. 1903.

95) JM to AM, 16 Feb. 1903.

96) JM to MM, 4 Nov, 1903.

97) *Ibid*, 25 Jan. 1904.

98) JM to AM, 10 Jan. 1904. The new employee, a Dr Hopkins, had worked on the *Advocate* as an associate editor and had just spent three years in Glasgow as Dominion Inspector of imported cattle.

99) See details on headed notepaper, JM to MM, 19 Sept. 1904.

100) *Ibid*; see also *ibid*, 18 Nov. 1904; and JM to AM, 5 Aug., 9 Oct. 1904.

101) JM to MM, 18 Nov. 1904.

102) JM to AM, 14 Nov. 1904; JM to MM, 18 Nov. 1904.

103) JM to AM, 26 Feb. 1905.

104) JM to MM, 3 Jan. 1905; JM to AM, 3 Feb. 1905.

105) JM to AM, 10 Apr. 1905.

106) *Ibid*, 5 Aug. 1904. See also below, pp. 90-2.

107) JM to MM, 16 Feb. 1906; JM to AM (n.d., early 1906); Hattie Davidson to MM, 23 Mar. 1906; A. P. Ketchen to AM, 27 Mar. 1906.

108) JM to AM, 5 July 1903.

109) *Ibid*, 18 June 1903.

110) JM to MM, 27 Sept. 1903.

111) See in particular JM to AM, 6 July, 21 Sept. 1902.

112) See, for instance, James Macgregor, 'Canada and the North West as an emigration field' in *Contemporary Review*, vol. XLII (Aug. 1882), pp. 218-36, in which the author spoke of the utter silence and loneliness of the prairie, and the almost total absence of life. See also above, pp. 60 and 76 for the comments of Lady Aberdeen in 1890 and of the female correspondents of *Chambers' Journal* in 1911.

113) JM to MM, 2 Sept. 1902.
114) *Ibid*, 23 Nov. 1902; see also JM to AM, 21 Sept. 1902.
115) JM to AM, 29 Dec. 1902, 3 Feb. 1903. At that rate, his earnings would have been less than the previous summer, when he had been engaged at $25 a month. Yet he noted on 3 February 1903 that $280 was a high yearly wage, the normal rate being $200. On 20 August 1902, however, he had said $20 a month ($240 a year) was the maximum pay for a 'greenhorn'.
116) JM to AM, 3 Feb. 1903.
117) JM to MM, 3 Feb. 1903.
118) See, for instance, JM to AM, 18 June 1903.
119) JM to MM, 20 Aug. 1902.
120) JM to AM, 21 Sept. 1902; JM to MM, 9 Jan. 1903.
121) JM to AM, 7 Apr. 1905.
122) See JM to MM, 20 Aug. 1902, 10 Mar., 15 May, 29 June 1903, 19 Sept. 1904.
123) *Ibid*, 25 Dec. 1902, 16 Feb. 1906. Professor Simpson of Winnipeg General Hospital was a native of Aberdeen and a graduate of Edinburgh University, while Dr Fraser of Brandon General Hospital came from the Beauly area of Inverness-shire.
124) JM to AM, 12 Mar. 1903.
125) JM to MM, 7 Mar., 9 Apr. 1903. McBean later met George Bain in Winnipeg on the latter's way home from a visit to Canada. On returning to Nairn, Bain was possibly to deliver lectures about his trip, which McBean encouraged his brother to attend. (JM to AM, 8 Sept., 27 Oct. 1905).
126) JM to MM, 23 Aug. 1903.
127) JM to AM, 15 Nov. 1903. He said the Scots were supplemented by the younger sons of the English nobility.
128) JM to AM, 18 Oct. 1903; JM to MM, 25 Jan. 1904. The Glaswegian settler, Alick Cameron, had brought over come Clydesdales and shorthorns from Scotland in 1902, and by 1904 was regarded as one of the wealthiest and smartest men in Manitoba.
129) JM to AM, 15 Nov. 1903, 5 Aug. 1904.
130) JM to MM, 9 Jan. 1903.
131) *Ibid*, 21 Mar. 1903. See also JM to AM, 10 Jan. 1904, for intimation of MacDonald's death.
132) JM to AM, 20 Jan. 1904. Other Scots mentioned in McBean's correspondence included the singer, Jessie Maclauchlin, whose concert he attended in May 1903 and who subsequently asked him to write an account of her Canadian tour for the *Scottish American* (JM to MM, 31 May 1903); Harry Cameron, a friend of McBean's who was the manager of the Electric Power Works in Winnipeg (JM to MM, 31 May 1903); and the son of a former Inverness minster who owned a dry goods store in Minto, Manitoba (JM to AM, 27 Oct. 1905).
133) *Farmers' Advocate and Home Magazine*, vol. xxxviii, no. 570 (20 Mar. 1903), pp. 247-9.
134) See also JM to MM, 14 Apr. 1904.
135) JM to AM, 14 May, 5 July 1903.
136) *Ibid*, 25 Apr. 1904; JM to MM, 14 Apr. 1904.
137) JM to MM, 31 May 1903; JM to AM, 18 June 1903.
138) JM to AM, 5 Aug. 1904.
139) See, for instance, JM to MM, 7 Mar. 1903; *ibid*, 14 Apr. 1904.
140) See also JM to MM, 23 Aug. 1903; JM to AM, 27 Oct. 1905.
141) JM to AM, 10 Apr. 1905.

142)   JM to MM, 2 Apr. 1903.
143)   *Ibid*, 27 Sept. 1903.
144)   JM to AM, 9 Oct. 1904; see also *ibid*, 5 Aug. 1904.
145)   *Ibid*, 10 Apr. 1905.
146)   *Ibid*; see also *ibid*, 7 Apr. 1905.
147)   JM to MM, 5 Jan. 1905.
148)   Mrs Lumb to MM, 27 May 1905.
149)   Mrs Lumb to JM, 3 Apr. 1905; Mrs Lumb to MM, 27 May 1905.
150)   But see above, p. 91: on 5 August 1904 John McBean had stated the price for the property was $10,000, then on 10 April 1905 he gave the total price demanded as $7,680.
151)   JM to AM, 10 Apr. 1905.
152)   See also *ibid*, 27 Oct. 1905, in which John McBean referred to the landlords at home as the 'Cawdor bloodsuckers' who had 'no sentiments with regard to their tenants'.
153)   When the McBeans' mother died in 1901, she left an equal share of her estate to all the family. Although Andrew had taken over the farm, he was expected to repay his five brothers and sisters their share.

CHAPTER III

'Nature's Gentlemen'

Most emigrants from North-East Scotland in the nineteenth and early twentieth centuries were people of only modest means. A significant minority, however, possessed substantial funds, which they often chose to invest in large-scale farming or ranching ventures, generally in Western Canada, and perhaps most notably in British Columbia. This capitalist exodus from North-East Scotland coincided with—and was undoubtedly stimulated by—a new enthusiasm for emigration among the wealthier elements in British society as a whole in the late nineteenth century. For most of the century emigration had been seen primarily as a means of relieving the economic problems of the poor, but in the 1880s and 1890s it became increasingly popular with the middle and upper classes. They were troubled by the growing difficulty of finding employment in overcrowded and competitive professions in Britain and began to see emigration as perhaps the only way to maintain their own or their children's standard of living in a changing economic and social climate. In their search to secure better prospects their motives matched those of many of their less wealthy counterparts; it was only the scale of their investment that was different. They were readily encouraged to settle in Canada by land and emigration agents who bombarded them with promotional literature extolling the social and economic advantages of the different provinces for 'gentlemen emigrants' and promised them a good return on their invested capital. The activities of wealthy agriculturists in particular in Canada around the turn of the century clearly merit some attention, not least because of the crucial rôle of one notable entrepreneur from North-East Scotland in inaugurating commercial fruit farming in British Columbia. The Earl of Aberdeen's investments in the Okanagan Valley provide the main focus for the following survey of the part played by 'gentlemen emigrants' and investors in the settlement and development of Canada in the late nineteenth and early twentieth centuries.

Tutoring the recruit: the pros and cons of pupilage

The children of middle and upper class families provided a major source of 'gentlemen emigrants' from Britain in this period. The problem of supernumerary younger sons who could not inherit the family estate began to manifest itself increasingly in the late nineteenth century as their traditional outlets in the Church, the legal profession and medicine became either less popular, overcrowded or too competitive in the face of the 'rise of the meritocracy'.[1] Dorothea Walker described how, as a youth, her husband had come to emigrate to the Okanagan Valley:[2]

> My husband was educated for the church. He was studying Theology and Greek and Latin and all the Classics. Nothing practical. He was at Oxford and he wasn't working ... so they took him from school and they had a tutor for him for a year, but even then he wasn't working ... And at 19 he kicked over the traces and told his father he was not going to be forced into the church. "Well," his father said, "It'll have to be the colonies." ... And so, the result was he was sent out here as a pupil to learn farming at $500 a year.

The issue of the 'younger son' provoked considerable contemporary debate, and periodicals such as the *Nineteenth Century* and *Chambers' Journal* regularly offered advice to parents on the best way to provide for the future of their unemployed—and sometimes unemployable—children.[3] Emigration to the British colonies was increasingly recommended as a profitable and socially acceptable outlet for boys who could take up farming alongside compatriots of their own class and therefore maintain the kind of social contacts and activities that they had enjoyed at home. In an age of increasing imperialist sentiment these emigrants were often portrayed as vital empire builders rather than the black sheep of wealthy families or, at best, the redundant products of British public schools for whom no outlet could be found at home. Advertisements offering specific openings to 'gentlemen emigrants' began to appear frequently in the press, and the new breed of emigrant also led to the publication of several specialist pamphlets and manuals of advice and information.

Yet much of the advice offered was contradictory and confusing. While most publications favoured settlement in Canada[4] and all were united in stressing the need for preliminary training before the emigrant launched out on his own, they differed on the form that such training should take and the way in which the emigrant should go about establishing himself in the colonies. Differences arose primarily over the advantages and drawbacks of the system of 'farm pupilage', under which the emigrant or his parents paid a premium to a colonial farmer who was then expected to board the emigrant and instruct him in all the essentials of colonial farming for a period of up to three years. Pupils were to be denied access to their own capital during this period, until they had gained enough experience to invest it profitably, and relatives at home were discouraged from sending out remittances. Inexperienced recruits were expected to work for little more than their board and lodging initially, while they or their parents were also to pay perhaps £100 a year to the employer in return for the instruction he provided. The system was found across Canada but was most widespread—and most expensive—in British Columbia, particularly in Vancouver Island, the dairylands of the

Fraser River and in the fruit growing regions. In the Okanagan Valley, according to one contemporary observer:

> The parents paid a farmer, we'll say $500, to give him [the son] work for the first year. And he was what they called 'a pupil'. Well, after he'd worked for about two months, then the farmer began paying him $5 or $10 a month back for it, according to how good he was. Well now, it seems a bit unfair, but at the same time, it wasn't altogether as unfair as you think, because some of these fellows could smash up machinery so quickly, or ruin a horse so easily, that the farmer did run a risk.[5]

So the fee was intended partly to compensate farmers for the loss of time and possible damage done by raw recruits. But advocates of the pupilage system also pointed out that it enabled parents to establish their sons in well-conducted households under responsible guardians of their own social class, who could be vetted in advance by the agents through whom the contracts were negotiated. These agents would then visit their clients periodically to ensure that each participant was keeping his side of the bargain. James Aspdin, one of the founders of the Anglo-Canadian Farm Pupil Association, recommended that pupils serve their apprenticeships on small mixed farms of from fifty to 200 acres, where the farmers would have time to give them more personal tuition than on larger units.[6] Once they had been trained there were various ways in which the emigrants could begin farming on their own account, and Aspdin recommended either the outright purchase of an improved farm for cash or share farming, in which the owner provided land, implements and seed and the pupil the labour, the profits being divided at the end of each season on a pre-agreed basis. He advised against buying on credit or taking up an uncleared homestead grant, and also discouraged emigrants from cattle ranching on the grounds that they would be subjected to a monotonous life in a harsh climate beyond the bounds of 'civilised society'.

Men like Aspdin and A. G. Bradley, who operated a farm pupil agency in London in the 1890s, upheld the pupilage system against the indiscriminate emigration of public schoolboys. They claimed it was only by paying a premium to suitable farmers that parents could ensure a proper training for their sons in an acceptable social environment, where they would be eased into their new surroundings and not taxed beyond their strength. They exploited parental fears that if they cut costs they would place their sons at a grave social and economic disadvantage. According to Bradley:

> Those who do not like paying have always ... the alternative of the ordinary farmer's household, where it is simply a question of food, good shelter, hard work, and a speedy dismissal if the youth proves troublesome or idle.[7]

But working farmers who employed all classes and nationalities of emigrants as hired labourers would not undertake to tutor them in colonial farming, and such emigrants were warned that they 'must not expect to get attentions they do not pay for, and that their teachers could not afford to give'.[8]

Even proponents of the premium system knew it was open to grave abuse. Both Aspdin and Bradley admitted that an emigrant's success depended on the calibre of the farmer to whom he was sent, and Aspdin urged parents to deal only with agents who, like himself, had practical colonial experience and contacts with reputable farmers. Bradley went further in suggesting that youths who had sufficient physical and mental stamina would stand a better chance of success in the long run if they sought employment with working farmers as ordinary hired labourers. Although they would have to sacrifice home comforts for a life of hard work and perhaps social deprivation, they were likely to become proficient in all branches of farm labour more quickly than recruits who opted for an easier introduction to Canadian farming.

The most glaring defect of the pupilage system was the ease with which pupils and their parents could be defrauded by unscrupulous agents and farmers. Exorbitant premiums were often charged for recruits who were then given only minimal instruction. Some were treated merely as paying guests and given no training at all, while others were regarded virtually as slave labour and assigned the most menial chores without ever being permitted to participate in essential farming operations. Many instructors themselves were only inexperienced farmers, and they regarded the premium system simply as a means of supplementing their own incomes. Canadian farmers often had little patience with 'gentlemen emigrants'. Men who had struggled to make a settlement out of nothing despised the arrogant, imperialistic attitudes of many 'remittance men', particularly those who had come from urban backgrounds and who had no knowledge whatsoever of farming, and very little interest in it. In the Okanagan Valley, for instance, some took up orchards but many spent their time in idleness while they waited for the next allowance to arrive from home:

> Kelowna was a rendezvous for remittance men by the hundreds, and they spent left, right and centre. They used to buy horses and play polo and tennis and they used to raise particular hell ... They got fabulous amounts of money, remittances, in those days. They'd have $300 or $400 a month remittance.[9]

Although Scots were generally considered to be hard-working and were therefore regarded favourably, such was the reputation of the English 'remittance man' that advertisements for farm workers in Canada towards the end of the nineteenth century increasingly stated that 'no Englishman need apply'.

The defects of the premium system and the unpopularity of farm pupils in Canada were repeatedly emphasised by the British press, the Emigrants' Information Office and the Canadian High Commission.[10] They all pointed out that the payment of premiums was completely unnecessary, since emigrants who were prepared to work hard would have no difficulty in finding work. Farm labourers were always in great demand and emigrants would be assisted in finding situations, without charge, by Canadian government agents stationed throughout the Dominion. Although the recruits might have to work for a time for only board and lodging, they would soon gain sufficient experience to be able to claim wages, and ultimately to launch out on their own. Their situation and prospects were therefore better than farm pupils who often received no wages, but on the contrary paid dearly for what was often an inferior introduction to Canadian farming practices.

The adverse publicity increasingly dissuaded parents from paying a premium to have their sons instructed by Canadian farmers. Those who were reluctant for them to take their chance with the majority of agricultural emigrants, in seeking hired labour with unknown employers, therefore looked for other ways in which the boys could be given an introduction to colonial farming. Although A. G. Bradley and James Aspdin both dismissed agricultural colleges as a means of training 'gentlemen emigrants' on the grounds that the controlled environment of a college bore no relation to actual farm conditions, such institutions became increasingly popular on both sides of the Atlantic. They were widely recommended in articles, pamphlets and official emigrant handbooks. The Ontario School of Agriculture and Experimental Farm at Guelph was the best-known training institution in Canada. It was founded in 1874 to offer advanced courses in stock breeding and farm management to existing farmers, but when enrolment fell towards the end of the decade it launched a successful campaign to attract young British emigrants. By 1880, when the school was renamed the Ontario Agricultural College, British students made up a third of its members.[11] Other training institutions in Canada included the Provincial School of Agriculture at Truro, Nova Scotia and the 640-acre St John's Collegiate Farm in Assiniboia, which functioned between 1885 and 1895. A number of institutions also sprang up in Britain to cater for would-be colonial farmers. From 1887 the Colonial Training College at Hollesley Bay in Suffolk taught students who subsequently went all over the British Empire. Although the fees were high[12] the curriculum was comprehensive, modern and practical, including subjects such as veterinary science, soil chemistry and geology. When Hollesley Bay College closed in 1905 some of its functions were taken over by the Royal Agricultural College at Cirencester, which introduced a special six-month programme for prospective colonists. Between 1907 and 1914 the Public Schools Emigration League also assisted about 300 British youths to emigrate to Canada. The League was formed as a result of an agreement between the Headmasters' Conference in Britain and the British Public Schools Association of Canada, under which the former vetted prospective emigrants and the latter gave successful candidates information, introductions and help in finding work in Canada.[13]

No specific training facilities for 'gentlemen emigrants' were available in North-East Scotland in this period,[14] but the local press regularly advertised openings for young men of means in Canada. On 18 January 1884, for instance, the *Aberdeen Journal* advertised for two or three young men with capital of £800 or £1,000 to enter into partnership with a farmer in Manitoba, in a ranching and wheat-growing venture.[15] Slightly less capital (£300 to £500) was required of a young man of 'good character, education and a respectable social position' who was invited to go into a farming or ranching partnership with a settler in North-West Canada in Spring 1887.[16] On 16 March 1903 a farmer with some capital who was about to emigrate to Canada advertised in the *Aberdeen Journal* for a partner to share his investment in a plot of land; and the following month, on 14 April, an Aberdeenshire farmer with land in the North-West Territories appealed for one or two young men with some means to join him in a profit-sharing enterprise on his Canadian farm. On 19 June 1913 W. A. Macdonald, a solicitor in the Aberdeenshire town of Insch, appealed to 'investors and settlers' to consider purchasing selected farms in the provinces of Manitoba and Saskatchewan, which were available in units of from 160 to 1,000 acres.

Advertisements were occasionally aimed at recruiting farm pupils, including one in the *Aberdeen Journal* on 13 June 1883 by the Canada West Land Agency of Ontario, based in Edinburgh and another on 2 January 1902 by a company in London. But the North-East press reflected the national suspicion of such agencies and the *Aberdeen Journal*'s warnings about the iniquitous premium system often quoted examples of emigrants who had been defrauded. On 18 April 1890 it published a letter from H. H. Wyllie of Lonmay, who had spent seven years in Ontario and whose letter was provoked partly by the recent murder of a young Englishman in Canada. He described the plight of a seventeen-year-old emigrant who, after paying a premium of £200, had been sent to a slovenly Irish household where he had been debarred from taking part in any essential farming operations. Wyllie urged that 'no young gentleman be so foolish as to pay a single penny to any agent or Canadian farmer in order to learn farming, unless he personally knows the man', advising them instead to invest their money in a course at the Agricultural College in Guelph. The following year, on 18 September 1891, the *Aberdeen Journal* published a letter from Alex Walker of Aberdeen and E. R. Townsend of Cork, further warning parents against sending their sons to Canada as farm pupils. They were the guardians of two boys whom they had sent to a so-called rancher in Alberta after paying him a huge premium. The guardians had met the rancher when he was visiting Scotland on holiday, and on the grounds that he was connected with a well-known Aberdeenshire family, they had believed his promise to board the boys for a year, during which they would be taught all aspects of ranch work. He claimed to own an extensive holding with a large stock and a profitable dairy, but the recruits had subsequently found these claims to be largely untrue, and the rancher's partner, from whom they were to have learned book-keeping, had refused to teach them.

Both H. H. Wyllie and another correspondent of the *Aberdeen Journal* on 22 June 1891 doubted whether public schoolboys made suitable recruits for Canadian farms. The 1891 correspondent blamed the many failures on inadequate training and the lack of congenial company, the remedy for which he claimed lay in the formation of community settlements. He based his remarks on the observations of Colonel Fane, one of the tenant farmer delegates who had visited Canada in 1890 and had encountered several disillusioned emigrants in the western provinces. Similar sentiments were expressed by a correspondent who wrote from Vancouver in 1889, complaining that Canadians in the North-West Territories were more eager to swindle newcomers than to help them settle in.[17] Having spent ten weeks on the parched prairie waiting unsuccessfully for his seed to germinate, he had moved west to Vancouver, where he had found the city full of disillusioned prairie farmers.

But these reservations must be set alongside the optimistic accounts of most observers and correspondents, including such notable figures as the Earl of Aberdeen.[18] The records kept by John MacLennan's office suggest that such recommendations to men of means to settle in Canada were heeded in North-East Scotland.[19] On several occasions in his weekly reports MacLennan mentioned the departure of emigrants of considerable means, including two good farmers from Dingwall, with £1,500 and £2,000 respectively, who booked for Canada in the week ending 25 April 1908. During the week ending 30 July 1910 he 'interviewed one farmer with 4000 dollars who leaves for Canada next week' and two months later, on 17 September, he reported an interview he had conducted at Alford with James Fife, a South African who was about to use his capital of £2,000 to take up a farm in Canada. Then on 14 January 1911 MacLennan mentioned a recent interview with a large farmer from Banff who had also decided to emigrate to Canada.

Contrary to James Aspdin's view that cattle ranching was a socially unsuitable occupation for 'gentlemen emigrants', several wealthy British settlers pursued this occupation in Alberta, which at the turn of the century was often described as 'the paradise of the younger son'.[20] W. Crawley Ricardo, for instance, the English cattle rancher and Cambridge graduate who from 1895 was largely responsible for making Lord Aberdeen's Coldstream Ranch one of the leading mixed farming enterprises in North America, gained his extensive knowledge of ranching in Southern Alberta[21] in the 1880s and 1890s. One of the wealthiest British investors in the prairie ranching industry at this time was Sir John Lister-Kaye, who in 1889 undertook a grandiose (but ultimately unsuccessful) colonisation scheme to attract British settlers to the North-West Territories. He formed the Canadian Agriculture, Coal and Colonisation Company, which acquired 110,000 acres of land from the Dominion Government and the Canadian Pacific Railway Company, located along the line of the railway in Southern Alberta. He divided this land into eleven, 10,000-acre properties, on which he provided some fencing, buildings, implements and stock. He then enlisted the help of land agents on a number of large English and Scottish estates to select an 'admirable class of agriculturist', preferably the sons of large farmers, from properties in Aberdeenshire, Dumfriesshire and Yorkshire. They were to undertake the management of his lands and put up £200 capital of their own to match the £246 that the Colonisation Company was to spend on each unit.[22] Lister-Kaye hoped to persuade the British government to promote a scheme of state-aided emigration to supply these managers with the labour force they required, but when the government refused to co-operate he sold his interest in the Company and withdrew from Western Canada by 1890. Yet although his colonisation scheme was short-lived, it was not without some effect in North-East Scotland, for during their first tour of Canada in 1890 Lord and Lady

Aberdeen encountered at least two Aberdeenshire emigrants who were living on properties recently established by Sir John Lister-Kaye.[23] John MacLennan's reports indicate that two decades later Alberta (his own home province) was still attracting wealthy North-East emigrants. In his report of 13 February 1910 he noted:

> There is an important movement among farmers of considerable means. I had the satisfaction last week of seeing a prominent farmer and his son change their minds from going to New Zealand and book to Canada. I drove 18 miles to interview them and [they] came into [the] city and booked to Calgary yesterday. They take with them over £2400. I went to Arbroath and interviewed another farmer who will go to Canada in April with over £3000. Two prominent farmers from Deeside are giving up their farms and going this spring. One of them is there now and has bought 960 acres east of Crossfields, Alberta. I am going to Elgin this week to see 2 brothers who intend going and who have nearly £3000 between them.

Later that year, during a visit to Carnoustie in September,[24] MacLennan met Alex Brown, a prominent farmer who was about to emigrate to Calgary taking £1,300 with him. A month later, on 23 October, in reporting a successful week of meetings among Morayshire farmers, he singled out for particular comment two brothers aged eighteen and twenty, the sons of a wealthy lawyer in Elgin. They had emigrated to Alberta the previous Spring to situations near Lacombe 'and the father is now sending money to Mr. Hutton, Supt. Experimental Farm there, to buy a farm for the boys'.

British Columbia: the gentleman's paradise?

The majority of MacLennan's wealthy clients, however, seem to have gone to British Columbia. On 6 June 1908 he reported:

> The last two weeks has seen the departure of a large number of good men to Canada from this district. Over 75[?] of them going west. British Columbia is receiving special attention at present, chiefly by people of some means.

On 6 August 1910 he noted that he had interviewed a man and wife who were taking £800 or £900 to British Columbia to invest in fruit farming, and a month later he interviewed John Burnett, a prominent fish curer in Fraserburgh and a man who 'controls considerable capital', just before Burnett left to re-establish his business in Nanaimo, Vancouver Island.[25] At this time MacLennan had several interviews with wealthy farmers and other men of means who proposed to emigrate to Canada, and he observed in his report of 9 October 1910:

> There are bright prospects of a large number of people of means leaving the North of Scotland for Canada in the near future. A gentleman left Aberdeen several weeks ago with his family for Vancouver taking with him £11,000 or

£12,000 ... One of the partners in a wholesale millinery store in this city has sold his interest and is leaving with his family in a few weeks to engage in a similar business at some point in the west. He will have about £2000 in money.

MacLennan's observations that several emigrants were leaving North-East Scotland to pursue business or professional opportunities in Canada are corroborated in the records of Aberdeen University. The *Roll of Graduates*[26] indicates that 128 graduates went to Canada between 1860 and 1925, all but thirty-seven of whom apparently remained permanently in the Dominion. Supplementary Records of the Arts Classes between 1864 and 1912[27] contain the names of a further twenty non-graduating students who also emigrated to Canada. As might be expected, the majority of these 148 emigrants— forty-two individuals—went to the old-established and traditionally 'Scottish' province of Ontario. But twenty-eight emigrants chose to settle in the newer, increasingly fashionable province of British Columbia, followed by twenty-one in Manitoba, fifteen in Alberta and thirteen in Saskatchewan.[28]

Eleven of these former students or graduates took up farming or farming-related occupations. They included George Bruce of Oldmeldrum (MA 1880) who after teaching in Aberdeen and Inverness went to Assiniboia in 1904 and began farming thirty-five miles north of Fort Qu'Appelle.[29] Sylvester Findlater of Mortlach (MB CM 1880, MD 1884), the son of the factor on the Earl of Fife's Banffshire estates, gave up a medical career to take up farming in Lacombe, Alberta in 1893, but later moved west to Vancouver.[30] Archibald Johnson (MA 1884) gave up teaching to become a farmer in Manitoba,[31] while George Rose of Perthshire (MA 1891) spent five years as a fruit-grower in the Okanagan Valley with his brother Hugh before trying his hand at gold-mining in 1896 and then entering the Canadian Civil Service in 1897. After serving as a sub-collector of Customs at Cascade, British Columbia, he subsequently returned to the Okanagan Valley to become the proprietor and editor of the *Kelowna Clarion*.[32] Alexander Cumming (BSc Agric. 1906), a farmer's son from Rothes, worked as a farmer and creamery inspector in Winnipeg before returning to Britain to become Chief Inspector of United Dairies in London.[33] George Jamieson from Newburgh retired from his post as the manager of a tea estate in Ceylon in 1909 to live at Priddis, Alberta.[34] The eldest of his eight sons took up tea planting in Ceylon, but three others were involved in horse and cattle ranching in the Priddis area. And Arthur Ligertwood retired from cattle ranching in Texas to Victoria, British Columbia in 1918, having been attracted to the province by its climate and good educational facilities.[35]

When Ligertwood's eldest daughter studied at the University of British Columbia she was taught by two graduates of Aberdeen University, A. G. Smith and E. B. Paul. The most commonly represented profession among the Aberdeen graduates who went to Canada was in fact teaching, thirty-four being employed as schoolteachers[36] and a further ten in institutions of higher education. They were followed by twenty-three ministers, nineteen doctors, fifteen lawyers, accountants or bankers and fourteen businessmen.[37] British Columbia initially attracted thirteen of the thirty-four schoolteachers, a further three settling there after having taught elsewhere in Canada; and the *Aberdeen Journal* on 23 August 1911 mentioned another two Aberdeen graduates, Duncan Stewart and James Strachan, after they had just been granted certificates of education to teach in British Columbia.

Perhaps the considerations which led Arthur Ligertwood to retire to British Columbia influenced several better-off emigrants from North-East Scotland. In 1891 at least three North-East men—John Grant of Alford, Dr George Lawson Milne of Garmouth and Joseph Hunter of Aberdeen—were serving in the British Columbian Provincial Parliament[38] and the belief that they would be among fellow-countrymen, surrounded by familiar and valued social institutions, may have encouraged other local emigrants to settle in that province. By 1891 it was already a popular destination, thanks largely to the extensive promotional activities of the provincial government, the transcontinental railway companies and a number of land developers. Then between 1891 and 1921 about 175,000 British settlers came to British Columbia, a significant minority of whom (about 24,000) fell into the category of 'gentlemen'.[39] The promotional literature repeatedly pointed out the province's strong links with Britain and the highly developed cultural and social amenities it offered, including first-class schools, libraries and municipal government.[40] On 8 April 1892 the *Aberdeen Journal* drew attention to the extension of railway facilities to British Columbia which it predicted, together with 'its beautiful climate and other attractions to home-seekers must secure a continuance of the development by which present investors will no doubt greatly benefit'. The most desirable settlers were those with 'a little money, brains and energy'[41] and all commentators were agreed on the exceptional opportunities available to those with sufficient capital. Lord Lorne, in a speech in Victoria quoted in the *Aberdeen Journal* on 25 November 1882, declared that a man with an income of from £200 to £600 a year could take up no better occupation than cattle or cereal farming in British Columbia.

The overriding emphasis on openings for monied emigrants, coupled with the warning to those of only modest means to avoid British Columbia, may have accounted for the seemingly disproportionate number of wealthy settlers in the province. Henry Murray, the Canadian government's emigration agent in Glasgow, noted after a trip to the Dominion in 1897 that 'British Columbia is not a poor man's country. There is no room for him there'.[42] And A. G. Bradley, too, while outlining profitable agricultural investments, reminded those with limited funds of the high cost of labour in British Columbia and suggested that they might find a more suitable outlet for their energies in the prairie provinces.[43] Similarly, the Scottish farming delegation which visited Canada in 1908 advised white emigrants with small means to stay away from British Columbia until they had saved enough money to become landowners and employers of labour.[44] Those who had to seek wage labour would, warned the delegation, feel out of place among the Oriental and Indian workers who were widespread in the province, unless they managed to secure higher employment as foremen or managers. It reported favourably on the way in which large corporations in the Okanagan Valley were selling small plots of land to modest investors, singling out Lord Aberdeen's Coldstream Ranch for particular commendation. But it warned emigrants against taking up such an offer unless they had at least £200 in savings, since 'those fine fruit valleys provide excellent openings for men with capital, but only for such' and the farm delegates predicted that even highly capitalised investors would have 'very hard times for some years' before their orchards became productive and profitable.[45] Then in 1912 the journalist J. S. Redmayne recommended that inexperienced emigrants intending to invest in fruit-farming should possess even more capital—at least £500 and preferably £1,000—to cover the cost of errors and time spent in training.[46]

Commercial fruit farming: Lord Aberdeen and the development of the Okanagan Valley

Fruit farming was undoubtedly the main incentive which attracted wealthy 'gentlemen farmers'—as well as several emigrants of lesser means—to British Columbia in the late nineteenth and early twentieth centuries. Land agents who extolled the profitability and social respectability of such an investment succeeded in diverting emigrants' attention from fashionable settlements in Vancouver Island to the inland valleys, which at the turn of the century witnessed a 'fruit mania' similar to the Albertan cattle mania of the 1880s. The industry first developed and was centred in the Okanagan Valley in southern British Columbia, where its establishment owed much to the enterprise of a few Scottish capitalists. Until the 1860s the area was little known and sparsely populated, familiar only to the native Indians and to a few isolated fur traders in the employment of the Hudson's Bay Company. Although its first orchards were allegedly planted in 1859 by a priest of the Oblate order, Father Charles Pandosy, when he established a mission in the Okanagan,[47] the commercial potential of large-scale fruit farming was not recognised until the closing years of the century. The influx of fortune-hunters to the Cariboo gold fields in the early 1860s also brought the Okanagan Valley some settlers, whose crops and cattle helped to supply the needs of the gold diggers to the north. A number of Anglo-Irish immigrants in particular were more successful at raising cattle and selling them to miners than they had been at prospecting for gold themselves, and from the 1860s to the 1880s the northern Okanagan was dominated by a few large Irish-owned cattle ranches.[48] Further south, in the area around Kelowna, Arthur Knox of Tarves, Aberdeenshire, who emigrated to the valley in 1874, after prospecting in the Cariboo, progressively added to his holdings until by 1890 he had accumulated 4,000 acres of ranchland. In the early 1890s he began to develop flourishing orchards on some of this land.[49]

The real birth of the Okanagan Valley in fact came in the 1890s. This was partly because the area then became more accessible, thanks to the inauguration of a steamer service on the Okanagan Lake in 1886, followed by the completion of a branch of the Canadian Pacific Railway from Sicamous

Junction to Vernon in 1892. A year after this Shuswap and Okanagan Line was opened the CPR extended its service to the rest of the valley by means of a new steamer service on the lake. With the promise of better access, wealthy entrepreneurs and land development companies began to buy and subdivide the large ranches of the Okanagan with the intention of encouraging settlement by selling off these smaller units as orchard properties. Well-to-do Scottish immigrants in particular exploited the Okanagan's new accessibility. Prominent among the entrepreneurs was John Gordon, seventh Earl of Aberdeen, and from 1893 to 1898 Governor General of Canada. When he was persuaded by a land agent to invest in property in the Okanagan Valley, large numbers of 'gentlemen emigrants' confidently followed his example; their intention was not only to take up an occupation which offered 'maximum profit with minimum risk'[50] but to maintain their social status by settling amidst compatible neighbours, men 'of education and refinement' who shared their own background and interests. The pioneer fruit farmers tried to lure like-minded emigrants to the Okanagan through promotional pamphlets and advertisements in the British press, persuading them that fruit farming was the ideal occupation for 'nature's gentlemen'. Their appeals met with an enthusiastic response and Lady Aberdeen noted approvingly in her *Canadian Journal* that by 1894 small parcels of her husband's land were being sold to selected British emigrants 'of a very good class', leading to the formation of a 'really high-class little community'.[51] In fact Lord Aberdeen's own personal investments in fruit farming were ultimately unsuccessful. Yet his contribution to the settlement and economic growth of the Okanagan Valley was positive and of permanent significance, not only for the valley itself, but also for the wider settlement of British Columbia. So how precisely did this Scottish earl contribute to the development of Canada's most westerly province, and why did his investments ultimately end in costly failure? It is clear that his failure was not unique. Nor was it complete, since Lord Aberdeen in the 1890s and early 1900s laid the foundations for future prosperity in the Okanagan and his more fortunate successors were able to learn from the mistakes of this prominent pioneer.

The attention of Lord Aberdeen and his wife was directed to British Columbia during their first visit to Canada in 1890.[52] In Vancouver they met George Grant MacKay, an engineer who had once constructed roads at Guisachan, the Inverness-shire estate of Lady Aberdeen's father. A real estate dealer in the Scottish Highlands and owner of the island of Raasay, MacKay had come to Canada in 1887, having found 'that land at home was getting to be a rather bad business'.[53] His intention was to see if British Columbia offered good prospects for his sons, after he had been attracted by a display mounted by the province in Glasgow. He was so impressed with its potential that instead of returning to Scotland he had sent for his family to join him. He had a real estate agency in Vancouver and in 1890 he established the Okanagan Land and Development Company with four associates and an authorised capital of $225,000. On his recommendation Lord Aberdeen purchased, for $10,000, a 480-acre ranch in the Kelowna area of the Okanagan Valley, which he named Guisachan (place of the firs). Lady Aberdeen rec-

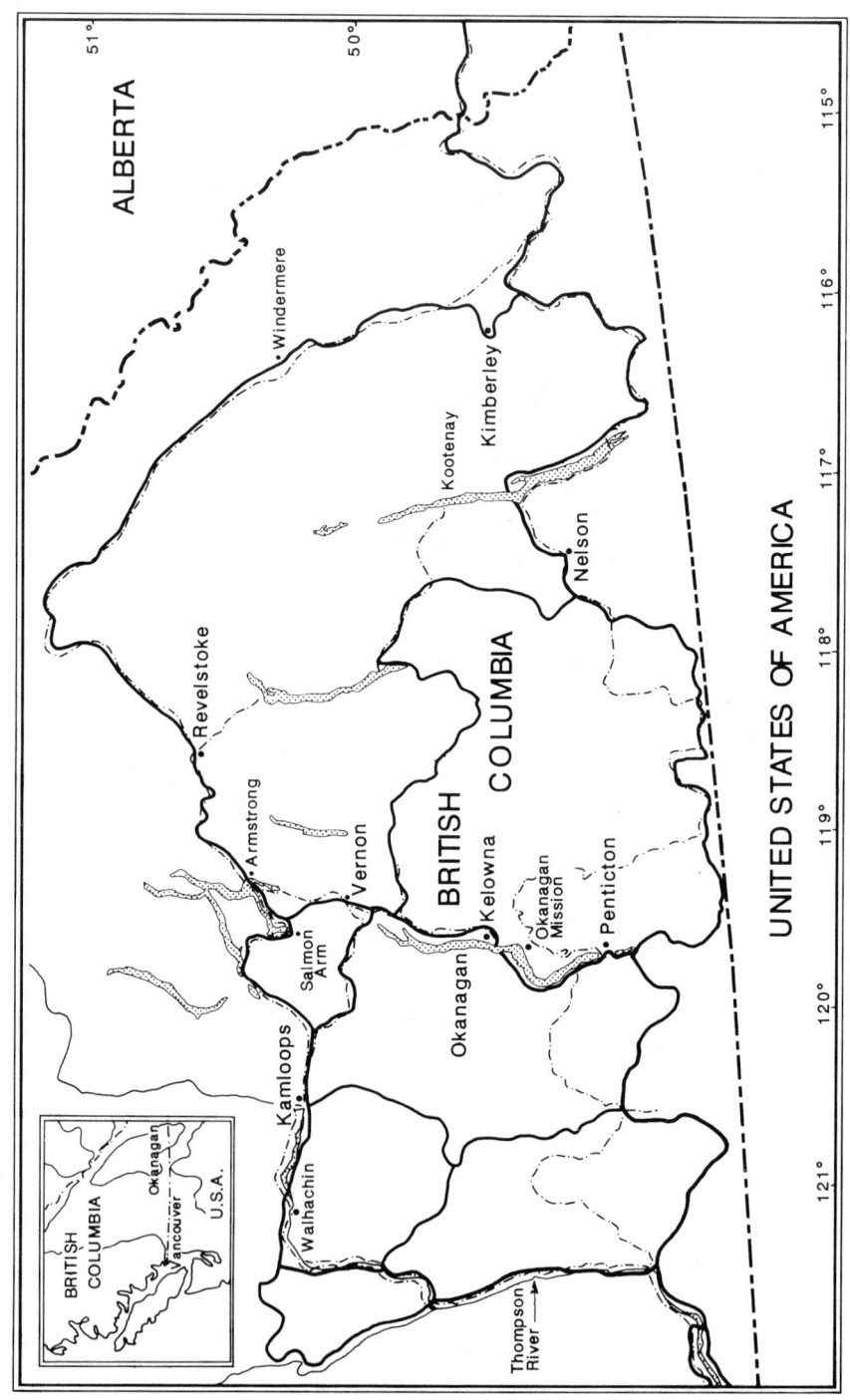

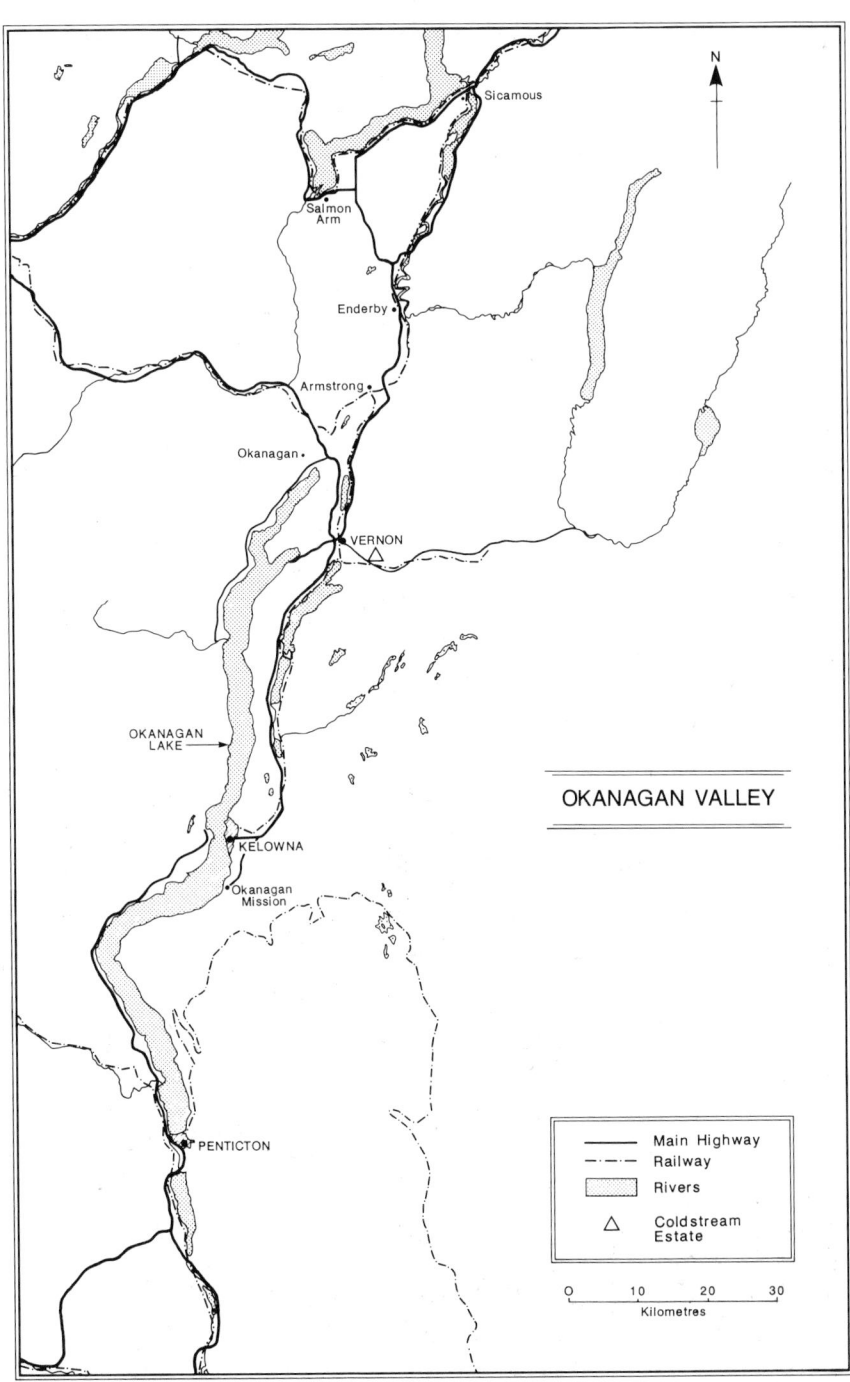

Sicamous

N

Salmon
Arm

Enderby

Armstrong

Okanagan

VERNON

OKANAGAN
LAKE

OKANAGAN VALLEY

KELOWNA

Okanagan
Mission

PENTICTON

Main Highway
Railway
Rivers
Coldstream
Estate

O   10   20   30
Kilometres

orded the meeting with MacKay and the subsequent transaction in her journal:

> Mr MacKay told us of another district about 21 hours from Vancouver whose reputation is even better & which is now in process of being opened up by a railway going South of the C.P.R. to Long Lake which Lord Lorne describes as the loveliest lake in Canada. The railway goes (or will go next September) to Vernon on the lake; 30 miles down the Okanagan Lake there is a farm, now belonging to a half-breed, 480 acres with a nice house, some 70 head of cattle, horses, wheat, implements etc etc. Mr MacKay was thinking of buying on his own account for 10,000 dollars a short time back ... [he] says that he is confident of the value of the land, that in a few years it would sell for double if not four times its present value & he has proved himself so fair & wise a man that we are safe in his hands.[54]

Guisachan was bought mainly in an attempt to persuade Coutts Marjoribanks, Lady Aberdeen's brother, to leave North Dakota, where he was not making a financial success of the 1,260-acre Horseshoe Ranch in McHenry County, of which he was the manager.[55] Both Coutts and his youngest brother Archie in fact typified the unsuccessful gentleman emigrant south of the border. Their father Lord Tweedmouth, a breeder of Aberdeen Angus cattle, had been attracted by the prospects of the Western USA as a source of profitable employment for his sons. The Rocking Chair Ranch in the Texas Panhandle was bought by a family syndicate and Archie was sent out as its assistant manager. But neither this venture nor Lord Tweedmouth's investment in the Horseshoe Ranch succeeded. In 1894, after the Texan experiment had been given up, Archie Marjoribanks went to Ottawa to work for Lord Aberdeen during his term of office as Governor-General of Canada.[56] Coutts duly moved to British Columbia and became the superintendent of the new Guisachan Ranch, where he was responsible for an international workforce, including an American foreman, Chinese domestic staff, and immigrants from Ontario, Yorkshire and Aberdeenshire.

Lord and Lady Aberdeen did not visit their new acquisition until 1891, when they travelled, along with their ten-year-old daughter Marjorie, on the first passenger train to run the forty-six miles between Sicamous and Vernon on the still unopened and incomplete Shuswap and Okanagan Line.[57] They arrived in time to see Guisachan Ranch take twelve prizes in the district's inaugural Agricultural Show. They were met in Vernon by Coutts Marjoribanks and taken by steamer up the Okanagan Lake to their property near Kelowna, thirty-five miles south of Vernon. Lady Aberdeen later described their first impressions of Guisachan in glowing terms:

> Now, knowing that the beauty of a country is often over-rated, we had schooled ourselves not to expect much, so as not to be disappointed. We imagined to ourselves, therefore, a flat plain with bare hills in the distance, a few scrubby trees and bushes here and there, and a house set down in the middle of the flat. Instead of which we found mountains looking more like the Inverness-shire mountains of my youth than any others we had seen in Canada, and about a

mile from the landing-stage we came to a gate leading into a wood ... with big trees of two hundred feet high, through which the moonlight fell in silvery streaks ... About half-a-mile brings us through the wood, and then, on emerging, we see our house a quarter of a mile away, standing against a background of purple hills, and commanding a charming view, with a peep of the lake from the verandah.[58]

Lord and Lady Aberdeen were so impressed with the Okanagan that they decided at this time to make another, more extensive purchase in the area. Their first intention was to buy from the Tarves emigrant, Arthur Knox, his 4,000-acre property adjacent to Guisachan, which would have given them access to the lake.[59] Knox, however, demanded $90,000 against the $36,000 offered by George MacKay on Lord Aberdeen's behalf, so MacKay directed his client's attention instead to the 13,261-acre Coldstream Ranch at the northern end of the valley, five miles from Vernon and near Long Lake (later known as Kalamalka Lake). It was bought, along with 2,000 cattle, seventy horses, pigs, implements, crops, hay and furniture, at a cost of £49,000 from the Irish pioneer, Forbes Vernon, who had built up a major ranch from his original acquisition of 1,450 acres.[60] Coutts Marjoribanks duly moved from Guisachan to manage his brother-in-law's second property, until in 1895 he bought land of his own in the same area. He was then replaced at Coldstream by W. Crawley Ricardo, the wealthy English cattle rancher from Alberta. Ricardo had first visited the Okanagan on a hunting trip in 1891 and he remained at Coldstream until 1914, making the property one of the major mixed farming enterprises in North America.[61] Lord Aberdeen himself first came to the ranch with his family in October 1894, for a short break from an official tour in Western Canada. It was, according to Lady Aberdeen's *Canadian Journal*, the first occasion on which the family had come together by themselves since Lord Aberdeen had become Governor-General over a year earlier, and she welcomed the opportunity to escape from Ottawa to a place where 'one need not ask permission from the Government before moving a plank or ordering a plate or a duster'.[62] In fact, throughout their five-year term of office Lord and Lady Aberdeen seem to have valued their British Columbia properties largely as a haven of rest and escape from their public duties, and an opportunity for their family to relax together in privacy at least once a year.

But Lord Aberdeen also had major ambitions for his ranches, proposals which he believed would benefit the local community as well as bring profit to himself. Many people in that community around Vernon felt prosperity in the area depended on the large ranchers' willingness to subdivide their properties in order to create for sale compact fruit farms of twenty to 100 acres each. This trend was actively encouraged by the land companies which bought up many Okanagan ranches in the 1890s and early 1900s, subdivided them and sold them off in small units for the development of orchards.[63] The Okanagan Land and Development Company established by George MacKay was one such concern. MacKay was convinced of the potential of commercial fruit farming in the valley and encouraged Lord Aberdeen to buy not only

Guisachan but also the much larger Coldstream property, whose previous owner, Forbes Vernon, had been heavily criticised in the locality for his refusal to sell off any part of the huge ranch to create orchards. MacKay persuaded Lord Aberdeen of the benefit he would confer on the district—and indeed on the whole province—if he would buy Coldstream and break up a large proportion of its 13,261 acres into compact lots for fruit growers. According to Lady Aberdeen, her husband's newly-acquired experience of British Columbian ranching at Guisachan had so fired him with enthusiasm for the prospects of the country that he required little persuasion from MacKay to make this major purchase.[64] Always ready and willing to invest money for the benefit of his fellow men, Lord Aberdeen complied with the wishes of the real-estate agent, who assured him that he was entering into possession of the finest ranch in the whole of British Columbia.

Part of the new property was entrusted to MacKay, who was to plant orchards and hop yards on a large scale and sell off the best land in twenty- to fifty-acre plots to buyers who wanted to go in for intensive farming and/or fruit growing. In 1892 200 acres at Coldstream and a similar acreage at Guisachan were planted out with fruit trees, an initial step towards large-scale fruit production which marked a turning point in the economic history of the Okanagan Valley. In 1895 the first forty- and fifty-acre units of the Coldstream estate were sold off to British emigrants for cultivation as fruit farms and other large landowners soon followed Lord Aberdeen's example. He arranged for the construction of a jam factory in Vernon, completed in 1893, to which growers, large and small, could send their soft fruit for processing. He also introduced the first irrigation system in the northern Okanagan, to bring a regular water supply not only to his own orchards but to the whole of that part of the valley. By 1907 ten- and twenty-acre irrigated (though unimproved) plots on the Coldstream estate were selling at £30 to £40 per acre,[65] and an emigration pamphlet in 1909 described Coldstream as the area's 'model estate'.[66] It declared:

> The ranch is under expert management; and provides employment for many labourers and skilled agriculturists ... Vistas of young orchards scurry away to the margin of Long Lake; and are the homes of many well-to-do English families.

But not only English families were attracted to the Okanagan. Among the specialists introduced to manage different parts of the Coldstream Estate were an experienced fruit foreman from Washington State and several Scottish immigrants, including a cattleman who had originally emigrated from Methlick, Aberdeenshire to Saskatchewan (and whom Lord and Lady Aberdeen had met on their first trip to Canada in 1890).[67] Among the first settlers who came out direct from North-East Scotland and bought land from the Aberdeens were William and Catherine Middleton from Echt, a middle-aged couple who arrived in June 1892 with their five children in order to develop dairying at Coldstream.[68] A year after they arrived they purchased a forty-acre plot east of Vernon, where subsequent emigrants from North-East Scotland sometimes stayed with them on arrival before moving on to their own properties. In 1900 thirty-year-old Billy Reid came out to Canada from Aberdeenshire to look for a farm for his father, and after searching unsuccessfully in the Red Deer area of Alberta, he purchased 160 acres and pre-empted a further 320 acres in the vicinity of Vernon. In 1903 he returned to the Vale of Alford to escort his parents, along with his three brothers and three sisters, to Canada, and the family stayed initially with the Middletons before moving on to their 1,000-acre Bennachie Ranch. Writing to his brother shortly after his arrival, William Reid sen. described his new property in glowing terms, being particularly impressed with the varieties of fruits, which 'are produced in amazing quantities, and of quality without equal'.[69] Reid's testimony—both about the quality of the land and the warm welcome given by the Middletons—was corroborated by Alexander Esson who, although well on in years, left Lumphanan in 1904 to settle with his wife and stepdaughter on the Midmar ranch near Vernon.[70] Both Reid and Esson contrasted agricultural conditions in Scotland (where 'the farmer's industry is rewarded with penalties, where he toils only to see the fruits of his labour reaped by others')[71] with the ease with which good land could be purchased in British Columbia.

Lord Aberdeen's confidence in the economic potential of fruit farming in the Okanagan Valley was bolstered by the phenomenal success of the industry across the border in Washington and Oregon and by the persuasive propaganda of the numerous land development companies. These factors all helped to bring about a sustained influx of wealthy British farmers, businessmen and ex-army officers, who bought fruit ranches at Kelowna and Vernon in the vicinity of the Aberdeen properties. Between 1901 and 1913 the number of fruit trees in the valley increased by 525 per cent and on the eve of the First World War there were about 30,000 people in the Okanagan who were involved in fruit growing.[72] The orchards extended virtually from Vernon to Penticton and covered not just the low-lying lakeside land but the benches above Okanagan Lake, where a number of land companies had built the essential irrigation systems. According to one estimate land values in the Okanagan increased dramatically from $1 per acre in 1898 to $1,000 per acre in 1910,[73] hence the preponderance of settlers with pensions or private incomes, for whom farming was 'an accessory rather than a main source of livelihood'.[74] It was reckoned in 1906 that the intending fruit farmer required about £1,000 to buy ten acres of land, build a house and keep the orchard going for five years until it became self-supporting,[75] after which he had to pay for a labour force to pick and pack his fruit. A large part of the initial purchase price often covered the cost of irrigation systems, which were usually installed in advance by the big development companies before they sold off their lands in small units; since this commonly involved the purchase of large tracts of useless land in order to obtain the water rights essential for irrigation, the price of irrigated land could be up to six times greater than land in unirrigated areas.

Intending fruit farmers were strongly advised to purchase irrigated land on the grounds that it was a safer investment. Development companies, it was argued, would not waste money on irrigating territory which was unsuitable for fruit cultivation; nor would they go to the expense of planting out such land with fruit trees before it was sold to smaller investors; nor indeed would the vendors then guarantee to maintain the orchards for a year after they had been sold. Under this arrangement new settlers who did not want to undertake the immediate responsibility of fruit farming on their own account could have the initial planting and cultivation of their orchards for a season or two performed by the skilled labour force of the vendors. This was one of the services offered by Lord Aberdeen's Coldstream Estate Company (formed in 1903), which also arranged to buy and market the fruit crop of neighbouring growers who did not want to seek a market for it themselves.[76] Investors were assured that their outlay would soon pale into insignificance in comparison with their high yields and profits of up to £70 per acre once their fruit trees had fully matured.[77] Since the Okanagan Valley lay between the highly populated coastal districts of British Columbia and the vast prairies to the east of the Rockies, fruit farmers were encouraged to believe that they would be in a prime position to tap a virtually unlimited market.

Emigrants were lured not only to the Okanagan Valley. Enterprising land developers, encouraged by the provincial government, took advantage of the enthusiasm for fruit farming among the British middle and upper classes to promote many other parts of the interior 'dry belt' of British Columbia. As in the Okanagan, settlers were persuaded that these areas were not only profitable fruit-farming locations but 'outposts of Empire' to which they could easily transfer their British assumptions and lifestyles. To the east of the Okanagan, the land around Kootenay Lake, which had received its first major influx of settlers during the silver and lead mining boom of the 1890s, was in the early twentieth century widely promoted as a haven for genteel British orchardists. Robert Randolph Bruce, a Scottish mining engineer who subsequently became a lieutenant-governor of British Columbia, first visited the area in 1897 while working as a land agent of the Canadian Pacific Railway Company. In 1912, in an attempt to cash in on the continuing fruit mania, he acquired 50,000 acres of land from the CPR, formed the Columbia Valley Irrigated Fruit Lands Company, and set out to attract wealthy British settlers to the Windermere Valley in East Kootenay. In an article in the British sporting magazine, *The Field*, in February 1912 Bruce told intending settlers that irrigation ditches had been constructed and that bench land was available for settlement at from £10 to £30 per irrigated acre. He assured them that for about £1,000 they could build a house and establish a profitable orchard in a location where they could share the company and leisure pursuits of aristocratic British colonists.[78] The settlement was promoted by Bruce's company in conjunction with the CPR Land Department and was advertised on at least four occasions in the *Aberdeen Journal*.[79] In January 1912 E. Mallandaine, the Company's manager who, like Bruce, was a former employee of the CPR Land Department in East Kootenay, visited Aberdeen to encourage emigration. He pointed out that Windermere's easterly location (close to the vast prairie market) and its proximity to the railway[80] gave it a distinct advantage over other fruit-producing regions of British Columbia. These promotional efforts were not made in vain, for in Spring and summer 1912 many more settlers than the Company had expected came to Windermere. On 10 March 1913 Alexander Longmuir, the emigrant booking agent in Stonehaven, intimated through the *Aberdeen Journal* that he could offer free passages to Windermere to twenty first-class ploughmen, who would be boarded at the colonisation company's expense and would receive wages of £60 per year. They were to sail on 14 April, and on 26 June 1913 the *Aberdeen Journal* reflected the continuing interest in the settlement when it published a notice from the CPR Company announcing that, owing to heavy demand, a conducted party was being organised to travel to Windermere in July. The following month MacKay Brothers, in correspondence with the Canadian Immigration Department, referred to two clients, a Mr and Mrs Craig, who had just left North-East Scotland to take up one of the CPR farms at Windermere.[81]

Two years before the Windermere settlement was conceived a similar community had been promoted to the west of the Okanagan Valley, at Walhachin, a 5,000-acre tract thirty-five miles west of Kamloops, bordering a seven-mile stretch of the Thompson River. It was confidently expected that this semi-arid valley (previously given over to cattle ranching) would rival the Okanagan as a fruit-producing and exporting centre once the waters of the Thompson River had been harnessed to irrigate the lands adjacent to the two railways which served the area.[82] The settlement of Walhachin was organised by a powerful London-based joint stock company, the British Columbia Development Association, in which the brewery baronet, Sir William Bass, played a formative rôle. It was publicised in Britain by skilled propagandists recruited for this purpose, including the journalist John Redmayne whose widely-circulated book, *Fruit farming on the 'dry belt' of British Columbia*, pointedly recommended fruit farming as an occupation for 'better class' emigrants. At Walhachin the British Columbia Development Association sold cottages for $1,000, undeveloped ten-acre plots for $3,000 and pre-planted ten-acre plots for $3,500. The Association also offered to plant and tend the estates of investors who could not take immediate possession of their holdings, a service which it particularly recommended to army officers about to retire and to public schoolboys seeking a career. The Association's highly selective recruitment campaign readily attracted aristocratic British colonists to Walhachin; within two years of its formation it boasted almost 200 residents, most of whom had bought their land unseen on the strength of alluring promotional literature.

Much of the impetus for the settlement of these areas sprang from the confidence inspired by Lord Aberdeen's large investments in the Okanagan Valley in the early 1890s. In fact, it was an agriculturist and an engineer from the Aberdeen properties (Messrs Palmer and Ashcroft) who helped to persuade Sir William Bass of the British Columbia Development Association of Walhachin's potential when they accompanied him on his first visit to the area in 1907.[83] Yet from the start there were clear signs that all was not well even with Lord Aberdeen's estates and despite his high hopes and good intentions, his promising investments soon became a severe financial embarrassment to him. G. A. Jamieson, a Scottish lawyer employed to assess the state and prospects of the British Columbia properties, submitted his report in November 1892, two years before Lord Aberdeen first visited Coldstream for himself.[84] He believed Guisachan, if well managed, would be a good investment, although he wished that the estate had been larger and had extended right down to the lake in order to include water rights. The property had been neglected by its previous owners, a family of mixed race who had pursued stock-raising on a small scale. The first concern of Coutts Marjoribanks on arriving at Guisachan had been to replace the existing frame house with a new and larger dwelling (which was then found to be grossly under-insulated against the Okanagan winters). Marjoribanks had also sold off the cattle from the ranch at $20 a head on the grounds that there would have been insufficient hay to see them through their first winter. Lord Aberdeen subsequently spent large sums of money on tillage, livestock and the planting of fruit and hops at Guisachan. In his report in 1892 Jamieson commented that this expenditure had been excessive, particularly since it would be at least 1896 before any reasonable return could be expected from the fruit crops.[85] He welcomed the cultivation of fruit, since the land was unsuitable for growing cereals; he also stressed that Guisachan 'never could be a cattle ranche' and for that reason 'it was in no respect suitable' for the relocation of Coutts Marjoribanks, probably Lord Aberdeen's main objective in this first purchase:

> Mr Marjoribanks was not the man to sit down and cultivate apples and pears or hogs: and I should most certainly have dissuaded Lord Aberdeen from going into the existing agreement about Guisachan and Mr Marjoribanks equally from undertaking it.

Jamieson felt Lord Aberdeen had been badly advised by George MacKay in respect of both Guisachan and Coldstream. He distrusted MacKay, who he thought had too much personal interest at stake in encouraging Lord Aberdeen to invest in the Okanagan.[86]

Jamieson was more critical of what he thought was the excessive price paid for Coldstream, although he admitted that it offered a good water supply and excellent land which was capable of being divided into lots of various sizes. He argued that Lord Aberdeen's interests had not been adequately safeguarded against the unprincipled actions of Forbes Vernon and his manager, who he maintained had deliberately overstocked the ranch with a view to its sale. MacKay held to his offer of $241,000 against Vernon's initial asking price of $250,000 but apparently failed to inspect the ranch or make a proper inventory of its assets before reaching an agreement. He put forward as a major asset in 1891 the fact that it was so well-stocked, but Jamieson believed there had been only about 350 cattle fit for sale at that time, and blamed MacKay for not counting the cattle which were to be included in the agreement. A final settlement was delayed until 30 July 1894 after a dispute arose regarding the number and quality of the cattle included in the sale, as well as the state of the fences. Jamieson alleged that the ranch was incapable of carrying 2,000 head of stock, that hardly any of the animals had been fit for sale in 1891 and that virtually no part of the £4,000 which Lord Aberdeen had expected to raise from their resale had been made. In a letter to Vernon on 26 October 1893 Jamieson appealed for a reduction in the overall price on these grounds. He also alleged that the hay which Vernon had laid in for the animals in 1891, without which they could not be maintained in a marketable condition, and which should have been sold with the ranch, had actually been stolen by the unprincipled manager, Wood. But his veiled threat of litigation against Vernon provoked a similar reply from the vendor, and despite Jamieson's opinion that the price was exorbitant he had to advise Lord Aberdeen to take out a mortgage on his Guisachan property to pay his debts.[87] The total annual charge on the estate in November 1892 was £4,290, and Jamieson stressed that under current management no part of this sum could be recouped from the estate. He estimated that the property needed an injection of almost $65,000 to make it viable.[88]

In January 1893, two months after Jamieson submitted his report, MacKay died suddenly. Coutts Marjoribanks proved to be a poor manager at Coldstream, and Jamieson laid some of the blame for the early failures, particularly in the management of stock, at his feet. Remembered as 'quite a gay blade', Coutts was more interested in breaking horses than in the business management of the ranch.[89] Not only was Coutts inexperienced, but his incautious generosity (similar to that of his brother-in-law) led him to employ too many workmen at excessive wages which were much higher than those paid on other properties in the area. Employees who were imported straight from Scotland caused friction when they failed to adapt readily to the new conditions and Jamieson strongly advised Lord Aberdeen to discontinue this practice until his affairs had been brought into better order:

I would venture very respectfully to warn Lord and Lady Aberdeen against as yet 'sending out' more people from Scotland in their own employment. For the present the position of matters at Coldstream is too critical to be trifled with: strangers coming out—especially men and women of mature years cannot at once assimilate themselves to a condition of matters totally different from all their associations and habits, and they must introduce elements of difficulty if not discord which ought, at the earlier stages of such an enterprise to be avoided ... Let Coldstream be brought into thorough order, with its own staff thoroughly organised, and working well, economically and harmoniously; and then draft out persons from the old Country who will find the system and machinery in full working order and will thus come easily to fill their proper place in its economy.[90]

The jam factory at Vernon was built before its time and was not wanted by the fruit growers who preferred to send out fresh produce on the CPR. Jamieson warned that the growers would probably find it more profitable to sell the fruit green than to have it preserved, and he also questioned the economic viability of a jam factory established as Lord Aberdeen's private property. His offer to buy their fruit direct for preserving would be valued by the growers only if he offered a higher price than the market value, and Jamieson felt that Lord Aberdeen's attempts to boost fruit farming should have been directed more to stimulating growers to help themselves.

To make matters worse, the jam factory's first manager, chosen by Lord

5   Coutts Marjoribanks.

6   First passenger train to Vernon, 14 October 1891.

7   Guisachan Ranch.

8   The Jam Factory, Vernon.

Aberdeen, was singularly unsuitable. Having advertised the post unsuccessfully in Scotland, Aberdeen eventually hired an itinerant tradesman, W. F. Krauss, who claimed to have managed fruit processing plants in several countries. He was employed on six months' probation and promised a free, furnished house, a salary of $17.50 a week and a share of the profits once production began. His lack of principle was clearly demonstrated even before he took up his post when he suggested a fraudulent scheme whereby Lord Aberdeen could fulfil his otherwise impossible ambition of exhibiting the produce of his jam factory at the World Fair in Chicago in 1893. Krauss suggested that preserves bearing an 'Okanagan Valley Preserving Works' label should be made ready in Scotland, and then be shipped out through British Columbia to Chicago. Lord Aberdeen refused to countenance any such deception, and although he still agreed—most unwisely—to employ Krauss, he inserted in his contract a stipulation that his manager was to engage in no such underhand practices.[91] G. A. Jamieson strongly opposed the employment of Krauss, whom he regarded as a scoundrel. This impression was confirmed when he discovered that the manager had personally pocketed $5,000 in return for a promise to the inhabitants of Okanagan Mission (near Kelowna) that the jam factory would be built there instead of at Vernon. He was also burdening his employer with huge debts. Not only was he personally extravagant (living in hotels while he furnished his free house elaborately at Lord Aberdeen's expense) but he ordered large consignments of implements and machinery for the new factory to be shipped out to Vernon from Britain. His wife, meanwhile, had apparently tried (unsuccessfully) to compromise Coutts Marjoribanks during a visit to Coldstream. For all these misdeeds Krauss was dismissed by George MacKay in December 1892 before his six-month probationary period had expired.

In response to the early failures and criticisms attempts were made to improve the management of Lord Aberdeen's British Columbian interests. After MacKay's death a new administrator, Edward Kelly, was appointed to oversee the estates while W. C. Ricardo, who took over from Marjoribanks at Coldstream in 1895, attempted to introduce a number of improvements on that property. Kelly reduced the herd, planted hops and fruit and began the irrigation works which successful fruit growing demanded. Although conditions did improve, almost two years after his first report Jamieson was still disappointed that Guisachan had not yet matched up to his expectations; crops there had failed repeatedly because of the alkaline soil, the choice of wrong varieties of fruit and the waterlogging of trees planted too close to the lake. On 3 September 1894 Jamieson wrote gloomily to Lord Aberdeen about the conflicting reports he had received of Guisachan's prospects:

> I don't know which to believe; it looked lovely when I was there; I preferred it infinitely to Coldstream; now I fear that it turns out that the soil is so alkaline as to be unfit for the growth of several kinds of vegetation.[92]

Lord Aberdeen took Jamieson's advice that he should not accept such a negative verdict without seeking an expert independent opinion, and in

December 1894 another adviser, Thomas Cunningham from the Provincial Department of Agriculture, reported at length to the Earl on the prospects of all his British Columbia interests.[93]

As far as Guisachan was concerned, Cunningham agreed with Jamieson that it was a much more valuable property than Coldstream, enjoying a better climate and producing better clover than the land around Vernon. Indeed, he believed that there were few bodies of land in British Columbia which offered such a good climate and declared that he had seen hundreds of valuable farms in Oregon and California with the same kind of alkaline soil. He was convinced that 'blundering mismanagement' rather than any defect in the land itself had caused Guisachan's crop failures and loss of money. He reiterated Jamieson's complaint that fruit trees, often of the wrong varieties, had been planted haphazardly in unsuitable locations and he criticised the 'ignorant butchery' of the person who had pruned them. He was particularly critical of Lord Aberdeen's decision to let out the work of tree planting by contract, since this was a skilled operation, not to be entrusted to anyone who had a financial interest in hastening the work. Stock had also been supplied in this way and Cunningham recommended that the cattle and pigs, which were of inferior quality, should be cleared off the ranch and replaced by well-bred stock.[94]

Several parties had already advised Lord Aberdeen to sell Guisachan, but Cunningham had confidence in its future prospects and believed that if his recommendations were followed it would eventually make better returns than any ranch in the whole Okanagan Valley. He not only advised Lord Aberdeen to retain Guisachan, but also suggested that he buy an extra 100 acres of well wooded land in the vicinity, for about $1 per acre, and promised to buy this land from him at any time if he later considered it to be a bad investment. He recommended the use of a subsoil plough to aerate the ground and arranged to consult his friends in Oregon and California as to the best methods for growing fruit in alkaline soil conditions.[95]

Cunningham was less enthusiastic about the situation at Coldstream. Like Jamieson, he thought too much money had been paid for this property, only one third of which was cultivable.[96] Here too trees had been badly pruned and mistakes had been made by the planting of inferior stock and the choice of unsuitable locations.[97] A serious lack of water meant that sheep, which might otherwise have been profitably grazed on the hill areas, would be an extremely expensive investment. Horse breeding could have been carried on more economically, but prices in this market had dropped to such an extent that Cunningham hesitated to recommend it.[98]

By the time Cunningham made his report Lord Aberdeen had begun to sell off the low-lying, cultivable part of the Coldstream estate in forty and fifty acre plots in the hope of making a quick—and much-needed—profit and of attracting a community of gentlemen farmers to the area. It was a policy opposed by the overseer, Edward Kelly, who thought that Lord Aberdeen should instead be patient and wait for the fruit and hop crops to bring in the profits; he was confident that the estate would eventually recoup both the initial purchase money and all that had since been spent on it many times

9 Coldstream Ranch.

over.[99] Thomas Cunningham also believed that, given good management, Coldstream could probably recover its losses, and he was equally opposed to selling off the best arable land at what he regarded as a ridiculously low price.[100] He acknowledged Lord Aberdeen's noble intention in offering the plots for sale, but argued that his hope of attracting desirable settlers to the Okanagan was unrealistic. Even if Lord Aberdeen had been able to select the initial purchasers himself, he would have no guarantee that they would remain in an area where 'changes are rapid ... and failures are frequent',[101] and he feared that these purchasers would become less agreeable as they became more independent. He reminded Lord Aberdeen that the best service he could render the area was to make a financial success of his own investment and he urged him to withdraw from sale those plots which had been set aside in such a central, strategically vital part of the estate. Cunningham declared that even the offer of as much as $100 per acre would not have tempted him to dispose of such valuable land, located on the stream, control of which was essential to the successful operation of the whole estate.

Part of Cunningham's task was to inspect the adjoining Kalamalka estate, which was for sale, and advise Lord Aberdeen on its purchase. He reported that it was a 'most valuable' property, with good soil, and well watered, containing the mouth of the strategically important Coldspring stream.[102] If Lord Aberdeen intended (as Cunningham hoped he did) to make his future home in the area, this property would be of much more use to him than to anyone else, and indeed was essential to give him control of the shore line of Long Lake.[103] The vendor was asking $60 per acre, but Cunningham warned Lord Aberdeen against spending more money unnecessarily when there had been such wastage at Coldstream, and suggested that an offer of $40 or less per acre, or a lump sum of $13,000 in cash, would be accepted.[104] A day later he wrote again to Lord Aberdeen, admitting that he had possibly overestimated the value of Kalamalka in his eagerness to secure more satisfactory boundaries for Coldstream through its purchase, and suggested that he offer instead a lump sum of $11,000.

Cunningham believed that if his recommendations were followed the Coldstream estate could become economically viable. On 11 December 1894 he wrote to Lord Aberdeen:

> I have no anxiety about the future, if your Lordship will introduce the necessary reforms in the conduct of the farms, but there must be very radical changes, and a definite policy adopted,—drifting and hoping will not win success. There must be definite aims, and every man connected with your estate must be made to understand them, and to take as much interest as if all depended on his individual exertions.

It was important that Lord Aberdeen forbid his employees at both Coldstream and Guisachan to speak disparagingly of the prospects of either ranch, and it was also essential that employees' wages be reduced. Contrary to the emigration agents' claims of plentiful work at high wages throughout British Columbia, both Kelly and Cunningham pointed out that there were

10   Lord Aberdeen and Edward Kelly at Coldstream.

thousands of unemployed men on the Pacific coast on the point of starvation
who would gladly accept farm labouring work in the Okanagan at $4 a
week with board and lodging; and Cunningham further suggested that Lord
Aberdeen should adopt branches of farming which required the least labour.
Barley crops should be planted at Coldstream, and drastic improvements
introduced in cattle breeding. Some investment in dairying might also be
profitable, since a friend of Cunningham, who farmed on the Cariboo road
on land 1,500 feet higher than Coldstream, and with a much inferior climate,
was barely able to meet the heavy demand for his butter at never less than
30 cents per pound. Cunningham also advised Lord Aberdeen not to dispose
of the premature and unsuccessful jam factory in Vernon, since a need for it
might arise in the future.[105]
    Provided that steps were taken to produce suitable and marketable com-
modities, Cunningham felt that Lord Aberdeen need have no fear for the
future of British Columbian farming. Given the small area of good land in
proportion to the 'sea of mountains' in the province, it was clear that his
agricultural land would one day be very valuable indeed. The area was filling

up and as Cunningham pointed out, 'We are not buying for to-day or for ourselves, but for our children. A country with such a climate will not be at a discount for very long'.[106] Cunningham was anxious that Lord Aberdeen should prosper, partly in order to vindicate his own belief in the prospects of Guisachan and Coldstream against the pessimism of many of his contemporaries. He also felt Lord Aberdeen had been unfairly treated in the initial purchase of these properties,[107] but more importantly he maintained that his success would be of provincial importance and would have far-reaching effects on the development of British Columbian agriculture.

Cunningham's optimism was seemingly misplaced, since in December 1895 an expert from the Government Experimental Farm at Ottawa, Professor Saunders, was employed to try to ascertain the reasons for continuing failures at Guisachan and Coldstream.[108] The following summer fruit and hops from Coldstream were still fetching far below the expected prices; forty acres of the estate had now been planted with hops, which were fetching only 13 cents per pound instead of the 25 cents needed to cover working expenses.[109] Ten years later 120 acres had been given over to hop growing, 250 acres to orchards and 1,200 acres to cereals, potatoes and hay. A further 1,220 acres were given over to timber, and the ranch also supported 900 head of cattle and 200 pigs, as well as some poultry and dairy stock. The annual labour bill was about $43,000 (£8,700).[110] In pursuit of success more and more cattle range was converted to orchards, but this policy demanded an outlay for irrigation and fencing that became intolerable when there was no corresponding improvement in profits. As Lady Aberdeen wrote later:

> the years came and went, and the golden age predicted always receded, and always more capital was called for, so as not to lose what had already been invested ... Neither the purchase money nor all that was spent on development ever came back, and the results of our investment in B.C. have been very sad.[111]

After more than a decade of deficits Lord Aberdeen sold Guisachan in 1903 and incorporated his remaining properties under the name of 'The Coldstream Estate Company Limited' with shareholders from South-East Scotland and Sussex. If the subdivision of land into orchards were to continue, a considerable injection of capital was required to expand the essential irrigation project begun in 1893. With the extra capital obtained in 1903 the irrigation system was extended and a further 4,000 acres were subdivided and offered for sale as orchard lots. For about fourteen years Lord Aberdeen remained a major shareholder of the Coldstream Estate Company, along with James Buchanan, later Lord Woolavington of Petworth, Sussex (who already owned property at Lavington in the North Okanagan). Aberdeen and Buchanan formed the White Valley Irrigation and Power Company for control and ownership of their irrigation works. In a system which served other properties than the Coldstream ranch and which by 1907 had cost approximately £20,000, they constructed canals along the north and south boundaries of the Coldstream valley to carry the water from their holding reservoirs at Lake Aberdeen and Lake Haddo. By 1913 a total of 2,375 acres

11   After a hunting trip, Guisachan.

of subdivided Coldstream land had been sold at an average price of $149 per acre, to English, Scottish and Canadian settlers. In 1921 the Coldstream Estate Company was dissolved. Lord Woolavington became the sole owner of the estate and Lord Aberdeen's involvement with farming in British Columbia came to an end.

What went wrong with Lord Aberdeen's promising investments? Perhaps some of the setbacks he suffered were the inevitable consequences of pioneering a new type of agriculture in an unfamiliar environment. In introducing commercial fruit farming to the Okanagan Valley he was confronted by a host of unforeseen problems, which were often only gradually overcome by trial and error. Unsuitable varieties of trees were planted, often in unsuitable locations where the soil was deficient or subject to waterlogging or inadequate irrigation. Some orchards were ruined by frosts, while others fell victim to sudden and unexpected blights. Some trees died inexplicably, but at Guisachan in particular most of the early orchards were lost within four years of planting largely because of the insufficient care and attention paid to the young trees. Lord Aberdeen's own naivety, inexperience and enforced and prolonged absences from his property were compounded by the mistakes made by his employees and advisers, who sometimes had conflicting ideas on how the estate should be managed. While Lord Aberdeen was selling off small fruit farms at what both Edward Kelly and Thomas Cunningham thought were ridiculously low prices, he was spending vast sums of money in replacing dead orchards and extending his irrigation systems, resulting in regular deficits rather than surpluses on both his properties.

But Lord Aberdeen was not the only pioneer to experience difficulties in farming on the 'dry belt' of British Columbia. Other settlers who followed him, often to the same area, did not always learn from his mistakes. They generally had the capital but not always the necessary skills; some planted their orchards in valleys with poor irrigation and transportation facilities, or too far north, where frosts devastated the yield, and several of these pioneers later abandoned their lands.[112] Once the fruit farmers began to send their produce outside British Columbia they had to face marketing problems, although in the pre-war period these difficulties were not so great as the problems of internal competition and improper distribution which were to plague the industry after 1920. The fruit growers could not reduce the price of their produce in external markets because of the high costs of production and transportation over extensive and difficult terrain. In the late 1890s the growers were helped by the demand for food provided by the Klondyke gold rush, and by an agreement which the provincial government negotiated with the CPR, whereby concessionary freight rates were allowed to Okanagan fruit so that it would not be at a disadvantage in competing with American produce in the prairie market. In 1903 a more distant export trade with Britain was initiated, but until 1912 the prairies remained the most profitable outlet for British Columbia fruit. In that year, however, the industry experienced its first real downturn, when after a bumper harvest in British Columbia, Washington and Oregon, the market was glutted and prices plummeted. The growers, whose capital was committed to their land and to the care of immature, non-producing orchards, could not weather the new market conditions and began to fall heavily into debt. In 1913, largely on the initiative of W. C. Ricardo, about 1,100 growers agreed to form a co-operative selling and distribution agency, the Okanagan United Growers Ltd. Through this Association the Okanagan growers managed to dominate the prairie market until 1921, when problems of excess production and internal competition began to reappear, showing the urgent need to create a more effective co-operative agency to market the region's fruit in the post-war period.[113]

Many immigrant farmers were deceived by the enthusiastic agents who persuaded them to come to British Columbia. They often failed to realise that fruit growing could not be prosecuted successfully all over the dry belt, and were equally unaware that it was a much more onerous occupation than the optimistic land agents and guidebooks indicated in their propaganda. C. W. Holliday, a Londoner who ranched in the Okanagan between 1889 and 1936, claimed that the real-estate agents, led by George MacKay, fraudulently depicted fruit farming as a 'lotus-eating existence in which you idled away the sunny hours while the dollars grew on the trees'.[114] Too many naive British immigrants believed these assurances that fruit cultivation required no effort on their part. Many of them, according to Holliday, purchased twenty-acre fruit lots on the Coldstream estate, 'and on these they built themselves little bungalows, planted fruit trees, and then proceeded to enjoy life with tennis, shooting and fishing, and all the social frivolities of Vernon, mistakenly imagining they could carry on thus indefinitely and that fruit trees took care of themselves'.[115] Perhaps these settlers should not be criticised too harshly, for they were generally acting on the land agents' misleading promises, although they often failed to alter their ways when they discovered that the reality of fruit farming did not correspond to their expectations. Certainly all too few heeded the advice of J. T. Bealby, a successful fruit farmer in the Kootenay region:

> Orcharding is a delightful occupation; but it is not an indolent life. No man can sit on his verandah all day and expect his ranch to buy him bread and cheese. Fruit-growing means work—solid, hard work—work from the first glinting of the dawn to the creeping up of midnight. It means an unceasing vigilance. It calls for the constant, daily exercise of a high intelligence. Once again, it calls for work, long and strenuous hours—at all events, thoughout the summer ... Nor will this imperative call to work by any means cease when you have guided your orchard through its childhood years. Even when it begins to repay you for your love and unremitting care, you will still find that it makes no light demands upon your energies. Spraying will have to be done, once, twice, perhaps three times, during the spring and summer. The soil will have to be kept free from weeds, and the surface maintained in a state of fine pulverisation. The fruit will have to be thinned, gathered, graded, packed, and loaded up for market. In fact, if you grow fruit that is worth growing, you must prepare yourself to lead the strenuous life.[116]

Most aristocratic fruit growers intended to employ hired labour, but this was often difficult and expensive to obtain. There was no ready supply of native workers in the interior of British Columbia and as Thomas Cunningham reminded Lord Aberdeen in 1894, hired labourers were often a costly waste of money. Yet Lord Aberdeen was also advised against importing Scottish employees who were unable to adapt to a new location and a new type of work. In fact, the inability—or refusal—to adapt to their new circumstances was a major cause of the failure of so many 'gentlemen' settlers in British Columbia. They came to Canada 'dominated by the pretensions and mores of the English middle class and quick to assume that what was different was inferior'.[117] With the aim of recreating the society they had left behind they formed insular, self-contained communities, in which they mixed only with those who shared their own background and interests. But they were 'players without most of their props',[118] living in communities which were socially and economically isolated from their surroundings. By refusing to acknowledge their need of expert advice to cope with the problems of pioneering and to acquire the skills necessary for successful fruit farming, they were virtually ensuring that most of their settlements would not survive in the long run.

The complete extinction of the settlement at Walhachin, for instance, within little more than a decade of its formation, was brought about by a combination of the settlers' insularity and refusal to adapt to a demanding new environment, their misplaced confidence in the promoters' promises, a lack of commitment to the interests of the settlers on the part of the British Columbia Development Association and the natural drawbacks of the site. Despite its proximity to the Okanagan Valley, Walhachin did not have the soil, climate or annual rainfall necessary to permit profitable large-scale fruit farming. Lacking the proximity of a lake to moderate temperatures, the area was vulnerable to severe frosts, so that only the hardiest fruits could survive. The vital irrigation system was poorly designed and hastily and badly con- structed by the Development Company, which was more concerned to make rapid profits for its shareholders than to ensure the long-term viability of the settlement. The 127-mile network was inefficient, impossible to maintain and soon became an expensive liability.[119] As early as 1912 shareholders began to see Walhachin as a poor investment and became less and less willing to pour capital into the project. Control of the settlement fell into the hands of the debt-ridden Sixth Marquis of Angelsey, a development which did little to inspire confidence among absentee investors; he appointed an inept manager at Walhachin, who was incapable of persuading the colonists to set aside their selfish (and often unattainable) ambitions and work together for the good of the community. Most of these colonists were ill-prepared for the difficulties of pioneer fruit farming. Some had come out to live the leisurely lives of semi-retired gentlemen farmers, on the strength of the promoters' assurances that Walhachin offered the ideal opportunity for that lifestyle. Others had been sent out in despair by their families from a background of personal scandal or expulsion from school or the military or civil service. They rapidly tired not only of a life which involved hard and continuous work but of a society where men vastly outnumbered women, a problem which was compounded by their self-imposed isolation from neighbouring communities.

Further east, the limitations of Robert Randolph Bruce's settlement at Windermere also became apparent before long. Insufficient work had been done on the site before the first settlers arrived in Spring 1912, so that many of the new arrivals had to be accommodated in tents until their houses were built. Among these settlers were Jack and Daisy Phillips, who came to Windermere from England in April 1912. In letters home they blamed their problems on the colony's promoters being 'too greedy and trying to build and do much more than they can possibly finish', as well as on misleading promotional literature.[120] By 1914 a Settlers' Association had been formed to oppose Bruce and his Columbia Valley Irrigated Fruit Lands Company and to press for compensation 'because our cisterns leak and we have paid too high a price for our land'.[121] For many of the Walhachin and Windermere colonists, and others in similar situations, the outbreak of the First World War seemed to offer a good opportunity to escape from a stultifying economic

GHOST OF WALHACHIN

Here bloomed a "Garden of Eden"!
The sagebrush desert changed to
orchards through the imagination
and industry of English settlers
during 1907–14. Then the men
left to fight - and die - for king
and country. A storm ripped out
the vital irrigation flume. Now
only ghosts of flume, trees, and
homes remain to mock this
once thriving settlement.

DEPARTMENT OF
RECREATION &   CONSERVATION

12   Walhachin today.

and social environment, and gentlemen farmers rushed to enlist from all over British Columbia.

The First World War was in fact a major watershed in the general history of settlement in British Columbia, marking the end of the era of the 'gentleman emigrant'. Capital from Britain, which had financed many pioneer fruit growers, was no longer available after the war broke out, and the orchards and irrigation works were abandoned as owners and their employees left for the front. Some survivors returned and tried unsuccessfully to revive their old lifestyles in a radically altered economic and social environment, but others had no desire to return. By 1919 the colony at Walhachin had virtually ceased to exist, while others collapsed soon afterwards in the face of the economic depression.

It was at this time, in 1921, that Lord Aberdeen relinquished his interest in British Columbian fruit farming. Yet, unlike many of his contemporaries, his failure was not complete. Despite his lack of personal success he still made a positive contribution to the development of the Okanagan Valley, and he was long remembered in the area as the major pioneer who broke up the big cattle ranches, introduced irrigation and laid the foundations of future prosperity. Coldstream was the largest and best-known property in the valley, and was for a long time regarded as the 'demonstration farm' for the whole district. Here he planted the first commercial orchards in the North Okanagan, and his continuing sale of small fruit farms and his use of irrigation brought about the first major influx of population to the area. Irrigation was essential to the development of orchards, and when Lord Aberdeen brought the first such scheme to the North Okanagan it made possible the more extensive subdivision of ranch land for this purpose.[122] The owners of other large ranches in the area began to follow his example and the growing population in the prairie provinces provided a ready market for these new fruit growers.[123]

Lord Aberdeen was always convinced that the area had benefitted from the disappearance of these large cattle ranches which had deterred settlement. His own enthusiasm for peopling the Okanagan was partly responsible for, and was certainly boosted by the subsequent campaigns of land companies, the provincial government and the CPR to attract population to the valley. His example helped to bring about the settlement not only of native Canadians (mainly from Manitoba and the North-West Territories) but also of wealthy British emigrants, including a significant number of Scots, many of them from Aberdeenshire.[124] During a visit to the Okanagan in 1907 John Murray Gibbon commented on the vital part being played by these Scottish farmers in the development of the fruit industry and commended Lord Aberdeen who, 'in the face of ridicule and early failures, has turned ordinary ranching country, hitherto considered only fit for grazing, into magnificent orchard land'.[125] A little earlier Lord Grey (then Governor-General of Canada) had visited Coldstream and had subsequently written to Lord Aberdeen, congratulating him on his achievements:

> I have paid two visits to your fruit ranch, and have been all over it, and am delighted with it all—with the appearance of the orchards, with the valley, with the admirable methods of management, and above all with the men in charge, and the general atmosphere of the whole place. Ricardo and Palmer both impressed me most favourably, and the men they have selected for subordinate but responsible positions, at least those I saw, appeared to be the very men for their respective jobs. I drove ... about seven or eight miles up the Valley to the ditch, which you are constructing ... and which, when finished, will provide a living for at least two thousand additional souls in your Valley ... You and Lady Aberdeen have every reason to be proud of what you have done, and I told the people of Vernon that I envied you the halo which sits round both your heads because of the splendid pioneer spade work you have done.[126]

While Lord Aberdeen himself incurred severe financial losses as a result of his British Columbian investments, it is clear that the Okanagan Valley—and indeed the province at large—profited greatly from his influence. He was one of the major developers of the area who had changed the direction of its economy from extensive cattle ranching to intensive fruit farming. In this way he had promoted immigration and employment, which were also helped by his construction of irrigation systems and ancillary workplaces. He and other contemporary developers succeeded in attracting the kind of population they wanted—so that the proportion of British settlers in the Okanagan grew from fifty-one per cent of the total population in 1891 to eighty-one per cent in 1911.[127] Neighbouring ranchers followed his lead in selling off small plots and providing facilities to help small fruit farmers establish themselves. In 1906 Olston Black commended Lord Aberdeen's success in attracting desirable settlers to the area by these measures:

> Thus there is growing up in the Okanagan Valley a community which will preserve the traditions and refinements of the old land while adopting the industry of the new; a community which owes its origin, as it is likely to owe its success, to the enterprise of Lord Aberdeen in establishing the Coldstream Ranche.[128]

It is ironic that the establishment of the Okanagan as Canada's major fruit-growing region was due largely to the initiative of this pioneer, yet at the expense of his own personal investments in the area and to the severe financial embarrassment of his estates in North-East Scotland, which supplied much of the capital for his British Columbian experiment.

NOTES

1) See Patrick A. Dunae, *Gentlemen Emigrants: from the British Public Schools to the Canadian Frontier* (Vancouver, 1981), pp. 49-50. Dunae maintains, however, that the real cause of the problem was the expansion of the public school system in England, which produced far too many youths who were 'ready for anything and fit for nothing'. See also report of the Canadian High Commissioner in Dept of Agriculture, *annual report on immigration, 1882*, in which he claimed that the professions 'are quite overdone, and gentlemen are looking round anxiously for other openings for their sons. The competition for the army is very keen, and the unsuccessful candidates numerous; and what becomes of those who have qualified for the other professions open to young men of education, is a problem difficult to solve'.

2) David Mitchell & Dennis Duffy (eds), *Bright sunshine and a brand new country: recollections of the Okanagan Valley 1890-1914* (Victoria, BC, 1979: Sound Heritage, vol. VIII, no. 3), p. 32.

3) See, for instance, W. Feilding, 'What shall I do with my son?' in *Nineteenth Century*, vol. 13 (Apr. 1883), pp. 578-86; W. Feilding, 'Whither shall I send my son?' in *ibid*, vol. 14 (July 1883), pp. 65-77; 'Colonial training for gentlemen's sons' in *Chambers'* (24 Oct. 1885), pp. 683-6; 'Colonial farm pupils' in *ibid* (20 Feb. 1886), pp. 118-9; G. J. Webster, 'Ranching in the Canadian North-West' in *ibid* (17 June 1905), pp. 453-7; and 'Cultured colonisation' in the *West. Rev.*, vol. 142 (1894), pp. 673-80.

4) *Chambers' Journal* on one occasion recommended emigration to South America, however, on the grounds that most British colonies were suffering from the same problems as the mother country in terms of excessive competition in overcrowded professions. (See 'Upper class emigration' in *Chambers'* (25 Apr. 1896) pp. 257-9). W. Feilding too, although he advocated the establishment of self-contained, 'aristocratic' colonies in Canada, preferred settlement in Australia (*Nineteenth Century*, vol. 14 (July 1883) pp. 65-77).

5) Paddy Acland, quoted in *Bright sunshine and a brand new country*, p. 32.

6) James Aspdin, *Our Boys: what shall we do with them? Or emigration the real solution of the problem, showing how youths and young men can be put into the way of obtaining a profitable living for the present and a competence for the future* (Manchester, 1890).

7) See 'Farm-Pupils in the Colonies' in *MacMillan's Magazine*, vol. LXII (July 1890), pp. 193-8. The article was anonymous, but Patrick Dunae attributes it to Bradley. (Dunae, *Gentlemen emigrants*, pp. 174-5).

8) 'Farm-Pupils in the Colonies', p. 195.

9) Bob Gamman, quoted in *Bright sunshine and a brand new country*, p. 34.

10) See, for instance, *AJ*, 28 Nov. 1890, 1 Jan. 1894 and 2 Apr. 1896 for the publication of warnings issued by the Canadian High Commission and the Emigrants' Information Office.

11) See Dunae, *Gentlemen emigrants*, p. 196.

12) £108 for the first year and £126 for the second year. (Dunae, *Gentlemen emigrants*, p. 201). One of the students at Hollesley Bay who later went to Canada was the younger son of the fifteenth Earl of Elphinstone, the Aberdeenshire laird. He acquired 9,000 acres near Virden, Manitoba, where he built a big house and tried unsuccessfully to establish two tenant farms. After abandoning this venture in the late 1890s he tried his hand at the Klondyke goldfields—also unsuccessfully—before returning to Britain.

13) The Headmasters' Conference dated from 1869 and the British Public Schools Association of Canada from 1904. Both organisations were concerned about the welfare and reputation of 'gentlemen emigrants'. The Public Schools Emigration League ceased to operate during the First World War and when it was revived in 1920 it was renamed the Public Schools Employment Bureau, which was concerned mainly with helping its clients to find work in Britain.

14) The North of Scotland College of Agriculture in Aberdeen was founded in 1904, but it was not until after the First World War that it took steps to train students in colonial agriculture. Even then, the 'Planters' Certificate' that was introduced in 1919 was aimed mainly at those who were going to take up appointments on rubber or tea estates, as well as the more general category who intended 'to proceed to Agricultural pursuits in the Colonies'. (See *North of Scotland College of Agriculture: Minutes and Proceedings*, 1917-18, pp. 168-9).

15) Application was to be made to R. G. Anderson of Reith and Anderson, cattle salesmen, Kittybrewster, Aberdeen.

16) *AJ*, 12 Jan. 1887.

17) *Ibid*, 20 Sept. 1889.

18) *Ibid*, 24 Nov. 1899.

19) PAC, RG 76, C-10294-5, vol. 405, file 590687.

20) Dunae, *Gentlemen emigrants*, pp. 87-105 and G. J. Webster, 'Ranching in the Canadian North-West' in *Chambers'* (17 June 1905), pp. 453-7. The Alberta ranching industry began in the mid-1870s near the North-West Mounted Police post at Fort MacLeod, but really took off during the 1880s and 1890s, as an offshoot of the cattle boom in the Western USA. The Dominion government offered leasing arrangements which aimed to attract large investors who could run big herds, leading to the creation of huge cattle empires. Ranchers could lease up to 100,000 acres of range land cheaply on condition that they acquired ten head of cattle for every 100 acres leased within three years of taking out the lease. They were also entitled to buy land within this tract for use as a home ranch at $2 per acre.

21) See below, pp. 117, 127 and 134, and Dunae, *Gentlemen emigrants*, p. 104. Until 1905 (when it was elevated to the status of a dominion province) Alberta was just one of the four main territories making up the vast North-West Territories, the others being Assiniboia, Athabasca and Saskatchewan.

22) *AJ*, 4 Apr. 1889.

23) See below, p. 118 & n. 67—John Will of Methlick later moved to British Columbia to work for Lord Aberdeen. For further details of Lister-Kaye's colonisation scheme, see James Hedges, *Building the Canadian West*, pp. 49-50; and PP 1906 [Cd. 2978], LXXVI, 533: *Report of the departmental committee appointed to consider Mr Rider Haggard's report on agricultural settlement in British Colonies*, vol. 1, Appendix XIII: memorandum by Sir John Lister-Kaye.

24) Report for week ending 10 Sept. 1910.

25) *Ibid.*

26) *Roll of the Graduates of the University of Aberdeen 1860-1900*, compiled by W. Johnston (Aberd., 1906) and *Roll of the Graduates of the University of Aberdeen 1901-1925*, compiled by Theodore Watt (Aberd., 1935).

27) *Record of the Arts Class, 1864-1868*, ed. W. S. Bruce (Aberd., 1912); *1870-1874*, ed. James Smith & J. F. Cruickshank (1896); *1878-1882*, ed. R. S. Kemp, R. A. Lendrum & J. S. Shewan (1927); *1880-1884*, ed. Henry Cowie (1923); *1881-1885*, ed. John Minto & W. G. Tulloch (1908); *1884-1888*, ed. Howard Gray & J. M. Bulloch (1938); *1888-1892*, ed. William Garden (1902); *1901-1905*, ed. Theodore Watt & J. M. Robertson (1951); and *1909-1912/13*, ed. J. Dunbar & William Taylor (1959).

28) Eight emigrants went to Quebec, four to Nova Scotia, three to Newfoundland and one to New Brunswick. Two of the pre-1905 emigrants went to the 'North-West Territories' (later Alberta/Saskatchewan) and eleven went to unspecified destinations. Nineteen of the 148 emigrants to Canada lived in more than one province. On each occasion their first destination has been taken as the province of settlement.

29) *Roll of Graduates 1860-1900*, p. 59.

30) *Ibid*, p. 164.

31) *Ibid*, p. 257.

32) *Ibid*, p. 461. Margaret Ormsby comments that Rose had a flourishing orchard at Kelowna in the early 1890s. (Ormsby, 'Fruit marketing in the Okanagan Valley of British Columbia' in *Agricultural History*, vol. 9 (1935), p. 81). George Rose's arrival was intimated by the *Vernon News* on 27 August 1891, when it reported that 'Mr Geo. C. Rose, MA of Aberdeen University, arrived on his way to the Mission, where he will enter into fruit culture extensively. He will reside in Dan Nicholson's house, adjoining which he has purchased 50 acres from G. G. MacKay'. See also Ursula Surtees, *Sunshine and Butterflies: a short history of early fruit ranching in Kelowna* (Kelowna, 1979), pp. 11-14; and 'Daily Journal of the Rose Brothers, 1893-5' (Kelowna Museum), which reflects the fairly leisurely, sporting life which the Rose brothers seem to have led at that time.

33) *Roll of Graduates, 1901-1925*, p. 117.

34) *Record of the Arts Class, 1864-1868*, pp. 80-1.

35) *Ibid, 1878-1882*, pp. 44-5. For other emigrants in farming or farm-related occupations, see *Roll of Graduates 1901-1925*, p. 221 (Gordon Grant), p. 372 (John MacLennan), p. 463 (Frank Oliver); and *Records of the Arts Class, 1884-1888*, p.50 (C. G. Ross).

36) Including fifteen women after 1900.

37) There were also three researchers, two journalists, two employees of the Hudson's Bay Company, one engineer, one policeman and one government employee, as well as twelve emigrants in unspecified occupations.

38) *AJ*, 30 May 1891.

39) Jean Barman, 'British Columbia's Gentlemen Farmers' in *History Today*, vol. 34 (Apr. 1984), p. 9. See also R. Cole Harris & Elizabeth Phillips (eds), *Letters*

from Windermere 1912-1914 (Vancouver, 1984), introduction, p. x: in the three decades preceding the First World War the upper and middle classes made up almost thirty per cent of British emigrants.

40)   *Canada's Western Heritage. British Columbia. Its Farms, Forests, Fisheries and Fruit* (1909). See PAC, RG 76, C-10621, vol. 530, file 803463.

41)   *Ibid*, p. 8.

42)   H. M. Murray's report to Clifford Sifton, Minister of the Interior, 29 Apr. 1897 (PAC, 7303, vol. 147, file 34873).

43)   A. G. Bradley, *Canada in the Twentieth Century* (London, 1905), p. 363.

44)   *Canada as it appeared to Scotch Agriculturists 1909-1910* (PAC, RG 76, C-10639, vol. 558, file 807176).

45)   *Ibid*, p. 24.

46)   J. S. Redmayne, *Fruit farming on the 'dry belt' of British Columbia* (London, 1912), p. 85.

47)   Pandosy (1824-1891) established a mission in the Okanagan in 1859, having spent the previous twelve years evangelising Indians in the Oregon Territory. He remained at the mission settlement he founded near Kelowna until his death in 1891. (George Woodcock, *Canada and the Canadians* (London, 1970), p. 109 and Paul M. Koroscil, 'A Canadian California' in *Horizon Canada*, vol. 3, no. 30 (Sept. 1985), pp. 710-15.

48)   For instance Cornelius O'Keefe, a disappointed goldseeker who became a drover. In 1867 he formed a partnership with two fellow drovers and established a ranch at the north end of Okanagan Lake. One partner dropped out four years later but the others expanded until by the 1890s they held 17,000 acres of land. The ranch was sold in 1907 to the Land and Agricultural Company of Canada, which was supported by Belgian investment. The Belgians had been attracted to the Okanagan by the publicity resulting from Lord Aberdeen's investments and their syndicate was the largest non-British development in the valley.

49)   See Paul M. Koroscil, 'Boosterism and the settlement process in the Okanagan Valley, British Columbia, 1890-1914' in Donald H. Akenson (ed.), *Canadian Papers in Rural History*, vol. V (Gananoque, Ont., 1986), pp. 86, 88. See also Margaret Ormsby, 'Fruit marketing in the Okanagan Valley', p. 81. Knox, the brother of one of Lord Aberdeen's Haddo tenants, had initially come to Canada to work on the farm of an uncle near Toronto, but had been lured west by the gold discoveries. (A. W. Gray, 'Arthur Booth Knox—pioneer rancher' in *Okanagan Historical Society Reports*, vol. 28 (1964), pp. 74-84).

50)   Redmayne, *Fruit farming on the 'dry belt'*, p. 25.

51)   *The Canadian Journal of Lady Aberdeen*, 30 Oct. 1894.

52)   As part of her convalescence after an illness, Lady Aberdeen chose to visit Canada with her husband in 1890, and they toured the Dominion from east to west. Lady Aberdeen's observations on the trip were recorded in a series of articles which she contributed to the *Onward and Upward* magazine (*Onward and Upward: The Journal of the Haddo House Association*, vol. I (1891), Aberd: Wylie & Son). The articles, entitled 'Through Canada with a Kodak', were later published separately in a book of the same name (Edin. 1893).

53)   The Journal of Lady Aberdeen, 1890-1899 (unpublished): entry for 14 Oct. 1890. (PAC, MG 27, C-1352 1L 1B5).

54)   *Ibid.*

55)   On their way to Vancouver in October 1890 Lord and Lady Aberdeen had met Coutts in Winnipeg, and Lady Aberdeen had expressed in her journal the hope that her brother would soon move north: 'To-night Coutts rejoiced our hearts

by turning up from Dakota ... He has had a bad time of it lately between droughts & losses of stock generally ... We are going to get Mr Clay to report on the possibility of selling the place which Coutts thinks would be cheap at 20,000 dollars, & then try to get Coutts over into Canada, into some more civilised part, probably Brit. Columbia.' (30 Oct. 1890).

56) Archie was taken on to the Governor-General's staff after it was discovered he was suffering from a progressive, and terminal, illness. He died in 1900, having been an invalid since 1897. (See *The Canadian Journal of Lady Aberdeen*, 14 Feb. 1894).

57) Lord Aberdeen chartered a special train for the occasion, which transported not only his own family but a number of other passengers who were going to the Agricultural Fair at Vernon. See *Through Canada with a Kodak*, p. 155.

58) *Ibid*, pp. 164-7.

59) Knox was in 1891 serving a term of imprisonment in Vancouver for burning a stack of hay. (See the Journal of Lady Aberdeen (unpublished): entry for 27 Oct. 1891).

60) The first settler at Coldstream was Captain (later Colonel) Charles Houghton, an Irishman who retired from the army in 1863 and came to British Columbia to take up a military grant. In May 1869 he relinquished his entire interest in the Coldstream property to his fellow Irish officers Charles and Forbes Vernon in return for a similar concession on their part, whereby they gave up their claims to a farm in the nearby Priest Valley in favour of Houghton. Forbes Vernon later became the sole owner of the Coldstream Ranch, after buying out his brother. He was also involved in government, entering the Provincial Legislature in 1875. From 1876 to 1878 and 1887 to 1894 he served as the Honorary Commissioner of Lands and Works and from 1895 to 1899 he was Agent-General for British Columbia, based in London. He also formed the Shuswap and Okanagan Railway Company which linked Vernon with the main line of the CPR at Sicamous in 1892. Arrangements for the sale of Coldstream by Vernon to Lord Aberdeen were made by George MacKay, who received commissions from both parties for his work. (See Koroscil, 'Boosterism and the settlement process', pp. 73-103; Jean Webber, 'Coldstream Municipality' in *Okanagan Historical Society Reports* (1951) pp. 77-85; and Diane Osborn, 'The Coldstream Ranch' in *ibid* (1958) pp. 118-21.

61) Koroscil, 'A Canadian California', p. 712.

62) Entry for 30 Oct. 1894. See also Doris Shackleton, 'Lord and Lady Aberdeen: Their Okanagan Ranches' in *The Beaver* (Autumn 1981), p. 17.

63) Arthur Knox's ranch near Kelowna, for instance, was purchased for $75,000 in 1904 by the Okanagan Fruit and Land Company. It was subsequently divided into parcels of one, two and five acres, which were offered for sale.

64) Quotation from *The Queen*, in Jean Webber, 'Coldstream Municipality', p. 78.

65) *AJ*, 7 Sept. 1907.

66) *Canada's Western Heritage*, p. 24.

67) See above, n. 23. John Will's wife died in 1891, leaving him with an infant daughter. In November 1891 he had an interview with Lord Aberdeen at Medicine Hat, and asked to be taken into his employment. At that time Will was employed as foreman on one of Sir John Lister-Kaye's farms in Saskatchewan, but was about to lose his job since this unprofitable farm was to be closed down.

68) R. M. Middleton (ed.), *The Journal of Lady Aberdeen: the Okanagan Valley in the Nineties* (Victoria, 1986), p. 51.

69) William Reid to James Reid of Backhill, Castle Fraser, 23 Sept. 1903, quoted in *AJ*, 24 Oct. 1903; see also *ibid*, 25 Aug. 1903, 25 Feb. 1904, 14 Oct. 1905, 19 June 1906, and Anne Pearson, *An early history of Coldstream and Lavington* (privately published, 1986). When Reid arrived by no means all the property was under cultivation, with only eighty acres in wheat and fifteen in oats. Hay had been cut on a further thirty acres.

70) *AJ*, 16 Mar. 1905. Among other references to North-East emigrants in the Okanagan in the *Aberdeen Journal* is an obituary notice on 28 October 1909 concerning James Cameron of Stonehaven, a gardener with the Summerland Trust Company, who was working there along with one of his six children, his wife and remaining family having stayed in Stonehaven.

71) *AJ*, 25 Feb. 1904.

72) Ormsby, 'Fruit marketing in the Okanagan Valley', p. 82.

73) Margaret Ormsby, 'Agricultural developments in British Columbia' in *Agricultural History*, vol. 19 (Jan. 1945), p. 13.

74) Bradley, *Canada in the Twentieth Century*, pp. 409-10.

75) See Olston Black, 'The Viceroy's Ranch: What Lord Aberdeen has done in the Canadian Far West' (1906), pp. 491-6; and *Canada*, 16 Feb. 1907. (NRA, survey no. 0055, Haddo House MSS: pamphlet box).

76) See Black, 'The Viceroy's Ranch'.

77) Redmayne, *Fruit farming on the 'dry belt'*, p. 27. J. H. Turner, the Agent-General for British Columbia, declared that in parts of the Okanagan Valley a gross profit of $500-600 per acre could be achieved (*ibid*, p. 8).

78) *Letters from Windermere*, introduction, pp. xiii-xiv.

79) 9 Jan., 13 Feb. 1912, 26 June 1913.

80) *AJ*, 9 Jan. 1912. Bruce's pamphlet had stated that a railway connection to the Canadian Pacific main line at Golden was 'virtually built' but in fact the branch line was not opened until 1917. (*Letters from Windermere*, introduction, p. xiv).

81) Letter dated 15 July 1913 from MacKay to W. D. Scott. (PAC, RG 76, C-10644, vol. 564, file 809010).

82) The Canadian Pacific Railway and the Canadian Northern Pacific Railway. See Dunae, *Gentlemen Emigrants*, pp. 162-70. See also Nelson Riis, 'The Walhachin Myth: a study of settlement abandonment' in *British Columbian Studies*, vol. 17 (Spring 1973), pp. 3-25.

83) Riis, 'The Walhachin Myth', p. 6.

84) See NRA, MS 0055/1/40, Bundle marked 'Coldstream 1894': memorandum by G. A. Jamieson on the property and affairs of the Earl of Aberdeen in British Columbia, 16 Nov. 1892. Unpublished archival material is used by permission of the Earl of Haddo.

85) *Ibid.* By 1892 Lord Aberdeen had spent a total of $44,972 on the estate but had received returns of only about $2,393.

86) *Ibid.* MacKay was in financial difficulties and was, Jamieson alleged, in the control of persons in the Okanagan who had only their own selfish interests to serve.

87) *Ibid.* See also Shackleton, 'Lord and Lady Aberdeen: Their Okanagan Ranches', pp. 14-16.

88) See Koroscil, 'Boosterism and the Settlement Process', p. 81.

89) See Jamieson's memorandum, 16 Nov. 1892 and also letter from Edward Kelly at Coldstream to Jamieson, 24 Jan. 1893 (MS 0055/1/40) asking him to send on the first financial statements that he had received from Coldstream and Guisachan so that he could see how the books were kept. All seemed to be in

chaos, and Marjoribanks knew nothing either about book-keeping or the practical management of the estate. See also Dunae, *Gentlemen Emigrants*, p. 104 and the comment of W. A. Middleton in Mitchell & Duffy, *Bright sunshine and a brand new country*, p. 12.

90) Jamieson's memorandum, 16 Nov. 1892.
91) Shackleton, 'Lord and Lady Aberdeen: Their Okanagan Ranches', p. 15.
92) MS 0055/1/40.
93) This correspondence is all contained in MSS 0055/2/62, Bundle 3.
94) See letters dated 5, 6, 7 Dec. 1894.
95) See letters dated 12, 13 Dec. 1894.
96) Letter dated 22 Dec. 1894.
97) Letter dated 3 Dec. 1894.
98) He suggested that Lord Aberdeen use his influence as Governor-General to try to secure a contract for supplying the army with horses.
99) In October 1894 Jamieson had suggested that Lord Aberdeen sell these plots on a system of deferred payments, so that purchasers could pay off their debts over a twenty-one year period. Kelly argued, however, that many people in Vernon would take up this offer, but would then be unable to make the repayments, and that Lord Aberdeen, as Governor-General, would be in an embarrassing position if he had to evict them.
100) A neighbour of Lord Aberdeen's had bought forty acres at $20 per acre. See letter dated 22 Dec. 1894.
101) Letter dated 10 Dec. 1894.
102) Letter dated 11 Dec. 1894.
103) Letter dated 7 Dec. 1894. Cunningham pointed out that in the future Long Lake might well become an upper class pleasure resort. A similar prediction was to be made regarding the Windermere Valley in 1913, when it was claimed that the sheer natural beauty of the area would make it the 'playground of Western America'. (*AJ*, 26 June 1913).
104) Letter dated 11 Dec. 1894.
105) See letters dated 12, 22 Dec. 1894. The jam factory was later incorporated into a cannery but was destroyed by fire in the 1930s. (Shackleton, 'Lord and Lady Aberdeen: Their Okanagan Ranches', p. 18).
106) Letter dated 12 Dec. 1894.
107) Cunningham reckoned that if he had met Lord Aberdeen in 1891, he could have saved him $70,000 on the price of the Coldstream estate.
108) Letter from Saunders to Lord Aberdeen, 19 Dec. 1895, enclosing report of his inspection of Guisachan and Coldstream. (MSS 0055/1/40).
109) The market for hops in Western America that year was so depressed that many growers in Washington and nearby states had not picked their crop at all.
110) See Olston Black, 'The Viceroy's Ranch'.
111) *'We Twa'; reminiscences of Lord and Lady Aberdeen*, pp. 90-1.
112) See J. L. Robinson (ed.), *British Columbia* (Toronto, 1972), p. 23.
113) After the war the fruit growers had the chronic problem of marketing excess production. For details see Ormsby, 'Fruit marketing in the Okanagan Valley', pp. 80-97; and 'Agricultural developments in British Columbia', pp. 11-20.
114) Charles W. Holliday, *The Valley of Youth* (Caldwell, Idaho, 1948), p. 180.
115) *Ibid*, p. 190.
116) J. T. Bealby, *Fruit Ranching in British Columbia* (London, 1909), pp. 194-5.
117) *Letters from Windermere*, introduction, p. xxii.
118) *Ibid*, p. xix.
119) Riis, 'The Walhachin Myth', pp. 11-14. For instance, since the ditches were

not lined with concrete, vast quantities of water seeped through the sandy, gravelly soil.

120) *Letters from Windermere*, pp. 81, 159. Letters dated 30 Aug. 1912 and 21 Feb. 1913.

121) *Ibid*, p. 208, letter dated 19 May 1914, from Daisy Phillips to her sister. Despite their early hardships, the Phillips' were in fact happy with their prospects at Windermere, but when war broke out they returned to England and Jack rejoined his old regiment. He died in 1915 as a result of wounds received at Ypres.

122) A few private irrigation systems had been constructed in the 1860s, and land companies had later provided similar facilities in their own territories. In the early twentieth century irrigation companies began to be established and shares in a distribution system were sold to farmers. (See Robinson, *British Columbia*, p. 23).

123) See Black, 'The Viceroy's Ranch' and *Canada*, 16 Feb. 1907.

124) In 1909, for instance, J. C. Dun-Waters, the former owner of the *Glasgow Herald*, bought a large estate at Short's Point on the west side of Okanagan Lake and named it Fintry. Entries in Lady Aberdeen's journal sometimes referred to emigrants from North-East Scotland. (See, for instance, entry for 23 Oct. 1891).

125) John Murray Gibbon, *The Scot in Canada: a run through the Dominion*, reprinted from *Aberdeen Daily Journal* (Aberd., 1907) p. 22.

126) Lord Grey to Lord Aberdeen, 8 Oct. 1906, enclosed in a letter from Lord Aberdeen to Howard Kennedy of *The Times*, 31 Oct. 1906; both contained in Earl of Aberdeen's correspondence (Provincial Archives of BC, E D A63).

127) Koroscil, 'A Canadian California', p. 715.

128) Black, 'The Viceroy's Ranch', p. 496.

CHAPTER IV

The Reluctant Emigrant

Most of the emigrants discussed so far viewed their removal to Canada primarily in positive terms, as a step towards independence and better opportunities for themselves and their families. Although undoubtedly they were also influenced by economic or social problems which restricted their prospects at home, for most these concerns took second place to the inducements to settle in Canada, and very few regarded emigration as a last resort. Their confidence was similar to that of the majority of emigrants who had left North-East Scotland earlier in the nineteenth century, positively persuaded of the benefits that would result from their decision to emigrate, and on the whole Canada met their requirements and expectations. But towards the end of the century it seems that an increasing number of emigrants were provoked to leave more by grievances than incentives, as they felt they were being pushed out—sometimes unwillingly—by adverse circumstances at home. On the whole working farmers and 'gentlemen emigrants' were not included in this category, which was made up mainly of unemployed urban tradesmen, thrown out of work during commercial recessions, and from time to time fishermen who were responding to a failure in the herring industry particularly. Clearly, by no means all emigrant tradesmen were destitute; the seasonal traffic of granite workers across the Atlantic, for instance, was for many years due primarily to the lure of high wages in North America, and even some tradesmen who emigrated in order to escape bad times at home ultimately did very well for themselves. But non-agricultural emigration was always controversial. It was given much less consistent—and much less favourable—coverage than settlement on the land, and the claims of its advocates were often contradicted by the complaints of disappointed settlers. Perhaps it is not surprising that many of those who had not been wholeheartedly committed to emigration soon became dissatisfied, often blaming their lack of success on the spurious promises of agents; but intending emigrants must have been greatly confused by the recurring disputes and conflicting accounts of conditions in Canada.

Sources in North-East Scotland contain far less information about the expectations and experiences of non-agricultural emigrants than their farming counterparts. No contemporary private correspondence has come to light; press coverage of the departure of tradesmen and fishermen was sporadic and rarely followed by published letters or reports of their experiences (except

147

in cases of controversy); and the Canadian government agent's reports do not suggest that either of these categories ever showed any particular interest in emigrating from North-East Scotland to Canada. To some extent this lack of evidence corroborates the view that interest was indeed sporadic, particularly in fishing communities, and perhaps the ambiguous and adverse publicity did prevent a more significant exodus of tradesmen. Yet press observations on contingents of emigrants leaving North-East Scotland clearly indicate that the movement was not entirely one of agriculturists and wealthy investors, and other categories of emigrants should be examined in order to build up as complete a picture of the local exodus as source materials allow.

Fluctuations in the fishing industry and emigration from fishing communities

Until the late 1880s the emigration movement seems to have bypassed the fishing communities of North-East Scotland. Since the 1820s those communities had been progressively transformed by the development of the previously insignificant herring fishing, which spread southwards from Caithness along the Moray Firth and Buchan coasts, and replaced the traditional dependence on line fishing for haddock, cod and other white fish. After the loss of its first export markets in the West Indies and Ireland in the 1840s, Scottish herring found new outlets in Northern Europe in the 1850s, which were to sustain the trade for the next three decades. The scale and profitability of the industry increased steadily, as herring fishers found they could earn more during the brief summer season (from mid-July to mid-September) than during many months of line fishing. The number of boats and men involved, the amount of capital invested, and the size of catches landed all increased steadily, and in the 1870s around 30,000 fishermen and an equivalent number of ancillary shore workers were employed during the herring season on the east coast of Scotland.[1] Activity was concentrated on a few ports, such as Peterhead, Fraserburgh, Buckie, Lossiemouth and Wick, which became major herring fishing centres, drawing in employees from the surrounding coastal communities and from further afield. White fishing operations had been conducted in small boats from a host of coastal villages, many of which had no harbours; but since the herring boats were much larger, fished close to shore and returned to port each morning with the night's catch, they required proper harbours and good landing facilities. Furthermore, from the start the herring industry was more highly capitalised than its predecessor; the curing process required that bulky and expensive stores be collected in advance, and it was also more convenient for buyers to deal with a few large centres, from where barrels of cured herring could be shipped quickly to the continental markets.

Many of the fishermen, however, still lived in their small, scattered coastal villages, from where they were recruited for the herring season by curers from the big ports. These curers were the linchpins of the trade, organising and controlling the activities of the crews they engaged. Most crews worked for a season under engagement to a particular curer, the bargain being made before the season began and applying to that season only. Under the agreement the crew was required to fish from a particular station and to pass on all the herring they caught to the curer, at a pre-determined price. The curers, who had accumulated the necessary stores in advance, then employed teams of women gutters and packers to prepare the fish for sale abroad. The demands of the herring trade therefore imposed major social changes on the communities concerned. It was not only that the fishermen had to migrate temporarily from their home villages to the big fishing centres, as did their wives and daughters who were employed in the curing yards. Herring fishing was also conducted on a much more impersonal basis than line fishing. The women gutters, for instance, were hired simply as wage earners to gut the catches of a large number of boats which were under engagement to their curing station, instead of working solely for their own family boat. The need for more extensive capital investment also eroded the self-sufficiency of the family unit, for although boats and tackle were generally owned by a small group of fishermen from the same community, working in the same boat, they increasingly made up the crew with hired men (often Highlanders) who had no personal interest in the boat. Many curers too came to have a stake in the herring boats, as they borrowed money not only to finance their own shorebased operations, but also sometimes to supply the fishermen with capital for investment in better boats and equipment.

Considerable financial risks were associated with the curing business. Variations in fish landings meant that gutters and packers were sometimes idle, and at other times unable to process a huge volume of fish in the short time available before it perished. More seriously, the curers might overestimate or underestimate the extent of stores to be bought in before the season began, and would then either be left with surplus stock or forced to buy extra stores at inflated prices in mid-season. But more serious still were the effects on the curers of a mid-season fall in fish prices. Since they made fixed bargains with their crews before the season began, they could not adjust these payments to take account of any subsequent drop in the price of cured fish; nor, if their profits were cut in this way, could they hope to repay the loans with which they had financed that season's curing operations. If the market were to remain depressed for a prolonged period, then the curers would be unable to set one year's losses against another year's profits, and many would be threatened with foreclosure.

For much of the nineteenth century, however, the herring market remained buoyant. Occasional price falls were cancelled out by the underlying upward trend of the market, and banks were also willing to carry over the short-term debts of a bad season and to extend credit, on the assumption that the trade would soon revive. Until the 1880s their confidence was vindicated, and many curers were encouraged to set up in business with the aid of loans, particularly from the North of Scotland Bank. But in 1884 the bubble burst, heralding the onset of a ten-year depression in the herring trade. The Lewis, Shetland and main east coast fishings that year all yielded catches which were plentiful in quantity but inferior in quality, so that prices collapsed dramatically, and the curers had to sell vast stocks of surplus fish at a loss of as much as one pound per barrel.[2] Assuming that this was just another temporary crisis, the banks carried over the curers' debts and advanced them fresh credit for the next season. It was only after further large catches and low prices in 1885 and 1886 that they realised the market was being greatly over-supplied and withdrew their support from curers, several of whom went bankrupt. The curers' failure adversely affected the fishermen, who now found it difficult to secure seasonal engagements for their boats, ancillary workers such as coopers were also thrown out of work, and the whole fishing enterprise slowed down considerably.

When the trade began to revive after 1893, daily quayside auctions replaced the pre-season contracts between fishermen and curers. This led to the appearance of a powerful new group of men, the fish salesmen, who, acting as agents of particular boats, were commissioned to dispose of their entire catch at the auctions. In this new era the herring industry also became more highly capitalised, and it was the fish salesmen—along with the banks, and other interested parties such as rope- and sail-makers—who supplied much of the capital for investment, particularly in steam-powered drifters after 1900. The high cost of converting from sailing boats to steam drifters meant not only that outsiders increasingly came to own shares in these vessels; it also meant that only a minority of fishermen could now afford to take up a share in a boat. Of the six or seven men who made up a steam drifter's crew in the early twentieth century, it is likely that an average of no more than three would have had shares in the boat, and in Peterhead at this time sixty per cent of all fishermen had no personal stake in the industry.[3] Furthermore, the hired crewmen were no longer transient Highlanders, but fishermen indigenous to the local communities where the owners also lived; so crews were increasingly polarised into employers and employees, a polarisation not dissimilar to that which at an earlier date had affected farming communities as a result of new agricultural practices.[4] The high capital cost of the drifters also meant that the industry had to be prosecuted more intensively in order to make maximum use of the expensive equipment, and the season was lengthened considerably by the addition of a winter fishing in the Minches and an important autumn fishing in East Anglia.

Meanwhile Aberdeen had been investing heavily in steam trawling since the early 1880s, so that by 1893 it had thirty-eight trawlers of its own and was the leading white fish port in Scotland. By 1914 it had 200 trawlers and accounted for seventy per cent of Scotland's white fish landings.[5] Initially its success was due to good catches being made in the vicinity, but even when more distant—and therefore more expensive—fishing grounds had to be sought, Aberdeen maintained its leading position, thanks largely to its efficient marketing facilities. Successive improvements made to the harbour in the course of the nineteenth century made landings easy, the city's fish market was opened in 1889, and the high quality product fetched a good price at Billingsgate, where most of it was sent immediately on special fish trains. The fishing industry greatly stimulated employment, so that between 1881 and

1911 Aberdeen was the fastest-growing city in Scotland. A vast army of shore-based workers supported a much smaller number of fishermen, and the *Aberdeen Free Press* of 4 January 1905 claimed that at that time the industry employed 9,200 non-fishermen in the city. Of that number, 3,000 were involved in the seasonal herring trade, but the rest were continuously employed in some aspect of the trawling industry and were recruited from the city's general labour market. Meanwhile the fishermen, who came from coastal communities stretching from Peterhead to Montrose, had to adjust— like the herring fishers—to major social and economic changes. Certainly the rewards and security in trawling were greater than those in small-scale, family-based line fishing; but deckhands on trawlers were simply wage-earners with no personal interest in the boats, which were owned mainly by shore-based concerns, or sometimes partly by their skippers.

Of what relevance is the history of North-East Scotland's fishing industry in a study of emigration from the region? To a much greater extent than any other aspect of the exodus, emigration from fishing communities was provoked by economic hardship and corresponded particularly clearly with periods of depression in the herring trade. While that trade remained buoyant, there is no evidence that the North-East's fishing population showed any interest in emigrating; however, once it became clear that the crisis of 1884 was not a temporary problem but the harbinger of a serious depression, the fishing communities began to experience a significant—if short-lived—boom in emigration.

In reviewing the state of trade in the region during 1885, the *Aberdeen Journal* on 1 January 1886 noted that the failure of the herring fishing had caused poverty and unemployment in Banff, Macduff and particularly in Peterhead, where the health of the herring was an index of the general health of the town. Parochial board or parish council records corroborate the repeated press claims of depression in fishing communities in the 1880s, and occasionally hint at the connection between economic hardship and emigration. Surviving parochial board records have been examined for all North-East Scotland's coastal parishes, from Bellie in the north to Banchory-Devenick in the south. Unfortunately the Inspectors' Visiting Books—potentially the most useful source of detailed information—do not survive, with the exception of one volume relating to Peterhead, but this volume covers the crisis period 1884-90, and the cases cited indicate the extent to which many people relied on a good fishing season to keep them above the poverty line. Among the paupers visited in 1886 were Margaret Fraser, 22 Queen Street, who had 'got no lodgers during the fishing and in consequence [fell] far behind with house rent'; M. A. Ritchie, 13 Backgate, who had 'made nothing at fishing this Season'; and Thomas Bowman, two of whose seven children had recently left for America.[6] Matters had not improved by 1887, when a number of paupers visited by the Inspector complained that they had been unable to make any money during the fishing season, and similar complaints were voiced in 1888 and 1889.[7] Three similar cases were documented in the Record of Applications for Poor Relief in Lonmay in 1890: the father of Barbara Buchan, an insane pauper, could no longer assist in her maintenance, as he had been unsuccessful at the fishing for some years and was deeply in debt; widow Mary Buchan, with two young children, 'has a share in a large fishing boat and also in a small boat but which presently is not worth anything to her'; and the two sons of widow Margaret Strachan could not support her, one having had his boat wrecked off Shetland and the other, who had had an unsuccessful fishing season, being 'overburdened with debt'.[8]

A number of applications for poor relief were made by individuals whose husbands, fathers or children, who might have been expected to support them, had emigrated, usually to North America. There were twelve such applications in Lonmay between 1881 and 1911, and twenty-three in Aberdour.[9] And among those admitted on to the Peterhead poor roll in this period was Elspet Lawrence, whose husband had drowned on Lake Huron in 1887.[10] Other applicants were the wives or mothers of coopers who had emigrated during the fishing depression: Margaret Chalmers and Isabella Will, for instance, both with several dependent children, were taken on to the poor roll in 1889 after their husbands had left Peterhead for North America and failed to send home any support; the two eldest sons of fish-worker Agnes McIntosh (admitted in 1892) were coopers in Newfoundland, while the son of widow Jane Wilson (admitted in 1894) was working as a cooper in Toronto but occasionally sent his mother some financial assistance.[11] The Fraserburgh parish records indicate that a number of 'emigrants' subsequently returned to the town and became chargeable; they included John Smith (71), a cooper, who applied for relief in 1897, two-and-a-half years after returning from North America, where he had spent over four years; and William Gray (38) and James Barrie (41), tradesmen who had spent eleven and three years respectively in North America.[12]

The press record confirms not only that emigration—sometimes temporary—was indeed taking place from fishing communities, but also that it was often controversial and regarded very much as a last resort. In remarking on the 'extraordinary rush' of emigrants from the country in 1888, the *Aberdeen Journal* mentioned—for the first time—that fishermen were participating in this trend, and predicted that before the end of the summer over 150 fishing families would have emigrated.[13] Throughout the Spring it went on to document departures from a number of fishing centres, and it is clear from these reports that the emigrants' decisions were closely bound up with the continuing depression in the herring trade, as fishermen, curers, coopers and also tradesmen whose businesses were suffering as a result of the crisis, decided to cut their losses. By January 1888, for instance, a number of Banffshire fishermen had sold their houses and gear in readiness for emigrating in the Spring, mainly to British Columbia, and about fifty individuals in Findochty, mostly families and young men, had made similar preparations to emigrate.[14] On 24 March and 10 April 1888 the *Aberdeen Journal* remarked on the large number of tradesmen emigrating from the Buckie district, some to Nebraska (where some young men from Buckie had previously settled) but many to Canada, particularly to British Columbia. As a result of these extensive removals, a large number of houses remained to let, rents had fallen considerably, and all along the coast fish-curing premises lay empty, as a result of the failure of so many firms.[15]

The east coast fishermen's interest in British Columbia had been aroused by publicity given to a proposal which was primarily intended to transfer Highland crofters to Vancouver Island. In 1887 Alexander Begg, a native of Caithness, was appointed as an (unpaid) emigration commissioner of the British Columbia provincial government, and he devised a scheme to establish a colony of Highland 'crofter fishermen' in the province. But although by the end of 1887 the British Treasury had agreed to Begg's proposal to set aside funds to transfer crofter families to Vancouver Island, the British Columbia government refused to take responsibility for securing the repayment of this loan; they feared not only that the settlers would be too poor to repay their advances, but also that they would become a public charge on the province. Begg therefore modified his scheme by suggesting that, in addition, a commercial company be formed to develop deep sea fisheries in which the emigrants could be employed, and an investment syndicate was duly formed in London to back the proposed fisheries company. The plan was not finalised until August 1892, when the British government agreed to advance a loan of £150,000 to British Columbia, in return for which the provincial government was to transfer up to 1,250 Scottish crofter families to Vancouver Island, provide them with land, houses and work, and guarantee the repayment of their advances. At the same time the investment syndicate was required to form a deep-sea fisheries company and to assist the provincial government in selecting and transferring the emigrants, and in supplying them with accommodation and employment. The company was to concentrate on fishing for halibut, which would be cured as well as exported fresh to eastern American markets, and the provincial government also agreed to grant the company up to 500,000 acres of public lands, of which 25,000 acres would be allocated to the colonists.[16]

But the scheme was never implemented. British enthusiasm cooled with the return of Gladstone's government to office in summer 1892, and the investment syndicate was unable to arouse sufficient interest among businessmen to form a fisheries company. A major stumbling-block then arose over the selection of emigrants, who, the British government insisted, should be recruited exclusively from Highland crofting counties. The British Columbians, on the other hand, planned to select colonists from a much wider area, in the hope of reducing the financial risk to the province that they feared would arise from the arrival of hordes of destitute Highlanders. Since these proposals coincided with the period of depression among east coast herring fishermen, it is not surprising that they hoped to be able to take advantage of the British Columbia scheme; and much of the exodus from the southern shore of the Moray Firth to British Columbia in 1888 was the result of publicity given to Begg's proposals. The cause of fishermen who wished to emigrate was taken up by two local MP's, C. H. Anderson (Lossiemouth) and P. Esslemont (East Aberdeenshire); and in February 1888 Esslemont was asked to present a petition to Lord Lothian, in which a number of Fraserburgh fishermen and fishcurers appealed to the Scottish Secretary to use

13   Herring boats, Fraserburgh Harbour.

his influence with the government to have them included in Begg's scheme.[17] Around 700 fishermen, coopers and tradesmen in the Fraserburgh district alone were said to be 'extremely anxious' to emigrate, provided they were given financial assistance, and they told Esslemont that the collapse of the herring fishing, coming on top of the general agricultural and commercial depression, had provoked considerable unemployment and distress among them.[18] Henry Marshall, one of the Fraserburgh activists, also submitted the fishermen's proposals to Begg, and received the following reply, published in the *Aberdeen Journal* on 12 April 1888:

Your scheme was duly received. I have been waiting for some definite news to send you, but have not yet received the decision of the B. C. Government as to whether they will accept my scheme or not. I have placed the whole matter before them in the most favourable light, and I hope they will adopt my plans. If I can get them carried out the organisation of your party will assist greatly, and much more can be accomplished than by parties going out singly. The expense of reaching British Columbia by railway is very great. I hope to get the fares reduced soon for through settlers to this point. I send you copy of my report on one of the proposed stations I would like to have occupied, and you will gather from that that I have not been neglecting the matter. I hope to be able to write you soon again to say that my plans are adopted, and that I am on my way east to lay them before you and others interested in this great fishing country.

During the Spring delegates were sent from Banffshire to Canada, supposedly to investigate Begg's claims. Some of them never even reached the west coast, but soon returned home to spread bad reports about Canadian fishing prospects, solely on the basis of their experiences on the east coast. On 23 March 1888 the *Aberdeen Journal* reported that James Reid and Alexander Stuart had gone from Buckie to Halifax, Nova Scotia, but had found the outlook there so depressing that almost immediately they had moved over to St John, New Brunswick. Finding prospects no better there, they had set off for British Columbia (their original destination) but in Toronto they met a man from Banff, who, on the basis of his own experience, strongly advised them against settling on the west coast, so instead of proceeding westwards in accordance with their instructions, Reid and Stuart decided to cut their losses, and returned to Buckie. Another Buckie emigrant, James Thain, who had accepted an engagement on board a Halifax fishing smack at this time, was also disappointed with his prospects and intended to return home, as did two fishermen from Portessie, who were equally unimpressed with conditions at St John, New Brunswick.[19]

These negative reports were highlighted by the *Fraserburgh Herald*, which was strongly critical of the emigration 'fever' which gripped the district in Spring 1888. On 14 February it disputed the claim that even seven—let alone 700—local people had expressed a desire to emigrate because of the depression in the fishing industry. While it did not object to the departure of redundant coopers and curers, it denied that there was any need for fishermen to leave and urged them to be patient:

That by and bye the business will assume its former flourishing condition we have no doubt whatever, and if any of our fishermen are contemplating going to British Columbia we ask them 'to look before they leap'. The field is unknown beyond what we hear of it through emigration agencies and other interested sources. No doubt fish abound in the waters, but so they do here—and by leaving home, fishermen may find when it is too late that they have sown the wind only to reap the whirlwind.

An editorial on 15 May reported with grim satisfaction that earlier warnings about smooth-tongued agents and the 'foolishness' of the British Columbia scheme had been vindicated by the unfavourable reports of Reid and Stuart:

In prospect, they breathed a purer air, and longed ... to escape from the inhospitable shores of Scotland to open up and develop the vast resources of the new Colony. From Fraserburgh alone a new township was to be formed, and a Chief Magistrate, Town Treasurer, Fishery Officer, Naval Constructor, Inspector of Works, Harbour Master and many other minor officials were elected, ready to assume office on their arrival. Mr Esslemont MP was interviewed, and he assured them of his good affairs in getting the Government to assist the Scheme with money grants ... [But] curer and fisherman alike, who have visited the Colony, report that it is unsuitable for the successful prosecution of the fishing industry; the two delegates from the Banffshire Coast, adding that they had seen as many fish landed in one day at Buckie, as they saw altogether in St Johns' during the whole period of their sojourn, and better prices realised for them. Fortunately for the fishermen on the East Coast, and particularly in the Fraserburgh district, our timely warning, and the refusal of the Government to assist emigration, were the means of keeping many at home, who in all likelihood would have gone out to their ruin.

This ambiguous report failed to point out that Reid and Stuart's comments were based on their experiences in Nova Scotia, 3,000 miles away from British Columbia on the opposite coast. And although a correspondent of the *Fraserburgh Herald* subsequently admitted that neither the Buckie nor the Portessie delegates had even set foot in British Columbia, he implied that the unfavourable conditions they described applied equally to the west coast fisheries, and commended the *Herald* for checking the 'ridiculous fit of imagination' which had provoked such unprecedented emigration from the locality. In a letter published on 22 May he declared that fishermen, after paying their passage, then required from £200-£300 capital in order to procure boats and nets, and in further correspondence, published on 29 May, he urged them not to leave their 'comfortable homes' for a land of 'questionable resources'. He alleged that a man could not make a living by fishing alone, but would have to supplement his income by farming; and—in another sweeping statement which failed to acknowledge the climatic differences between the east and west coasts of Canada—he claimed that the emigrants would have to endure an annual period of enforced idleness from Christmas until April when the weather prevented the prosecution of either fishing or farming. Then on 25 May the *Aberdeen Journal* added its voice to the criticism of Canadian fishing prospects when it claimed that earlier experiments in combining fishing and farming in 'crofting' settlements in New Brunswick and Nova Scotia had failed, and that the two activities should be kept distinct.

Alexander Begg's scheme had provided the only clear encouragement to North-East fishermen in this era to treat emigration as a positive opportunity, rather than simply as a negative response to bad conditions at home. When it foundered on local press hostility (including the publication of deliberately misleading statements) and particularly on the British government's refusal to allow non-crofters to participate, it ensured that emigration from these fishing communities would henceforth be regarded as nothing more than a last resort. It is hardly surprising that many of those who left with such a negative attitude did not succeed. Emigrants who felt they were being pushed out by adverse circumstances would be less likely to plan their removal carefully and less prepared to adapt to their new environment than those who left for mainly positive reasons, after considering all the advantages and drawbacks of such a move. Many fishermen in fact abandoned their previous occupation when they emigrated, sometimes perforce, since few had the capital required to obtain a boat on arrival or the particular skills necessary to make an immediate success of Canadian fishing. Had they been offered financial assistance—public or private—in establishing a fishing enterprise in Canada, then emigration might have been a more attractive—and more viable—proposition, but since the only such scheme to be mooted was still-born, this theory was never put to the test.

After 1888 the North-East press once more fell silent on emigration from fishing communities, partly because the movement declined sharply in the wake of a better herring season in 1889. In reviewing the year's trade on 27 December 1889, the *Aberdeen Journal* noted that fishing had been fairly remunerative all along the coast, and in Fraserburgh, as predicted, this had led to renewed confidence that better times lay ahead:

> Emigration from the district fell off considerably during the year, and this fact, coupled with the poor inspector's most favourable report upon the year's progress and condition of the poor, guarantees that the wave of depression has commenced to roll back.

A year later, on 26 December 1890, the *Aberdeen Journal* confirmed that many fishing communities had indeed revived considerably during the year, particularly Fraserburgh, where the herring season had been very successful, and where

> Another proof of better times is the marked falling away of emigration. For two or three years back there was a continual stream going from the town and district to America and other parts of the world, but within the last twelve months comparatively few people have considered it necessary to leave the old home.

When from time to time in later years there were signs of a revival of interest in emigration among fishing communities, the local press often published cautionary reminders about the drawbacks of fishing in Canada. On 21 April

1908, for instance, the *Aberdeen Journal* published a letter from A. S. King in Vancouver, warning Scottish fishermen to disregard recent advertisements inviting them to come to that city. Claiming that he had seen more fish lying at Aberdeen fish market in one morning than he had seen at Vancouver in three months, he pointed out that there were up to 600 redundant fishermen in Vancouver. Most of the fishermen and curers were Japanese or Chinese, who were accustomed to lower wages and a much lower standard of living than their Scottish counterparts; he therefore advised no one to break up his home and come to British Columbia on the strength of spurious advertisements which greatly overestimated the health of the fishing industry in that province. And in 1911 James Pennie, a Fraserburgh settler in Vancouver, responded negatively to the many enquiries he had received from home regarding prospects there, advising none but intending farmers to emigrate, and then only to the prairie provinces.[20]

Given all these warnings, it is not surprising that fishermen in North-East Scotland tended to emigrate only when prospects were so bleak at home that they felt there was no alternative. On the whole, the period from 1893 until 1914 was one of prosperity and growth in Scottish fishing, and there is little evidence of emigration, although ancillary tradesmen such as coopers sometimes emigrated if they could not attract sufficient business. For instance, Isabella Milne, a cooper's wife, applied to Fraserburgh parish council for assistance in 1909 after 'her husband left for America 2 months ago because he could not get work in Fraserburgh'.[21] Among the seven Fraserburgh emigrants whose departure was reported by the *Aberdeen Journal* on 24 September 1909 were three coopers, all bound for Toronto; and on 9 January 1911 the newspaper predicted that around 300 emigrants, mainly coopers and their families, would leave Fraserburgh that season for Canada, particularly for British Columbia, as a result of the competition created by barrel factories in the town. On 26 December it confirmed that such an exodus had indeed taken place, and that 350 people had emigrated from Fraserburgh, mainly to Canada or the USA. Perhaps it was because Fraserburgh depended on fishing more exclusively than any other coastal town in the region, that a slight downturn in the trade provoked emigration from there whereas it did not have this effect in—for example—Peterhead.[22]

Again on 10 May 1912 the *Aberdeen Journal* reported that several hundred people had emigrated from Fraserburgh that Spring, mostly the families of coopers who had already settled abroad. But it went on to indicate a more serious problem in the North-East fishing community. Whereas in 1890 110 boats had fished out of Stonehaven, by 1911 this number had fallen to fifty-two, and competition from German trawlers had greatly reduced the value of the catch. For many, emigration seemed to be the only way out:

> Even little Stonehaven with its 4577 people has arranged for a special train to be run from its station to Glasgow this month to take 200 men, women and children from the neighbourhood for whom Scotland is so hopeless that they are leaving her for ever. Sturdy fishing folk these whose forbears came over with the Danes. But what can their little 15-ton cutters and yawls do against the thirty

German steam trawlers that are constantly flooding the market of Aberdeen with shots of 700 tons of cod caught on a three weeks' voyage to Iceland?[23]

A government report in 1914[24] indicated that the major problem facing North-East fishermen was their inability to afford the huge cost of converting to steam drifters or steam trawlers. Witnesses questioned in a number of fishing centres claimed that financial hardship was the main reason for renewed emigration from these communities; indeed, perhaps more fishermen were emigrating now than during the earlier crisis, for in the 1880s many more had had their capital tied up in boats, and had therefore been unable to emigrate. By 1914, however, far fewer fishermen could afford to take up a share in a steam drifter or a steam trawler, and those who faced the prospect of simply becoming deckhands on a vessel in which they had no personal interest might well prefer to emigrate. John May and James Sim, fishermen in Inverallochy and Fraserburgh respectively, claimed that fishermen and their families were taking the unprecedented step of emigrating from these localities to Canada, simply because they could not accumulate enough capital to buy a share in a boat or nets. According to May:

There are thirteen emigrants leaving St. Combs because of the hard living. If the Government could advance money at reasonable rates, I know that we could save £100 annually, which would mean a very large sum out of a fisherman's earnings ... I have never seen a fisherman emigrating from my locality in my life before. These are the first of our fishermen that I have ever seen emigrating. There is something in a fisherman's life to compete for, and besides, you have your own independence.[25]

Robert Stephen, President of the Peterhead Fishermen's Association, confirmed that emigration was indeed a rare phenomenon in fishing communities; for although eleven emigrants had left Peterhead and Buchanhaven in 1911 and 1912, he was aware of only one family who had emigrated previously—and that was nineteen years earlier.[26] And W. D. Clark, Honorary Treasurer of the Peterhead and Fraserburgh Fishermen's Association, pointed out that fishing emigration, once insignificant, was increasing steadily; most emigrants went to Canada, and particularly to Vancouver, where they either continued to work in fishing or found general labouring work.[27]

On the Moray coast, Alexander Cowie, a fish salesman in Lossiemouth, told the same enquiry that about six young men had emigrated from there to Canada within the previous two years, not necessarily to pursue a career in fishing, but prepared to take 'anything that turned up'. They too had been discouraged by the difficulty of raising enough money to participate in fishing on a shareholding basis.[28] And James Slater, a fisherman in Buckie, alleged that the capital needed to acquire and maintain a steam drifter was often not offset by the vessel's subsequent earnings; he claimed to know of at least one skipper and mate who were emigrating because they could not afford the high operating costs of this new, highly capitalised fishing.[29] R. W. Crowly, an engineer and journalist in London, advocated that the government should advance loans to fishermen to equip their boats with motors, for unless some such incentive were offered, the current 'constant emigration' would continue and increase. John Buchan, a retired Peterhead fishermen, supported Crowley's view that state loans should be advanced to young fishermen in order to prevent further emigration, for several such emigrants had already left his district for Canada, forced out by financial hardship.[30]

Clearly emigration from fishing communities in North-East Scotland was much more the result of grievances than incentives, and after the abortive Vancouver fisheries experiment, Canadian agents rarely went out of their way to encourage Scottish fishermen to settle in the Dominion. On at least one occasion, however, the Canadian government agent in Glasgow, H. Murray, tried to exploit difficulties in the herring industry in order to secure emigrants for a totally different purpose. As he wrote to his superior in Ottawa on 25 August 1897:

> Having noticed lately in the newspapers that the Herring fishing over Scotland has this year been a failure and that great distress prevailed amongst the men so employed, I have sent our agents on a visit to the districts directly interested for the purpose of working up a party for the Crows Nest Pass Railway.[31]

But Murray's recruitment campaign was directed mainly at the crofting communities, and there is no evidence that fishermen in North-East Scotland took advantage of his offer.

In 1903, however, John Cowie, a fish-curer in Lossiemouth, was engaged by Raymond Prefontaine, the Canadian Minister of Marine and Fisheries, to examine fishing stations in Canada and report on the advisability of introducing Scottish practices in the catching and curing of herring. Cowie recommended that a steam drifter, crewed by Scottish fishermen, should spend the following summer on the eastern seabord of Canada, demonstrating Scottish fishing practices to the Canadians; and on 11 March 1904 the *Aberdeen Journal* reported that he had engaged three fishermen and six female gutters (all from Lossiemouth) and a cooper (from Burghead) for this purpose. The party was to leave in early May and would spend four months in Canada. On 5 May the *Aberdeen Journal* duly reported that a steam drifter, commanded by Captain Shaw of Aberdeen, had left Lossiemouth the previous day, with its crew of three local fishermen, as well as two fishermen from Campbeltown, who were working their passage out, and an engineer and fireman. Cowie himself was to leave a few days later from Glasgow for his headquarters at Kanso, Nova Scotia, taking with him the six gutters and the cooper, as well as supplies of barrels and salt. The *Aberdeen Journal* predicted that 'Much interest will be taken in the expedition, for its success will open up great possibilities for the fishing population, for which there has hitherto been small field for emigration'. But despite the apparent success of the experiment, this prediction does not seem to have been fulfilled, and the short-term venture did not lead to any long-term emigration. The *Aberdeen Journal* mentioned Cowie's experiment only once more, on 1 July, when it noted that private letters received from Nova Scotia indicated that although the fishermen were handicapped by their unfamiliarity with the coast, they clearly felt the experiment was worthwhile, and they had found the Canadian catch to be of a much higher quality than its Scottish counterpart. But thereafter incentives given to North-East fishermen to emigrate seem to have been confined to occasional press advertisements for specific—and sometimes temporary—posts. On 1 July 1911 coopers interested in going to Newfoundland were asked to apply to Redman, at Bellslea Temperance Hotel in Fraserburgh; on 10 January 1912 a free passage and good wages were offered to coopers willing to sail for British Columbia ten days later; and on 11 June 1913 MacKay Brothers in Aberdeen offered six months' employment to three women kipperers in Vancouver, commencing 1 September, at wages of $45 (£9) per month. The Canadian government emigration agents in Aberdeen were not concerned to recruit fishermen; on only one occasion was it mentioned that 'frequent enquiries' had been made at the Aberdeen office by men interested in the fishing industry in Canada,[32] and the lack of evidence of such settlement in Canadian sources confirms the impression that fishermen played only a minor and intermittent part in the overall emigration movement from Scotland.

Scottish emigrants in the Canadian granite industry

G. G. Archibald reported in 1914 that frequent enquiries were coming in to his office not only from fishermen but also from granite workers. Granite was probably the industry which accounted for the greatest number of tradesmen who emigrated from North-East Scotland, and each Spring the local press reported the departure of trainload after trainload of masons and quarrymen, seeking lucrative employment on the other side of the Atlantic. Unlike the fishermen, they were often responding to positive stimuli, and also participating in a seasonal emigration movement which had been gathering momentum since the 1860s, when the United States first purchased the skills of Scottish tradesmen in order to develop its own infant granite industry.[33] By the 1880s it was customary for around 200 granite tradesmen to leave Aberdeen each Spring for the American quarries and stoneyards. While some settled permanently, or stayed away for a number of years, many of these men commuted annually across the Atlantic, returning home temporarily when winter brought a large part of the North American granite industry to a standstill, then re-emigrating at the opening in Spring of each succeeding season. Although most of the emigrants went to the USA, particularly to New England, the North American granite industry straddled the Canadian border, and many emigrants moved freely and frequently between granite centres in Vermont and the Province of Quebec, or between Maine and New Brunswick. The demand for skilled Scottish tradesmen was not confined exclusively to the USA, as one commentator pointed out in 1902:

Never before in the history of the Granite trade of this great country has there been a time which showed such a general and continued demand for men. Not from one place or State only, but from one end of the vast Continent to the other—from the Atlantic to the Pacific comes the cry for more men. Nor is this demand a sudden one, or is it likely to come to a sudden stop. The nature, extent, and design of the majority of granite jobs throughout the country are of such dimensions as to guarantee employment for many months to come; indeed, at the present time, on the very verge of winter, advertisements are being scattered broadcast o'er the land calling for granite cutters, most of them stating there is a certainty of a winter's work to those who answer the odds.[34]

Advertisements for granite tradesmen, particularly stone cutters, in various parts of Canada, appeared from time to time in the Aberdeen press and in the local *Granite Cutters' Journal*. On 4 September 1888, for instance, John Donald of Mile End, Aberdeen, appealed in the *Aberdeen Journal* for twenty quarrymen to go to Canada; on 18 April 1906 John Cook's agency appealed for twenty granite cutters; on 27 April 1912 MacKay Brothers advertised for forty sett-makers for Vancouver, and two days later R. & J. Davidson also offered work to paving cutters in Vancouver. Among situations offered in Montreal were a post for a granite letter cutter (3 March 1904), positions for fifty marble and granite cutters (9 June 1904) and 'steady work' for a stone cutter, interested parties for this last post to apply to W. F. Pratt, 1 Adelphi, Aberdeen (10 October 1906). Other posts advertised included a foreman for a monumental granite works in an unspecified part of Canada (13 September 1910) and on 23 August 1912 R. Brown in Ottawa appealed in the *Aberdeen Journal* for a granite polisher and also a foreman to take charge of a cutting shed in that city.

Several Aberdonians who ultimately either returned home or gravitated to the centre of the American granite industry in Barre, Vermont, had worked at a number of locations in Canada and the USA. Peter Florence, for instance, made several trips to America in connection with contracts at Dick's Island, New York, and also worked in Canada, from where he eventually returned permanently and went into business on his own account in King Street, Aberdeen.[35] William Brown, on the other hand, set up in business in Barre in 1886, having served his apprenticeship in Aberdeen and then having worked at several locations in the USA and Canada.[36] William Barclay from Fraserburgh was apprenticed to a granite cutter and builder in New Pitsligo before going out to Montreal for a year in 1875. He subsequently worked in Aberdeen, but spent two seasons in the USA before emigrating permanently to Barre in 1886, setting up his own business there the following year.[37] And Charles McMillan from Aberdeen, who launched his own business in Barre in 1888, had previously pursued his trade in Massachusetts, Maine and Quebec.[38]

Although trade union journals periodically publicised opportunities for Scottish granite tradesmen across the Atlantic, they also regularly issued warnings against going to places where work was scarce or where there were industrial disputes. In 1904, for instance, the secretary of the Montreal Granite Cutters' Union asked the assistance of his Aberdeen counterpart in preventing further local emigration to Montreal, in view of current industrial action there:

> We found out your address from two men, "Granitecutters," who have come here from Aberdeen. No doubt they came here not knowing the exact condition of affairs, and to come here from the old country and no work to do can only end in hardship for all. We would wish you to inform all Granitecutters within your jurisdiction of the trouble that exists here, and stop them from coming this way, so as to give us a chance to win our cause, which we vouch for is a just one.[39]

Presumably this advice was heeded, for there was no more public correspondence on the subject; but on the few occasions when such warnings failed to dissuade granite workers from emigrating, the Aberdeen recruits came into bitter conflict with the granite trades' unions on the other side of the Atlantic. The most acrimonious incident as far as Canada was concerned was probably the lengthy dispute over the use of non-union labour from Aberdeen by the Stanstead Granite Quarry Company of Toronto and Beebe Plain, Quebec.

Vacancies in this firm were advertised from time to time in the Aberdeen *Granite Cutters' Journal*. In March 1902, for example, it intimated that the Company required at least twenty building-work cutters at its Beebe Plain plant in the province of Quebec, on the Canadian-American border, payment being 35-40 cents per hour for an eight-hour day, and two years later J. W. Stearle of the same firm wrote to the secretary of the Aberdeen Granite Cutters' Union, asking him to advertise vacancies for fifteen or more cutters at Beebe Plain.[40] Then in 1905 Alexander Robertson, a trade union activist, who had worked at various granite centres in Canada and the USA, and was also a former president of the Aberdeen Trades Council, tried to unionise the Stanstead Company's firm in Toronto, where he himself was then employed. Some years earlier, while working in Victoria and Vancouver, British Columbia, Robertson had organised branches of the Journeymen Stonecutters' Union of North America and the Bricklayers' and Stonemasons' Union, and had also served as President of the Victoria Stonecutters' Union until 1892.[41] In 1905 the jurisdiction of the American Granite Cutters' National Union was extended to Canada and Robertson therefore attempted to form a branch of the renamed 'American Granite Cutters' International Union' among the Stanstead Company's Toronto workforce. This involved pressing for an eight-hour, three-dollar working day, which would have brought the firm— the largest in Toronto—into line with other unionised granite works. But Robertson's demands were rejected by the company, which instead tried to persuade employees to sign long-term agreements and to take out shares. When those who refused to do so were dismissed, the remaining workers came out on strike. Then from 12 March 1906 men employed at the quarry at Beebe Plain refused to cut the granite required by the Stanstead organisation to fulfil a contract, unless the employers would agree to the demands of the union in Toronto. From that date members of the American Union boycotted the works at Beebe Plain, as well as in Toronto, and a stalemate seemed to have been reached.

During a previous attempt to unionise the Stanstead works, the employers had threatened Robertson that they could easily recruit all the non-union labour they required in Britain. In an attempt to forestall any such action subsequently, Robertson warned Aberdeen granite workers against the activities of agents who might be sent to the city to recruit strike breakers.[42] Robertson died early in 1906, but his campaign was maintained by James Duncan, General Secretary of the American Granite Cutters' International Union, who similarly asked Aberdeen tradesmen to ignore advertisements offering work in Toronto.[43] Potential recruits were warned that Toronto, far from being a granite centre, had no local quarries, the stone being brought from a distance. Even at the height of the season no more than sixty men were employed there, so it would be extremely difficult for recruits to find work once the Stanstead job had been completed.[44] The company's tactic was to import men in the hope that lack of alternative work and financial necessity would compel them to fulfil their obligations even if they objected to the circumstances, once these had become evident to them after their arrival.

Despite these warnings, a number of men were recruited by Stanstead Company agents who visited Aberdeen from 1906 to 1909.[45] Many of the recruits had no money, and were indebted to the company for part of their passage, repayments to be made out of their wages. In this way the company was guaranteed their services at least until such bills were paid.[46] The recruitment of strike-breaking Aberdonians for Beebe Plain caused particular bitterness, since many of the tradesmen who had stopped work there were Aberdeen emigrants, often settled in the area with their families. One Aberdonian, James Palmer of Barre, recounted a visit to Beebe Plain in a letter to the *Granite Cutters' Journal* in 1907.[47] Up to forty of his fellow-countrymen were employed there, with more on the way, all of them having been recruited under false pretences. Many men who had refused to work when apprised of the circumstances had insufficient money even to buy a meal, and were searching desperately for legitimate work in order to earn enough money to return home.

The *Granite Cutters' Journal* indicates that the Stanstead Company's efforts to employ Aberdeen tradesmen as strike-breakers were largely unsuccessful. First-class workmen were deterred from going by the low wages and long hours, so that a large number of the recruits consisted of the city's most inept granite workers. Despite their straitened circumstances, a majority of the recruits then apparently refused to undertake the work when they realised they had been deceived. Those men who were not thus persuaded were regarded with great disfavour by the trade unions on both sides of the Atlantic. The names of strike-breaking Aberdonians were forwarded to Aberdeen by American union officials and published in the *Granite Cutters' Journal* with the intention that on their return to Scotland they would be disciplined by the home union;[48] and when an updated list of thirteen recruits' names was published in October 1907 local union branches were asked to check their books and to strike off any of these men who were members.[49] By this time, however, a compromise agreement had been reached in the dispute, after the employers had offered to recognise an alternative union, the Canadian Granite Cutters' Union. Having consulted their colleagues at other granite centres in the Dominion, the Stanstead Company employees decided to support this purely Canadian body and relinquished their membership of the international union. By early September 1907 around eighty cutters at Beebe Plain had joined the new union, which was granted a charter by the Canadian government, allowing it to establish branches throughout the Dominion and ensuring that it would be recognised by its British counterpart.[50]

By the time of the Stanstead dispute granite tradesmen were emigrating from Aberdeen not only in order to take advantage of opportunities across the Atlantic, but also to escape unemployment and financial hardship at home. Whereas in the late nineteenth century the granite industry on both sides of the Atlantic was generally buoyant, and economic need was not an instrumental factor in the decisions of most emigrants, after about 1902 the Spring exodus began to be seen increasingly as a means of relieving the overcrowded labour market in Aberdeenshire. Many emigrants no longer left willingly, as branch secretaries of the Granite Cutters' Union all over the county reported the virtually enforced departure of unemployed men impatient at continuing stagnation in trade, or men who could no longer make ends meet at home; and indeed in some years emigrants seem to have been barely able to scrape together enough money to pay for their passage.[51] Their plight was highlighted by the editor of the *Granite Cutters' Journal* in March 1906, when he declared that while he welcomed the good employment prospects across the Atlantic, 'still there is a pathetic side to the picture. It is often a heartbreaking sight to see fathers tearing themselves away from their beloved ones to cross the ocean in search of that work which their own country is unable to provide for them'.[52] In some years even this large exodus did not dilute the home labour pool sufficiently to permit full employment among those who remained,[53] and even worse problems arose on those occasions when the North American industry could not absorb an extensive influx from Scotland. A depression across the Atlantic in 1907 and 1908 resulted in the return of several granite tradesmen to Aberdeenshire, at a time when the North-East was already experiencing considerable economic hardship. Their untimely reappearance was first noticed in February 1907, and in July and August the continuing lack of work in North America resulted in a greater number of men than usual coming back to Scotland for the winter.[54]

A two-month strike in Aberdeen in 1913 coincided with the opening of the season in North America and considerably exacerbated the normal Spring exodus. In March 1913 the Granite Cutters' Union appealed to the Aberdeen Granite Association for a reduction in working hours and an increase in wages.[55] When both the union's original demand, and its subsequent compromise proposals were rejected by the manufacturers, a strike was called from 1 April. Virtually the whole granite labour force of about 1,500 was affected by this strike, which continued until 23 May, and which clearly resulted in an increased departure of tradesmen; the *Evening Express* on 19 May, for instance, reported that, according to the union's records, 350 men had left for Canada and the USA since the beginning of the strike.

Booking agencies in Aberdeen undoubtedly helped to stimulate this movement, losing no opportunity to remind granite workers both of general shipping facilities and of specific openings across the Atlantic. R. & J. Davidson especially requested granite cutters to book early passages,[56] while Paton's similarly invited tradesmen to call and arrange transatlantic passages through their office.[57] They advertised the service of free, up-to-date and reliable advice regarding work and wages in Canadian towns, and on 22 April they appealed directly to those on strike in Aberdeen, announcing that they had definite situations in Canada for stone cutters and other tradesmen. MacKay Brothers repeatedly advertised for tradesmen for Beebe Plain, where a new stone cutting shed was under construction. The first advertisement, which appeared in the *Aberdeen Journal* on 4 April, intimated that twenty-five granite cutters were required and that they would earn 38 cents per hour for an eight-hour day, while the ten quarrymen required would earn 25 cents per hour for a nine-hour day. Assisted passages would be given and the recruits were to leave on 10 May. But when the advertisement was repeated ten days later, a new agreement had been completed, and thirty granite cutters were now required, at a wage rate of 41 cents per hour. According to the *Evening Gazette* of 11 April, about 100 tradesmen had gone to Beebe Plain since the start of the strike, and it later announced that seventy recruits had gone out there under the auspices of MacKay Brothers, the lure of high wages being 'intensified by the shadow of poverty and starvation at home'.[58]

Economic depression and artisan emigration

So by the early twentieth century emigrant granite workers crossed the Atlantic not only in pursuit of higher wages and better opportunities, but in order to escape the effects of a trade recession in Scotland. Meanwhile, other categories of tradesmen had been emigrating in protest against such adverse conditions from a much earlier date. The commercial and agricultural depression of the 1870s and 1880s caused hardship both in Aberdeen and among country craftsmen, many of whom moved to the city to swell the ranks of the unemployed there. In late 1885 the *Aberdeen Journal* commented almost daily on the extent of unemployment and distress in Aberdeen, where two major factories, Broadford Works and the Bannermill, had reduced wages by five per cent, and where in addition 100 employees at Broadford (mainly young girls on half time working) had been made redundant.[59] By 9 December 808 people had added their names to a list of the unemployed being drawn up by J. C. Thompson, President of the Aberdeen Trades Council, with the intention of assessing the extent of the problem and organising relief measures. On the same day the *Evening Express* opened a subscription fund, to be spent in meeting cases of urgent distress, and the *Aber-*

deen Journal on 10 December re-emphasised the gravity of the crisis when it claimed that 'It would be difficult to over-estimate the extent of the destitution to relieve which the fund is established. The bare necessities of life are no longer within the reach of the wives and families of hundreds of working-men who formerly earned fair wages.' By 11 December donations to this fund amounted to £60 and a parallel town council fund for the unemployed stood at £1,026.

At this juncture the town council did not set aside any funds to assist emigration. Although a number of trade organisations tried to reduce pressure on the overstocked home labour market by giving financial inducements to members to emigrate,[60] most of the 'large batches of tradesmen' who left in the 1880s—as at all other times—financed their own removal. Their departure was often noted in the local press. Among those driven away from Ellon by the dull state of trade in 1882, for instance, were a mason, emigrating to Manitoba, and a carpenter, tailor and blacksmith, all emigrating with their wives and families, while the emigrants from Fyvie included three merchants, three carpenters, two blacksmiths, two shoemakers and three or four masons.[61] On 14 April 1888 the *Aberdeen Journal* complained that the extensive exodus from the county—which it blamed mainly on the unfavourable economic situation and prospects at home—was taking away the cream of the many different classes participating in it. On 19 April 1889 it mentioned the departure of a large party of joiners, carpenters, masons and plasterers from Fraserburgh, mainly for Canada; and two months later, on 7 June, it noted that sixteen artisans, all from the Woodside district of Aberdeen, had left for Montreal and Ontario.[62] From time to time public attention was drawn to the departure of particular occupational groups. Among seventy emigrants leaving Aberdeen in March 1906, for instance, were three members of the Aberdeen City Police Force, who had resigned in order to take up farming in Canada;[63] and on 10 May 1912 a *Daily Mail* article quoted in the *Aberdeen Journal* mentioned that seven members of the Aberdeenshire County Constabulary had emigrated to Canada during the previous year. This report also commented on significant emigration among railway company employees, corroborating an earlier observation made by the *Aberdeen Journal* itself on 20 April 1911. A local railway official interviewed at that time told the newspaper three employees at the Aberdeen Joint Station were to leave that week, following in the footsteps of many other recent emigrants. These vacancies would not be filled easily, as all the Scottish railway companies were finding it increasingly difficult to recruit and retain staff; in addition to several experienced railwaymen who had emigrated already that season, a number of young recruits who had been given free passes from the North of Scotland to busy rail centres further south had remained in their employment for only a few weeks before leaving for the colonies.

However wealthy or impoverished these emigrants may have been, they were nearly always obliged to finance their own removal, unless, of course, they received assistance from friends, relatives or some other private source. But in 1906 and 1907, in a short-lived—and largely unsuccessful—experiment, municipal funds were set aside to finance the removal of a limited number of unemployed Aberdeen workmen to Canada. The Unemployed Workmen Act of 1905 allowed local authorities to create special distress committees to monitor and alleviate the problems of the unemployed; they could make use of money from local rates, supplemented by charitable donations,[64] to establish labour exchanges and assist the migration or emigration of suitable candidates. From 1905 to 1912 almost £200,000 was spent nationally in assisting over 21,000 emigrants, over 13,000 of whom came from London.[65] Although the act had most impact in England, distress committees were also constituted in nine Scottish burghs with populations of over 50,000, only four of which, however—Aberdeen, Edinburgh, Leith and Glasgow—made use of their powers to assist the emigration of unemployed workmen.

The Aberdeen Distress Committee was formed in 1906, initially to disburse a donation of £250 that had been allocated to the local Chamber of Commerce by the charitable 'Queen's Unemployed Fund'. Its activities were first mentioned in the press on 9 June, when the *Aberdeen Journal* noted that among the (largest ever) party of 200 emigrants which had left the city for Canada the previous evening were seventeen men who were being sent out under the auspices of the Distress Committee. Then a week later, on 15 June, it published a letter which had been sent to John Croll, Clerk to the Distress Committee, by one of the first emigrants assisted under the scheme. This correspondent had arrived in Toronto with his wife and four children on 1 May, and had immediately begun work, driving a wagon which supplied stores with fruit and vegetables. He was earning $9 a week, which he expected soon to increase, and he was well satisfied with his situation and prospects, although he admitted that the scarcity of housing in Toronto made for extremely high rents. But he encouraged the committee to continue its policy of sending needy families to Canada, adding that 'There are lots of Aberdeen fellows around here, and they all seem to get work. I should think there would be plenty of work here for some years to come'.

By the time the Aberdeen Distress Committee abandoned its emigration policy in May 1907 it had spent nearly £500 on sending away sixty emigrants, all to Canada. Applicants were required to be medically examined and to appear personally before the Distress Committee, and those selected were guaranteed work on arrival by Canadian emigration agents.[66] The emigrants all agreed to repay their advances by instalments so that others could be similarly assisted to emigrate, but in fact the Salvation Army, which was the agency used by the Distress Committee to organise the removals and collect the repayments, had great difficulty in recovering these loans. Indeed, it was financial problems, coupled with the seemingly very limited success of the scheme in improving the condition of those assisted, that led to the abandonment of officially-sponsored emigration as a means of helping Aberdeen's unemployed. The Salvation Army supported the theory of the scheme, but blamed its failure partly on the Aberdeen Distress Committee's inclusion of unmarried men among the assisted emigrants. Some committee members opposed the emigration of married men (the only category recommended for assistance under the Act) if their wives and families were left behind and then might have to be supported by the parish authorities. But on the other hand they also deplored the loss to the community that was usually constituted by the removal of entire families. Some members therefore preferred to sponsor single men in the hope that they would ultimately return home to invest the money they had made in Canada.[67] But Colonel Lamb of the Salvation Army warned the committee that he anticipated problems in collecting repayments from single men, who, instead of returning home, were much more inclined to disappear to the United States without trace; and he stressed that while his Canadian colleagues would seek to recover these loans, they would not accept responsibility if this proved impossible. Lamb's warning was vindicated by the fact that only two of the seven single men who were given loans of £9 12s. 6d. each to emigrate in June 1906 made any effort to repay their advances, while a married man with five children had struggled to make a small repayment; and in June 1908 the Distress Committee resigned itself to writing off £100 in unpaid debts.[68]

Incentives, expectations and experiences

Even impoverished emigrants who were given assistance to settle in Canada were not usually driven away by totally negative considerations, since Canadian demand for artisans and labourers often coincided with periods of commercial recession at home. In its annual report for 1881 the Canadian Department of Agriculture complained that the number of artisans and mechanics arriving in the Dominion had fallen far short of demand, especially in the western cities, where twice the number of settlers could have been satisfactorily placed. A year later the *Aberdeen Journal* attributed the upsurge in local emigration not only to the trade depression in Scotland, but also to the complementary revival of trade and manufactures across the Atlantic, a revival which by 1887 was attracting the attention of tradesmen-emigrants from all over Britain and Europe.[69]

Employment opportunities in Canada were often brought to the notice of potential emigrants through advertisements inserted in the North-East press by local booking agents. The jobs offered included posts for paper-makers,[70] shop assistants,[71] millwrights, fitters and other employees in a lumber mill,[72] general labourers, moulders, steel workers, miners and bricklayers.[73] There was a particular—and continuing—demand for railway construction workers: on 29 January 1907 R. & J. Davidson advertised railway work in Winnipeg, at $2 a day, to various tradesmen who were able to pay their own fare of £9 10s. each; and on 1 October 1907 the Salvation Army Emigration Office in Aberdeen intimated that immediate railway construction work at Reid Station, Quebec, was available for 100 able-bodied men who were willing to sail from Glasgow on 5 October. The recruits were offered assisted passages, and in special cases an advance of the full fare. On 10 February 1910 MacKay Brothers offered railway construction work in Canada to twenty-five men, and later that year the *Aberdeen Journal* reported the com plaints of the President of the Grand Trunk Railway regarding the serious shortage of labour in the Dominion. The Company urgently needed 5,000 men in order to fulfil its schedule for opening a mountain section, but only 1,600 were available; on the Pacific coast even ordinary labourers could not be obtained, and further east trainloads of settlers were absorbed into other employment as soon as they reached Winnipeg.[74]

But in spite of the demand for labour, opportunities for tradesmen in Canada were given much less extensive and much less positive treatment than settlement on the land. Non-agricultural emigration was always more controversial than its farming counterpart, and intending emigrants must have been greatly confused by the many acrimonious exchanges and conflicting accounts of conditions of labour in Canada. The encouragement of those who supported artisan emigration was often neutralised by the complaints of disappointed settlers, and indeed more contradictory advice was given to tradesmen-emigrants than to any other category of settler in the Dominion. Perhaps it is not surprising that those who had left primarily in order to escape from economic hardship at home soon became discontented; many had probably given insufficient consideration to the advantages and drawbacks of emigrating and were therefore not wholeheartedly committed to their new life—especially, of course, if they only intended to remain in Canada long enough to recover their finances. By this time the United States offered fewer openings to these emigrants, since it was being bombarded with unskilled settlers from southern and eastern Europe to such an extent that it began to legislate against indiscriminate immigration. But in turning their attention to Canada, these artisan-emigrants perhaps forgot that the Dominion's much smaller labour market could not yet cope with an unremitting and unregulated influx of urban tradesmen. While it always welcomed working farmers who would populate and make productive its vast empty territories, it was not always made clear that the demand for tradesmen was likely to be more erratic, as well as secondary to and dependent on the establishment of a thriving agricultural population.

Dissatisfied emigrants often blamed their inability to find lucrative employment on misleading press reports about the state of Canadian trade, and in particular on the spurious promises of agents. The *Aberdeen Journal* is peppered with examples of conflicting advice and complaints from disillusioned settlers. On 17 June 1903 it reported that W. T. R. Preston, the Canadian Commissioner of Emigration in Britain, had clashed with the Winnipeg Trades and Labour Council over the latter's claim that there was no work for mechanics and artisans in Canada. Preston claimed that he had received 20,000 applications for such employees, and repudiated the Trades Council's warning to intending emigrants not to go to Canada. But in 1907 James Coutts of Aberdeen urged intending emigrants to beware of self-interested agents who often sent out unsuitable people, even in winter, when no work was available. Writing to a friend at home shortly after he arrived in Toronto, Coutts spoke of hundreds of tradesmen and labourers idle in that city and reiterated a common complaint, that the high cost of living in Canada cancelled out the higher wages earned there.[75]

Later that year conflicting accounts began to reach Aberdeen concerning the experiences of a contingent of 180 local emigrants who had been sent out to Portage La Prairie, Manitoba, by the James A. Smart Company in order to work on the construction of the Grand Trunk Railway. Six months later the Smart Company opened an office in Aberdeen, and within a week had sent out thirty more recruits, fulfilling the prediction of the Canadian government emigration agent in Aberdeen that 'a large number [would] go out with them as times are very poor here and money scarce'.[76] On 23 October the *Aberdeen Journal* published a letter which had been sent to the editor by one of the March emigrants, Alexander Sandison, who had gone out to Canada in company with a number of friends, all from the Broad Street district of Aberdeen. Having come from a very poor home background, he was well pleased with his accommodation (an encampment of 300 men) and his wages of $2 a day. He had already managed to save £30, and he strongly recommended young men in Aberdeen who were earning less than 30 shillings a week to follow his example. But Sandison's advice and claims were refuted in a letter from Joseph Kempen, published on 20 November. Kempen too had emigrated to Portage La Prairie in March to work on the railway, but contrary to his expectations he had found the work very badly paid. The men were charged $4.50 a week for board, so that they were unable to save anything out of their wages, and he claimed that Sandison, whom he knew, had been unable to save even 30 cents, let alone £30. Kempen was not alone in his criticisms; several other Scottish recruits had arrived at Portage La Prairie to discover that the local contractor of the Grand Trunk Railway Company was unable to give them immediate work, and after numerous complaints, the Canadian government made an official investigation into their treatment. Its findings were published in the *Aberdeen Journal* on 13 December, when it was reported that, thanks to the intervention of the immigration commissioner at Winnipeg, these early problems had been overcome, all the men were now employed and there had been no further complications.

By this time, however, complaints were reaching Aberdeen from other parts of Canada. On 26 December, for instance, the *Aberdeen Journal* published a letter from A. Gerrard in Toronto, warning emigrants who intended to leave the following Spring not to take for granted the assurances of 'grossly misinformed' agents that trade had revived and employment was plentiful. Recent emigrants to Toronto—where unemployment in December stood at almost 6,000—were highly critical of agents who had promised abundant work to skilled and unskilled alike, and since October, said Gerrard, 10,000 disappointed settlers had sailed from Quebec on their way back to Britain. On 24 January 1908 another Aberdeen correspondent in Toronto, Henry Massie, reiterated the warning about unemployment in the overcrowded Canadian cities, and advised tradesmen against emigrating; the same issue contained excerpts of a letter from Calgary which complained that thousands of emigrants were being duped into coming to Canada on the strength of advertisements in the British press which fraudulently promised work for all. Another correspondent the following month[77] pointed out that many men who had preceded their families to Canada had barely been able to earn enough to keep themselves from starving, let alone send for their dependents to join them. And another Aberdonian in Toronto, complaining that the city had experienced its worst winter for forty years, warned those aged over thirty against emigrating and maintained that the country was 'not what it is represented to be' by over-enthusiastic agents.[78] Winnipeg too was suffering similar problems of unemployment, according to an Aberdeenshire settler in Manitoba, who advised even farm servants (provided they were in work at home) not to emigrate during the current overstocked condition of the labour market.[79]

Emigrants were periodically warned against taking advantage of assisted passages offered by Canadian contractors, who sometimes had to recruit British labourers after native Canadians had refused to agree to their terms and conditions of employment. Some of the risks involved in emigrating under contract are indicated by the experiences of a large contingent of unskilled labourers from Aberdeen at Clarke City, Quebec, which provoked a great deal of conflicting correspondence in the North-East press in 1907 and 1908. The men were recruited by the Aberdeeen booking agent, R. B. Arthur. On 17, 18 and 19 September 1907 he advertised in the *Aberdeen Journal* for 100 general labourers and carters to work for six months for the North Shore Power Railway and Navigation Company, sawmillers and manufacturers of wood pulp, at Clarke City, near the mouth of the St Lawrence River. Within a week he had obtained all the men he needed— indeed, he could have recruited twice as many—an eagerness which both the newspaper and John MacLennan declared was testimony to the continuing trade depression in Aberdeen.[80] The men sailed from Glasgow on the SS *Cassandra* on 20 September, having been seen off from Aberdeen Joint Station by a large crowd of wellwishers. While they were required to provide a deposit, and also pay their own way to Glasgow, their transatlantic fare was advanced by their employers, who were to recover this expenditure by weekly deductions of 15*s.* from the men's wages. A further deduction of 12*s.* 6*d.* per week would be made for board and lodging out of the recruits' promised earnings of 11*s.* a day.

The emigrants who arrived at Clarke City at the end of September were not the first to be sent out there by Arthur. The company, of which he was a regular agent, apparently preferred Scottish recruits to native French Canadians, and since, according to John MacLennan, 'the reports from those who have been there for some time are very favourable ... they get their men easily'.[81] But some of the reports which began to filter back to Aberdeen from this latest contingent were far from favourable. On 28 October 1907 the *Aberdeen Journal* published a catalogue of grievances which had come to light since the men had arrived at Clarke City. They were quickly disappointed in their expectations of sending home money to their dependents, who as a result soon began to suffer severe financial hardship. Not only were the men's earnings to be just 8½*d.* per hour for a nine-hour day; they were not to receive any payment at all until their passage money had been repaid in full, and men with families, who had been promised a £2 bonus on arrival, were never given this gratuity. The men were not employed under cover, as they had been led to believe, but were labouring in the open air, and some time had already been lost through bad weather, a problem which could only increase with the onset of winter. Furthermore, Clarke 'City' was in a remote, inaccessible location, 350 miles from Quebec; and since the St Lawrence was closed all winter, and the company owned the only road communications as well as the only store, the Aberdeen recruits were effectively prisoners until the following Spring.

An equally critical report appeared in the *Evening Gazette* on 28 October, highlighting the plight of a number of women whose husbands had been unable to send home any money from Clarke City. James Troup's wife had expected that her husband would soon save enough money to bring her and their five children out to Canada, but he had not sent back a single remittance, and she had been forced to apply for parish relief to support her family. Two other women, a Mrs Main of Summer Street and a Mrs Jamieson of Claremont Street, declared that their husbands had given up steady jobs 'because of the great inducements in respect of wages' which Arthur had held out to them; and the wife of George Troup had sold all her personal effects in order to allow her husband to get fitted out for Clarke City. There were, claimed the *Evening Gazette*,

> numerous other cases in the city, in which inquiry will reveal the same story of suffering. Husbands have left their wives and families at home, and as the promises which induced them to give up their situations have not been fulfilled, they are barely able to keep themselves far less to send money home for support of those near and dear to them. The unfavourable reports which have come home have had a deterrent effect on several young men who intended to leave for Canada shortly, and some official statement would be welcomed to allay the feelings of many as to the prospects which Canada affords for the industrious artisan.

R. B. Arthur was quick to defend himself against these allegations and in a letter published by the *Aberdeen Journal* on 30 October, he blamed the 'misleading information' published two days earlier on a few 'hysterical' wives. Insisting that he had made full enquiries into the Clarke City firm's business standing before sending out any emigrants, he noted that recruits who went out in Spring 1907—and their dependents—had so recommended the arrangements that around 200 men left behind were eager to join them as soon as work became available, and some wives too had made plans to join their husbands once the St Lawrence reopened. Arthur's position was supported by a letter from John MacLennan, which appeared in the *Evening Gazette* the same day, in which he claimed that the recruits had not been at Clarke City long enough to form proper opinions and noted regretfully that many people who went to Canada by means of advanced passages 'are careless and indifferent respecting those they leave behind'. Arthur was also backed up to some extent by an editorial in the *Evening Express* on 1 November. It too felt it was easy for emigrants who had expected the new land to be 'overflowing with milk and honey' to blame their subsequent disappointment on the misleading promises of agents, and pointed out that most agents were unlikely to risk the heavy penalties imposed on those who wilfully deceived emigrants, just for the sake of a few shillings' commission. But it added that the complaints coming back from Clarke City seemed to be of more substance, and merited the official enquiry which by that time had been promised by the Canadian immigration authorities.

Letters from disillusioned emigrants began to appear in the Aberdeen press from late October. On 31 October the *Evening Gazette* published two such letters, from a boxmaker and a sawyer, who had found the conditions at Clarke City intolerable. The boxmaker, in a hastily-written note, complained that recruits were not even told when there was to be a postal collection, for fear they would abscond on the mail boat. He went on bitterly:

> God knows when we are to get any money. They don't even pay us on pay day. It is always a week or so past the time before we get paid. There are some boys here getting all their passage money kept off them this pay day, so they will be left without a penny, but ... if they don't watch themselves there will be a riot here, for we are getting played on too much now. I have been seriously thinking of doing a bolt before the snow comes here, as everybody that is here is leaving with the last boat. It is sickening working here, as the gaffer is a French Canadian, and he gives all the best work to his countrymen, and they all speak French, so we don't know what they are saying, and can't follow them with the work. We have been digging out trenches every day we have been working, and my legs and feet are soaking wet every night. It is an awful place. It is always raining in torrents, so bad that we cannot work. We have lost four days already since we started.

On 2 November the *Aberdeen Journal* published a letter from another recruit, which had been sent on for publication by his mother in Skene. He claimed that on arriving at Quebec the men had been advised not to proceed to Clarke City. A number of recruits had heeded this advice and had taken advantage of the abundant opportunities for employment then available in Quebec city. He, however, had gone on to his destination, but in disgust at the living conditions and the employers' withholding of wages, he had left, along with a companion, on 7 October, having managed to catch a small boat leaving from a fishing village about nine miles down river. James Troup, in an interview with the *Evening Gazette* on 20 November, described Clarke City as nothing more than a collection of wooden huts in the bush, where the men were housed in rough bothies:

> On the second day after arrival most of the men commenced to work. They were divided into squads; some worked at concrete, some filling holes in the river ... Work had not been in operation but a few days when a great many of the men complained of illness, due to the water, and a general feeling of discontent as to the class of work at which they were engaged, the belief having been that they were to be employed at a pulp mill.

A delegation of up to fifty recruits had then marched on the site manager, complaining that they had been employed under false pretences, but although the manager promised to redeploy them at more congenial work, many grievances remained, particularly over the non-payment of wages. Troup went on to relate how after three weeks—by which time he had earned £9 but had not received a single payment—he had returned to Quebec along with three companions. By now it was too late in the season to find work, and they were forced to seek help from the St Andrew's Association, which arranged for them to be fed by the Salvation Army and then sent them on by steamer to Montreal. But employment prospects were even worse there, and after pleading unsuccessfully for a passage on several transatlantic vessels, Troup stowed away in the coal bunkers of a Dundee steamer and in this way returned to his home at 127 Union Grove, Aberdeen.

On 9 January 1908 John MacLennan wrote a lengthy letter to the *Aberdeen Journal* in support of Arthur and refuting the allegations made by Troup and other complainants. He denied that the men had ever been promised either wages of 11s. a day or a bonus of £2 on arrival. George Somers of Aberdeen, whose sons had gone to to Clarke City, confirmed that no such promises had been made by the agent, and even Troup, when interviewed by MacLennan, admitted that Arthur had never held out these specific incentives. The misunderstanding had apparently arisen because one of the June recruits had written home saying he was earning 11s. per (twelve-hour) day, and another emigrant who had gone out in June had sent home a £2 bonus to his wife before he had even begun work. But MacLennan, having scrutinised all the Clarke City Company's correspondence with Arthur, said the bonus was never intended to be the universal right of all employees; it was to be granted at the Company's discretion and furthermore, it had been made perfectly clear that no wages would be paid until the passage money had been fully recouped. Nor were the men ever promised anything other than general labouring work, despite the claims of some that they had been engaged to work indoors at specialist tasks such as box-making; and MacLennan spoke scathingly of the inability of some recruits to cope with outdoor labour. He also pointed out that the Company had incurred substantial financial losses as a result of the desertion of some recruits and the incompetence of others. Of ninety-eight men who had sailed from Glasgow, twenty-three had refused to proceed from Quebec to Clarke City, and although denied their services, the Company was still obliged to pay £126. 10s. to the steamship company for their fares. Some of the other recruits had clearly never done a day's manual labour in their lives, and MacLennan ventured to suggest that emigrants who received pre-paid passages, or who took advantage of charitable schemes, were often less committed, less adaptable, and much more ready to complain than men who paid their own way to Canada.

These criticisms did not go unchallenged. Within two days MacLennan's claims had been contradicted by an anonymous correspondent, who followed up his letter of 11 January with a second onslaught four days later. Pointing out that there were more ways of misleading people than telling out-and-out falsehoods, he insisted that the full conditions of their employment had not been adequately explained to the Clarke City recruits. If, for instance, they had really been told—as MacLennan claimed—that they would not be able to send home any funds until their fares had been paid off (a period of up to four months) then clearly they would not have abandoned their dependents without the means of support. And if, as MacLennan also suggested, the men were shiftless and lazy, then surely this reflected badly on R. B. Arthur's selection procedure. In his second letter, the unnamed correspondent went on to complain that MacLennan's statement had replaced the original promise of an impartial Canadian government enquiry into the grievances of the Clarke City recruits. Instead of taking evidence on the spot, from the men actually involved, the Canadian Immigration Department had simply commissioned a report from MacLennan in Aberdeen, who had reached his assumptions without a full knowledge of the facts, and largely on the evidence of two witnesses; one of these witnesses, George Somers, had never even been to Clarke City, and the other, James Troup, had just written to the *Aberdeen Journal* protesting about MacLennan's misinterpretation of his statement. In his letter, which appeared on 14 January, Troup agreed that the men had never been promised 11s. a day. They had, however, been told that they could work as many hours as they wished at 22 cents per hour, but on arriving at Quebec they discovered that the wage rate was to be only $17\frac{1}{2}$ cents per hour and the working day restricted to a maximum of ten hours. When they refused to accept these terms, the employers had promised that if they carried on to Clarke City they would be given the £2 bonus and would have all their grievances settled; but the seventy-five men who proceeded on the basis of this verbal promise soon discovered they had been greatly deceived.

The last public word on the Clarke City dispute went to R. B. Arthur, whose advertisements had initiated the whole controversy. On 27 January he wrote to the *Aberdeen Journal*, again denying that the men had been misled in any way: while interviewing applicants, he insisted, copies of an Official Circular, quoting a minimum wage rate of 15 cents and a weekly boarding charge of $3, had been clearly displayed on his desk; he had also pointed out the position of Clarke City on the map and had passed round letters from previous recruits. In response to Arthur's request of late October 1907 that the company should investigate the complaints which had been appearing in the Aberdeen press, some of the recruits had taken it upon themselves to defend their employers' interests, and Arthur duly enclosed two items of emigrant correspondence along with his letter of 27 January. These letters, dated 18 and 19 December, came from George Robertson, a satisfied recruit, who wrote in praise of the Clarke City Company and to dispel the damaging rumours which had been circulating in Aberdeen. His first letter dealt with the general situation and prospects of Clarke City, which he declared was in a healthy—and increasingly accessible—location. It also had a brilliant future, for once the construction of the mills was fully completed, around 500 new hands would be required. In his second letter, which was countersigned by five other Aberdeen emigrants, Robertson described the favourable way in which the Aberdeen recruits had been received and treated at Clarke City, despite the incompetence of some men to perform manual labour. He also noted that all employees who had requested an advance had been told this would be allowed once they had got some time in, and during November most of the married men had in fact been able to send home $35-$40 (£7-£8) to their dependents.

But perhaps the adverse publicity had made its mark, for after 27 January no further reference was made to Clarke City in the *Aberdeen Journal*, and never again did R. B. Arthur advertise on behalf of the Clarke Company. In fact, there were relatively few press complaints about Canada until 1913, when at the beginning of May news reached Aberdeen of the plight of a number of tradesmen who had gone out to Saskatchewan the previous month on the promise of situations which had not then materialised. The first intimation of the problem was contained in a letter from one of these emigrants at Prince Albert, which appeared in the *Evening Gazette* on 1 May:

> I arrived here a week ago, but the job we were going to was a hoax. There are any amount going idle here. The Board of Trade gave us a job to break sticks ... We are living in a small shack, which costs us 10 dollars a month between six of us ... Canada is not the place it is said to be. You are far better at home with a small wage, because everything is so dear here ... I am sorry I left to come here, as I would have had a comfortable job at home still. I would not go away again if I was at home, because this place is boomed too much.

Having received several other letters in the same vein, the *Evening Gazette* sought an explanation from G. G. Archibald at the Canadian government emigration office in Aberdeen. In his press statement, published on 2 May, Archibald admitted there were problems in Saskatchewan, which he blamed on unscrupulous agencies which guaranteed situations to tradesmen and then left them in the lurch. Restating the official government policy that only agriculturists and domestic servants were guaranteed employment in Canada, he urged all intending emigrants to seek advice from his office before making arrangements with a booking agent, and pledged that, whenever possible, he would take action against those who held out spurious promises of employment.[82]

Archibald's statement was welcomed by another correspondent of the *Evening Gazette*, who also suggested that those who had been induced to emigrate through false representations should have recourse to the Merchant Shipping Act, which imposed a penalty of three months' imprisonment or a fine of £50 on such unscrupulous agents.[83] The plight of the Aberdeen tradesmen in Saskatchewan—who in June were still suffering great hardship as a result of their prolonged unemployment—also led the Aberdeen Trades Council to consider a plea from a former member, James Cock, himself resident in Saskatchewan.[84] He wanted the Aberdeen Trades Council, in conjunction with its counterparts throughout the country, to take steps to curb the activities of Canadian emigration and shipping agents, who, despite complaints, were continuing to introduce large numbers of unwanted settlers to Canada in the hope of reducing the price of labour. Cock's allegations were confirmed by subsequent press statements and correspondence. On 17

July, for instance, the *Aberdeen Journal* published a notice, authorised by G. G. Archibald, telling booking agents not to send any more non-agricultural emigrants—especially building workers—to Western Canada until the labour market had become less congested, and suggesting that they also reduce the number of these settlers being sent to the eastern provinces. This plea was then reinforced by gloomy letters in the *Aberdeen Journal* on 1 August and 8 September (again warning of severe unemployment in Toronto, Winnipeg, Edmonton and Vancouver, blaming the situation on over-zealous agents and advising non-agricultural emigrants to stay at home); and by the annual report of the Aberdeen Savings Bank on 25 December, which noted that many recent emigrants to Canada were returning to Scotland because they had been unable to find work. In his annual report for 1913-14 Archibald suggested that recent emigrant failures had arisen largely because many skilled and unskilled labourers had gone out to various Canadian cities on the strength of nothing more than a vague belief that their friends were doing well there; they had not taken the precaution, strongly recommended by the Immigration Department, of having a definite assurance of work before leaving home, and often failed to realise that the Dominion was unable to cope with a 'promiscuous emigration' of unwanted tradesmen from Scotland.

The emigration of tradesmen was clearly a source of considerable controversy and provoked more ambivalent advice, warnings and complaints than any other aspect of the movement. Although there were undoubtedly successes, and many emigrants were attracted by positive incentives, a significant number of tradesmen—and almost all fishermen—who emigrated did so reluctantly, driven away from Scotland more by economic grievances than by a conviction that they could secure a better future for themselves and their families in Canada. Perhaps their lack of commitment and their negative attitudes help to explain their apparently high failure rate, their readiness to lay the blame on 'fraudulent' agents and also the frequent complaints of Canadian employers about the calibre of tradesmen-emigrants. Many, indeed, treated their emigration as a temporary expedient, and the seasonal exodus which had been initiated by the granite workers for positive reasons later came to be composed primarily of unemployed tradesmen seeking a quick (if short-term) solution to their financial problems at home. Whereas many agriculturists emigrated in families, prepared to start life afresh with the aim of ultimately attaining independence and prosperity, emigrant tradesmen often went to Canada on their own, leaving their dependents at home until they could afford to rejoin them. Many therefore looked no further than their employment as wage labourers on short-term contracts, and since they had no personal stake in their work, it is not surprising that they easily became discouraged and discontented.

Despite the fact that these fishermen and tradesmen had often been driven away from home by unemployment and economic pressures, they were rarely given financial assistance to go to Canada. Most had to finance their own removal, although some—such as the Clarke City recruits—took advantage of pre-paid passage schemes, and a limited number benefitted from the emigration fund of the Aberdeen Distress Committee in 1906 and 1907. There were, however, many other emigrants from North-East Scotland in this period who were systematically assisted to settle in Canada, and the part played by a variety of philanthropic agencies in organising and financing this exodus merits detailed examination.

NOTES

1) Malcolm Gray, 'Organisation and growth in the east-coast herring fishing, 1800-1885' in P. L. Payne (ed.), *Studies in Scottish business history* (London, 1967), p. 187.
2) Malcolm Gray, *The fishing industries of Scotland, 1790-1914: a study in regional adaptation* (Oxford, 1978), p. 147.
3) PP 1914 Cd. 7221, xxxi, 533: *Report of the Scottish departmental committee on the North Sea fishing industry*, app. 19, p. 222.
4) See vol. I, pp. 156-62.
5) Gray, *The fishing industries of Scotland*, p. 167.
6) GRA, MS 6/64/25: Visiting Book of Registered Poor, Peterhead, 1884-90, pp. 59, 210, 182 (nos 142, 478, 430).
7) *Ibid*, pp. 79 (no. 188), 131 (no. 324), 161 (no. 379), 162 (no. 384), 163 (no. 385), 193 (no. 447), 220 (no. 502).
8) GRA, MS 6/50/7: Lonmay Parochial Board, Record of Applications for Poor Relief, 1855-1902, pp. 76, 78.
9) *Ibid*, MS 6/50/5: Lonmay Parochial Board, General Register of Poor, 1845-1930; and MS 6/1/9: Aberdour Parochial Board, Record of Applications, 1891-1915.
10) *Ibid*, MS 6/64/17: Peterhead Parochial Board, General Register of Poor, 1869-1931, p. 141.
11) *Ibid*, MS 6/64/14: General Register of Poor, 1853-92, pp. 755, 779, 951; and MS 6/64/15: General Register of Poor, 1857-1903, p. 427.
12) *Ibid*, MS 6/27/22: Fraserburgh Parochial Board, Record of Applications, 1894-1907, pp. 53, 115, 190. Gray applied for relief in 1900 and Barrie in 1904.
13) *AJ*, 22 Mar., 14 Apr. 1888.
14) *Ibid*, 23 Jan. 1888.
15) See also 13 Apr. 1888, 28 May 1889.
16) For further details on this scheme, see Jill Wade, 'The "Gigantic Scheme"; crofter immigration and deep-sea fisheries development for British Columbia, 1887-1893' in *BC Studies*, no. 53 (Spring 1982), pp. 28-44.
17) 'We have, upon due and careful consideration, and at full meetings, decided that British Columbia is a likely field for our occupation and what we now crave is that should your lordship see fit to extend assistance to fishermen and others on the east coast of Scotland your lordship will not overlook the necessities of our case.' (*Fraserburgh Herald*, 7 Feb. 1888). See also *ibid*, 27 Dec. 1887, 31 Jan. 1888.
18) *Ibid*, 7 Feb. 1888.
19) *AJ*, 18 May 1888. See also *FH*, 15, 29 May 1888.
20) *FH*, 25 Apr. 1911.
21) GRA, MS 6/27/23: Fraserburgh Parochial Board, Record of Applications, 1907-1911, p. 24.

22) In 1902 Fraserburgh had 551 boats as against 375 in Peterhead, and employed one thousand more local people in various aspects of the industry. (See Sydney Wood, *The shaping of nineteenth century Aberdeenshire* (Stevenage, 1985), p. 267).

23) *AJ*, 10 May 1912.

24) PP 1914 Cd. 7642, xxxi, 733: *Report of the Scottish departmental committee on the North Sea fishing industry*, vol. II, minutes of evidence.

25) *Ibid*, p. 22.

26) *Ibid*, p. 171.

27) *Ibid*, p. 5.

28) *Ibid*, p. 90.

29) *Ibid*, p. 101. Another witness, however, claimed that there had been no emigration from Buckpool, and Joseph Addison, a merchant in Portknockie, told the enquiry that he knew of no-one having emigrated from there because of the poor prospects of acquiring part ownership of a boat (p. 37).

30) *Ibid*, pp. 128, 42.

31) Murray to James Smart, in PAC, C-7312, vol. 155, file 39501, part 1: arrangements made that Scottish and Welsh farm labourers and farmers wishing to settle in Manitoba and the North West Territories will be given work on the railway, 1897.

32) G. G. Archibald's report, incorporated in *Dept of the Interior, annual report on immigration, 1913-14*. Archibald also noted that such advice was not entirely within his scope.

33) See vol. I, pp. 254-9.

34) *Granite Cutters' Journal*, vol. I, no. 9 (Jan. 1902), p. 2. The author of the article was a native of Aberdeen, resident in the USA.

35) *In Memoriam* (APL), 1900, p. 46.

36) Arthur Brayley, *History of the granite industry of New England* (Boston, 1913), vol. II, p. 62.

37) *Ibid*, pp. 38-9.

38) *Ibid*, pp. 52-3.

39) *GCJ*, vol. IV, no. 2 (June 1904), p. 6. See also *AJ*, 27 May 1904.

40) *GCJ*, vol. I, no. 11 (Mar. 1902), p. 7; vol. IV, no. 4 (Aug. 1904), p. 6.

41) See Robertson's obituary in *AJ*, 6 Mar. 1906.

42) *GCJ*, vol. V, no. 6 (Oct. 1905), p. 3.

43) *Ibid*, vol. V, no. 10 (Feb. 1906), p. 12.

44) *Ibid*, vol. VI, no. 3 (July 1906), p. 8.

45) See, for instance, *ibid*, vol. VI, no. 3 (July 1906), p. 8; no. 6 (Oct. 1906), p. 8; vol. VII, no. 6 (Oct. 1907), p. 7.

46) *Ibid*, vol. VII, no. 5 (Sept. 1907), p. 1: letter from James Duncan who again asked the *Granite Cutters' Journal* to publicise the fact that the Stanstead Company was a non-union concern, and to urge unionists to stay away. Sometimes extra money was also deducted from recruits' wages for tools sold to them by the company when they arrived.

47) Vol. VII, no. 7 (Nov. 1907), p. 3.

48) E.g., *ibid*, vol. VI, no. 3 (July 1906), p. 8.

49) Vol. VII, no. 6 (Oct. 1907), p. 7: James Allathan, James Barbour, David Beattie, James Beattie, William Beattie, James Clark, John Clark, William Cruden, Alexander Garden, John Grieves, Charles Raeburn, George Rennie, Francis Smith. Subsequent comments in the *Granite Cutters' Journal* indicate that returning strike-breakers were in fact disciplined. In August 1908 (vol. VIII, no. 4, p. 4) the Aberdeen monumental branch of the union reported difficulties

experienced with men returning from Beebe Plain who thought they were being harshly treated. The branch secretary noted, however, that the union had the support of its general membership in the (unspecified) action taken.
50) See *AJ*, 4 Sept. 1907, article reprinted from the *Sherbrooke Daily Record.* The American Granite Cutters' International Union refused to recognise the legitimacy of the Canadian union. Aberdeen tradesmen continued to patronise the Stanstead Company, however, for John MacLennan, in his report for the week ending 19 November 1910, noted the recent or imminent departure of twenty stonecutters from Aberdeen to work at Beebe Plain. (PAC, RG 76, C-10294, vol. 405, file 590687, part 1).
51) *GCJ*, vol. V, no. 8 (Dec. 1905), p. 5; no. 12 (Apr. 1906), p. 4.
52) *Ibid*, vol. V, no. 11 (Mar. 1906), p. 8.
53) See, for instance, annual reports of the Granite Cutters' Union in Aberdeen in *ibid*, vol. V, no. 10 (Feb. 1906), p. 2; vol. VI, no. 10 (Feb. 1907), p. 2.
54) *Ibid*, vol. VI, no. 10 (Feb. 1907), p. 8; vol. VII, no. 4 (Aug. 1907), p. 5; no. 5 (Sept. 1907), p. 4.
55) *AJ*, 18 Mar. 1913. The union asked that hours be reduced from nine to eight per day for the first five days of the week, and from six to four hours on Saturdays. They asked for an increase in wages from $7\frac{1}{2}d.$ to $9d.$ per hour.
56) *AJ*, 4 Apr. 1913.
57) *Ibid*, 7 Apr. 1913.
58) 25 May 1913.
59) *AJ*, 11, 14, 15, 16, 18, 19, 21, 23 Dec. 1885.
60) *Ibid*, 29 Apr., 24 May 1882.
61) *Ibid*, 26 May 1882.
62) See also, for instance, *ibid*, 14 Apr., 26 May 1882, 26 Apr. 1905, 1 Apr. 1911.
63) *Ibid*, 13 Mar. 1906.
64) In November a public appeal was launched, headed by Queen Alexandra, and by the end of the year the 'Queen's Unemployed Fund' had reached £125,000.
65) Carrothers, *Emigration from the British Isles*, p. 252. See also PP 1905 [306], V, 507.
66) *AJ*, 12 Apr. 1907.
67) *Ibid*, 1, 2 Mar. 1907.
68) *Ibid*, 20 June, 3 July, 11 Aug. 1908. By August 1908 only £19 13s. 2d. had been recovered from assisted emigrants. During the course of the experiment almost 64 per cent of those who applied to the Distress Committee in Aberdeen were assisted to emigrate, as against only nine per cent in Glasgow. (*Ibid*, 4 Dec. 1907).
69) *Ibid*, 26 May 1882, 6 Apr. 1887.
70) *Ibid*, 5 May 1890, application to be made to the newspaper office.
71) *Ibid*, 14 July 1893, application to be made to A. S. Stewart, George Street, Aberdeen.
72) *Ibid*, 8 Jan. 1907.
73) *Ibid*, 27 Apr. 1910 (Northern Ticket Office); 21 Aug. 1911 (MacKay Bros).
74) *Ibid*, 17 Aug. 1910.
75) *Ibid*, 2 Apr. 1907.
76) John MacLennan's report for week ending 21 Sept. 1907.
77) *AJ*, 18 Feb. 1908.
78) *Ibid*, 26 Feb. 1908.
79) *Ibid*, 15 Apr. 1908. See also 21 Apr. 1908 and 4 Feb. 1909 for further warnings about unemployment in Canada.
80) *Ibid*, 21 Sept. 1907; and MacLennan's report for week ending 21 Sept.

81) MacLennan's report for week ending 21 Sept. 1907.
82) He was careful to point out, however, that the Canadian Immigration Department was in no way responsible for statements made by such emigration and employment bureaux (*EG*, 2 May 1913).
83) *Ibid*, 9 May 1913.
84) *AJ*, 12 June 1913.

CHAPTER V

Philanthropy and Emigration

The late nineteenth century was in one sense the age of the philanthropist. Social and economic problems in late Victorian Britain spawned the creation of a number of charitable societies, both national and provincial, which tackled pressing problems from a variety of motives and in a variety of ways. Many of their leaders were inspired primarily by an evangelical Christian commitment to give both practical and spiritual help to needy individuals. Others stressed the general benefits to the nation and empire to be derived from their particular programmes of social reform. Some societies concentrated exclusively on encouraging emigration, while others incorporated a degree of emigration into a home-based programme of reform or assistance, sometimes as an integral part of that programme. Indeed, it was partly on the grounds that charitable societies espoused the cause of emigration so enthusiastically that the government consistently refused to accede to demands for systematic state aid to emigrants. The societies sent the bulk of their recruits to Canada, and among the categories singled out for assistance were destitute children, the deserving unemployed and single women. The following two chapters will consider the experiences of some of these settlers, with particular reference to their origins in North-East Scotland, the purpose of their emigration, the degree to which it was successful and the nature of Canadian reaction to them.

Origins and development of charitable emigration agencies

Although there was considerable precedent for assisted emigration schemes, until the second half of the nineteenth century the numbers sent abroad in this way were relatively small and interest was sporadic, fluctuating according to the extent of economic distress at home. But the government's consistent refusal to undertake any major programme of state-aided emigration helped to ensure a continuing rôle for charitable emigration societies and individual philanthropists, and in 1886 over sixty private societies throughout the British Isles espoused the cause of assisted emigration.[1] The National Association for Promoting State-Directed Emigration and Colonisation numbered representatives from at least nine emigration societies among its members, including Maria Rye, Annie Macpherson, Thomas Barnardo and Ellen Joyce.

Although the Association did not achieve many of its objectives, it did bring pressure to bear on the government over a number of years; and it could perhaps claim some credit for the two minor state-aided Highland settlements at Killarney and Saltcoats, as well as the establishment of the Emigrants' Information Office[2] and the setting up of the select committee enquiry into colonisation in 1889. That enquiry, of course, did not ultimately recommend state-aided emigration, and fifteen years later another parliamentary committee reported negatively on Rider Haggard's proposals for government-assisted agricultural settlements in the colonies. It emphasised the failures of past experiments in state-aided colonisation, but praised the work of numerous emigration societies all over Britain, which it said had vastly raised standards in private emigration. These societies carefully selected suitable emigrants, gave them reliable advice and financial assistance, and looked after them on the voyage and in terms of finding situations for them in the colonies. They were, declared the report, largely responsible for improving the image of emigration since the 1860s, when many emigrants had complained about the fraudulent accounts of advertising agents who had a financial interest in despatching large numbers.[3]

So while the campaigns of national organisations for state-aided emigration were only sporadic and ultimately failed, the private emigration societies which periodically lent support to these national campaigns continued to operate in their own spheres and indeed increased in number. Public interest had been aroused by the debates surrounding state-aided colonisation, so the government's ultimate refusal to implement any such programme created a vacuum and probably helped to focus attention on the philanthropists. Different individuals and societies had different priorities, though many were influenced by evangelical Christian beliefs. Thomas Barnardo and William Quarrier were interested in juvenile emigration, as part of a wider programme of rescue work among destitute and orphaned children. Ellen Joyce and the Countess of Aberdeen were involved in specifically female emigration, while General William Booth of the Salvation Army favoured the removal of suitable people of both sexes as one solution to the problems of unemployment and destitution in Britain. The long-lasting economic depression of the late nineteenth century in fact influenced many of the philanthropists. They asserted that emigration would not only help Britain by alleviating overpopulation, but would open up better prospects for the emigrant at the same time as meeting the incessant colonial demand for certain categories of labour, particularly female domestic servants.

Then in the early twentieth century when the eugenics movement took hold in Britain arguments of racial purity and the importance of perpetuating the British race in the empire were used to justify a wide variety of emigration schemes, including those of a number of philanthropists.[4] They believed that such schemes could be used to solve social, economic and moral problems alike, and argued that their emigrants would be 'the bricks with which the Empire would be built'.[5] Dr Barnardo, for instance, spoke of the national and imperial advantages which would arise from his juvenile emigration scheme. He was determined that the colonies should not be burdened with the physically weak or morally undesirable of the British nation, so all his emigrants were to be physically sound and of certified moral character, as well as being of practical use to the recipient countries.[6] Although the Salvation Army aimed to relieve the overcrowded home labour market by means of emigration, it did not advocate an indiscriminate exodus. Any emigration scheme should benefit the mother country, the recipent colony and the individual emigrant in equal measure, and General Booth always stressed that he would not send abroad the dregs of British society, but only those who would be an asset to the empire. He aimed to build up the empire partly by exporting that section of the unemployed, destitute surplus which had shown some aptitude for emigration and which had been given some training in necessary colonial skills; at the same time assistance and supervision were to be offered to better-off (but often still poor) individuals and families who wished to improve their prospects by emigrating, and to the wives and children of men who had already gone abroad. General Booth put great emphasis on the development of the British empire by good British stock, and only very reluctantly agreed to parties of emigrants being sent to foreign countries. One of his supporters claimed in 1909 that the future of the empire lay with British emigrants, and spoke of the necessity of pouring into the colonies (particularly Canada) a continual stream of British blood.[7]

For most philanthropists, however, the philosophical justification of emigration on the grounds of empire-building or eugenics was subordinate to practical issues. They regarded it primarily as a legitimate way to help needy individuals across a wide spectrum of society. In the field of child welfare, for instance, Thomas Barnardo and William Quarrier both incorporated assisted emigration schemes into their rescue and rehabilitation programmes, in England and Scotland respectively. Although Barnardo's fame rests mainly on the Homes for all kinds of destitute children which he established throughout England, he had also sent over 31,000 juveniles abroad by 1914, 28,689 to Canada and 2,342 to Australia.[8] In 1867, with Lord Shaftesbury's patronage, Barnardo founded the East End Juvenile Mission, and opened his first Boys' Home in London three years later. Boys from this Home who he thought would not prosper in Britain were sent to Canada provided that £10 could be obtained to defray the cost of passage, while a few other children were sent to South Africa, Australia and New Zealand, mainly to positions of domestic service.

Until the 1880s Barnardo refused to implement his own emigration scheme, partly because he was making use of other specialist agencies in this field, notably that of Annie Macpherson, the East End social worker and evangelical daughter of a Scottish Quaker. She had begun to take parties of destitute children from London to Canada in 1869. Her recruits were first received into Homes in Britain, where they were prepared for emigration and taught marketable skills, while arrangements were made for their supervised passage, reception and distribution in Canada. She accompanied the first party of 100 boys, along with her friend Ellen Bilborough, who then remained in Canada for thirty years to manage a distributing home which was provided by the mayor and council of the town of Belleville, Ontario. Macpherson's sisters, Rachel Merry and Louisa Birt, at first helped to run receiving centres in London and Liverpool, but as the work expanded they moved to Canada to superintend distributing homes which were subsequently opened at Galt, Ontario and Knowlton, Quebec, respectively. Not only Barnardo but also several other evangelical children's organisations, as well as a number of English poor law unions, used Annie Macpherson's agency to emigrate children who were under their care, and whom she undertook to provide with homes across the Atlantic.[9]

Barnardo had also been discouraged from implementing his own emigration scheme by the restrictions placed on Maria Rye's removal of pauper children after 1874, when she was accused of lining her own pocket and providing inadequate after-care facilities.[10] By 1882, however, financial constraints on his work in Britain and the encouragement of supporters like Samuel Smith had convinced him that emigration should form a more integral part of his rescue work. Smith, an industrialist and from 1882 Liberal Member of Parliament for Liverpool, had been impressed by Louisa Birt's work in that city and particularly favoured emigration as a 'safety valve' which would defuse social tensions at home.[11] In 1882 Smith gave Barnardo a special donation to be used for emigration, and on 20 August Barnardo shipped his first party of fifty-one boys from Liverpool to Canada. The success of this venture, in which all the boys were soon placed out in employment, encouraged him to repeat the experiment the following year, when he also sent a party of girls to the Dominion. At this time he acquired a house in Peterborough, Ontario, which was used as a distributing home for the children. This house (Hazelbrae) later became the distributing centre for girls, and other premises in Toronto and Winnipeg were acquired as distributing centres for the boys.

In 1884 Barnardo himself paid the first of several visits to Canada, mainly in order to find a site for an 'industrial farm' which he proposed to establish in the Far West. He was concerned that some boys who had been located in rural Ontario had drifted into the cities and into their old lifestyles. He believed this problem could be solved by establishing in the Far West, well away from any city, an industrial farm which could train up to fifty boys a year for a career on the land. Many western farmers were in need of labourers, and it was hoped that some boys would ultimately take up homesteads of their own. Barnardo found a suitable site near Russell, Manitoba, close to a branch line of the Canadian Pacific Railway, and on his second trip to Canada in 1887 he successfully completed negotiations for the acquisition (by grant and purchase) of 8,000 acres in this area. Selected boys aged over seventeen were sent to the industrial farm for a year's training, after which they could take situations as farm labourers or apply for homestead grants.[12]

Barnardo insisted that all his emigrants should be carefully selected and should receive some preliminary training before they were sent abroad. A small percentage was aged under ten, and these children were boarded out with Canadian families at the expense of the Barnardo organisation, or occasionally adopted, while older children were allocated places by the distributing homes. To ensure their future well-being, they were to be well supervised and followed up by visitation and correspondence; he was adamant that they should not be 'cut adrift', as he thought abdication of responsibility was the rock on which many emigration schemes had foundered. The network of depots and distributing homes across Canada was not only to take in new arrivals and place them in employment, but should keep in regular contact with them; and if the settlers were ever ill or in need in later years they were invited to return to these homes for assistance.

Financial pressure and inadequate facilities elsewhere meant that Barnardo's work was confined mainly to Canada, although he always hoped that it would be extended. In 1883 he had sent an unescorted group of boys to Australia, but lack of protection during and after the voyage led him to send out only isolated cases in the custody of friends thereafter. In 1902 he sent his son to South Africa to assess the feasibility of setting up children's training homes there. Stuart Barnardo's report was discouraging, in that it spoke of an unsuitable social climate, Dutch hostility to further British immigration, and the government's refusal to give financial assistance at a time when Barnardo's overseas work could not have been extended without outside funding.

Barnardo's emigration work was opposed in some quarters in both Canada and Britain. During the economic depression of the 1890s unemployed Canadians resented the influx of assisted settlers under the Barnardo scheme, and attempted to discredit them by claiming that they comprised the dregs of Britain's city slums.[13] Barnardo refuted these allegations, on one occasion providing evidence for an enquiry into juvenile immigration instituted by Lady Aberdeen. During her husband's term of office as Governor-General of Canada she had become concerned at allegations of excessive criminality among young immigrants; she was prompted to write to the Ministry of the Interior after the death of a Barnardo boy, George Green, had led to his employer being tried for manslaughter, a case which resulted mainly in extensive derogatory publicity about the introduction of defective children to Canada.[14] The reports and statistics which A. M. Burgess at the Ministry obtained from various receiving homes in Canada and philanthropic emigration societies in Britain led him to write to Lady Aberdeen

> that the immigration of juveniles is not the unmitigated evil which some of the opponents of the system so positively assert. For the country it involves no disadvantage, so far as the information at our disposal discloses. For the children themselves it means in many instances salvation from moral ruin.

Burgess made no attempt to answer her query about the conditions under which the children lived, but merely tried to convince her that they were essentially law-abiding.[15] Meanwhile critics in Britain claimed Barnardo was depleting the ranks of female domestic servants and male farm workers. In reply he pointed out that the vast majority of his children were placed in situations at home, even though it made financial sense to send abroad as many as possible. He became increasingly convinced of both the practical and the moral justification for emigration and argued the case for the effects of environment over heredity in forming character, echoing Burgess's statement of 1896. He claimed that many of the children came from such bad environments that if, after they had been trained in one of his Homes, they were returned to their families, much of the benefit of this preliminary training would be lost. It was therefore preferable to remove them entirely and irrevocably from the evil influences of their homes.

Barnardo's rescue work was centred on the English city slums, particularly in London, although many of the children had come originally from other parts of the country, and sometimes even from abroad.[16] According to the *Aberdeen Journal* of 19 January 1905, 'not a few' of the 60,000 children helped by Barnardo since 1867 had come from the North of Scotland. Certainly people in the area were kept informed about the various aspects of his work and contributed financially to it, often as a result of fund-raising tours undertaken in the region by Barnardo children. In January 1905, for instance, a group of Barnardo boys gave musical performances in a number of North-East villages as part of a fund-raising programme. And in October 1910 during a similar tour (aimed specifically at defraying the emigration costs of two participants) the Homes' deputation secretary, Maurice Snellgrove, explained to audiences the work of the Barnardo organisation. Then in June 1912 Barnardo's warden for Scotland, W. H. Fuller, came to Aberdeen to address a meeting in the YMCA.[17]

But despite the *Aberdeen Journal*'s claims, it seems that North-East Scotland—indeed Scotland as a whole—supplied very few recruits for Barnardo's Homes and emigrant parties. Of a random sample of 5,655 emigrant boys taken for the years 1882-94 and 1910-12, only forty were Scottish, and of this number only five had North-East origins. Only two of these five had been admitted to Barnardo's straight from their home area: an orphan, whose case had been taken up by the Superintendent of a Mission Sunday School in Aberdeen, but who had been refused admission to the City's School of Industry because he was over age; and an illegitimate infant, who had been refused entry to Quarrier's Homes after his grandmother in Aberdeen became too ill to look after him. Two of the other North-East emigrants had previously been admitted into Barnardo's Edinburgh Home, having moved to the capital from Aberdeen and Fraserburgh respectively. The remaining Aberdeen-born emigrant, another orphan, had spent most of his childhood with relatives in Somerset before being sent to Barnardo's Homes at the age of thirteen, and then to Canada a year later. Most of the Scots recruits in fact only came into contact with Barnardo's once they had left home, often after they had become destitute following a fruitless search for work in Edinburgh or London.[18]

Barnardo's limited involvement with destitute children in Scotland did not mean he was unaware of the relief measures provided by others in this sphere. In the late Victorian network of evangelical philanthropy he was well aware of the activities of contemporaries such as Lord and Lady Aberdeen. Lord Aberdeen had in fact laid the foundation stone of Barnardo's Cottage Homes in 1876 and had spearheaded the formation of a committee which took over the responsibility for his work.[19] In 1884 Lady Aberdeen established a female orphanage in the village of Methlick on the Haddo House estate, and the *Aberdeen Journal* indicates that some of these orphans were subsequently sent to Canada, perhaps in imitation of the schemes of Barnardo or William Quarrier.[20] Barnardo and the Aberdeens alike were acquainted with William Quarrier, another Scottish evangelical and philanthropist who specialised in child welfare and who implemented his own scheme of Canadian emigration. Barnardo was present at the opening of Quarrier's Orphan Homes at Bridge of Weir in 1878 and there were many similarities in the emigration policies and practices of the two men.

Quarrier's Orphan Homes: rescue, rehabilitation and emigration

If Barnardo's link with assisted emigration from North-East Scotland is very tenuous, Quarrier's scheme had more direct relevance for the area. When the Countess of Aberdeen first promoted assisted female emigration under the auspices of the Aberdeen Ladies' Union after 1883, candidates were initially to be sent out to Canada under Quarrier's arrangements, and to his Receiving Home.[21] By the 1860s William Quarrier had a prosperous boot and shoe business in Glasgow, but the memory of his impoverished childhood, coupled with his evangelical zeal, meant that he was already devoting much of his profit to the relief of needy children in the city.[22] As a result of a meeting with Annie Macpherson in 1871 and financial backing from Thomas Corbett, a Scottish businessman living in London, Quarrier was encouraged to establish an orphanage in Glasgow by the end of that year. By 1872 the premises were so full that new accommodation was obtained at Cessnock House, Govan for the boys and at two locations in Govan Road for the girls. Four years later he acquired the property near Bridge of Weir which in 1878 was opened as The Orphan Homes of Scotland. Children qualified for admission if they were 'Orphan boys and girls deprived of both parents, children of widows or others with no relative able or willing to keep them, from 1 to 14 years of age, from any part of the country'.[23]

The voluntary emigration of suitable children was an important part of Quarrier's rescue programme from the start.[24] On 23 June 1872, ten years before Barnardo, he sent his first party of thirty-five Glasgow and Edinburgh children to Canada, having received sufficient donations to cover the transportation costs of £10 per emigrant. They were supervised on the voyage and taken on arrival into Annie Macpherson's Receiving Homes at Knowlton, Belleville and Galt, from where they were hired or those under twelve were adopted into private households. In the first of thirty-one annual reports on his work issued at this time Quarrier stated his faith in juvenile emigration on practical as well as moral grounds:

> By the emigration feature of the work we are enabled to place these children in Christian homes in Canada, where they will be kindly cared for and watched over by Miss Macpherson and her helpers. By this means we hope to be enabled yearly to rescue a fresh set of boys and girls, whilst, without this providential

14   William Quarrier.

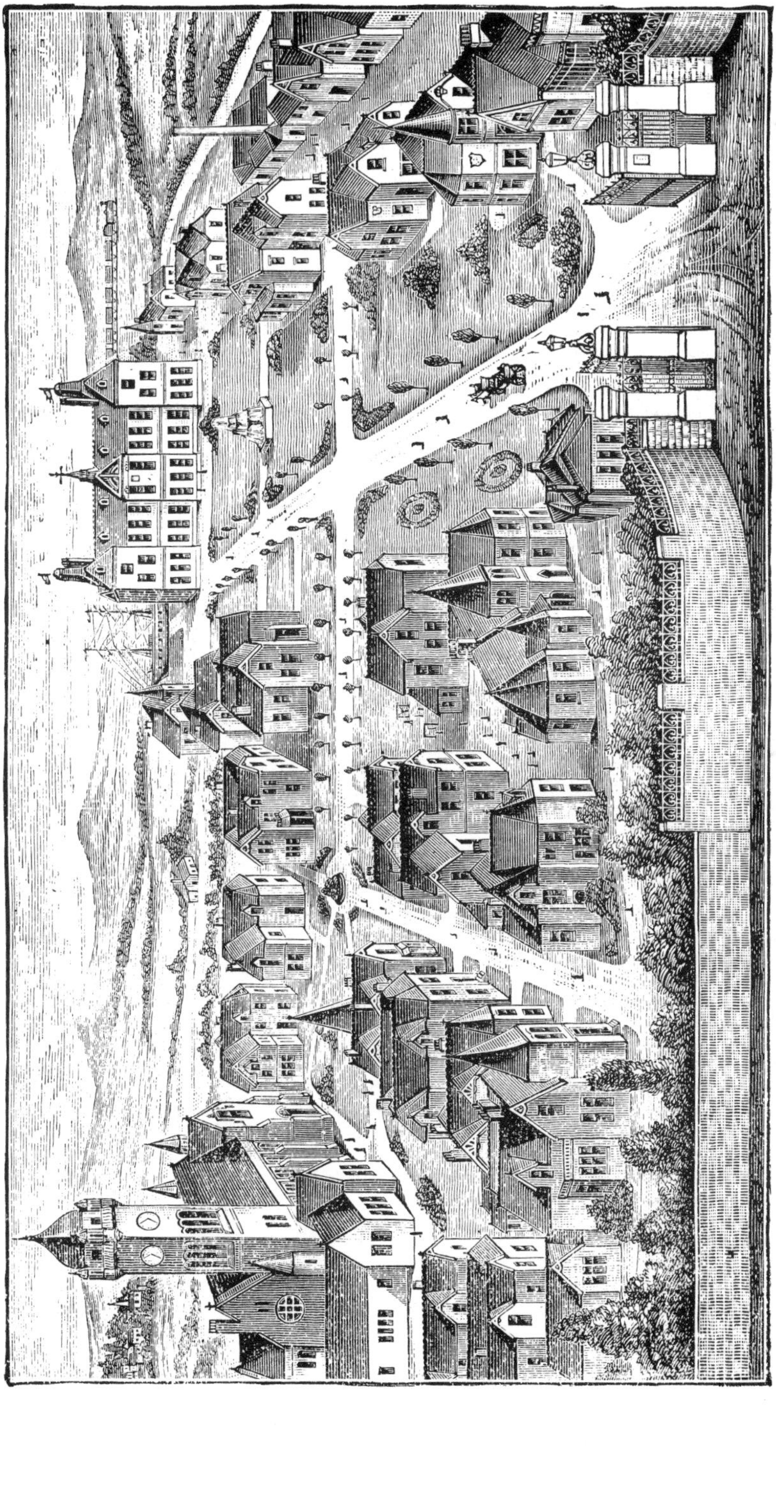

15   Quarrier's Orphan Homes of Scotland.

outlet, we should be stocked up with the same set of children for four or five years, and unable to rescue more.[25]

The success of his first experiment encouraged Quarrier to make emigration a regular part of his work, finances permitting, and within seven years 400 of the 700 children received into his orphanages had been sent to Canada.[26] In May 1878 he accompanied a shipload of seventy-eight children, sixty-six of whom were from his orphanages. During his visit he met many of those he had sent out in the previous seven years, and came home resolved to despatch even more emigrants, convinced 'that we can do nothing here for the class of children we help that will at all compare with what can be done in Canada.'[27] Quarrier paid several further visits to Canada in pursuit of this work. Until 1887 he used Annie Macpherson's facilities and the services of Ellen Bilborough at Belleville in supervising and placing the children. In 1878 Miss Bilborough was put in sole charge of the Marchmont Home at Belleville, which by that time was catering primarily for Scottish children.[28] But faced with rising numbers of emigrants each year, Quarrier in 1887 built his own reception and distribution centre, 'Fairknowe', at Brockville, Ontario. Here he employed a resident superintendent, matron and staff to find situations for the children and to supervise their after-care until they were twenty-one. In the months before an emigrant party arrived these staff advertised in the press and in church circles for farmers who would either adopt a child or employ an (older) one under indenture. After Quarrier's death in 1903 the work in Canada was taken over by his daughter Agnes Burges and her husband, and by the time the depression put an end to it in 1933, a total of 6,987 children had been sent to Canada under the auspices of The Orphan Homes of Scotland.[29]

In contrast to Barnardo and Maria Rye, but following the example of Annie Macpherson, Quarrier did not advertise his financial needs publicly, relying instead on freewill gifts to keep the scheme going. Contributions flowed in from all over Britain, not least from individuals and organisations in North-East Scotland. In his 1879 *Narrative of Facts* Quarrier noted the particular generosity of Aberdonians and quoted from one correspondent who had regularly contributed to the emigration work and who now enclosed

£10 to take a lassie to Canada, unless you want it much for any other purpose, in which case use your discretion. I am glad to see that you aim at sending out 100 this season. That's right, the more the better; we can easily spare them, particularly girls, and they will do good in Canada.[30]

The emigration scheme was brought to public notice in the North-East by representatives such as Ellen Bilborough, who spoke in Aberdeen in 1878 and by Quarrier himself, who gave three addresses in the city in September 1891, making reference to the success of the Canadian work.[31]

Like Barnardo, Quarrier was criticised both by those who thought any reduction of the labour supply in Britain damaged national well-being, and by some who claimed that he was exporting the dregs of Scottish society, to

Canada's detriment. Like Barnardo, he replied that many of the children were in fact placed in situations at home, while the emigrants were offered prospects of independence and employment which would never have been possible in Scotland. In his very first *Narrative of Facts* in 1872 he challenged his critics:

> And to those who object to emigration as withdrawing labour from this country, we would say, 'Come and see the children as we take them in, and you will perceive that not the labour market, but the crime market, is likely to be affected by our work of rescue'.[32]

The removal of the children also opened the way for an acceleration and expansion of the rescue work at home. Although many of his emigrants had been taken from utter destitution, he claimed that the preliminary training they received in his Homes prepared them adequately for colonial life and that the failure rate of his Canadian settlers was minimal.[33] This claim was apparently accepted by the Canadian authorities, for when Quarrier complained in 1897 about a new act to restrict juvenile immigration to Ontario, he was told that in contrast to the children introduced by some British agencies, his candidates had always been entirely satisfactory, and would continue to be welcomed as settlers.[34] The act subjected the activities of the Canadian receiving homes to much greater scrutiny, but Quarrier regarded it as a personal insult and an unwarranted interference by the Ontario government in charitable schemes which it did not support financially, and from 1897 he refused to emigrate more children. But after his death in 1903 his family resumed the scheme, convinced that the 1897 act offered better protection for the children, rather than being a hindrance to their removal.

Most of the children in Quarrier's orphanages and emigrant parties were drawn from Glasgow and the surrounding area. But there was by no means an exclusive concentration on the west of Scotland. Children from all over Scotland and from several parts of England were also received into the Homes, often as a preliminary to their being sent to Canada. In 1885, for instance, several boys from the Isle of Man Industrial School passed through Cessnock on their way to Canada, and Manchester and Cambridge were among other English towns which despatched emigrants through Quarrier's agency. North-East Scotland did not only make substantial financial contributions to the emigration scheme; the area was also represented among the emigrants themselves. In forty case history books of emigrant children examined for the years 1879-1919 there are 121 cases of children with Kincardine, Aberdeen, Banff, Moray and Nairn origins being admitted and subsequently sent to Canada, after a suitable period of training. They form just over two per cent of the total number of emigrants sent out by the Orphan Homes of Scotland during this period, while a number of other children with North-East backgrounds were taken into the Homes but not subsequently sent abroad.[35]

Why were these children taken into care? As might be expected, several were destitute orphans who had no-one to look after them, and whose cases

16   Fairknowe Receiving Home, Brockville, Ontario.

had been brought to Quarrier's notice by relatives who could not cope, concerned friends or employers, inspectors of poor, local ministers or visiting 'Bible women'. In some cases a parent had fallen ill or become disabled and could no longer support the family. Other children were illegitimate and had been abandoned or neglected by one or both parents, cases which sometimes involved the intervention of the Society for the Prevention of Cruelty to Children. Occasionally a child was left destitute when a parent was committed to prison. Before a child was admitted into the Orphan Homes detailed enquiries were always made into its background and exhaustive efforts made to find relatives who could take responsibility for it. Unlike Barnardo, Quarrier tried to follow Annie Macpherson's lead in ensuring that no child was sent to Canada without its own consent and the consent of its nearest relatives; even though he was firmly convinced that for many children emigration offered the only chance of a fresh start in life, away from the corrupting influence of their home environments.

Several children from North-East Scotland who were taken into Quarrier's care had simply been orphaned. In August 1885 two brothers and a sister from Aberdeen aged between five and nine were admitted to Bridge of Weir, having been brought in by their grandmother after both parents had died. The boys were subsequently sent to Canada in March 1890 and their sister two months later.[36] John, aged thirteen, was admitted in August 1886, claiming that his mother had died the previous month and his father six years earlier. On his mother's death the landlord of their house in the Gallowgate, Aberdeen, had sold all the furniture and paid John's fare to Glasgow, where he could more easily earn his living selling papers than was possible in Aberdeen. John was very anxious to be sent to Canada, but his story could not be verified by any of Quarrier's contacts in Aberdeen, and two years later he disappeared without trace.[37]

A family of five children from Lossiemouth aged between two and thirteen was admitted and sent to Bridge of Weir in 1888 after their father and mother had both died of TB in August and October respectively:

> Before her death she [the mother] was much comforted by the knowledge that the children would be cared for here. Rev Mr. Riddell Baptist Church Lossiemouth visited her made application for their admission had emigration paper sent which she signed and now brings them through the Inspector of Poor promising to pay railway fares &c. There are a good many relations as grand father uncles aunts half brothers &c but none of them have taken any interest in or helped the family.[38]

A paternal uncle had been traced to Assiniboia, and two girls and a boy were subsequently sent to Canada in May 1889. Another girl who was sent out in May 1890 died of TB two years later and the final brother emigrated in 1896. A family of four children from Inverallochy was sent to Bridge of Weir in September 1892, following the deaths of their parents earlier that year. An aunt in Cairness had been paid by the parochial board of Rathen to keep the children since their mother's death but no relatives were able to assume this responsibility permanently. Three other children were in farm service and another, aged eleven, had been adopted by a woman in Lonmay. Of the three girls and a boy sent to Bridge of Weir, one girl and the boys were subsequently sent to Canada in 1894 and 1899 respectively.[39]

In 1894 James Denoon of Lossiemouth recommended that Archie should be admitted to the Homes at Bridge of Weir, following the death of his mother and father in 1888 and 1894 respectively. No relatives could be found to support him and he was admitted and sent out to Canada the following year.[40] Donald and Willie aged five and seven from Aberdeen were taken in by Quarrier after their father, a street porter, had died. Their mother had died the previous year and their half-sister in Aberdeen had signed the necessary emigration papers. Willie in fact went to sea, but Donald was sent to Canada in 1905.[41] James from Aberdeen went to Bridge of Weir on 14 July 1902. His maternal uncle had written from Edinburgh to recommend his admission after both parents had died, and although James ran away back to Aberdeen soon afterwards, he was returned to the Homes and subsequently sent to Canada in 1904.[42] John and Helen from Forres were cared for by their grandfather after their parents died but on his death they were boarded out by the parish until they were sent to Bridge of Weir in 1903 and from there to Canada in 1907.[43] Of a family of seven children from Botriphnie sent to Bridge of Weir in 1904, all but one girl (who died) later went to Canada in 1909, 1910, 1911 and 1920. After their father had died of TB in 1902 the parish had paid ten shillings a week to the family, but when the mother and another child also died of the same disease her brother in Exeter requested that the family should be admitted to the Orphan Homes. On enquiry it was found that the mother's half-brother would have taken the eldest girl, but he agreed with the recommendation that the family should be kept together, accompanied the children to Bridge of Weir, signed the emigration papers, and periodically visited them thereafter until they were sent to Canada. A paternal aunt in Buckie had also given her consent for the children to be sent to the Orphan Homes, although she was a Roman Catholic.[44] Alice and Grace, aged five and nine, were admitted from Aberdeen in 1906, having lost both parents. The three children of their father's previous marriage were unwilling or unable to take them, and after being sent to Bridge of Weir Grace was ultimately emigrated to Canada in 1910 while Alice went into service in Britain eight years later.[45]

Luke, aged seven, was sent to Bridge of Weir from the Aberdeen Poorhouse at Oldmill in 1912, where he and his mother had lived since his father's death two years earlier. His father's employer, Robert Duthie, had taken an interest in the family and when Luke's mother died in 1912 he recommended that the child be sent to Bridge of Weir and obtained Luke's grandfather's consent to this move. Duthie retained an interest in the boy, sending him savings certificates in 1918 and writing appreciatively to Mary Quarrier after Luke had been sent to Canada in 1921. When the boy's grandfather died in an Aberdeen poorhouse at the end of 1921, leaving a small sum of money, Duthie remitted this legacy to Miss Quarrier on Luke's behalf and asked her to supply him with his address in Canada.[46]

Sometimes the death of the breadwinner in a family caused such hardship that the children were admitted to the Orphan Homes even if the remaining parent was still alive. The disablement of one or both parents could have similar consequences. In 1885, for instance, there were two cases involving disabled fishermen. On 2 June two brothers, aged four and seven, were sent from Aberdeen to Bridge of Weir after their father had given written consent for their removal to Canada, where they were then sent in 1886:

> Father ... got frost-bitten while on board a Polar Whaling Vessel and is not quite fit to provide for these. His wife has a baby at the breast and is a very worthless low character. The Inspectors of Poor at Old Machar & St Nicholas Aberdeen say they have had a great deal of trouble with her but cannot take the children from her and board them out as they are not orphans.

To send the children to the Orphan Homes was presumably a legitimate way to remove them from their mother's influence, a device which was again adopted twelve years later in respect of the baby girl who had been born in the Old Machar Poorhouse in 1884:

> Mother an extremely bad character tramps the country, & it is feared might have an evil influence over ——————— if not removed from danger.

At the father's request the Rev John Calan of Old Aberdeen asked for the girl to be admitted to the Orphan Homes, with a view to her being sent to Canada. The father, who since 1885 had moved from Peterhead to Aberdeen to work as a shoemaker, was in receipt of 2s. 6d. per week from the parochial board, having lost both his feet and the partial use of his hands. He signed the girl's emigration form in the presence of two Bible women, one of whom then accompanied her to Bridge of Weir, but she was not in fact sent to Canada, returning to her father in Aberdeen in 1900.[47]

Also in 1885 two of the five children of a disabled Aberdeen fisherman were sent to Bridge of Weir in March, then to Canada in June:

> Father James who was a fisherman has lost an arm and since trawling boats began to be used has been able to earn almost nothing. Mother Ann used to bait his hooks etc but it seems a mystery how they manage now to make a living.

A Mrs Edmond had had the two sisters admitted to 'some sort of Day Feeding School' in Aberdeen three years earlier, but now they had to leave she was anxious that the good work done in the school should not be ruined and therefore offered to pay their passage and outfit to Canada.[48]

Three children from Udny were taken in by Quarrier in 1889 on the recommendation of Robert Stephen of Fraserburgh, who was acquainted with the children's circumstances through their maternal aunts. Their father, a farm servant, had died in Fraserburgh in 1881, since when their mother had

> struggled on and earned a living by washing &c but has now fairly broken down

through privations it is believed. She was not able to come here but after full explanation of the work signed the paper. It is feared she is consumptive. She has been confined to bed but it is hoped that relieved of the burden of the children she may rally to be fit for a light situation. She is a very respectable person.

The children were brought to Bridge of Weir by one of the aunts, and the two boys were subsequently sent to Canada in 1894 and 1895.[49] There was a similar case in Aberdeen in 1891 when two brothers, aged eight and one, were sent to the Orphan Homes. Their father, a mill worker, had died the previous year, since when the family had received four shillings a week from the parish. The mother, who was consumptive and unfit for work, signed the boys' admission papers but kept one child, a girl aged six, on the understanding that if she died this child was to join her brothers. Since the mother was unable to travel to Bridge of Weir, the boys were brought down by a Miss Sinclair, a dress-maker in Aberdeen, who had interested herself in their case, and one of them was sent to Canada in 1894.[50] In 1900 a brother and sister from Aberdeen were taken in since their mother had died and their father, a stone polisher, was said to be dying, once more from tuberculosis. No relatives could help the children, who were both sent to Bridge of Weir, the boy being sent to Canada in 1908.[51] A dispute arose in 1909 over a boy from Woodside, Aberdeen, who had been sent to the Orphan Homes four years earlier. His father had died and the widow and child were in receipt of 2s. 6d. per week from St Nicholas Parochial Board, since the woman was not strong and unable to earn enough to support herself and the boy. No help could be expected from the three children of the father's former marriage or from any other relatives, and the case was recommended by the Rev Andrew Dickson of Hilton Church, Aberdeen. Although the mother herself accompanied the child to Bridge of Weir, signed the admission papers and said she was quite willing for him to be sent to Canada, in May 1909 she requested that he be returned to her at Raemoir, Banchory. Her request was blocked by Mr Dickson, who warned that it would be a great mistake to return him. In reply to a second application the mother was told that the Homes would not hand over her son without the minister's permission, and in September 1909 he was sent to Canada.[52]

Some illegitimate children were admitted when they were left destitute by the death or desertion of their mothers. Four such children from Macduff, aged between six and twelve, were sent to Bridge of Weir after their mother died in 1886. No-one could be found to admit paternity, and the children were being maintained by the parochial board but left in the charge of their maternal grandmother in Macduff, who was 'old and deaf and quite unfit to look after them'. Their admission to the Orphan Homes was recommended by the minister, Mr Hunter, and two boys were subsequently sent to Canada in 1887, another boy in 1888 and their sister in 1893.[53] John, aged seven, was admitted from Aberdeen on the death of his mother in 1891. His father was unknown and no relatives were able to assist him. His stepfather, a lamplighter, had four children already and could not take him in, but agreed to hand him over to the Orphan Homes after their work was explained to him, and John was sent to Canada the following year.[54] In 1898 Jeannie, aged six, was sent from Elgin to Bridge of Weir on the recommendation of the Inspector of Poor at nearby Urquhart. Two years earlier her mother, who had several other illegitimate children, had boarded her out with a woman in Elgin, promising to pay her upkeep, but she had then disappeared and responsibility for maintaining the child had fallen on the parochial board. Jeannie was sent to Canada in 1906.[55] Charles's mother died of TB in Keith in 1910 when the boy was eleven. His reputed father could not be located and none of the relatives traced through the Homes' investigations (including a half-brother, two half-sisters, a maternal grandmother and an uncle in Keith, and another uncle and two aunts in Ayrshire) was able to take him. He was recommended for admission by the Rev Hugh Fitzpatrick of Keith and was sent to Canada in 1912.[56]

William Quarrier shared the philosophy of contemporary emigrationists such as Barnardo and William Booth, that to send people abroad was a legitimate means of offering them a better chance in life, often with the aim of removing them irrevocably from corrupting influences at home. On these grounds some children from North-East Scotland, most of whom were illegitimate, were sent to Canada under the auspices of Quarrier's Orphan Homes. Bella and Jane, aged five and four, were admitted in 1886 and sent to Canada in 1888. They were two of the three illegitimate children of an unemployed mill worker in Aberdeen, and were said to have been brought up 'horribly' by their mother. This was one of at least three local cases recommended to Quarrier by A. C. Barker of 79 Chapel Street, Aberdeen and the children's initial clothing and later Canadian outfit were supplied by a Mrs Fraser of 8 West Craibstone Street, Aberdeen.[57]

Two nine-year-old children, both illegitimate, were sent to Quarrier's Homes in December 1887 through the agency of Miss Donaldson, a Bible woman in Inverness. Bella was removed from the custody of a woman in Inverness who was allegedly keeping her for immoral purposes; while John, who had begged the Inverness police authorities to give him a chance in life by sending him away from home, was handed over to Miss Donaldson for removal to Bridge of Weir. Both children were sent to Canada in 1888, though John returned to Inverness in 1894.[58]

There were three cases of a similar nature in 1889. In February Albert, aged fourteen, was sent to the Orphan Homes at the suggestion of Mrs Anderson, 26 St Swithin Street, Aberdeen. Little was known of his background but he was very anxious to be sent to Canada, perhaps because a farmer for whom he had worked had recently emigrated:

His mother lived with her father, a respectable man, at Aboyne till his death and then removed to Aberdeen. She was much given to drink but seems somewhat improved. Besides Albert she has another illegitimate boy aged 12 by different man. She would gladly send him too. Mrs A. thought best to see how Albert got on and not relieve her all at once. Albert was employed on a farm but master emigrated and the mother failed to get him suitable work in the city and he is very anxious to get to Canada himself.[59]

In July William, another illegitimate child from Aboyne, was sent to Bridge of Weir, again at Mrs Anderson's instigation. Nothing was known of his father and the emigration form was signed by his mother. Although William went to Canada in 1890 he apparently returned to Aberdeen in 1897 to trace his mother but left again for Canada within a year.[60] In November 1889 George, aged five, was sent to Bridge of Weir after the Rev J. J. Tindall of Kinellar had applied for his admission through Mr Barker of Chapel Street, Aberdeen. George was illegitimate, but his mother had since married another man and according to Tindall, 'the child has been subjected to constant and cruel maltreatment at the hand of the step-father'. His mother, who had just given birth to twins and could not cope with the elder child, signed the emigration form and George was sent to Canada in 1892.[61]

There was some dispute over the custody of John, an illegitimate child originally from Pitsligo, who went to the Homes in 1891 at the age of ten. When his father had stopped paying his maintenance in 1888 responsibility for the boy fell entirely to his mother, a domestic servant, who by 1891 was working in a laundry in Edinburgh. Since the person with whom her son was boarded was a drunkard who abused the boy, she applied to have him taken into Quarrier's care, but within a month a woman in Edinburgh had requested the return of the boy, whom she said she had adopted. Her request was supported in a letter three months later from John's reputed father in Ellon, Aberdeenshire, but he was told he had no control over the child, and since John's mother claimed that the woman was not telling the truth, John was kept at Bridge of Weir until he was sent to Canada in May 1892.[62]

In 1893 the Wesleyan minister in Banff recommended that Annie (7) and Jessie (5), two of a family of six illegitimate children, be sent to Bridge of Weir. Three of the children had died and the mother was about to enter a Salvation Army Rescue Home in Glasgow with the youngest child. No support had ever been offered by the fathers, and a Salvation Army officer accompanied the woman to Bridge of Weir when she came to sign the admission papers. The elder girl died soon after admission but Jessie was sent to Canada in 1896.[63] Alexander, from Duffus, was admitted in 1893 at the age of thirteen, primarily because his mother wanted to give him a better chance in life. She had divorced his father, a ploughman, and in 1893 was working for a sheriff's wife in Bridge of Weir, so was familiar with Quarrier's work. She felt that her son needed better care and training than he was receiving from the woman in Elgin with whom he had been boarded for nine years, so when this woman married and refused to keep him his mother applied to have him admitted to the Orphan Homes. Alexander was sent to Canada the following year.[64]

Richard (13) and Jane (6) were taken to Bridge of Weir in 1894 after the courts had given a custody order to Quarrier. Their father, a collier, had died in Aberdeen about five years earlier and their mother, an alcoholic, had recently been convicted at Dundee for allowing the children to beg and sing on the streets. She had nò fixed residence but was accustomed to travelling the country with the children. Although she had re-married she had left her husband and was now living 'with some low character of a man in a common lodging-house and they are both living off proceeds of children's earnings'. Richard died two years after entering the Homes but his sister was sent to Canada in 1897.[65] In 1902 two brothers from Elgin, aged eleven and five, were admitted to the Homes eight months after the death of their father. Formerly a prosperous grain merchant in Elgin, he had died of alcoholism in the asylum and their mother, who was similarly addicted, had recently been in the poorhouse. During that period her four children had been boarded out in Elgin, but the boys were returned to her when she went to live with her brother in Orton, Fochabers. In view of the mother's condition, however, the boys' removal to Bridge of Weir was recommended by a Miss Smart in Elgin, who also accompanied them to the Homes. The elder boy was sent to Canada in 1907 and the younger one in 1909.[66] Still in the same area George, aged twelve, was sent to Bridge of Weir from Elgin in 1906. His parents had both died in Glasgow in 1897 and 1904, since when he and his fourteen-year-old brother had been looked after by a step-mother in Elgin, with regular help from the parish and occasional help from the boys' older brother and sister in Glasgow. But the fourteen-year-old had just been sent to a reformatory for housebreaking. His crime was attributed partly to defective supervision on the part of the step-mother by the Rev R. Macpherson of Elgin. He therefore recommended that George be sent to Bridge of Weir to escape the danger of a similar fate, on the grounds that his step-mother 'is careless and does not attend to the boy & it is desirable that he be removed at once, before going astray as did William'. George's elder brother in Glasgow accompanied him to the Homes and signed the emigration form, George being sent to Canada four years later.[67]

Still in Morayshire, two brothers and a sister from Forres, aged between eight and eleven, were admitted to the Homes in 1908 after the intervention of the Society for the Prevention of Cruelty to Children. All were illegitimate and nothing was known of their fathers:

> Mother ... who signs form is a notorious character. She married a labourer ... about 2 years ago and by him has four children, three before marriage and one since. He is a very bad character having been several times in jail for theft assault & housebreaking and twice for neglecting the children. They were brought by Mr Masson Inspector S.P.C.C. Forres who says the case has been on their books as under supervision &c since 1902. Maternal grandmother is old and gets Parish help while mother has often been in receipt of same.

All three children were sent to Bridge of Weir, from where the elder boy was sent to Canada in March 1913 and the younger one a year later. Requests by the mother at this time to have the girl returned to her (the step-father having died) were strongly opposed by the SPCC Inspector at Forres. Not only did the mother have to support her younger children at home, with the aid of parish relief, but the inspector implied she was a prostitute, whose house was under constant police surveillance.[68] Four children were removed from Aberdeen to Bridge of Weir in 1909 on the recommendation of Mr Allison, missionary, Orchard Street, partly on the grounds that the mother was unfit to care for them. Their father, a mason, had died in 1907, since when the mother had been supported by the parish but this income had been stopped owing to the birth of an illegitimate child. There were two other children, a boy who was kept by his grandfather in Glasgow because he refused to live with his mother, and a girl of three who was with a paternal aunt in Aberdeen. According to this aunt, who brought the family to Bridge of Weir after the mother had signed the admission forms, 'the children have literally been in starvation, sometimes picking things off the street and eating them. They look very much neglected.' All four were subsequently sent to Canada between 1911 and 1916, and in 1912 Mr Allison asked the Homes to forbid the children to correspond with their mother because of her extremely bad influence.[69]

The SPCC was involved in the case of John from New Pitsligo, who was sent to the Orphan Homes in 1913 at the age of nine. His father was unknown and his (unmarried) mother was an unemployed domestic servant, 'much given to drink & immorality & lives in squalor & dirt.' His case was recommended by both the congregational minister in New Pitsligo and the SPCC, whose inspector in Peterhead accompanied the boy to Bridge of Weir. He was then sent to Canada in 1919.[70]

Some children were sent to the Orphan Homes as a direct or indirect result of crimes committed by their parents. They included three brothers from Stonehaven, aged eight, six and three whose father, an agricultural labourer, was sentenced to life imprisonment in 1893. He had shot dead a fellow servant and wounded another at the farm where he was employed and the mother, who handed over the children, 'sees the desirability of removing them as far as possible from scene of father's crime'. In addition, she had two illegitimate daughters and a baby to support, and the report noted that the children would not lose much by being separated from her. After friends in Aberdeen and Stonehaven had raised £60 to help the children, a committee which was appointed to disburse these funds applied to have them admitted to the Orphan Homes. All the boys were later sent to Canada, the elder ones in 1897 and the youngest ten years later.[71]

The following year saw the admission of 'a very nice boy, with a very bad history'. This was the three-year-old product of an incestuous relationship between a domestic servant in Aberdeen and her father. After the case came to light the father was imprisoned and the family scattered. The boy's admission was recommended by a local minister and the admission papers were forwarded to the mother, who had emigrated to Boston, for her signature. The child was sent first to Bridge of Weir and then to Canada in 1904.[72]

Annie Harper's plight was graphically described in the press in 1910 when her mother and step-father were charged with ill-treating and neglecting her the previous autumn. Annie, aged fourteen, was illegitimate and had received no support from her father, although his mother had contributed to her maintenance until she was ten years old. Her mother, Jemima Harper, had married a farm servant, John Johnstone, of Birkenhill, Gartly and there were four children from this marriage. According to the girl's evidence in court, she was not treated like these other children but was deliberately victimised:

She did not get the same food, and had to take her meals at another table, and often had to take what the others left ... She had to get out of bed at 5.30. when her step-father rose, and had to clean all the boots, and sweep and wash out the floor, carry water and provide firewood. Her bed was made in the floor among some bags, but the others had a bedstead to lie on ... Her mother often beat her with her hand and sometimes with a stick. The boys had not to do any work, and were well treated. She hoped she had not to go back to her mother; she would rather go any where.

Annie's claims were corroborated by the evidence of the fiscal, who reported that

The girl had to lie on the bare floor, the only protection from the floor being two pieces of wet and filthy sacking. She had no under-clothing for months and months. She had to go about in the cold weather with boots which were quite worn done, and to such an extent that her feet got broken out in chilblains, and then in open sores, and while she was so suffering her mother never gave her any treatment whatever. After a time a pair of new boots were got, and the girl was obliged to put these new boots upon the open sores. There were four other children in the family, and they were not ill-used.

On Christmas Day 1909, when she had been ordered to rise at 5.30 am to wash the floor, Annie had run away to a neighbouring farm, where she had been taken in and given fresh clothing. The farmer, a Mr Ingram, reported the case to the police in Huntly, and an inspector who visited the Johnstone home that night saw for himself the appalling conditions under which the girl was kept, in contrast to the other children. John Johnstone's plea of not guilty to ill-treatment was accepted by the court, but his wife pleaded guilty and was fined £7, with an alternative of forty days in prison.

A number of prosecution witnesses, including the police inspector, the Ingrams and another neighbouring farmer, stressed the danger of sending the girl back to the guardianship of her mother and step-father. On the recommendation of the SPCC Inspector, a petition was presented in court to have Annie dealt with under the Industrial Schools Act, but after the mother claimed that neither she nor her husband could afford to pay anything towards the child's maintenance in an industrial school, it seems that the authorities considered her admission to the Orphan Homes of Scotland as an alternative. Annie's case was recommended by James Bruce, a farmer and chairman of the Gartly School Board, the admission schedule was signed by the child's mother, and Annie was sent first to Bridge of Weir and then to Canada in 1912.[73]

William Cumming (11) and his brothers George (9), John (5) and Charles (1) were sent to the Quarrier Homes in February 1911 after their father, a labourer, had been convicted of killing his wife at their home in Cairnie. The case, which came before the High Court in Aberdeen, was reported in the local press, particularly the evidence given against their father by William and George Cumming. At 2.30 am on 20 December 1910 William Cumming and his mother had come home after searching fruitlessly for the father, who had not returned from a trip to Huntly. On finding him in the house in a drunken state, a quarrel arose between the parents, and when their father began to attack their mother, William escaped with George, who had already suffered a head injury at the hands of his father. The boys ran to the police office in Huntly, but when officers went back to the Cumming household they found Mrs Cumming dead on the floor alongside a bloodstained poker and ladle. Her husband was asleep in the same room. Cumming was sentenced to ten years' imprisonment, and by the time the case came to court it had apparently been decided that the children should be sent to the Orphan Homes. The children's maternal grandparents in Portsoy were unable to assist with their maintenance and in any case the parish council of Cairnie, to which the children were chargeable, thought it desirable to remove them from the 'gruesome associations' of their father's crime. The parish council promised to make a yearly donation on behalf of the boys and sent them to Bridge of Weir, accompanied by the Inspector of Poor and a woman neighbour, after their admission had also been recommended by Provost Smith of Huntly and by a Mr Davidson, farmer, of Newton, Cairnie. William and George were sent to Canada in 1913, and John and Charles in 1921.[74]

Three brothers and a sister from Fordyce in Banffshire, aged between five and ten, were sent to the Orphan Homes in 1915. Their mother had died and their father, a farm servant, 'is drunken & lazy & a very bad influence on the children. At present doing 2 months in prison for neglecting his children.' There were two other children, one of whom was illegitimate and worked as a farm servant in the locality, and the other a baby who had been adopted by a family in Cullen. The case was recommended by the registrar and minister in Portsoy and the father signed the necessary admission papers. An uncle and aunt had been located in Fordyce and another aunt in Pitmedden had agreed to contribute £20 a year to the Orphan Homes in the event of the children being taken there. All four were first taken to Bridge of Weir and subsequently sent to Canada between 1921 and 1925.[75]

On some occasions children were admitted to Quarrier's Homes because they were beyond the control of their parents or guardians. These were the grounds on which George (14) from Aberchirder and Henry (6) from Elgin, both illegitimate, were admitted in 1886 and 1887 respectively, both being sent to Canada later.[76] James, aged twelve, was admitted in 1895 on the advice of James Collie, an advocate in Aberdeen, since his mother had died and his father had been in the asylum for ten years, with little hope of recovery. He had one brother in the army, another who was a drunken labourer in Aberdeen, a sister who was a mill-worker and a younger sister who was in the North Lodge Industrial School in Aberdeen. Another sister who worked as a charwoman in Aberdeen was reluctant to take him since he was accustomed to wandering the streets day and night, and she feared she would not be able to control him. But she signed the admission papers and after a period at Bridge of Weir James was sent to Canada in 1897.[77]

Robert, aged fourteen, was sent from Dysart (Fife) to Quarrier's Homes in 1908, since 'of late he has got beyond control and would not attend school &c although not a bad boy'. His father, a shore labourer, had died in Aberdeen four years earlier and his mother had since moved to Dysart to work in a factory. She had also to support a five-year-old daughter, so Robert was sent to Bridge of Weir and to Canada in 1911.[78] Duncan's mother had died at Inverkeithing (Fife) in 1898 when the boy was three weeks old. His father's name and whereabouts were unknown and throughout his childhood he had been maintained by the parish of Huntly, presumably his mother's place of origin. But in 1911 when he began to get beyond the control of the people with whom he was boarded, it was suggested that he be sent to the Orphan Homes of Scotland, where the Huntly council would be willing to contribute to his support:

> the Parish as 'guardians' think it is best for the lad to be put into an Institution and give him a chance of being educated under proper authorities. He and a few other boys had been getting into trouble anent a school boys' strike in connection with his school.

His removal to the Orphan Homes was recommended by the Inspector of Police, while the Inspector of Poor at Huntly signed the admission forms and another official from the same institution accompanied the boy to Glasgow. He was sent to Bridge of Weir and to Canada in 1913.[79] Another case recommended by the Huntly Parish Council in 1912 was that of Thomas, allegedly born in 1899 in Aberdeen. His father, a labourer, had not been heard of for four years, and he was looked after by his mother, a laundry worker in Aberdeen who earned nine shillings a week, 'but being of delicate nature, the boy has got beyond her control'. She had two other children to support and signed Thomas's admission papers, the Huntly Parish Council having expressed its willingness to contribute to the boy's support. He was sent to Bridge of Weir and to Canada in 1915.[80]

References in the initial registers of Quarrier children who were sent to Canada indicate that regular reports and communications continued to be received from or about them after their transfer to the Dominion. No such correspondence or reports survive, but occasional comments on their where-abouts and circumstances can be found in Ellen Bilborough's accounts of her supervisory work at Belleville, reproduced in the annual *Narrative of Facts*. In 1877, for instance, in the context of a report about Glasgow children who had been placed by the Belleville Home in Bruce County, Ontario, she noted that

> Near Hughie, and going to the same school, is Henry McLean, adopted by Scotch people, who came about six years ago from Aberdeen ... Henry is a bright intelligent child, very honourable and straightforward.[81]

It is clear from the case histories that a few children were sent to the Orphan Homes because their parents wanted to give them a better chance in life than they could offer, preferably across the Atlantic. But in many cases the parents, if they had not died, had abdicated their responsibilities or were felt to be physically or morally unfit to bring up a family. It then fell to the parish authorities, the local clergy or public-spirited benefactors to undertake responsibility for the children. Some might be maintained by the parish, either in the poorhouse or through being boarded out in the locality. Others might be placed with suitable relatives, and Quarrier's organisation always initially investigated the family circumstances thoroughly to see if any relatives were able or willing to take children who had been referred to them. If this were not the case, and if children had been particularly recommended as likely to benefit from Quarrier's emigration scheme, arrangements would be made to have them transferred to the Glasgow or Bridge of Weir Homes for training, before having them sent to Canada.

Reformatories, industrial schools and emigration

Some of North-East Scotland's destitute or otherwise needy youth was catered for in this way. Others were assisted to go abroad through locally-based agencies, perhaps after receiving training or correction in an industrial school or reformatory. Part of the policy of the industrial and reformatory schools all over Britain was to encourage the assisted emigration of suitable inmates through charitable or governmental agencies, and special training was sometimes given with this in mind. The policy was implemented most extensively by the Liverpool Education Authority, which by 1914 had sent out nearly 1,200 children to Canada. Agencies such as the Salvation Army, Dr Barnardo's, the Children's Aid Society and the Catholic Emigration Society were used by various schools to send children abroad, mainly to Canada, where younger children were either boarded with families or occasionally adopted, and older emigrants were sent to situations of farm and domestic service. In 1909 a Treasury grant in aid of emigration allowed half the expenses of removal (not exceeding £8) to be advanced to children under thirteen, and one third of the expenses (not exceeding £5) to be advanced to children aged thirteen or fourteen. No similar provision was made for children over fourteen, but a departmental committee which reported on reformatory and industrial schools in 1913 urged that the full grant be extended to older candidates, who made up the majority of the emigrants. The committee highly recommended emigration as 'one of the best means of disposal open to the schools, especially for children coming from bad homes',[82] similar sentiments to those of philanthropic emigrationists such as Barnardo and Quarrier.

On the whole, relatively few delinquent children were sent abroad from Scotland, to the surprise of a parliamentary committee which reported on Scottish reformatory and industrial schools in 1914.[83] The most significant exodus probably took place from Kibble Reformatory, Paisley, which in the early twentieth century had an arrangement with the government of New South Wales to send out forty boys a year for agricultural settlement.[84] As far as Aberdeen was concerned, the first recorded emigrant from a reformatory left in 1861, when a boy from Oldmill Reformatory emigrated to South Africa when his time had expired, along with two sons of the school's governor. This was an event which, according to the school's directors, 'excited interest among the other boys, and it is hoped it may yet lead to a spirit of emigration among them, which the Directors think it proper to encourage.[85] Fifteen more boys seem to have emigrated from Oldmill before its closure in 1897, while a total of nine girls also left from the equivalent female reformatory in Aberdeen before it was closed in 1901.[86]

During the 1860s the governors of the Aberdeen industrial schools, Farquhar Spottiswoode and his wife, worked hard to raise funds to assist the emigration of former inmates.[87] But while their interest in emigration began with industrial school children, particularly girls, they soon wished to extend the net of assistance to other vulnerable groups in society, particularly the growing army of unemployed labourers in Aberdeen. And in appealing for funds through lectures, correspondence and pamphlets, they expressed views common to many contemporary emigrationists: they contrasted the excess of labour in Britain with its dearth in the colonies, recommended emigration as an effective and necessary solution to pauperism, and stressed environment over heredity as the vital factor in the formation of character.

The annual returns sent to the Chief Inspector of Industrial Schools do not record any direct emigration from the Aberdeen schools until 1878, when one girl went from the King Street establishment. It was, however, quite common for a child to be taken into care because a parent had emigrated. Seven of the seventeen boys admitted to the Aberdeen industrial school between 1868 and 1877 because a parent had emigrated were illegitimate; in six cases the father had gone abroad, in one instance the mother, and their whereabouts were generally unknown. Six more boys had been admitted because their fathers or mothers had abandoned the family when they emigrated.[88] Between 1886 and 1918 the admission minute books record at least a further fifteen boys who were admitted because a parent was abroad and the child was either without proper guardianship or beyond the control of the remaining parent or guardian. In most instances the parent was in North America, and in two cases the boys' fathers had crossed the Atlantic as masons or stonecutters, perhaps as temporary emigrants.[89]

Between 1878 and 1915 the records show a total of thirty-three children who emigrated from the various schools of industry in Aberdeen. The largest number (fifteen) came from the Female School of Industry in King Street; twelve of them left in the three years 1884-6, while the one girl who left in 1878 was the only emigrant from a Scottish industrial school that year. We know very little about these female emigrants, although it appears that the five girls who emigrated from the King Street establishment in 1885 were sent to Canada under the auspices of the Emigration Committee of the Aberdeen Ladies' Union, this committee having paid part of their passage money.[90] There was also a single reference in the *Aberdeen Journal* to two girls who were sent out from the Whitehall Industrial School to situations in New Zealand. Their departures are not recorded in the official statistics, however, which indicate that only one girl was emigrated from this institution in the period 1862-1915, and she left in 1886.[91] The *Aberdeen Journal* of 29 January 1910 reported on the annual meeting of subscribers to the Whitehall school.

Thirty-four girls had been discharged and found work during the previous year, and reference was made to very satisfactory reports which had been received from the employers of two girls who had been sent to New Zealand. With reference to their success, the chairman of the school committee mentioned his own visit to Australia and New Zealand in 1909, in particular how he had been struck by the great demand for domestic servants in these countries. The committee, he said, would willingly send more girls abroad provided they received assurances as to their favourable reception and employment. Aberdeen maintained no separate industrial school for Roman Catholic boys, but from 1878 girls could be sent to Nazareth House. Two emigrants left this institution in 1899, and the Chief Inspector in his report for that year noted and commended the new development:

> There seems to be, in the neighbourhood of the school, good openings for girls on leaving, but it is interesting to note that a beginning has been made with the emigration of girls. This experiment seems to be succeeding; it is certain that where a child has a really bad home there is no means of disposal so effective.[92]

Two more girls emigrated from Nazareth House in 1900, but after that no such departures are reported in the annual returns.

On at least one occasion the inmates of Oakbank Boys' Industrial School were given an illustrated lecture on Canada by the local Canadian government agent.[93] On two occasions between 1875 and 1947 the visiting directors at the school mentioned emigration in their reports. On 25 April 1906 J. Fleming 'took the opportunity when here to assemble the boys and address a few words to the scholars upon the occasion of a boy G. S. Lawrence leaving for Canada'. Twenty-three years later, on 20 June 1929 it was reported that one boy was preparing to set out for Canada the next day.[94] Eleven emigrants or prospective emigrants are mentioned among the 800 entries in the school's discharge book between 1881 and 1900, the only such book which survives for any of the Aberdeen industrial schools. Perhaps four of these emigrants can be matched with the official statistics, which indicate that a total of thirteen boys emigrated from Oakbank in the period up to 1915.[95] The emigrants mentioned included Charles Scorgie, discharged in 1883, who emigrated to an unspecified destination in May 1885, and Peter Whittle, who after his discharge in 1885 worked in Aberdeen for a year before going to America with his father. Brothers Thomas and Andrew Dalgety both went to join their father in Astoria, Oregon, after being discharged in 1885 and 1886 respectively, and similarly Andrew Wallace, who attended the school for only eight months in 1891, emigrated in October to the USA, where his father was employed as a mason. Daniel Levack, who worked in a wool mill at Pitcaple after his discharge in 1891, was said in a progress report a year later to be 'doing well, but anxious to emigrate if he could get assistance'. Several boys went to Winnipeg, where the school had secured the services of a clergyman to take charge of new arrivals and look after their welfare.[96] These emigrants included Charles Jackson in 1894, John McDonald, who was sent out under the auspices of the Children's Aid Society in 1899,[97] and former inmate John Robertson of Peterhead, who also went out in 1899 but returned to Aberdeen a year later. The *Aberdeen Journal* on 17 June 1899 remarked on the emigration of an (unnamed) Oakbank boy to Winnipeg as a farm servant, since this was the third case sent there by the school's directors that year.

Industrial school children were sent abroad under various agencies. On 3 February 1894, for instance, the *Aberdeen Journal* noted that the Emigration Aid Union had recently written to the Aberdeen schools, intimating that a party was to leave shortly for Canada, and asking whether any Aberdeen boys would be joining it. Mention has already been made that at least one emigrant from Oakbank went to Canada under the auspices of the Children's Aid Society. An official report in 1912 noted the part played by the Salvation Army, among other agencies, in organising the removal of reformatory and industrial school inmates and poor law children to Canada and their subsequent supervision there for four years. The children were accommodated and trained in Homes in Toronto and Winnipeg before being allocated to foster parents, although the Salvation Army remained legally responsible for the child's welfare until it was eighteen.[98]

The Salvation Army: the world's largest emigration agency?

The Salvation Army's rôle as the agency through which the Aberdeen Distress Committee sent sixty emigrants to Canada in 1906 and 1907 has already been noted.[99] The Army in fact assisted a number of local distress committees in this way, but it did not undertake to remove emigrants only on behalf of other institutions. Carefully-regulated emigration was an integral part of the social strategy of William Booth, who favoured it on the grounds that it offered a viable means of relieving the twin pressures of overpopulation and unemployment at home, as well as being advantageous to the Empire. He thought it offered a more immediate solution than legislation to Britain's problems, and in the early twentieth century the Salvation Army became probably the largest emigration agency in the British Empire and perhaps in the world.[100]

It has already been noted that Booth, like Barnardo, stressed the Empire should be filled up with good British stock, and insisted emigration should be carried out on principles which would satisfy both the old and new countries, as well as the emigrant himself. He was practical, determined both that the settler should be prepared for his new home and that the new home should be prepared for the settler. He rejected the argument that emigration was a panacaea for all ills, asserting that it was criminal to transport penniless, untrained men and women to a strange land:

> Emigration, by all means. But whom are you to emigrate? These girls who do not know how to bake? These lads who never handled a spade? And where are you to emigrate them? Are you hoping to make the Colonies the dumping ground of your human refuse? On that the colonists will have something decisive to say,

where there are colonists; and where there are not, how are you to feed, clothe, and employ your emigrants in the uninhabited wilderness?[101]

In Booth's opinion the international network of the Salvation Army made it ideally suited to supervise both the selection of suitable emigrants and their relocation in the colonies. From the 1890s his efforts were directed partly towards the relief of the utterly destitute by such means.

General Booth first went abroad in 1886, to France and Switzerland, then to Canada and the USA later the same year. Four years later he launched a major scheme for transforming the estimated tenth of Britain's population which was permanently destitute into a useful, self-respecting part of the population, a scheme in which emigration played a major rôle. In his book, *In Darkest England, and the Way Out*, Booth first discussed the causes and consequences of social and economic deprivation, then outlined his threefold solution. In the first place, the needs of the destitute would be met in city-centre refuges, where they would be fed and provided with temporary work and religious counselling. Candidates suitable for further training (in terms of their honesty and capacity for hard work) would be sent to a farm colony in the provinces, where they would be given basic agricultural instruction and expected to derive their support from the land. From the farm colony, as from the city colony, some would be returned to friends or found permanent employment. But it was expected that the majority, once thoroughly trained, would be sent abroad to fulfil the third part of the scheme, the establishment of an overseas colony of former paupers who, thanks to rigorous training, preparation and selection, would be an asset to the Empire. Booth hoped to secure a tract of land in one of the colonies which would be well prepared for the gradual settlement of suitable colonists. As time went on, he expected that the movement would become self-perpetuating, as colonists, once comfortably settled, would save money and assist their friends and relatives to join them. If the scheme were successful, he predicted that the pioneer colony would be the forerunner of many such settlements.

When he launched his 'Darkest England' project in autumn 1890, Booth asked for donations of £100,000 to set it on foot and £30,000 a year for five years at least to maintain it. City refuges were created, and 3,000 acres secured for the establishment of a farm colony at Hadleigh, Essex, where colonists spent three years in agricultural training. Between 1892 and 1909 hopes alternately rose and fell regarding the formation of the overseas colony. In 1905 Rider Haggard was appointed by the Colonial Office to enquire into Salvation Army settlements in the USA, with a view to establishing similar colonies in the British Empire. Like Booth, Haggard believed it was preferable to send a suitable urban surplus abroad to build up the Empire than to abandon them to 'rot in the towns like herrings in a barrel'.[102] His report recommended that a charitable loan of £300,000 should be raised so that eligible candidates could be removed from British cities to prepared colonies within the Empire. The land, which was to be sold to the colonists and paid for in instalments, would provide security for the loan, and interest repayments should be guaranteed by the British government. The scheme

17   William Booth.

was to be administered by the Salvation Army or a similar organisation under government supervision. Haggard's immediate plan was to send about 1,500 families to 160-acre homesteads on a tract of 240,000 acres in North-West Canada which the Dominion government was prepared to grant for the purpose. He estimated the cost of the operation at £200 per person, which was to cover passage, the provision of housing, implements and seed and the maintenance and instruction of the emigrant until the first harvest had been gathered. The colony was to be managed by the Salvation Army, whose representatives would collect annual instalments of the funds which had been spent on training and equipping the colonists until all the outlay had been recovered with interest.

Beginning in 1901, a few suitable trainees were sent annually from the Hadleigh farm to Canada and Australia. In 1906 eighteen families, chosen from Hadleigh, were placed with a few experienced farmers from Ontario in a small bloc settlement at Tisdale, Saskatchewan, on land owned by the Independent Order of Foresters. But both this settlement and a similar experiment on Vancouver Island in 1910 came to nothing, largely because of financial problems.[103] In fact the overseas colony, the main focus of Booth's tripartite scheme, was never implemented, either in Canada or in Rhodesia (where Booth himself had hoped it would be established). The parliamentary committee of 1906 appointed to consider Rider Haggard's proposals criticised them as unworkable, mainly on the grounds of excessive cost and earlier unsuccessful experiments in colonisation, compared with simple emigration.[104] Insufficient public money was provided to fund the scheme, which was also opposed by the colonies, unwilling to admit Britain's surplus slum population.

But the Salvation Army's interest in emigration was not limited to the relief of the utterly destitute through the provision of special colonies. Booth also favoured the emigration of working-class people who wanted to escape from the threat of poverty, or who generally wished to improve their prospects: these might include agricultural labourers who wanted to be their own masters or secure land for their children, young women looking for work, or the wives and families of pioneer emigrants. He rejected the argument that those already in employment should not be assisted to emigrate by pointing to the large number of able candidates who applied for every position that became available. While some emigrants (such as the Distress Committee recruits) might require partial assistance from municipal authorities or charitable organisations, supplemented by a Salvation Army loan and help in their relocation, Booth believed that many could meet their own expenses; they just required the reassurance of the Salvation Army's advice and protection in making their arrangements, travelling to their new homes and securing employment. As early as 1887 an advertisement in the *War Cry* advised Salvationists who were contemplating emigration to contact Army headquarters in advance in order to secure favourable and well-remunerated situations as domestic servants and farm hands in Canada.[105] But Booth intended that the selection of emigrants should be made without reference to the applicants' religious affiliations, depending instead on their apparent potential for making the most of the new opportunities afforded them, and he was anxious that they should repay all expenditure made on their behalf as soon as possible.

By the time the Migration and Settlement Department came into existence as a distinct branch of its organisation in 1903, the Salvation Army already had considerable experience of this kind of work. In the first nine months of its life up to November 1891 its Social Wing received applications from 700 potential emigrants, ninety-five of whom subsequently paid nearly £900 in booking their passages through the Salvation Army.[106] The Social Wing continued to supply advice and letters of introduction to an increasing number of applicants, who settled, independent of the Salvation Army, in places of their own choice, although their passages and employment were often secured through the Army's agency. In May 1894 an Emigration Board was formed and three years later William Booth announced that, pending the establishment of the overseas colony, the Army would concentrate on expanding its labour exchanges, so that emigrants could be sent to places where their skills were in particular demand.

In order to implement Booth's proposals more effectively, a separate Migration and Settlement Department was set up in 1903 under the control of Colonel David Lamb. A native of Friockheim in Angus, Lamb had joined the Salvation Army while serving his apprenticeship as a chemist in Aberdeen, and in 1903 was governor of the farm at Hadleigh. He was put in charge of the Emigration Department after returning from a survey trip to Canada in autumn 1903, and remained in this position until the Department was wound up in 1932, by which time he had been round the world four times and had visited Canada almost annually in pursuit of his work.

The creation of a separate emigration department immediately increased the Salvation Army's work in this field. In one week in April 1904 200 men left Hadleigh for Canada,[107] and Lamb was forced to remove his London headquarters four times, to ever bigger premises. General Booth was emphatic that the department existed to meet, not to create, a demand, pointing out that in the busy season from mid-January to May the office often received 4,000 personal enquiries and 3,000 written applications per week.[108] In 1904 approximately 1,500 emigrants were sent to Canada, a figure which increased to 3,970 in 1905 and to 13,000 in 1906, these 13,000 having been selected from over 100,000 applicants. About sixty per cent of the emigrants came from urban areas, most were aged between twenty and thirty and almost seventy per cent was male.[109] The popularity of the Salvation Army's emigration facilities was maintained well into the twentieth century, and by 1930, despite the interruption of the First World War, it had sent out a total of 200,000 emigrants, mainly to Canada, less than one per cent of whom had been deported or had returned dissatisfied.[110]

Emigrants who could not afford the passage money were assisted by means of a Loan Fund, made up of all the donations, subscriptions and business profits of the Emigration Department. Those who were helped in this way were required to repay the loan in annual instalments, so that the money could be used to assist other needy emigrants, and most seem to have responded to this demand. For instance, about 500 of the 3,970 emigrants in 1904 were given assistance amounting to £1,000 and by 1906 a quarter of this sum had been repaid as stipulated. Of the 36,308 settlers sent to Canada by the Salvation Army between October 1903 and July 1908, 9,400 received loans amounting to £38,375, of which £5,112 had been repaid by the latter date.[111] But although the Loan Fund had helped nearly 10,000 people to emigrate by 1909, they made up only a small proportion of the total sent out to Canada by the Salvation Army, most of whom paid their own fares. For them the main function of the Emigration Department was to facilitate their travelling arrangements and their relocation.

The Salvation Army publicised its emigration scheme in pamphlets (many of them written by General Booth himself), press advertisements and lectures all over Britain.[112] Free information was issued both by the main office, by seven branch offices (at Aberdeen, Glasgow, Belfast, Liverpool, Bedford, Plymouth and Southampton) and by hundreds of individual Salvation Army officers scattered throughout Britain, each one of whom was a 'potential migration agent'.[113] When an intending emigrant applied for information he was given a package of literature (including government circulars) on the area of his interest, or, if he had no destination in mind, he was advised on general prospects within the Empire and on the advantages and drawbacks of different destinations. He was also required to complete an application form, on the basis of which the emigration officers in both London and Toronto judged whether he was a suitable candidate or not; and those who required financial assistance had to provide references of character and competence.

The information and assistance referred almost exclusively to Canada. In return for the Salvation Army's selection and supervision of emigrants the Canadian government until April 1906 paid the organisation a bonus of twelve shillings for each adult settler and six shillings for each child, once it had satisfied itself that the emigrants belonged to the eligible categories of agriculturists or domestic servants.[114] The Salvation Army also allocated the Canadian Immigration Department a regular column in each of its two main publications, the *War Cry* and the *Social Gazette*; in return the immigration authorities contributed not only towards the cost of these publications, but also towards the expenses of lecturing in Britain and to caring for new arrivals in Salvation Army hotels and rest homes across Canada.[115] The Emigration Office had special arrangements with all the leading steamship and railway companies so that Salvation Army emigrants could book their passages with the company of their choice through Army agents in any part of Britain. Emigrants were often grouped together on specific ships and sent out in 'conducted parties' under the care of a Salvation Army officer who had experience of transatlantic travel and Canadian conditions. The size of the conducted parties varied from twenty to 200 people, who were looked after from the time of embarkation until they were delivered into the care of Salvation Army officers in Canada to be taken to their final destination. The conducted parties soon proved to be so popular that in 1905 the Salvation Army began to charter its own steamships, in which the whole accommodation was reserved for its emigrants. The first such ship was the SS

Vancouver, which left Liverpool for Canada on 26 April 1905 with almost 1,100 passengers, including a contingent from Aberdeen. According to the *Aberdeen Journal* of 26 April, eleven emigrants had left the railway station the previous night under the charge of Captain Smythe from the Salvation Army's London headquarters. A further twenty-one passengers joined the party between Aberdeen and Stirling, and all thirty-two were booked on the SS *Vancouver*. Frequent sailings followed—in 1908, for instance, there were seven chartered sailings in four vessels, including a party of 800 which left Liverpool on the SS *Kensington* on 20 February. Five hundred of them were destined for British Columbia and paid £16 a head for the sea and rail journey from Liverpool to Vancouver.[116] Such was the demand that in some weeks both a conducted party and a chartered sailing left Glasgow and Liverpool. Departing emigrants were presented with a Bible and a small book of advice compiled by Colonel Lamb, on how they should conduct themselves during and after the voyage. They were urged to be self reliant:

> While we are looking out for work for you, don't wait for us. Look out for yourself. Take the first likely job which offers, and better it at the first opportunity. If perchance the first place to which you are sent is not quite what you expected, remain at it while you are looking for a better.[117]

Yet although the colonists were encouraged to stand on their own feet, the Salvation Army made positive efforts to secure employment for those who emigrated under its auspices. Emigrants' particulars were sent in advance to Salvation Army agents in the appropriate parts of Canada, who were in close touch with potential employers, particularly farmers. Those officers who came over from Canada to escort the passengers on the SS *Vancouver* in 1905 opened a Labour Bureau on board, with the result that all passengers who required situations had secured them before they arrived. Similar facilities were subsequently offered on all chartered ships, and to the larger conducted parties. The officer in charge of the Labour Bureau on the SS *Kensington* in 1908, for instance, brought with him a register of applications which had been received at the Salvation Army's Vancouver office for help needed by farmers, fruit growers and other employers of labour in British Columbia. As the voyage proceeded, each passenger was interviewed and the needs of the employers were gradually matched to the colonists' skills. On every occasion when these facilities were used the number of vacant situations on the employment register was apparently much greater than the number of passengers requiring work.[118] Provision was also made for passengers in smaller conducted parties who did not have access to a labour bureau on board ship. In such cases a detailed list of the requirements of the passengers was mailed ahead to a Salvation Army agent in Canada who, having studied the list in conjunction with an up-to-date register of employers' applications for workers, would try to board the ship some time before it docked, in order that the emigrants could secure work before they landed. Once employment had been decided the emigrants were issued with through tickets to their various destinations, and the Salvation Army agents always tried to ensure that they were met at each transit point and forwarded immediately to their new employers.

The Salvation Army obviously encouraged most of its emigrants to seek agricultural work, and about seventy-five per cent of them apparently followed this advice,[119] generally settling either in Ontario or further west. Only a few could afford to buy land and most became farm labourers. Farmers who required wage labour applied to the Salvation Army's Toronto office specifying their needs (in terms of the workers' required experience, marital condition and often nationality) and stating the terms and conditions of employment. Of the 800 people brought out on the SS *Kensington* in 1908, 600 settled on the land, while the remaining 200 found positions in domestic service. A special women's branch of the emigration department dealt with the large number of unaccompanied females who sought such work in Canada under the Salvation Army's auspices, providing supervised accommodation until they had been put in touch with their new employers. The Salvation Army also took care of the dependents of married men whom it sent to Canada in advance of their families to prepare a new home. In November 1905, in response to the severe unemployment in Britain, they took the unusual step of organising a winter sailing of several hundred selected men for whom they had secured work on lumber camps and farms in Ontario, with the promise of Spring work to follow; undertaking to look after the men's dependents until they were in a position to send for them.[120] The wives and families of pioneer emigrants were brought out in special parties, often after the main emigration season was over; and in the last three months of 1907, for example, 430 women and 696 children were brought to Canada in this way.[121]

The Salvation Army believed the success of its emigration work was reflected in the widespread public confidence in its methods, particularly in the large number of applications it received to take young, unaccompanied children to Canada to join their parents.[122] Certainly the Canadian government, employers of labour and the colonists themselves seem to have been well satisfied with the facilities provided. The emigrants welcomed the efficiency of an international network which escorted them from port of embarkation to final destination and which also found them employment.[123] The Government Commissioner of Immigration who inspected (at Winnipeg railway station) the emigrants for British Columbia brought out on the *Kensington* in 1908 wrote afterwards to Colonel Lamb that he had 'yet to see a finer body of immigrants brought into Canada from the Old Country'.[124] The Salvation Army's methods were also praised by W. T. R. Preston, the Canadian Emigration Commissioner for Europe, and by J. P. Whitney, Premier of Ontario, who welcomed the policy of conducting settlers straight to their new employment and noted the very low failure rate of the Salvation Army scheme.[125] Sir Wilfrid Laurier, the Premier of Canada, was 'well pleased' with the Salvation Army settlers, and urged them to 'send us more, and send some English and Scotch lasses for the North-West'.[126] Canadian employers seem to have favoured Scottish workers; at least 'R.W.I.' of Kamloops, British Columbia, having received two Scottish workers in 1908 (probably from the *Kensington*) soon requested another employee of the same nationality:

We had placed with us two Scotch gardeners, a few weeks ago, by the Salvation Army. These are very satisfactory men, and are of a class we desire. Can you place a maid with us in a month? We pay 25 dollars a month, and would prefer a Scotch help here now, and the company would serve to make them contented.[127]

On 24 August 1911 the *Aberdeen Journal* reported that of 1,000 emigrants who had recently left Scotland under the auspices of the Salvation Army, fifty per cent had come from Glasgow and the south-west, thirty per cent from Edinburgh and the south-east, twelve per cent from Aberdeen and the north and the remaining eight per cent from the central counties of Scotland. It is in fact impossible to distinguish precisely the number of Scottish emigrants sent out by the Salvation Army. During the Second World War the Army's London headquarters suffered a direct hit from a German bomb, and records relating to individual emigrants were destroyed. An incomplete series of duplicate records held in Toronto, however,[128] seems to confirm that the majority of the Salvation Army's Scottish emigrants came from Glasgow. Out of 740 Scottish emigrants who went to Canada under its auspices between 1913 (when the record begins) and 1922, 298 came from Glasgow and several others were from nearby towns such as Paisley and Greenock. But at least eighty-eight individuals or family groups came from North-East Scotland, seventy-three of them from the city of Aberdeen. Small numbers of emigrants also came from Peterhead, Huntly, Stonehaven, Ellon, Elgin, Fochabers, Rothes and Inverness. They were made up of thirty-three families (seventy-nine individuals), thirty-three single women, fourteen single men and eight widows, six of whom were accompanied by a total of fifteen children. Only eight of the emigrants belonged to the Salvation Army.[129] In only four cases (all in 1913) did a family group include a man and wife travelling together; twenty married women travelled to Canada either alone or accompanied only by their children, presumably to join their husbands; and on nine occasions a married man went out either alone or accompanied only by his children.

The emigrants followed a variety of occupations, the largest number being domestic servants (twenty-nine) and housewives or housekeepers (seventeen). Surprisingly, there were only six farmers,[130] and there were also very few professional people among the emigrants: three female teachers and a nurse, a typist and a clerk. There were five factory workers, five unskilled labourers, three tradesmen, one merchant and ten emigrants of no specified occupation, one of whom was going out to join her sister. All the six fishermen or fish workers and curers among the Scottish emigrants came from Aberdeen. The emigrants settled in a variety of locations right across Canada: the majority (fifty-one) went to Ontario, sixteen went to British Columbia, six to Manitoba, five each to Quebec and Saskatchewan, three to Alberta, one to the United States and one to an unspecified destination. Very few of the Salvation Army's Scottish emigrants, and none from the North-East, went to the Maritime

Provinces, and a grocer from Peterhead was one of only eight from Scotland who moved over to the USA in the whole period 1913-22.

Potential emigrants from North-East Scotland were made well aware of the Salvation Army's facilities through regular advertisements and reports in the local press and through the periodic visits of General Booth and Colonel Lamb to Aberdeen and the surrounding area. Interested parties could obtain free information from the Salvation Army Citadel at 26 Castle Street, Aberdeen, or from Army agents in the rural towns, through whom they could also book passages on chartered vessels or conducted parties. Army representatives travelled north to escort emigrant parties to their port of embarkation, as in May 1907 when a Captain Taylor accompanied twenty emigrants from Aberdeen to Glasgow. There they were joined by other Salvation Army emigrants and embarked, under Colonel Lamb's direction, on the SS *Ionian*, making up the fourteenth conducted party to leave for Canada under the Army's auspices that year.[131] Special Salvation Army agents visited North-East Scotland from time to time to boost emigration. In January 1908 Edward Adair, a British Columbia fruit grower, came to Aberdeen to recruit young women for that province.[132] He was followed a month later by Staff Captain William Patterson, the eastern representative of the Salvation Army Immigration Department in Canada, who since 1905 had been responsible for finding employment for all Salvation Army recruits arriving at Quebec. He was therefore, reported the *Aberdeen Journal*, well qualified to advise all enquirers on their suitability as emigrants and also on the best locations to choose. During his brief visit to Aberdeen he was 'besieged' by intending emigrants seeking advice, mainly unemployed people but also a number of moderate capitalists interested in using their savings to begin a new life in Canada. In an interview with the *Aberdeen Journal*, Patterson pointed out that of 15,000 emigrants sent to Canada by the Salvation Army in 1907, less than 100 were unemployed; and of that number, some had not sought work, while others were sick. He reaffirmed his faith in Canada's future, despite the current commercial depression. He maintained that the emigrant tide was still flowing strongly towards the Dominion: the Salvation Army had booked ten steamers already for the coming season, and he himself was to take charge of a full shipload of over 1,000 agriculturists, general labourers and domestic servants sailing to British Columbia on 20 February. He acknowledged that emigrants from Aberdeenshire were well represented among the Salvation Army's recruits, although he was unable to state the exact number involved, as the emigrants were spread over different sailings. He did admit, however, that they included some people with considerable capital who were going out to investigate the prospects for purchasing fruit farms.[133]

On 14 November 1909 Lieutenant-Colonel T. Howell, the Canadian Secretary for Immigration in connection with the Salvation Army, came to Aberdeen unexpectedly and gave an unscheduled lecture in the Citadel. He spoke about the good prospects of Western Canada for emigrants who were prepared to work hard on the land, and reiterated the importance of populating the Dominion with British settlers in order to counter the recent large influx from the USA. He was followed only two days later by the Rev

Dr John Robbins, an ex-chaplain of the British army in Canada, who lectured (again under the Salvation Army's auspices) on the opportunities offered to the unemployed workman who emigrated to Canada.[134] In February 1910 a representative from British Columbia spent a week at the Army's Aberdeen headquarters to advise intending emigrants and also to promote emigration by giving public lectures in the city.[135] Then in January 1913 Major John MacGillivray from Canada addressed a large audience, mainly of young people, in the Salvation Army Hall in Huntly. His two-hour lecture, on the subject of 'Homes across the Seas', was reported by the *Aberdeen Journal*[136] to have been full of practical information for all kinds of emigrants, and it seems to have borne fruit, for on 26 March the newspaper remarked that several people were preparing to leave the Huntly district for Canada and the USA. While many had booked their passages through an ordinary ticket agent in the town, some had made use of the Salvation Army's facilities, and the Army's Toronto immigration statistics record that two single men from Huntly came out to Ontario under the auspices of the Salvationists in May and August 1913.[137]

But female domestic servants made up by far the main contingent of Salvation Army emigrants from North-East Scotland, as well as from the country at large,[138] and an increasing amount of the Army's local and national work was devoted to catering for single women. They were encouraged to emigrate not only because their removal would relieve the labour (and marriage) markets at home, but because their 'hallowing influence' would be much welcomed in the colonies;[139] and General Booth himself was of the opinion that 'to the proper building up and cementing of the British Empire thousands of godly, healthy, strong women are immediately absolutely essential to the Colonies'.[140] Assisted passages for women and guaranteed employment at wages of up to £50 a year were advertised in the *Aberdeen Journal*[141] and women were urged to take advantage of the Army's trustworthy service instead of relying on less reputable emigration agencies. Itinerant female agents from the Army emigration department's women's branch visited the North-East periodically to recruit candidates. In March 1909 and February 1912, for instance, Staff Captain Ella Macnamara came to Aberdeen, on the second occasion spending a week in the city to recruit domestic servants for a conducted party which she was to accompany to Canada.[142] In December 1909 the Salvation Army sent a Mrs Thompson of Toronto to Aberdeen, Kirriemuir, Forfar and Perth to advise intending female emigrants; and in February 1913 Miss Winifred Leal visited Aberdeen on her return from an extensive Canadian tour in order to advise women emigrants on current employment opportunities in the Dominion.[143]

For the Salvation Army the removal of suitable women to the colonies was only a part—if perhaps the major part—of its wider emigration policy. Many emigration societies, however, were concerned exclusively with women, particularly in the late nineteenth century, when it was increasingly believed that the twin problems of a redundant female population in Britain and a lack of women in the colonies could be solved by exporting the surplus. Several of the early charitable emigration societies had been concerned with women's welfare, and the activities of their successors merit detailed examination, since organised female emigration constituted an increasingly significant part of the national exodus in the late nineteenth and early twentieth centuries.

NOTES

1) W. A. Carrothers, *Emigration from the British Isles*, p. 228.
2) Many of its unpaid staff were drawn from the ranks of the private emigration societies.
3) PP 1906 [Cd. 2978] vol. lxxvi, p. 533: *report of the departmental committee appointed to consider Mr Rider Haggard's report on agricultural settlements in British colonies*, vol. 1, pp. 3, 5-6. 14. For further details on Rider Haggard's scheme, see below, pp. 210-12.
4) See A. James Hammerton, *Emigrant gentlewomen: genteel poverty and female emigration 1830-1914* (London, 1979), pp. 169-71. After the First World War, however, emigration was criticised by many eugenists, who argued that priority should be given to building up the depleted nation in Britain itself. For further details on the eugenics movement in general, see Francis Galton, *Inquiries into human faculty and its development* (London, 1883), Montague Crackenthorpe, 'Eugenics as a social force' in *Nineteenth Century*, vol. 63 (June 1908) pp. 962-72; J. A. Lindsay, 'The case for and against eugenics' in *ibid*, vol. 72 (Sept. 1912) pp. 546-57; E. Lyttleton, 'Eugenics, ethics and religion' in *ibid*, vol. 74 (July 1913) pp. 155-63; H. S. Shelton, 'Eugenics' in *Contemporary Review*, vol. 101 (Jan. 1912) pp. 84-95; H. S. Shelton, 'The political aspect of eugenics' in *ibid*, vol. 107 (Jan. 1915) pp. 105-12.
5) Gillian Wagner, *Children of the Empire* (London, 1982), xv.
6) One of Barnardo's biographers wrote in 1904 that 'The lads and lasses Dr. Barnardo selects to send to Canada constitute an increment of industrial wealth wherein are stored interminable possibilities of augmentation and National and Imperial advantage.'. (John H. Batt, *Dr Barnardo: the foster father of 'Nobody's Children'. A record and an interpretation* (London, 1904), p. 128.
7) Harold Begbie, quoted in *The Surplus: being a restatement of the emigration policy and methods of the Salvation Army, together with a report on last year's work, and introductory note by General Booth and prefatory remarks by representative men on the subject of emigration and colonisation* (London, 1909), p. 14.
8) A. E. Williams, *Barnardo of Stepney: the father of nobody's children* (London, 1943), p. 217. See also Wagner, *Children of the Empire*, xiv. Almost a third of the children sent from Britain to Canada between 1870 and 1941 went under Barnardo's auspices, making it the leading child emigration agency of its day.
9) Wagner, *Children of the Empire*, p. 75.
10) These accusations were made in a report by Andrew Doyle, an inspector of the English Local Government Board who had been sent out to Canada to examine the operation of assisted emigration schemes. He also complained that Rye brought over far larger parties than she could manage, and highlighted her general lack of organisation and management. Child emigration was not officially sanctioned again until 1883, although Doyle largely exempted Annie

Macpherson's work from censure, and she continued to send out destitute street children and orphans to Canada.

11) Wagner, *Children of the Empire*, pp. 112-3.

12) The industrial farm continued to function until 1905, but never paid its way, and after Barnardo's death the council which took over responsibility for his institutions decided to sell it.

13) For instance, opponents in Canada drew public attention to a court case in 1896, in which a Barnardo settler on the industrial farm had been charged with indecent assault. (Gillian Wagner, *Barnardo* (London, 1979), pp. 247-8.

14) *Ibid.* In this case the critics alleged that the boy had been physically and mentally defective and argued from this unsubstantiated allegation that the medical examination of children before embarkation was extremely slipshod. The manslaughter case was dropped by default after the jury had disagreed over conflicting evidence.

15) Letter from A. M. Burgess to Lady Aberdeen, 2 May 1896. (Provincial Archives of Manitoba, Lady Aberdeen Enquiry regarding juvenile immigration, 1895-1901, file 28735. In support of his claims Burgess quoted figures supplied by Barnardo concerning the ultimate fate of his children, and also enclosed figures showing that out of 3,725 children placed out by Quarrier's Homes only seventeen had apparently committed any offence. (Wagner, *Children of the Empire*, p. 153).

16) Batt, *Dr Barnardo*, p. 134.

17) *AJ*, 19, 27, 28, 30 Jan., 1, 2 Feb. 1905; 19, 21, 22 Oct. 1910; and 6 June 1912.

18) See Dr Barnardo's Homes: Chronological Listing of Boys sent to Canada, 1882-94 and 1910-12. (Liverpool University Archives, D2/1/a1—D2/1/a31 and D2/1/a79—D2/1/a87). The registers of girls sent to Canada did not supply places of origin. All Barnardo's personal records of children are embargoed for 100 years, so exact details of individual cases cannot be disclosed.

19) The need for such a committee had arisen after Barnardo had become involved in controversy over his financial integrity and the management of his homes. He was opposed by another mission leader in the east end of London who thought Barnardo was encroaching on his territory, a disgruntled Baptist minister who complained he was losing his congregation to Barnardo's mission, and by the Charity Organisation Society, which disliked the proliferation of private societies which they feared would undermine the existing poor law system. In order to protect Barnardo's work Lord Aberdeen led a group of evangelicals in the formation of a committee which took over responsibility for the work and appointed Barnardo as their Honorary Director. They warded off the Charity Organisation Society's demands to conduct an investigation into Barnardo's, but a court of arbitration set up in 1877 to investigate all the allegations against him subsequently cleared him completely of any malpractice. And the committee, whose first action had been to investigate his books, had found them completely in order. (Wagner, *Children of the Empire*, p. 109).

20) *AJ*, 17 Jan. 1894. One of the emigrants from Barnardo's London Home in 1892 was a Scot who had been taken into the Home initially at the request of Lady Aberdeen (Barnardo Archives, D2/1/a23).

21) Haddo House MSS, news cuttings, volume marked 'May 1883—May 1885', pamphlet opposite p. 30.

22) He began in 1865 by setting up 'Brigades' of shoeblacks, newspaper and parcel boys, which offered work, education and training to destitute Glasgow streetboys.

23) Quoted on the cover of the annual *Narrative of Facts* published by Quarrier

from 1872 to 1903. (Full title: *A Narrative of Facts relative to work done for Christ in connection with the Orphan and Destitute Children's Emigration Homes, Glasgow*).

24) *DNB* (1901-11), pp. 146-7; and Rev John Urquhart, *The life story of William Quarrier: a romance of faith* (Glasgow, 1900).

25) *A Narrative of Facts* (1872), p. 9.

26) Alexander Gammie, *A romance of faith: the story of the Orphan Homes of Scotland and the founder William Quarrier* (London, 1936), p. 108.

27) *Ibid*, p. 105.

28) Liverpool University Archives: records of Dr Barnardo's Homes—D6(iii) [c] 1-20: Marchmont Home History Books, list of boys and girls sent to Canada, 1870-1914. Until 1874 and again from 1888 most children received into the Marchmont Home at Belleville were English, although there was a scattering of recruits from Scotland, including two brothers from Banff in 1871 and two boys from Aberdeen in 1872. From 1875 until 1887 however, the majority of recruits were Scottish, most of them being sent out under Quarrier's auspices. Of the nine children with North-East origins received into Marchmont in this period, six can also be traced in the records of Quarrier's Homes.

29) Gammie, *A romance of faith*, p. 90.

30) *A Narrative of Facts* (1879), p. 3.

31) *Ibid* (1878), p. 7 and *AJ*, 1 Sept. 1891.

32) P. 28.

33) Urquhart, *A romance of faith*, p. 377. See also above, n. 15.

34) Entitled 'An Act to Regulate the Immigration into Ontario of Certain Classes of Children', this legislation was intended to appease public opinion regarding the quality of juvenile immigrants, and was later adopted by the other Canadian provinces. Under penalty of a $100 fine or three months' imprisonment, it required that each distributing home be licensed, and that a regular written account be given of each child's antecedents and early years, along with details of, and reasons for any subsequent change of situation in Canada. The work of each agency was to be inspected four times a year and proper facilities were to be provided for the reception of children and for their subsequent shelter in times of need. Juvenile immigrants had to produce certificates authorising their admission, and it was made an offence to introduce to Ontario any physically or mentally defective or criminal child. Children taken into the distributing homes were to be placed under official control from the time of their arrival until they were eighteen. Each child's subsequent situation was to be inspected at least once a year by both an independent government officer and representatives of the various emigration agencies. (See Wagner, *Children of the Empire*, p. 154).

35) See table I for total number of emigrants sent out by Quarrier's Homes.

36) Vol. 6 (1884-5), p. 267. In the examples quoted here the names of the children have been altered, abbreviated or omitted to avoid the possibility of identification.

37) Vol. 7 (1885-6), p. 246.

38) Vol. 9 (1887-8), p. 256.

39) Vol. 13 (1891-2), p. 354. In 1901 the two girls who had remained at Bridge of Weir were returned to their brother and sister in Aberdeen.

40) Vol. 15 (1893-4), p. 368.

41) Vol. 18 (1896-7), p. 3.

42) Vol. 23 (1901-2), p. 136.

43) Vol. 24 (1902-3), p. 153.

44) Vol. 25 (1903-4), p. 142. The Orphan Homes were positively Protestant and evangelical in their approach.
45) Vol. 28 (1906-7), p. 17.
46) Vol. 34 (1912-13), p. 146. When Luke was admitted to Bridge of Weir in 1912 his grandfather was in receipt of parochial relief, while his uncle, who lived at the same address and worked in a sawmill, earned 14 shillings a week. In 1921 Duthie told Miss Quarrier that both Luke's grandfathers were alive, one being an invalid in the poorhouse and the other a cabinetmaker in Aberdeen.
47) Vol. 6 (1884-5) p. 210 and vol. 18 (1896-7), p. 166.
48) Vol. 6 (1884-5), p. 139. The Mrs Edmond was probably the same woman who was on the committee of the Aberdeen Ladies' Union from 1884 to 1890. (See below, pp. 259-76).
49) Vol. 11 (1889-90), pp. 38-9. The other child died in 1894, a year after the mother's death.
50) Vol. 12 (1890-1), p. 252. The other boy died in 1897.
51) Vol. 21 (1899-1900), p. 112. The girl was returned to her grandmother in 1907, as she was to be admitted to the Aberdeen Educational Trust, following in an older sister's footsteps.
52) Vol. 27 (1905-6), p. 32.
53) Vol. 7 (1885-6), p. 177.
54) Vol. 12 (1890-1), p. 78.
55) Vol. 20 (1898-9), p. 29.
56) Vol. 32 (1910-11) p. 96.
57) Vol. 7 (1885-6), p. 128. According to the 1875 *Aberdeen Directory* Barker was a manufacturer, with business premises at 3 Jopp's Lane, Aberdeen.
58) Vol. 9 (1887-8), pp. 22, 23.
59) Vol. 10 (1888-9), p. 104. No information about Mrs Anderson can be gleaned from the *Aberdeen Directory*, but it seems that after she had supervised the removal of the children to Canada she may have lost touch with their mothers. When Albert asked the Orphan Homes for his mother's address in 1898 Mrs Anderson was unable to supply it, and William, who was sent abroad in July 1889, was also unable to obtain any information about his mother through Mrs Anderson when he wrote to the Orphan Homes in 1894.
60) *Ibid*, p. 262.
61) Vol. 11 (1889-90), p. 5.
62) Vol. 12 (1890-1), p. 193.
63) Vol. 14 (1892-3), p. 185.
64) *Ibid*, p. 81.
65) Vol. 16 (1894-5), p. 7.
66) Vol. 23 (1901-2), p. 103.
67) Vol. 27 (1905-6), p. 189.
68) Vol. 30 (1908-9), pp. 90-1. In fact, after two unsuccessful attempts to place her in service in the west of Scotland, Jane was ultimately returned to her mother in Forres in 1916. She had been sent back to the Homes by both employers, who complained of her insolence and disobedience. The elder brother was killed in action in August 1917 and a sum of £9 6s. 6d. which had been in the care of a Mr Winters at Fairknowe was remitted to the mother in Forres.
69) Vol. 31 (1909-10), pp. 88-9.
70) Vol. 35 (1913-14), p. 75.
71) Vol. 14 (1892-3), p. 328.
72) Vol. 15 (1893-4), p. 154.
73) Vol. 32 (1910-11), p. 58. Evidence from the court case is taken from an undated

cutting from an unnamed newspaper attached to the entry in the record book. The Orphan Homes traced an uncle in Forfar and two of the child's three known aunts in the Gartly area.

74) Vol. 33 (1911-12), pp. 66-7. Evidence from the court case taken from an undated cutting from an unnamed newspaper attached to the entry in the record book. This report 'hoped that the memory of these sad days will be dimmed and that a more joyous time awaits the boys when they are residing in Quarrier's Homes or some similar institution.'

75) Vol. 36 (1914-15), pp. 38-9.

76) Vol. 8 (1886-7), pp. 13, 94.

77) Vol. 16 (1894-5), p. 271.

78) Vol. 30 (1908-9), p. 117.

79) Vol. 33 (1911-12), p. 209.

80) Vol. 34 (1912-13), p. 156.

81) *Narrative of Facts* (1877), p. 16.

82) PP 1913 [Cd. 6838] xxxix, 1, p. 60: *report of the departmental committee on reformatory and industrial schools.* See also p. 59, and *Evidence,* (PP 1913 [Cd. 6839], xxxix, 117, pp. 178, 285).

83) PP 1914-16 [Cd. 7886] xxxiv, 491, p. 76: *report of the departmental committee on reformatory and industrial schools in Scotland.* They thought the low numbers surprising in view of the large emigration from Scotland in general to the colonies. But Gillian Wagner says that in Britain as a whole, public support was not readily forthcoming for emigration from reformatories and industrial schools. (Wagner, *Children of the Empire,* xiii).

84) *Ibid, evidence and appendices.* (PP 1914-16 [Cd. 7887], xxxiv, 609, pp. 93-4).

85) Fifth annual report of the Oldmill Reformatory School, 1862 (King pamphlet collection, AUL, Special Collections, K380/5). The reformatory school differed from the industrial school in that it had power to detain children under sixteen who had been convicted of a criminal offence. It was meant to provide a middle way between prison and society.

86) See table II.

87) See vol. 1, pp. 145-8.

88) Aberdeen School of Industry, admission minute book III, 1867-1874.

89) *Ibid,* 1886-98, entry no. 1555 (Andrew Wallace, admitted 7 Feb. 1891). See also below, p. 208, he himself emigrated at a later date. See also *ibid,* 1898-1916, entry no. 2174 (Andrew Kane, admitted 5 Apr. 1911, for theft, aged ten). He had apparently been up before the court on several occasions. His father was a stone cutter, whose address was given as Barre, Vermont.

90) Second annual report of the Aberdeen Ladies' Union. (See below, pp. 259-76 and table II, pp. 228-30).

91) See table II.

92) PP 1900 [Cd. 408], xliii, 1: *forty-third report of H. M. Inspector of Reformatory and Industrial Schools of Great Britain,* for the year 1899, p. 451.

93) *AJ,* 8 Apr. 1912.

94) Oakbank Industrial School: Visiting Directors' Report Book (1875-1947).

95) Like the emigrants in the Spottiswoodes' era, several boys from Oakbank emigrated some time after their discharge from the school, so their removal would not have been recorded in the official statistics.

96) *AJ,* 17 June 1899.

97) McDonald was illegitimate, supposedly the son of a farmer in Resolis, Easter Ross. Later progress reports (in November 1899 and August 1900, 1901 and 1902) indicate that he was living at Oak Lake, Manitoba. For details of the

eleven emigrants mentioned in the discharge book, see entries for 31 Dec. 1883 (Scorgie); 12 May 1885 (Whittle); 16 Oct. 1885 (Andrew Dalgety); 3 July 1886 (Thomas Dalgety); 5 Oct. 1891 (Wallace; see also admission book, 1886-1898, entry no. 1555); 3 July 1888 (Levack); 10 May 1894 (Jackson); 24 Sept. 1899 (McDonald); 14 May 1895 (Robertson); 30 Apr. 1898 (James Ferguson); 25 Apr. 1899 (John Campbell).

98)   PP 1913 Cd. 6839, xxxix, 117, p. 87: *report of the departmental committee on reformatory and industrial schools*, evidence. See also *AJ*, 6 Sept. 1913, 11 Apr. 1914.

99)   See above, pp. 168-9.

100)   *AJ*, 24 Aug. 1911.

101)   William Booth, *In Darkest England and the Way Out* (1890), p. 76.

102)   William Booth, *The Surplus*, p. 90.

103)   Twelve English families were settled at Coombs on Vancouver Island in 1910. But within a few years the colonists at both locations had moved away to take up free homesteads, the debt for land, houses and implements having been too great. See R. G. Moyles, *The Blood and Fire in Canada: a history of the Salvation Army in the Dominion, 1882-1976* (Toronto, 1977), pp. 138-49. See also *The New Settler: a review of the Salvation Army Immigration Work for 1906* (Jan. 1907), pp. 8-9; and *The Surplus*, pp. 31-2.

104)   It was argued that settlers in special colonies had a greater tendency to be dissatisfied than individual emigrants who were more readily absorbed into existing colonial communities; and that in any case, such individuals were being well catered for by existing emigration agencies.

105)   1 Oct. 1887.

106)   See *War Cry*, 28 Nov. 1891, p. 11.

107)   *Salvation Army Year Book* (1975), pp. 13-17.

108)   *The Surplus*, p. 35.

109)   *The New Settler*, pp. 14-15: report from Brigadier T. Howell, Secretary for Immigration, Toronto, to Commissioner Coombs, 12 Jan. 1907.

110)   Anon., *Organised Empire Migration and Settlement* (London, 1930), p. 8.

111)   *Statistics of emigration work*, October 1903 to 31 July 1908 (Archives, Salvation Army International Headquarters, 101 Queen Victoria Street, London); and *The Surplus*, p. 51.

112)   In winter 1908-9, for instance, it was proposed that Salvation Army emigration officers should deliver at least 250 lectures in country towns and villages throughout Britain, as well as organising special emigration conferences at central points. (PAC, C-4768, vol. 105, file 17480: Salvation Army immigration records, general file).

113)   *Organised Empire Migration and Settlement*, p. 9.

114)   The 12-shilling payment was made up of the 7-shilling bonus paid to ordinary booking agents, together with an extra sub-agent's bonus of 5 shillings, before the general bonus was raised to £1 in April 1906. (For further details see PAC, C-4728, vol. 60, file 26/4, part 5: bonus to booking agents; and C-4768, vol. 105, file 17480, part 1: Salvation Army immigration schemes, letter from Commissioner of Emigration to James Smart, 27 Nov. 1903).

115)   Annual payments made by the Canadian Immigration Department to the Salvation Army included £1,000 towards the expenses of its London office, £500 for special articles in its newspapers in Britain, £250 for special pamphlets and $2,500 towards the distribution of settlers in Eastern Canada (raised to $7,500 in December 1907). It also paid £20 per month for its columns in the *War Cry* and the *Social Gazette*. (See PAC, C-10421, vol. 487, file

752538, part 1: philanthropic societies which assist immigrants to Canada, 1907-1929).

116) *The Surplus*, pp. 41, 52, 55-7.
117) David Lamb, *Notice to Passengers* (n.d.), p. 1.
118) *The Surplus*, pp. 43-4.
119) But see below, n. 130.
120) William Booth, *The recurring problem of the unemployed. One permanent remedy. Emigration—colonisation. Proposals for the better distribution of the people, and incidentally an appeal to local authorities for the judicious application of the emigration provisions of the Unemployed Workmen Act, 1905* (London, 1906), pp. 37-9.
121) *The Surplus*, pp. 37-8, 51.
122) *Ibid*, p. 34.
123) *Ibid*, p. 81: letter from 'E.G.', Reston, Manitoba, 24 May 1908, thanking the Salvation Army for finding him a good situation on a farm and asking their help in finding homesteads for himself and a friend.
124) *Ibid*, p. 58; letter dated 6 Mar. 1908.
125) *The recurring problem of the unemployed*, p. 44 and *The Surplus*, p. 91. Preston declared that 'The Salvation Army is the greatest emigration factor Great Britain has ever seen'.
126) *The Surplus*, p. 91.
127) *Ibid*, p. 84.
128) The Salvation Army (Canada and Bermuda): George Scott Railton Heritage Centre, Toronto, Archives and Museum: immigration cards (Scottish immigrants), 1913-1922.
129) There were 47 Presbyterians, 14 'Protestants', 2 Episcopalians, 2 Conregationalists, 2 Plymouth Brethren (both fishermen), 2 Roman Catholics, one Baptist and 10 entries where no religion was specified.
130) In fact, only 26 of the 740 Scottish Salvation Army emigrants between 1913 and 1922 had been involved in farming, either as farmers, farm managers or farm workers.
131) *AJ*, 4 May 1907.
132) *Ibid*, 8 Jan 1908.
133) *Ibid*, 14, 15 Feb. 1908.
134) *Ibid*, 16, 17 Nov. 1909.
135) *Ibid*, 18 Feb. 1910.
136) *Ibid*, 31 Jan. 1913.
137) A 24-year-old labourer, a member of the Salvation Army, came out in May on the *Grampian*, and a 20-year-old farm worker left in August, also on the *Grampian*.
138) Of the 740 Scottish emigrants listed in the Toronto records between 1913 and 1922, 271 were said to be 'domestics'.
139) *The Surplus*, p. 22.
140) *The recurring problem of the unemployed*, p. 42.
141) See, for instance, 3 Jan., 17 Feb. 1910; 23 Feb. 1912.
142) *AJ*, 17 Mar. 1909; 23, 26 Feb. 1912.
143) *Ibid*, 9 Dec. 1909; 1 Jan., 3 Feb. 1913.

TABLE I
EMIGRANTS SENT TO CANADA THROUGH QUARRIER'S HOMES, 1872–1921

YEAR	FIRST PARTY	SECOND PARTY	THIRD PARTY	TOTAL
1872	64			64
1873	81			81
1874	71			71
1875	65			65
1876	49			49
1877	56			56
1878	79			79
1879	130			130[1]
1880	117			117
1881	64	92		156
1882	73	65		138
1883	97	89		186
1884	118	127		245
1885	100	99	140	339
1886	*	*	*	*
1887	*	*	*	*
1888	120	120		240
1889	129	123		252
1890	121	128		249
1891	129	103		232
1892	130	120		250
1893	128	140		268
1894	140	117		257
1895	138	124		262
1896	132	122		254
1897	117	118		235
1898†	—	—		—
1899	3			3
1900	4			4
1901	12			12
1902	12			12
1903	18			18
1904	71			71
1905	188			188
1906	191			191
1907	177			177
1908	163			163
1909	138			138
1910	188			188
1911	180			180
1912	184			184
1913	185			185
1914	151			151‡
1915	33			33
1916	56			56
1917	—			—
1918	—			—
1919	—			—
1920	63			63
1921	51			51
TOTAL	4,516	1,687	140	6,343

Source: A Narrative of Facts, 1872–1922
[1] James Ross states that only 18 emigrants left in 1879. (James Ross, The Power I Pledge (Glasgow, 1971), p. 61.
* Figures missing.
† Emigration was suspended from 1899 to 1903.
‡ Two emigrants were also sent to Australia and New Zealand.

TABLE II

CHILDREN EMIGRATED FROM REFORMATORY AND INDUSTRIAL SCHOOLS, 1854–1915

| | REFORMATORIES | | | | INDUSTRIAL SCHOOLS | | | | | | | | |
| | | | Aberdeen | Aberdeen | | | | Aberdeen | Aberdeen | | | | |
Year	England	Scotland	Oldmill (boys)	Mount St. (girls)	England	Scotland	Boys	Girls (1)	Girls (2)	Girls (3)	Total (R.S.)	Total (I.S.)	Grand Total
1854–58	*	*	*	*	*	*	*	*	*	*	42		42
1859	*	*	*	*	*	*	*	*	*	*	108		108
1860	46	14	1	*	*	*	*	*	*	*	60		60
1861	102	8	—	—	*	*	*	*	*	*	110		110
1862	116	15	—	—	1	3	—	—	—	—	131	4	135
1863	101	25	—	—	4	—	—	—	—	—	126	4	130
1864	76	19	—	—	1	—	—	—	—	—	95	1	96
1865	77	18	—	—	9	11	—	—	—	—	95	20	115
1866	57	12	—	1	2	2	—	—	—	—	69	4	73
1867	78	11	—	—	3	—	—	—	—	—	89	3	92
1868	91	11	—	—	8	1	—	—	—	—	102	9	111
1869	107	14	—	—	11	2	—	—	—	—	121	13	134
1870	148	9	2	—	34	15	—	—	—	—	157	49	206
1871	163	15	2	—	49	10	—	—	—	—	178	59	237
1872	124	9	3	—	56	6	—	—	—	—	133	62	195
1873	132	13	—	—	59	8	—	—	—	—	145	67	212
1874	105	12	—	—	104	2	—	—	—	—	117	106	223
1875	74	10	—	3	48	2	—	—	—	—	84	50	134
1876	42	3	1	—	28	1	—	—	—	—	45	29	74
1877	24	4	—	—	21	3	—	—	—	—	28	24	52
1878	40	2	2	—	23	1	—	—	1	—	42	24	66
1879	39	3	1	—	36	—	—	—	—	—	42	36	78
1880	51	5	—	—	48	4	—	—	—	—	56	52	108

Year													
1881	60	6	1	1	58	5	1				66	63	129
1882	82	7			82	10					89	92	181
1883	129	6	1		86	19					135	105	240
1884	125	7			118	24			3		132	142	274
1885	108	7			132	22			5		115	154	269
1886	106	11	2		110	30	2	1	4		117	140	257
1887	99	22		2	108	45					121	153	274
1888	132	11		2	90	29					143	119	262
1889	95	12			151	35			1		107	186	293
1890	64	10			91	16			1		74	107	181
1891	74	8			106	23	1				82	129	211
1892	51	7			113	12					58	125	183
1893	44	6			127	25					50	152	202
1894	40	4			87	13	2				44	100	144
1895	37	4			83	15					41	98	139
1896	32	3			118	3					35	121	156
1897	33	4			94	4					37	98	135
1898	24	4			103	15				2	28	118	146
1899	17	11	+	+	105	8	1			2	28	113	141
1900	21	3	+	+	80	3					24	83	107
1901	23	7	+	+	86	2					30	88	118
1902	31	4	+	+	107	13					35	120	155
1903	29	9	+	+	136	7	2				33	143	176
1904	36	8	+	+	110	8					45	118	163
1905	36	7	+	+	209	16	1				44	225	269
1906	46	13	+	+	169	22	1				53	191	244
1907	39	8	+	+	197	15					52	224	276
1908	13	18	+	+	188	8	1				21	202	223
1909§	12		+	+	205	9	1				30	214 (219)	244 (249)

continued

TABLE II—continued

| | REFORMATORIES | | | | INDUSTRIAL SCHOOLS | | | | | | | | |
| | | | Aberdeen | Aberdeen | | | | Aberdeen | Aberdeen | | | | |
Year	England	Scotland	Oldmill (boys)	Mount St. (girls)	England	Scotland	Boys	Girls (1)	Girls (2)	Girls (3)	Total (R.S.)	Total (I.S.)	Grand Total
1910	24	6	†	‡	151	10	—	—	—	—	30	161	191
1911§	11	16	†	‡	167	5	—	—	—	—	27	172	199
												(179)	(206)
1912§	42	15	†	‡	172	14	—	—	—	—	57	186	243
												(194)	(254)
1913	*	*	†	‡	*	*	*	*	*	*	51	176	227
1914	*	*	†	‡	*	*	*	*	*	*	39	169	208
1915	*	*	†	‡	*	*	*	*	*	*	7	66	73
GRAND TOTAL	3,508	500	16	9	4,484	553	13	1	15	4	4,146	5,466	9,724

Source: Annual Reports of the Chief Inspector of Reformatory and Industrial Schools of Great Britain, nos. 1–59, 1854–1915. (British Parliamentary Papers).

The Aberdeen Schools of Industry were:
—Aberdeen School of Industry (for boys): in Skene Square until 1878, then at Oakbank;
—Aberdeen School of Industry for Girls: in Skene Square until 1881, then at Whitehall (no. 1);
—Aberdeen Female School of Industry, King Street: certified 1870 (no. 2);
—Aberdeen Industrial School for Roman Catholic Girls, Nazareth House: certified 1878 (no. 3).
* Individual totals not specified.
† Oldmill Reformatory was closed in 1897, for financial reasons.
‡ Mount Street Girls' Reformatory was closed in 1901, owing to low numbers of inmates.
§ For the years 1909, 1911 and 1912 the total numbers of emigrants from industrial schools given in the inspector's reports do not correspond to the figures arrived at if the emigrants from individual industrial schools (or even the total number of emigrants from England and Scotland) are added together. The figures in the table have been arrived at by adding together either the emigrants from individual industrial schools or the totals of industrial school emigrants from England and Scotland. The figures in parentheses are taken from the same reports, and are said to be the totals of industrial school emigrants from Britain for the years concerned.

CHAPTER VI

The Female Emigrant

The late Victorian era saw a notable upsurge of support throughout the British Isles for schemes of specifically female emigration. Various categories of women were encouraged to emigrate to a number of destinations, under the auspices of various agencies and with varying degrees of success. Yet an indiscriminate exodus was not encouraged and there were fierce opponents of female emigration both in Britain and in the recipient colonies, although their opposition was generally based on opposing viewpoints. Women and girls from North-East Scotland participated fully in the exodus. Most were simply recruited by booking agents eager to export as many domestic servants as possible to Canada in order to claim the Dominion government's bonus on these eligible settlers. Some, however, were sent abroad by societies which were governed less by commercial motives than by a desire to redress the imbalance of the sexes at home and abroad and to stamp the woman's 'hallowing influence' on the colonies. And around 300 female emigrants also left North-East Scotland under the auspices of one locally-based organisation, the Aberdeen Ladies' Union, which for over a quarter of a century despatched recruits to Canada under the direction of its visionary and enthusiastic patron, the Countess of Aberdeen.

The specific encouragement of female emigration had begun in the early 1830s, when the philosophy of systematic colonisation replaced more negative attitudes to the colonies, and a higher view came to be taken of these lands and their requirements. Attempts were made to persuade more women to emigrate, not solely in order to redress the imbalance of the sexes which was prevalent in most colonies, but also to rid the British Isles of large numbers of unemployed young women. These efforts were channelled through the Colonial Office, provincial governments in the colonies concerned, and a number of philanthropic societies and individuals such as Caroline Chisholm, Lord Shaftesbury and Sidney Herbert.[1] The nature and extent of assistance given varied according to the motives of the organisers, economic conditions in Britain and the requirements of the colonies. Initial efforts were directed at Australia where transportation had provoked a particularly acute imbalance of the sexes in the early nineteenth century, but philanthropists soon became interested in sending female emigrants to more popular and accessible destinations in British North America. In the 1840s the Irish poor law unions began to send women to Canada as well as to Australia, and in 1850 the London Female Emigration Society sent its first contingent of eighteen working women out to Toronto.[2] In the 1850s Maria Rye became involved in promoting employment opportunities for middle class women in Britain, but the difficulties of the task soon led her to advocate some form of assisted female emigration.[3] She became Honorary Secretary of the Church of England Emigration Society, and in 1862 founded the Female Middle Class Emigration Society with the support of Lord Shaftesbury, five years before she turned her attention exclusively to juvenile emigration. During its thirty-year existence the Society gave interest-free loans to about 400 women, mainly teachers and governesses, to enable them to emigrate to Canada, Australasia and South Africa.

The period from 1880 until the First World War saw a notable resurgence of interest in female emigration. A variety of national and provincial societies, some of them short-lived, others which endured for over a quarter of a century, organised the emigration of over 22,000 women.[4] Many more women did not belong to any society but simply booked their passages through ticket agents, who for financial reasons targeted their recruitment campaigns at domestic servants as well as agriculturists. Canada was the preferred destination of most societies, since it was 'nearer home, and in morals and sobriety superior to the Australian and African colonies'.[5] Yet, although Canada also voiced the most consistent demand for female settlers, they were generally expected to pay the full steerage fare of around £5, the Dominion government offering few financial incentives to women emigrants. This meant that emigration societies and agents with limited funds were often forced to send applicants to those Australasian colonies which continued to offer free passages to suitable women, although the gradual termination of such schemes, combined with higher fares to the Antipodes, helped to concentrate activities on Canada before the end of the nineteenth century. Then for a brief period at the turn of the century, South Africa took over from Canada as the main resort of Britain's assisted female emigrants, when large numbers of women responded to pleas to settle there in the aftermath of the Boer War.[6]

The leading agencies involved in female emigration at this time included the Women's Emigration Society (1880-83), out of which grew the Colonial Emigration Society (1883-92) and the British Women's Emigration Association[7] (1884-1919). The latter society, under enthusiastic leaders such as Ellen Joyce and Adelaide Ross, soon became the most influential agent in the organisation of assisted female emigration from Britain, absorbing the Colonial Emigration Society and the Female Middle Class Emigration Society in 1892 and supervising the work of many smaller provincial associations. After 1901, in response to the great upsurge of interest in South Africa, its work in this area was conducted independently by the South Africa Colonisation Society,[8] with an additional body, the Colonial Intelligence League, being formed in 1910 to ensure that only educated and properly trained women were assisted to emigrate. In 1919 these three leading emigration societies were amalgamated to form the Society for the Overseas Settlement of British Women.[9]

Practical needs and imperial duties: promoting female emigration

The revival of interest in female emigration was provoked largely by the impact of the economic depression in late Victorian Britain. The twin arguments which had produced the earliest schemes to assist women emigrants— 'civilising' the colonies and reducing the chronic surplus of women in Britain—both took on a new dimension in the late nineteenth century. Although the depression damaged the employment prospects of working class women, increasing concern was expressed at the plight of the educated 'distressed gentlewoman' who had been unsuccessful in the marriage market and who was often left without the means of support when her parents died. Such women, struggling to maintain their lifestyle against the rising cost of living, were often forced to seek paid employment, but they were less adaptable than their working class counterparts. They rejected domestic service (where demand for employees exceeded supply) as too menial and sought instead all too few positions as governesses or 'lady companions' in the hope of retaining some of their social status and respectability.

Emigration was increasingly seen as a legitimate means of elevating the position of these women as well as the traditional, working class female emigrants, and at the same time of serving wider British and colonial needs. This attitude was reflected in the concern of the leading emigration societies to cater for both categories of women, the Female Middle Class Emigration Society pioneering the policy of sending out educated recruits.[10] The societies commonly cited the widely publicised and continuing shortage of domestic servants in all the British colonies as a major justification for their programme; but they also pointed out that in the colonies a woman who had to earn her own living and who was competent was not looked down on socially, but was treated as an equal by her employers. Women were also encouraged to believe that they would not only find remunerative and congenial employment, but that they would, given the imbalance of the sexes in the colonies, stand a better chance of making a 'good marriage' than they would at home. This opportunity to marry well was stressed by A. J. MacMillan of Brandon, Manitoba during a lecture in Aberdeen in 1888. There were, he claimed, thousands more men than women in Manitoba, and female emigrants would be much welcomed, initially as domestics but before very long as wives.[11] Meanwhile, middle class women who still baulked at the idea of domestic service were encouraged to emigrate to Canada by the assurance of ample opportunities for employment in those fields which were so restricted in Britain—as teachers, nurses and mother's helps. Those with some capital to spare were told that they could profitably invest in raising fruit, vegetables, flowers, poultry or dairy produce, although they were warned not to rush into any such venture until they had acquired the know-how and stamina to cope with a pioneering life.[12]

In the early years of the twentieth century the case in favour of the emigration of educated women was greatly strengthened by the popularity of the eugenics movement and the upsurge of imperialistic sentiment. The twin arguments of the woman emigrant's civilising mission and the imbalance of the sexes at home and abroad were adopted by the eugenists, who feared that the surplus female population in Britain was hindering the attainment of their ideal, racially pure society. While they favoured a reduction of the birth-rate to a level where all children would be wanted and carefully reared, they recommended emigration as a short-term means of eradicating the female surplus. More importantly, the emigration of suitable women would be the means of promoting racial purity in the colonies, where many more 'respectable' white women were needed to prevent British settlers marrying either native women or 'inferior' immigrants, and to ensure the reproduction of British society abroad. These ideas were promoted in a number of contemporary pamphlets and periodicals,[13] and were readily adopted by all the female emigration societies, which increasingly upheld the wider, imperial function of their clients. Recruits were told that they were 'missionaries of Empire',[14] who were going out not only to fill positions of employment but ultimately, and more importantly, to become the wives of British settlers and the mothers of a future British colonial generation. Societies which catered for middle class female emigrants were particularly interested in these theories, since their recruits seemed to meet most satisfactorily the requirements of the eugenists in terms of their birth, breeding and general attitudes. Potential recruits were assured that they would suffer no shame or deprivation in emigrating to Canada, which 'wants some of our educated women to live their lives, to make their history, to chronicle the joyous, vigorous robust tone of a young and prosperous country' and where 'no educated woman need fear that her talents will get rusty'.[15] On the contrary, these women would play a vital rôle in the Dominion's social development, whether they went out as teachers, nurses, homemakers to bachelor brothers or as home helps in families where they would unquestionably be treated as the social equals of their employers.

Eugenic arguments in favour of female emigration were given a fillip by the Boer War, after which several ex-soldiers remained as farmers or tradesmen in Britain's extended South African possessions, aggravating the existing problems of an excessively male-dominated society. Suitable British women were urged to follow these pioneers to South Africa where, as colonial wives, their rôle would be 'to exalt the tone of social life, [and] to bring a softening, elevating, intellectual influence'.[16] In 1910 some members of the BWEA and SACS joined together to form the Colonial Intelligence League. It concerned itself exclusively with promoting the emigration of educated, professional women, who it wished to ensure were also adequately trained in the essentials of colonial life. The League then endeavoured to find situations or investment openings in Canada and South Africa for its clients, some of whom were women with capital whom it had encouraged to go into business on their own account in the colonies.

Persuading, training and removing the female emigrant

There were various ways in which female emigration societies went about their task of attracting and selecting suitable candidates, training them if necessary, supervising their removal and settlement, and finding them employment. Their approach depended partly on the intelligence and occupational background of their clients, who in the early days of the movement were often semi-literate and more likely to respond to a personal invitation than to a written explanation of the advantages of emigration. The leading society, the BWEA, worked through local committees scattered across Britain, made up of voluntary workers who were responsible for publicising the Society's activities and for making an initial selection of candidates. By 1901 there were 150 such workers, who organised public meetings to discuss emigration, supplied interested parties with information about life abroad, helped them to complete their application forms and checked all references. Each applicant who requested an advance of passage money from the Loan Fund and asked that employment would be secured for her in Canada also undertook 'to accept the situation selected for me ... and to remain in that situation until I have discharged the sum advanced to me'.[17] The loan was to be recovered in monthly instalments, usually of fifteen shillings, deducted from the girl's wages. Completed application forms were returned to the BWEA headquarters for final approval or rejection by Ellen Joyce. Successful applicants then had their passages booked by the central office, while local workers were to pass on precise instructions about preparations for departure and the repayment of loans. Financial assistance was given to women who were going out to follow professions, trades or domestic service (provided they had not been in domestic service at home), to families, and also from 1890 to a small number of men and boys, usually the relatives of the female emigrants.[18]

As the idea of middle class female emigration became popular, the emigration societies put increasing emphasis on books, pamphlets and articles as a means of attracting recruits. The *Imperial Colonist*, the monthly organ of the British Women's Emigration Association and the South Africa Colonisation Society, appeared from 1901 to 1927, initially under the editorship of Ellen Joyce. As well as advertising the facilities and reporting the achievements of the societies it represented, it provided a forum for the publication of numerous articles which described the experiences of emigrants, offered practical advice on particular occupations and recommended various destinations. Georgina Binnie-Clark,[19] for instance, wrote a number of articles for the *Imperial Colonist* between 1907 and 1912, which covered such topics as 'Horticulture as a career for women' (February 1908), 'Women's chances in the West' (March 1909) and a three-part survey entitled 'Are educated women wanted in Canada?' (February to April 1910). One of the first projects of the Colonial Intelligence League was to sponsor an enquiry into a widely-recommended occupation for middle class women in Canada—that of the home help. The writer and journalist Ella Sykes spent six months in Western Canada in 1911 posing as an impoverished gentlewoman, in order to investigate claims from disgruntled emigrants that the home help was nothing more than a general servant. Her account of her experiences appeared in her book, *A Home-Help in Canada* (1912), in which she assessed the advantages and drawbacks of middle class emigration, stressing the need for competence and hard work, but recommending Canada to women who could meet these requirements. The same requirements were repeatedly emphasised in articles in a number of general periodicals, notably *Chambers' Journal*, which regularly devoted space to the emigration debate. In August 1911 it appealed to readers, particularly women, to submit their accounts of the daily routine of colonial life, accounts which it thought would be more truthful and less vague than the usual emigration agents' propaganda, and which it hoped would be of practical use to intending emigrants. The appeal produced a big response, and selected articles covering a number of destinations appeared in *Chambers' Journal* in February 1912. Three of the letters were from women who had had experience of ranch life in Alberta,[20] one was from an emigrant who had spent twenty years as a general servant on a farm in Manitoba, and another was written by an English woman who had gone out to assist her brother on a fruit farm in British Columbia. All the correspondents spoke well of Canada as a land of challenge and opportunity, although they all stressed repeatedly the need for energy and hard work.

It was a cardinal principle of the BWEA that only diligent girls of proven capability and good character should be sent abroad. It sent away not only its own recruits but also those of smaller, provincial societies which wanted to make use of the facilities of the larger organisation; but even applicants who did not receive a loan and only wanted the assurance of supervision on the journey were required to conform to the same standards as the BWEA's own assisted recruits. All applicants were vetted and their references checked; then as more and more middle class women became interested in emigrating, the societies began to put increasing emphasis on the formal training of candidates. Perhaps it was felt that middle class recruits, though educated to a higher level than the traditional female emigrants, were less likely to possess the practical skills essential for colonial life. At any rate, a residential training home for 'genteel' emigrants was opened at Leaton in Shropshire in 1909 where, for ten shillings a week, twelve students at a time were given a three-month course in colonial housework. The practical training of emigrants, both before and after their removal, was also a major concern of the Colonial Intelligence League. In 1912 it purchased fifteen acres of the Coldstream Estate in the Okanagan Valley in British Columbia, where it established the Princess Patricia Ranch to train women specifically in farming skills. Students were to give their labour in return for a year's board, lodging and instruction, at the end of which it was expected that they would find salaried posts on farms or take up land on their own account, as individuals or in groups.[21]

The encouragement given to men of means to settle in British Columbia in the early twentieth century was matched by similar attempts to persuade 'genteel' women of its attributes as an emigrant destination. Specific openings for teachers, dressmakers and particularly home helps were regularly advertised in the *Imperial Colonist*, and in provincial newspapers,[22] with committees being set up in the province to arrange for the employment of home helps under the auspices of the BWEA, and to vet prospective employers. Preference was given to women who had been trained at Leaton, and successful candidates were offered a minimum wage of £30 a year. The area around Vernon and Kelowna in the Okanagan Valley was particularly highly recommended because of its congenial society:

> It is on the ranches in the neighbourhood of these places that the Home Helps will find the happiest home, as there are large settlements of people from the old country, connected with good families, who will preserve the traditions and refinements of the old land while adopting the industry of the new.[23]

In April 1913 the Joyce Hostel was opened at Kelowna, one of the final achievements of the BWEA before the First World War. It was named in commemmoration of Ellen Joyce's thirty years of work for female emigration and was intended to provide accommodation for the increasing numbers of women who were by that time turning away from domestic service to non-resident work in shops and offices.

Facilities for the protection, reception and employment of female emigrants had existed long before 1913 on both sides of the Atlantic. In the 1880s the BWEA set up hostels in London and Liverpool to house emigrants on the night before their departure, and employed matrons to escort 'protected parties' across the Atlantic. These facilities were open to all approved female emigrants, not merely to those who were receiving assistance from the BWEA's funds, and they were widely used by a number of other societies, including the YWCA, the Girls' Friendly Society and provincial organisations such as the Aberdeen Ladies' Union. On arrival in Canada the emigrants were first taken to reception centres run by the government, the YWCA or the Girls' Friendly Society,[24] where they were generally allowed to stay free of charge for the first twenty-four hours. Most societies tried to secure work in advance for their clients, so that they could move straight from the reception centres to their new employment. The Canadian Manufacturers' Association periodically supplied the BWEA with lists of factory jobs on offer; and most female emigration societies and agents had employment registries and local correspondents in Canada who kept them informed about openings in the female labour market.

The female emigration debate: opposition, complaints and counter-arguments

The activities of the female emigration agencies did not go unopposed, either in Britain or in the colonies. Mistresses in the colonies made repeated requests

18   Immigrants for domestic service, Quebec, c. 1911.

for cooks, housemaids and general servants, the very categories of workers which were in such short supply in Britain. The insatiable colonial demand for domestic servants provoked much criticism at home that emigration societies were depleting the country of precisely the class of women which it most required to retain. Charitable emigration societies were in a dilemma, for they could not afford to alienate potential subscribers by assisting the removal of women whom these potential subscribers wished to employ themselves. They therefore pointed out that the shortage of domestic servants was due primarily to these girls seeking less onerous and more remunerative employment in shops and factories at home, and that it was from such occupations, not from domestic service, that most working class emigrants were recruited. They also stressed that the kind of servants most sought after in Britain were generally not suitable candidates for domestic service in the colonies, where employees were not required to be highly specialised in any one branch of domestic work but to be capable of undertaking a wide range of duties. The societies' enthusiasm for middle class female emigration was not due just to concern at the plight of unemployed 'gentlewomen' or to the impact of eugenic theories; by encouraging the emigration of women who would never consider going into service at home they hoped to stem the criticism that they were denuding Britain of large numbers of domestics.

The emigration societies claimed that their failure rate was minimal, and that most recruits repaid their loans promptly and adapted successfully to their new life. Yet despite the continuing demand for female settlers, colonial employers regularly complained that the societies were more concerned with removing a surplus female population from Britain than with meeting colonial needs. From the inception of female emigration schemes in Australia in the 1830s colonists had complained about the moral and physical shortcomings of female settlers, who at that time were selected mainly from workhouses and charitable institutions in England and Ireland.[25] It was argued in 1882[26] that Maria Rye had disproved the theory that the bad hereditary tendencies of many pauper girls would prevent their succeeding in Canada, but this optimistic feeling was seemingly not shared by the Canadians, who complained that there was often no demand for the type of girls she sent. Complaints were also voiced about the calibre of 'genteel' emigrants who were said to be pretentious and incapable,[27] despite the societies' assurances that, once trained in basic domestic duties, these recruits would be more adaptable, reliable and socially acceptable than traditional working class emigrants.

Female emigrants from North-East Scotland did not escape criticism; but the complaints seem to have been directed more at women who left under the auspices of general booking agents than at those who were chosen by specifically female emigration societies. It seems that the various emigration agencies and servants' registries in Aberdeen and North-East Scotland did not exercise such strict standards in the recruitment of female emigrants as did the BWEA and its affiliated organisations. It is impossible to state precisely how many women left the region under the auspices of these agencies, but correspondence between H. W. J. Paton and the Canadian Immigration Department suggests that they probably catered for the majority of female emigrants. By November 1910, eighteen months after he had opened his emigration bureau, Paton had sent out well over 200 girls, all to Ontario; by July 1911 he had despatched over 150 more women to Canada, so that in a period of little more than two years one agent alone had sent away as many female emigrants as were recruited by the Aberdeen Ladies' Union in its entire thirty-year existence.[28]

Most of these emigrants were domestic servants, deliberately recruited by the agents so that they could claim the Canadian government's commission on them. But quantity and quality were not always synonymous, and on a number of occasions the agents' bonus was rescinded when the emigrants refused to take up the occupations for which they had been recruited or failed to satisfy their employers. In September 1910, for instance, two women sent out to Canada the previous April by Paton were recommended for deportation after they had refused to repay their fares to the booking agents and had also turned down remunerative employment secured for them by Paton's representative in Toronto.[29] In May 1913 a strong protest was made in a solicitor's letter from Napanee, Ontario, to the Canadian Department of the Interior, concerning two unsatisfactory domestic servants from Aberdeen who had been sent to Napanee:

> We desire to report to you the case of two servant girls, who were shipped to this Country by Mackay Bros. & Co ... Aberdeen ... the one girl, Mary Rait was secured by Mr. Taylor, Emigration Agent at Perth [Ontario], who claimed to have obtained her through Mackay Bros. & Co. We are informed ... that she belonged to the criminal class before she left the Old Country and has since been deported. She was sent to Mrs. W. J. Dollar of Napanee and defrauded her out of her passage money and was absolutely useless as a servant and was of a very bad moral character. The girl, Isabella Mitchell was hired through the same agent as a cook for Mrs. F. F. Miller of this town. She did not profess to know anything about cooking, was absolutely filthy about her personal habits and no respectable housekeeper would want her about the premises ... We submit it is not right that people should be permitted to defraud Canadians out of passage money for useless so-called servants, as neither of these girls were fit to enter the premises of any respectable person.[30]

The following year the Department turned down Mackay Brothers' request for a bonus on a girl who had shown no serious intention of taking up domestic service:

> She has already been in service in two or three different places and the reports received concerning her habits are not at all to this girl's credit and I may also add that at one time one of her employers had to take this girl out from the police court where she was detained on the charge of vagrancy.[31]

The letter went on to point out that this was 'only one of several cases which have lately come to our attention where girls booked by you to Canada have not made good and ... if this state of affairs is going to continue the Department will ... be obliged to report unfavourably upon the class of immigrants selected by your officials'. In February 1917 the bonus was disallowed on a female client of Paton's agency who was completely untrained in domestic service and had clearly failed to satisfy her three employers in Toronto:

> Rose McIntyre was first employed at Mrs. Edwards ... for about one week and was then let go. She was not much use as a domestic, had no experience and was careless, indifferent and lazy. She does not want to stay in domestic service, but wants to play the piano in a moving picture show. She was next employed by Mrs. Rominisky ... from November 25th till shortly after Christmas. Mrs. Rominisky told me that she was very unsatisfactory. She took the baby out one afternoon at 2:00 o'clock and should have returned at 5:00 o'clock, but did not come back till 10:00 o'clock with the baby. On another occasion on her Sunday off she did not return until Wednesday ... Miss Carmichael [Paton's representative in Toronto] told me that Rose McIntyre had sent to her sister in the United States for $30.00 to finish paying her advance passage, but had only paid $5.00 of this money on the passage ... I was also informed that she smokes cigarettes, and altogether from the reports I have had, she appears to be most unsatisfactory in every way.[32]

McIntyre then spent six weeks with another employer, a Mrs Gregg, who had known her in Scotland and who was aware that she was difficult to manage. She left that position to work in a munitions factory, owing Mrs Gregg over $24 for board and other debts which she had run up, but by May 1917 she had apparently married and gone to the USA, her mother repaying the outstanding passage money to Paton's office.[33]

Criticism of female emigration from North-East Scotland was not only voiced by the Canadian Immigration Department and dissatisfied employers. From time to time the emigrants themselves or their parents complained about the treatment they received at the hands of agents. In October 1909, for instance, nine young women from Aberdeen were induced to emigrate temporarily to Nova Scotia by Joseph Christie, a former Aberdeen town councillor who had failed in business. On 13 October he advertised in the *Evening Express* for experienced herring filleters and gutters to work for him in Halifax, promising recruits a free passage to and from Nova Scotia, free accommodation and twelve months' employment at wages of $4 a week. But Christie's intemperate habits meant that he was subsequently unable to fulfil these promises, and in June 1910 the girls' case was taken up by John Croll, a solicitor in Aberdeen, after he had been approached by a number of parents. As a result of Croll's intervention the complaints were investigated by the Canadian government's immigration agency in Halifax, which discovered that the girls' plight had ultimately been relieved by the local agent of the Society for the Prevention of Cruelty to Children. Having been asked for help by one of the recruits, she found that Christie (who had disappeared, leaving his debts behind him) had no intention of meeting his obligations, and she had therefore removed the girls to the Society's hostel. The North British Society had agreed to pay their board until suitable employment was found for them; one girl subsequently got married and two more returned to

Aberdeen after their father sent for them, but the remainder were placed in domestic service and, according to the government agent's report on 4 August, they were all 'well satisfied, and are doing well in their several positions, and have made no requests to be sent home, since leaving Christie'.[34]

Most complaints by female emigrants either appeared in the local press or in correspondence with the booking agents. According to the daughter of William Miller, a jeweller in Aberdeen, her party which sailed from Liverpool to Quebec in May 1913 was treated no better than cattle, being confined in a customs shed for a day on arrival and then despatched to Montreal without food. In Montreal they were accommodated ten to a room, and the following day prospective employers 'came to interview the live-stock', those who did not receive appointments being sent on to Toronto where the procedure was repeated.[35] Also in 1913 a domestic servant sent out through Paton's agency by Mrs Stewart's registry in Aberdeen complained about inadequate liaison between Mrs Stewart and Miss Mary Carmichael, Paton and Stewart's Scottish representative in Toronto:

> I did not think much of the reception we got when we arrived in Toronto. Miss Carmichael said she did not expect me nor had she a place for me as she had never had any papers from you concerning me, but in the course of the forenoon a lady phoned for a maid so I saw her in the afternoon and came here the next morning.[36]

The agents hotly refuted allegations of the maltreatment of emigrants under their care. Mrs Stewart claimed that she had received hundreds of letters from satisfied clients, one of which, from Maggie Masson, formerly of Whitehills, Banffshire, was quoted in the *Evening Gazette* of 30 May 1913:

> It is five months since I arrived, and I find my people just as nice as when I met them in Aberdeen. Everything is so much different, and so much easier than in the homeland. We have a lovely electric washing-machine, so we can sit and eat breakfast and have the washing going on at the same time. We dine at the same table as the master and mistress, and travel first-class with them. I cannot thank you enough for recommending me to a good family.

Although most girls were homesick to begin with, Mrs Stewart said this phase soon passed, and none of her clients had returned home dissatisfied. On the contrary, most strongly advised their contemporaries to follow their example and were often determined to give financial assistance to other members of their families to join them as soon as possible. Mrs Stewart commended the provision made by Mary Carmichael for the reception of emigrants in her own home and at the Toronto YWCA; the girls could rest here before being interviewed by a number of prospective employers and choosing for themselves the situation they liked best.

Paton similarly praised Miss Carmichael's reception facilities and defended his own treatment of female emigrants in a statement to the Canadian Immigration Department in 1914:[37]

The girls travel under the care of an experienced conductor from Aberdeen to Glasgow; they are taken on board the steamer, seen into their cabins and the brightest girl of the party personally introduced to the "Ship's Mother" when the girls are sailing on the Allan Line steamers and to the Chief Stewardess when travelling by the Donaldson Line. The girls wear a distinctive badge; they are all berthed together on the steamer and are looked after specially in *every* way till they arrive at Landing Port. Ten days before the vessel sails the Glasgow Office of the C.P.R. is advised the names of the girls and the name and sailing date of the steamer on which they are to travel—they in their turn advise their officials at Landing Port and a man is specially detailed to look after the girls on their arrival, see to their luggage, see them on board the proper train and advise their Montreal office of the number who have arrived and when they have left Landing Port. Montreal Office in its turn checks the girls and wires our Lady Super-intendent, Miss Carmichael ... when the train will arrive at Toronto Station and she meets the girls and takes them home with her.

While booking agents might state categorically that they did not mislead or mistreat emigrants, they could not deny the accusation that many of their clients fell into precisely that category of emigrant which was in keen demand at home. Since they could claim the Canadian government bonus only on farm workers and domestic servants, their main efforts were directed at attracting such recruits, which incurred the wrath of those who were con-cerned at the growing dearth of domestic servants in Britain. Occasional comments in the Aberdeen press echoed this national complaint, as in 1913 when one correspondent suggested importing domestic servants from Switz-erland and Norway to alleviate the shortage brought about by the emigration of so many local girls to Canada that year.[38] The agencies responded to the universal colonial demand for domestic servants by regularly advertising specific openings in the local press. Most such advertisements in the *Aberdeen Journal* related to North America, and between 1887 and 1914 at least twenty-one agencies in Aberdeen and the North-East advertised posts for domestic servants in these regions.[39] Some agencies dealt exclusively with women. A Miss Minty of Canal Terrace, for instance, was the Aberdeen representative of the Montreal-based Women's Canadian Employment Bureau, which claimed to vet clients strictly in order to ensure that no unsuitable girls were permitted to emigrate. The Bureau was set up in 1907 by Jane Radford to 'supply a reliable medium between Employer and Employed, and to secure Local and Emigrant Domestic Ser-vants and Other Women Workers of good character and ability; also to insure to Emigrants, disinterested advice, protection, and carefully selected situations, and introduction to their respective religious denomination'.[40] Mrs Radford was particularly anxious to secure Scottish recruits, not least from Aberdeen, and of sixty-three domestic servants from North-East Scotland placed by her agency between 1907 and 1913, all but eight came from the city of Aberdeen. The Women's Domestic Guild of Canada, which sent out over 1,000 girls a year, also claimed to impose rigorous methods of selection, its agents subjecting the girls' references to close scrutiny. The Guild was represented in Aberdeen by a Mrs Joss, who regularly sent women to Canada.

On 23 March 1907, for instance, the *Aberdeen Journal* noted the departure of fifteen such women from the city, and in an interview with that newspaper on 24 June 1908 Mrs Joss quoted letters of thanks she had received from satisfied clients, who spoke of the comfortable situations and high wages obtainable in Canada. Protected parties of recruits (who could obtain an advance of their fare if necessary) left Liverpool regularly during the emigration season, and on arrival they were taken to the Guild's headquarters at 71 Drummond Street, Montreal. From there they were sent to situations which had been secured for them in advance, and according to Mrs Joss, Scottish girls were held in particularly high regard both by employers and by the Canadian authorities. Some of the general booking agencies employed lady superintendents specifically to organise female emigration, and also invited Canadian representatives to their offices to interview and select prospective emigrants, whom they would then accompany back across the Atlantic. Mrs Niblett from Winnipeg, for instance, selected recruits at Paton's and Stewart's Aberdeen offices in February 1913, and the following month Mrs Winifred Scott of Toronto, the secretary of the British Women's Domestic Guild, came to Aberdeen to interview women who wished to go out to specific posts as domestic servants in Canada.[41]

Not all the female emigrants sent out to Canada as domestic servants by the Aberdeen booking agents were leaving similar employment at home— some were acting on the assurance that it was socially acceptable and beneficial to take up such employment in the Dominion. Bella Farquhar, for instance, who was recruited by Paton in 1913, had 'kept lodgers in Aberdeen, but to better herself went to Toronto, her intention being there to enter domestic service, which she did not care to do in this country'.[42] Then as time went on the booking agents began to advertise an increasing number of non-domestic situations, in Canadian factories, offices and shops,[43] with preference being given to those who had had similar experience at home.

Despite these qualifications, however, the vast majority of women who emigrated under the auspices of general booking agents continued to be recruited from the ranks of domestic service and the agents' activities therefore continued to draw the criticism of British employers. But not all female emigrants from North-East Scotland made their arrangements in this way. Some left through charitable women's emigration societies which categorically denied that they sent away domestic servants. The best-known— and certainly the most highly-regarded[44]—such agency in the area in this period was that run by the Aberdeen Ladies' Union under the direction of Lady Aberdeen.

Lady Aberdeen and schemes of women's welfare

Ishbel Gordon, Countess of Aberdeen, was a prominent figure among those individuals who saw in emigration a remedy for some of the economic and social ills of the 1880s and 1890s, as well as a means of benefitting the colonies.

Her active support for female emigration should be seen in the context of her lifelong crusade to elevate the general condition and status of women. Some of her enterprises had national and international repercussions, including the formation of the Women's National Health Association of Ireland,[45] and a successful crusade against tuberculosis, also in Ireland. She advocated the admission of women to the ministry and as President of the Liberal League she demanded the extension of the franchise to include women. From 1893 to 1936 she was President of the International Council of Women, a body which worked to improve the social and economic condition of women, and in 1893 she was instrumental in setting up a branch of this movement in Canada.[46] Out of meetings of the Canadian Council of Women there came the beginnings of a Dominion-wide health service through the creation in 1898 of the Victorian Order of Nurses.[47] Even the social welfare projects which she instituted in North-East Scotland often had implications beyond the region. The Haddo House Association, for instance, which began as an educational project for the servants on her husband's Aberdeenshire estates, evolved into the Onward and Upward Association, with branches throughout Britain and the Dominions. At the same time the Aberdeen Ladies' Union, which was created under her presidency in 1883, became part of the National Union of Women Workers and exerted its influence both at home and abroad. Lady Aberdeen's encouragement of emigration through this organisation was integral to her welfare activities in the city and county of Aberdeen and drew support from a considerable number of people in the area who had become convinced of the value of a local scheme of assisted female emigration.

Lady Aberdeen's faith in the efficacy of emigration was part of an overall campaign to improve the physical, economic and social condition of women which had begun even before her marriage, at the age of twenty, to John Gordon, seventh Earl of Aberdeen. Among a number of religious and political leaders who had visited her parents' home, William Ewart Gladstone had been the most influential in inspiring Ishbel not only to lifelong Liberalism but also to philanthropic work. In her youth she became associated with rescue work among London prostitutes, which no doubt strengthened her resolve later to save unemployed and under-employed young women in Aberdeen from the fate which Sheriff Watson had alleged had befallen them in the 1840s.[48] On 7 November 1877 she was married and her home, her Liberal and evangelical zeal and her charitable activities were transferred to North-East Scotland. Among her early activities in the district were the establishment of a cottage hospital and district nurse at the village of Tarves and a female orphanage at Methlick, the latter being opened by Gladstone in 1884.[49] Having organised Bible study, needlework and history classes for her own servants at Haddo, she then tried to encourage domestic and farm workers (of both sexes) from the surrounding district to continue their education by attending Saturday and evening classes at a community centre which she established in Methlick. Although few mistresses would allow their female servants to go out at night in this way, they were generally sympathetic to Lady Aberdeen's aim of promoting the physical, moral and material welfare of women by means of education, and in December 1881 the wives of several tenants on the Haddo estate joined with her in forming the Haddo House Association. Correspondence courses, compiled by Lady Aberdeen, were sent out every two months to 'associates', who were thus encouraged to broaden their horizons through study. By involving employers as 'members' of the Association, Lady Aberdeen hoped to restore mutual understanding and loyalty between mistresses and servants; and girls were rewarded not only for success in study, but for remaining in the same situation for two years, as well as for consistent moral conduct.[50] The Haddo House Club, formed in 1889, subsequently catered in a similar way for Lord and Lady Aberdeen's own household. Aware that apparently more attractive and independent openings in shops, factories and offices were depleting the ranks of domestic servants, they encouraged their own servants to develop outside interests through the provision of educational and recreational activities, and encouraged other employers to follow their example.[51]

The Haddo House Club continued to operate until 1920, not only at Haddo House itself but also in London, Dublin and Ottawa when the household was resident in these centres. Of similar duration but much wider influence was the Haddo House Association, which within a year of its formation had enrolled over 800 girls and 500 mistresses. By 1894 it boasted 8,600 associates and members and 120 branches, including two in Canada and one in South Africa.[52] Indeed, so far beyond North-East Scotland had its influence extended that in 1891 its name had been changed to the less parochial Onward and Upward Association, and from 1891 to 1930 the *Onward and Upward* magazine was distributed monthly to the various branches as a mouthpiece of the Association. This journal offered quizzes, articles on general knowledge, items of fiction, accounts of the Aberdeens' travels and a regular children's pamphlet, as well as a record of the activities of the Association and its branches. The theologian Henry Drummond, a close friend of Lord and Lady Aberdeen, supported its launch and contributed to several early issues, while Lady Aberdeen enlisted the help of the journalist W. T. Stead in having it produced cheaply in London and transported free to hundreds of emigrant associates.[53]

Lady Aberdeen's interests were not confined to domestic and farm servants in rural communities. She also wished to eradicate the causes of female degradation in the city of Aberdeen where, despite the efforts of churches and charitable societies, she felt moral standards were still disgracefully low. Thus in November 1883 she launched the Aberdeen Ladies' Union

> with the object of uniting together, in one body, all workers for the welfare of women and girls in Aberdeen, with the view of their strengthening one another in their common work, and with the special aim of striving to raise the moral standard in all ways possible.[54]

On these grounds leaders of organisations such as the Girls' Friendly Society and the YWCA, along with those connected with industrial schools, prisons and poor houses, were urged to join the new organisation. It was proposed, for instance, to rescue young female inmates from the poor houses and help them to make a fresh start, as well as to seek out and remove girls from bad localities and influences, while a free registry was to be established with the particular aim of supervising and finding work for school-leavers. Circulars and application forms were sent to interested ladies, who were asked to associate themselves with whichever branches of the work most appealed to them. More generally, they were urged to further the aims of the Union by means of subscriptions, donations and gifts of cast-off clothing; by supporting monthly prayer meetings at which committee members also reported on the various branches of the work; by distributing wholesome literature to girls with whom they came into contact, and by passing on the names of needy girls to the appropriate committees.

Within a month of its formation over 200 women had apparently joined the Aberdeen Ladies' Union.[55] Within a year a free registry had been opened in Marischal Street and over seventy girls provided with employment through this agency. A club for young working women, mainly factory girls, offered educational and recreational facilities in twice-weekly meetings, while a 'Lily Band', formed to cater for children who were still at school, but who worked half-time in the factories, had attracted 180 members.[56] Over 500 signatures had been obtained for a petition requesting better protection for women under the 1885 Criminal Law Amendment Act, this petition being presented to the Upper House by Lord Aberdeen. In subsequent years the Ladies' Union added to the activities and institutions designed to improve the condition and prospects of working women. In a number of recreational clubs girls were given practical instruction in such diverse subjects as cookery, needlework, singing, reading and musical drill.[57] A strong religious theme pervaded all the clubs' activities, and girls were rewarded for good conduct. The Seabank Rescue Home in Aberdeen was a refuge for destitute women, inebriates and ex-prisoners from poor houses and jails all over the North of Scotland; a lodging house was provided for working girls, and from 1889 a Training Home improved their employment prospects by instructing them in the duties of domestic service.[58] When the closure of the Bannermill cotton factory in February 1904 led to great distress in the east end of the city, the Union organised a mill-girls' club and dining room with the aid of the Aberdeen Association for Improving the Condition of the Poor.

The Aberdeen Ladies' Union was one of several provincial associations in Britain dedicated to the 'care and protection' of females. The various ladies' unions were incorporated in the National Union of Women Workers in 1895 and in 1897 the Aberdeen branch changed its name to the Aberdeen Union of Women Workers in accordance with other branches. The National Union, based in London, aimed both to federate existing women's organisations and to assist in the formation of further local unions and councils. In this way it hoped to promote women's welfare in general and to collect and disseminate information which would be of use to working women in particular. It held annual conferences which were attended by delegates from the various branches and their associated societies. Although in 1889 and 1892 national conferences were held in Aberdeen, the Scottish branches complained of

19   The Countess of Aberdeen in her going-away dress, 1877.

20   Haddo House, Tarves, Aberdeenshire.

isolation, and in 1903 an attempt was made to overcome this by creating five district unions in Scotland, the city of Aberdeen forming the centre of a North-East Union which consisted of Aberdeenshire, Banffshire, Elgin and Kincardine.[59] Close relations were also maintained with the Scottish Mothers' Union, the British Women's Temperance Association and the Travellers' Aid Society, a branch of the latter being formed in Aberdeen under the auspices of the local Union of Women Workers in 1896.[60]

Some of these organisations were peripherally involved with emigration. The Travellers' Aid Society, for instance, maintained branches in various parts of Britain, the colonies and the USA, where emigrant girls were met and assisted on their way. At Liverpool, the major port of embarkation, they were met at the railway station and conveyed to their ships, and the annual reports of the Aberdeen Union of Women Workers indicate that some local emigrants made use of the Society's services.[61] When Lady Aberdeen appealed in the *Aberdeen Journal* on 6 November 1888 for funds to establish a training home, she stressed the need to educate girls not only for domestic service at home but also for emigration, pointing out that those untrained in household skills would stand little chance of bettering themselves by being sent abroad. The Servants' Registry run by the Ladies' Union advertised a number of foreign situations as well as local posts, including a cook and general servant for Canada, a children's nurse for Australia and a nursemaid to accompany a family to New York.[62]

But the Aberdeen Ladies' Union went much further than merely advertising situations and mentioning emigration. The Countess of Aberdeen was personally convinced of the value of emigration as a means of benefitting not only the emigrants themselves, but the society which they left and the countries where they settled. Her support for well-conducted female emigration was governed by the same moral and social principles as her philanthropic activities at home and was indeed just one aspect of her campaign to improve the status and prospects of women. Under the control of a special committee, the positive promotion of emigration was integral to the work of the Aberdeen Ladies' Union from its foundation. In February 1884 Lady Aberdeen herself made a public appeal on behalf of this committee for funds to assist the 'Emigration of Friendless Girls',[63] and in the next thirty years, aided by special donations and legacies, the Emigration Committee assisted or supervised the departure of over 330 female emigrants from North-East Scotland.

Lady Aberdeen and the promotion of emigration

How did Lady Aberdeen herself come to be convinced of the case for assisted female emigration, and how did she personally promote the welfare of emigrants? Her faith in the advantages of emigration was confirmed by her extensive foreign travels and her encounters with successful emigrants from North-East Scotland. In 1887 she and her husband paid their first visit to the USA, on their way back from a tour of India, Australia and New Zealand.

Lady Aberdeen's brothers Archie and Coutts were then managing cattle ranches in Texas and Dakota respectively, and Lord Aberdeen was a major shareholder in the 200,000-acre Rocking Chair Ranch in Texas. In a number of cities they visited on their journey across America from San Francisco to New York they met deputations of prosperous Scottish settlers, several of whom had come either from their own estates or from other parts of Aberdeenshire. Nearly fifty years later, looking back on the encounters she had had with the children of Haddo and Cromar tenants all over the world, Lady Aberdeen wondered why their elders had not also emigrated to countries where they were always made welcome and where they could easily and quickly come to own their own land.[64]

In 1890, after Lady Aberdeen had been ordered by her doctors to take a long rest, she and her husband chose to pay their first visit to Canada, partly in order to investigate the case for emigration as a solution to economic and social problems at home. Among members of their household who accompanied them on this trip were eight servants—six women and two men—who wished to remain permanently in Canada. One girl had to return to Scotland because of the death of her father, but later reports indicate that the other emigrants all found good situations, and Lady Aberdeen attributed their success largely to the wholehearted way in which Canadians welcomed newcomers to their country.[65] During her tour of the Dominion Lady Aberdeen showed a keen interest in all matters pertaining to emigration and her observations were recorded in a series of descriptive articles which she contributed to the *Onward and Upward* magazine, and which were later published as *Through Canada with a Kodak*. She noted the arrangements made at Quebec by the government, the Canadian Pacific Railway and the Women's Protective Immigration Society for the reception of newly-arrived settlers. She was favourably impressed with a 'pleasant little Home for Female Emigrants' which she subsequently visited at Montreal,[66] as well as by the good employment opportunities for suitable women. In a number of places she saw proof of the successful settlement of emigrants from North-East Scotland. At Kingston, for instance, she and her husband visited a daughter of one of their tenants, as 'her people had not heard from her for some time & were anxious. We found her all right however, at the same address ... with Mrs Davies, the wife of a photographer who continues to give her a v. good character indeed.'[67] Shortly afterwards, during a train journey to Winnipeg, Lady Aberdeen met and had a long talk with the child emigrationist Annie Macpherson, and in Winnipeg itself she had a meeting with Ellen Joyce of the BWEA.[68] Among the agricultural labourers she met on the prairie was John Will from Methlick, who was about to buy a farm of his own near Edmonton, on which he was to be joined by his Aberdeenshire bride, a Haddo House Associate from Ellon.[69] Further west still, at Banff, Lord and Lady Aberdeen met two sisters from their Deeside estate. Both were well satisfied with Canada, one being employed at Banff Sanatorium and the other with her brother on one of Sir John Lister-Kaye's farms in the area.[70] On this trip the Aberdeens also visited the Highland crofters' settlement at Killarney, which Lord Aberdeen had subsidised,[71] before moving on to Vancouver where they met George Mackay and arranged to purchase Guisachan Ranch. On their first visit to the Okanagan the following year they met yet another prosperous emigrant from the Haddo House estate, a woman who with her husband was farming a seventy-five acre plot adjacent to the Shuswap and Okanagan Railway. As well as keeping cows and poultry they grew fruit and vegetables to sell to the miners and railway construction workers in the area.[72]

In 1893 Lord Aberdeen became Governor-General of Canada and from then until 1898 he and his wife were resident in the Dominion. Only a fortnight after their arrival they welcomed a party of 300 new emigrants at Quebec, a visit which Lady Aberdeen later recorded in her journal:

> We started off immediately after breakfast to the Emigrants' receiving place near the docks in order to welcome a party of some 300 emigrants arrived this morning by the *Parisian*. The arrangements are all v. well made. There is a large long central sort of hall where they go on arriving with their baggage & sit & rest. In this place there are stalls where they can buy provisions for their journey & also socks, books etc. We asked what they bought most & found it was cheese—then tins of condensed milk, coffee, tongues, sausages etc. Out of this room there is the dining room, where preparations for very comfortable meals, breakfast, dinner were being made. Each meal can be had for 25c. Then there are a limited number of rooms upstairs where girls arriving without friends or who are not well can stop for a few days free, or are found places for. Then there is the place where all the steerage passengers baggage have to be fumigated, with the exception of articles of leather, & books, & then we looked through one of the colonists sleeping cars where the seat makes into berths for which bedding can be purchased for $2.25.[73]

In 1895 Lord and Lady Aberdeen were still welcoming new settlers to Canada. In the report of her visit to the International Conference of Women Workers in Toronto that year Mrs Duff of Hatton told the Aberdeen Ladies' Union that

> she had a distinct recollection, when in Quebec on a Sunday morning, seeing Lord and Lady Aberdeen going down about eight o' clock and receiving the emigrants, who always landed on Sundays at the Canadian Line Stores. From the citadel one looked sheer down 300 feet to the deck of the steamers, and they could distinguish everybody on board, and observe the kind welcome which the emigrants, and especially the Scotch and Aberdeen emigrants received from Lady Aberdeen on their first landing in a strange land.[74]

On taking up their appointment in 1893 Lord and Lady Aberdeen had in fact been presented with a formal address of welcome by forty-three Aberdeenshire settlers in the North-West Territories,[75] and in the course of their travels over the next five years they were repeatedly reminded of the importance of Scottish settlement, particularly on their trips to the West.[76] But they were interested in wider aspects of emigration than that from their home county, including the colonisation schemes of a number of English philanthropists. In October 1894 they visited settlements in Manitoba estab-lished by Dr Barnardo[77] and the Young Colonists' Aid Society[78] and early the following year Lord Aberdeen had discussions with General Booth regarding the latter's plan to establish a Salvation Army colony in Canada.[79] Their faith in emigration had already been confirmed by the success of their own servants whom they had left behind in 1890, and on the whole their extended opportunity to witness the practical results of immigration from 1893 to 1898 further strengthened their belief in the value of well-conducted settlement. On returning to Britain they both continued to promote the colonisation of Canada. In the 1890s, for instance, Lord Aberdeen was President of the Self-Help Emigration Society, and in a speech to the International Congress of Women in 1899 he predicted imminent prosperity for Canada.[80] Both he and his wife recommended women to settle in British Columbia, where they themselves had purchased property and where hard-working Scots were always welcomed.[81]

If Lord and Lady Aberdeen's support for emigration was part of their general interest in female welfare, and if their views were confirmed by their transatlantic travels and the experiences of the emigrants they encountered, then their enthusiasm must also be seen as a product of the age in which they lived. Lord Aberdeen's speech to the 1899 International Congress of Women, for instance, was delivered in the course of a general debate on emigration in which several speakers reiterated familiar arguments about the value of emigration. There is little doubt that Lady Aberdeen in particular was influenced both by previous and contemporary experiments in assisted emigration from Britain, and the involvement of women from North-East Scotland in some of these schemes. Perhaps her interest was kindled partly by the example of predecessors such as Maria Rye and by the emigration scheme operated by the governors of the Aberdeen School of Industry.[82] Furthermore, she was participating in a movement for which there was not only local precedent, but in which we have seen there was considerable contemporary national interest. The Aberdeen Ladies' Union came into being at the end of a year which saw the foundation of the National Association for Promoting State Colonisation and shortly after Lady Gordon Cathcart's settlement of crofter families from her Hebridean estates on land in Western Canada, a scheme which was given considerable publicity in the Aberdeenshire press.[83]

It has been demonstrated that female emigration in the 1880s and 1890s was no novelty either to its promoters or participants. But while Lady Aberdeen certainly reflected a general interest and utilised existing facilities in the 1880s and 1890s, she also wanted to create a special movement of her own. Although her Canadian travels widened her knowledge of emigration and confirmed her belief in its efficacy, they also brought home to her (as to Ellen Joyce on her first trip in 1884) the hardships of the pioneering life and the importance of sending only those who were resilient enough to withstand these hardships. She believed that several schemes had failed through insufficient preparation and was anxious to learn from the mistakes of her predecessors in implementing her own scheme. On visiting settlements such as Killarney she made careful notes on the development of the colony, its successes and failures and the progress of individual colonists. In her public statements she always stressed the pitfalls as well as the advantages of emigration, realising that the claims of guidebooks and advertising agents were sometimes deceptive.[84] On her first visit to Canada she met several emigrants among her fellow passengers on the SS *Parisian*, where the standard of accommodation caused her to note that the emigrants' problems often began even before they reached their destination:

> Poor wretches, they fill me with compassion: one would never have had the pluck to emigrate if one knew this had to be gone through first. They are not allowed to use their hammocks by day, and there is nowhere for them to sit, so the poor ill ones lie about the deck anyhow in abject misery.[85]

In Canada itself she was particularly struck by the barrenness of the prairie, the destination of most late nineteenth-century settlers. Although she recommended its rich soil to farmers, she repeatedly warned of the loneliness and isolation experienced by many settlers in this region where she felt the struggle merely to live swallowed up all one's energy,[86] and she stressed that the life of the female emigrant was especially hard.[87]

Lady Aberdeen echoed the pleas of Mrs Gillespie, President of the Montreal Women's Protective Immigration Society, that intemperate or delicate women, and those without practical skills, should remain at home. Although good domestic servants were in demand, Mrs Gillespie claimed in 1890 that the higher wages in Canada did not always offset the high cost of living, and she discouraged even capable women from giving up secure posts at home in order to emigrate.[88] Lady Aberdeen was particularly critical of Ellen Joyce for encouraging the emigration of girls who she felt were ill-suited to Canadian needs and ill-prepared for pioneer life. In 1894 she supported the efforts of a Miss Dent to open a boarding house in Winnipeg for disillusioned and sometimes destitute middle-class female emigrants:

> It is doubtless a need, for girls come out misled by advertisements or by descriptions of situations & find themselves stranded. Miss Dent agreed in the main that girls of the better class should not be invited to come out unless they clearly understand that the only opening for women here is domestic & that of a rough & exacting character. The wages of course are good though nothing extraordinary. $12 to $15 a month would be the average here & $20 the exceptional wage for a good cook—further west $15 to $20 & $25 to $30 for a good cook. Harm has been done by Mrs Joyce & others painting this country as an elysium for girls, & thereby bringing out a wrong class unfitted for the work required ... a large proportion of the girls brought out by Mrs Joyce definitely as servants have been failures, many being London & South of England girls with a physique totally unfitted for this country & many others altogether too airified.[89]

On a visit to Fort Qu'Appelle the following year she witnessed the folly of sending to remote Canadian farms and villages girls who had been trained for service in the houses of the British gentry. The Hudson Bay Company agent's servant at Fort Qu'Appelle was an English emigrant who had come to Canada in search of higher wages and with the expectation that she would be one of several servants in a well-conducted household. Instead, she had been employed as a general servant at wages of $10 a month, and was so disillusioned that she intended to return home as soon as possible. Following her meeting with this servant, Lady Aberdeen wrote critically in her *Journal*:

> it is utterly wrong & cruel for the G.F.S., or Mrs Joyce, or any Emigration Society, to encourage such girls to come out. It must result in utter failure both for themselves & for their employers & creates a prejudice against girls from the old country at all. Good strong general servants, ready to fall in with the ways of the country, & who have *not* been told that they are sure to marry comfortably as soon as they set foot in Canada are what are wanted. And Scotch & Irish girls do better than English girls—of this there is scarcely a doubt.[90]

Both she and Lord Aberdeen deprecated the encouragement given to girls to emigrate only in order to find a husband, which they felt induced pride, restlessness and a tendency to take service only as a temporary expedient until they secured a proposal of marriage.[91] Lady Aberdeen commented in 1894 that a girl would have to be 'very desperately in love' before she would marry a pioneer settler, and she reiterated this view in 1896, after visiting a newly-married and newly-arrived Scottish couple in the Okanagan Valley, who were struggling to subsist on an unproductive twenty-acre holding.[92] Lady Aberdeen urged emigrationists to recognise Canada's requirements, so that only those women who could improve their own prospects by emigrating, and who would be an asset to the British Empire, should be sent out. On her return from her first visit there in 1890 she told members of the Aberdeen Ladies' Union that while Canada was a land of promise, only those who were willing to work hard and adapt themselves to the country's ways should consider emigrating. On this basis she recommended 'our hearty Aberdeenshire lasses, who knew what hard work was, and were not afraid of it'.[93] Four years later she contrasted the failure of many of Ellen Joyce's English settlers with the success of those from North-East Scotland, when she recorded in her *Journal* that Aberdeenshire women had proved to be just the kind of settlers that Canada required.[94] Was this claim justified, and if so, how much credit was due to Lady Aberdeen herself for preventing an indiscriminate exodus from Aberdeenshire, and ensuring that the desired categories of emigrants came to Canada?

By various means over a sustained period the Countess of Aberdeen tried to ensure that female emigrants who left North-East Scotland were well-informed, advised, trained, selected and ultimately followed-up in their new locations. In concluding her series, 'Through Canada with a Kodak' in the *Onward and Upward* magazine in 1891, for instance, she expressed her desire to make known the Dominion's needs and to promote its well-being:

> if these little sketches have added somewhat to your knowledge of what Canada is, if it has increased your pride in her, if it has kindled a desire to do what may be in your power to build up its fortunes, I shall feel they have not been written in vain. The high moral and religious character of her present populations, the wise and true foundations that they are laying for future development and

prosperity makes one long that those remaining in the old country should thoroughly realise how much reason they have to rejoice in our common kinship, and that those thinking of coming out to Canada to try their fortunes should come with a hearty desire to do the utmost for the land of their adoption.[95]

In her attempt to interest only suitable settlers, Lady Aberdeen had offered guidance on Canada's labour requirements as well as general information on the Dominion gleaned during her tour in 1890. She noted the constant demand for servants all over the country, at wages ranging from $8-$12 in the East to $20 a month in the West. Girls who passed through the Female Emigrants' Home in Montreal, for instance, often found situations within twenty-four hours.[96]

Yet as in her later *Canadian Journal* Lady Aberdeen stressed the importance of flexibility; while hard-working and adaptable general servants would do well, those who were unskilled, or who had been trained in only one domestic skill should stay at home, since most Canadian mistresses employed just one servant, who was expected to turn her hand to a variety of tasks. The great value put on girls who had received some general training vindicated Lady Aberdeen's emphasis in her appeal of 1888 (for funds to establish a Servants' Training Home) that girls had to be trained in the duties of domestic service in order to benefit from emigration. There was a particular shortage of suitable servants in British Columbia. Many mistresses preferred to employ Chinese servants, since

> the general verdict is that, after all, they are better than girls who come out from the old country with all sorts of foolish notions in their heads as to what work they should or should not do. I regret to say that the general tone of the girls who have gone to British Columbia, and who get high wages (12, 15 and 20 dollars a month, and even more), has not been such as to make employers very anxious to repeat the experiment. Still, girls going West to the Pacific coast are certain to find good places, and if only they will be sensible, and ready to turn their hands to anything, and to do as they are bid, they will command first-rate wages and happy homes.[97]

The 'Aberdeen Association'

On her way back to Eastern Canada after this first visit to British Columbia in 1890 Lady Aberdeen was asked to address a gathering of ladies in Winnipeg on various aspects of women's work. The result of this meeting on 19 October 1890 was the creation of an organisation which from 1891 until the First World War attempted to mitigate the isolation and hardships experienced by many prairie settlers. She told her audience of 1,400 how on her journey westwards a few weeks earlier she had been struck by the isolated situation of many immigrants, particularly the recently-settled Scottish crofters and also some of her Onward and Upward Association girls who were working on ranches in the North-West Territories and British Columbia, located forty to fifty miles from the railway. In order to brighten their drab lives and stimulate their minds with news of the outside world and general reading material, she suggested that a collection of suitable magazines, books and newspapers be made from homes in Winnipeg. The ladies of the city could then make up parcels of reading material, along with packets of flower seeds and small decorations for the home, and despatch these parcels periodically to isolated prairie homesteads. On 12 November 1890 the Winnipeg ladies met again to consider these recommendations, and the outcome was the creation of the 'Aberdeen Association for the Distribution of Literature to Settlers in the West'. A committee of women undertook to send monthly parcels to settlers whose names were furnished by the Winnipeg clergy and immigration authorities, this list to be regularly updated as new settlers arrived and went out on to the prairie. The women also promised to write to the recipients at least twice a year and it was hoped that in time the scheme could be extended to all small prairie towns, whose women would establish and maintain personal contact with families on isolated farms and ranches. The Association was undenominational and it was stipulated that no propaganda of any description should be included in the parcels.

After leaving Winnipeg Lady Aberdeen herself continued to promote the new Association. On 3 November 1890 (a week before it was formally launched) she wrote to W. T. Stead, her collaborator in the production of *Onward and Upward*, asking him to publicise the Association's needs in the *Review of Reviews*. She pointed out that the Winnipeg ladies, despite their enthusiasm, were not rich, and although they would probably be able to obtain some periodicals from friends in Eastern Canada, literature from Britain would be more welcome. Stead responded by asking his readers to co-operate in making up a Christmas parcel for despatch to Canada.[98] Lady Aberdeen also appealed to readers of *Onward and Upward* either to send reading material and other small gifts to friends in Western Canada or, if they had no connections there, to send books and magazines to Madame Gautier of the Aberdeen Association in Winnipeg:

> The ladies of this Association are deluged with applications for monthly packets of such literature, and find that packets containing consecutive issues of the same magazine are those most valued. They will be very gratified for all contributions, helpful for mind, and heart and soul, and tending to give thoughts which will uplift the common daily work which would otherwise be drudgery.[99]

In a later appeal in the *Aberdeen Journal*[100] she declared that settlers preferred Scottish newspapers to all others and urged people in North-East Scotland to send their surplus reading material to her for despatch to Canada.

The first batch of eighty-two parcels was sent out by the Winnipeg committee on 12 January 1891, and grateful letters subsequently poured back from the recipients, all craving more news of the outside world.[101] By the time of the Association's first annual meeting in November 1891, attended by Lady Aberdeen, two hundred families were in receipt of monthly parcels sent out by the Winnipeg committee. The costs of wrapping paper, twine, labels, cartage and postage had been met partly by a gift of $100 by Andrew Carnegie[102] but Lady Aberdeen had persuaded the Allan and Dominion steamship lines, and the CPR to transport future parcels free of charge. A petition was sent to the Dominion government requesting free postage for the Association's parcels, and in 1894 the Postmaster General agreed to grant this concession up to a certain weight.[103]

Interest continued to grow on both sides of the Atlantic. For three years the Winnipeg committee worked alone, but in 1894 a branch of the Association was formed in Halifax, Nova Scotia, and further branches were later formed in all the chief Canadian cities. When Lord Aberdeen was Governor-General of Canada his cousin (and the wife of his secretary), Carry Gordon, brought all the branches together into a federation, and supervised the work of the Ottawa branch from her residence in that city. When Lady Aberdeen visited Mrs Gordon on 5 April 1895 to see the work in progress, she found the Ottawa branch was sending out eighty-five parcels a month, while those in Halifax and Winnipeg were sending out eighty-seven and two hundred respectively. She recorded in her *Journal* the impact of the literature and the continuing gratitude of the recipients:

> It is extraordinary to read some of the grateful letters which are received & which show what an amount of good can be done amongst these isolated people by even a magazine. An article will often suggest thoughts there which change the whole course of life & are carried into actual action.[104]

After her return to Britain Carry Gordon continued to work on behalf of the Aberdeen Association in co-operation with the Marchioness of Dufferin. In order to meet the growing demand for parcels, branches were formed in London, Liverpool and Glasgow, and the Beaver Line, as well as the Dominion and Allan steamship companies, granted free carriage to these consignments of literature. In 1899 Messrs William Thomson and Sons gave similar carriage concessions in their ships sailing from the Tyne, Dundee and Aberdeen. In a letter to the *Aberdeen Journal* in which she intimated this extension of facilities, Lady Aberdeen suggested that it merited the formation of a branch of the Association in Aberdeen itself.[105] She instructed parties interested in such a scheme to contact either Carry Gordon (now at Ellon, Aberdeenshire), William Smith of Canada House, 201 Union Street, Aberdeen, or herself. William Smith was also responsible for collecting the parcels of literature which were to be sent out in one of Thomson's ships early in June, and any material intended for shipment was to be sent to him by 31 May. There were now, Lady Aberdeen continued, fifteen branches of the Aberdeen Association operating in Canada, from Victoria to Halifax, all sending out monthly parcels. Each lady helper had a number of families under her specific charge, with whom she corresponded regularly, and Lady Aberdeen believed the friendships thus formed were of equal and perhaps superior value to the gifts of literature. The Aberdeen Association continued to operate in this way in Canada until the First World War, although in Britain its functions were taken over by the Victoria League in 1903. By that time the League had begun to supply literature on a similar plan to settlers in other British possessions across the world.

On her first visit to Canada Lady Aberdeen had been impressed with the facilities of the Women's Protective Immigration Society, which she subsequently recommended to intending emigrants. The society took charge of all female settlers disembarking at Quebec, whether they were travelling alone or with one of Ellen Joyce's 'protected parties'. Despite her later criticism of Mrs Joyce's choice of emigrants, Lady Aberdeen also recommended that girls travel with a protected party at a fare of £4. 10s. and with the promise of securing work on arrival.[106] Indeed in 1889 the emigration committee of the Aberdeen Ladies' Union had become affiliated to the United British Women's Emigration Association and thereafter took advantage of its facilities in making travelling arrangements for girls whom they sent out from North-East Scotland.

Emigration and the Aberdeen Ladies' Union

It was through the establishment of this Union that Lady Aberdeen exercised her most direct influence on female emigration from North-East Scotland. The information and advice offered in instalments of *Onward and Upward* was only a very indirect means of providing Canada with suitable settlers, while the Aberdeen Association was devoted to improving the quality of life of those who had already emigrated, from whatever part of the world. But for a quarter of a century the emigration department of the Aberdeen Ladies' Union was an important vehicle for advising, selecting, sending out and following up a large number of female emigrants from Aberdeenshire to a number of destinations, mainly Canada. Support for emigration was, as has been mentioned, integral to the Union's activities—when explanatory circulars regarding the new society were sent out in December 1883 it was suggested that ladies interested in emigration should help the cause by finding out the names of girls who would benefit from being sent abroad, by assembling an outfit for them, and by collecting the money required for their passages.[107] Although the assisted emigration scheme was inspired by Lady Aberdeen, it soon gained a momentum of its own, arousing the interest and support of a number of middle-class women in the city of Aberdeen. Miss Anne Macdonald of Queen's Terrace headed an emigration committee of up to ten members which supervised all aspects of this work and which formed a very active and important branch of the Aberdeen Ladies' Union.

In trying to stimulate and sustain interest in its work, the emigration committee followed Lady Aberdeen's example in regularly publicising the case for emigration. In her initial appeal for funds in February 1884 Lady Aberdeen declared that the committee aimed 'to discover friendless girls of tender years, and have them sent to Canada, under the arrangements made by Mr. Quarrier of Glasgow', who some years earlier had established his Home in the Dominion, from which children were readily adopted by colonists.[108] Thanks to careful supervision, the scheme had been successful, and the committee felt that by using this facility to find new homes for friendless Aberdeen girls, they were not only giving them a new start in life but were also eradicating a potential source of social disorder and misery at home. Over the next twenty-five years the need for selective emigration and its advantages to all concerned were regularly brought before the North-East public in the annual reports of the emigration committee, issued separately from the general reports of the Ladies' Union. In her first report in 1885, for instance, Anne Macdonald echoed Lady Aberdeen's plea of the previous year that

> no better channel exists for the philanthropic to extend their charity than to rescue friendless Girls from the risk of falling into evil courses and to put them in the way of obtaining respectable employment abroad.[109]

These reports appeared both in pamphlet form and in the columns of the Aberdeen press. They not only reflected the emigration committee's own views, but drew on the experiences of the emigrants themselves and also quoted the opinions of influential emigrationists at home and abroad.[110]

Further publicity was achieved through the debates on emigration which took place at occasional conferences convened by the Aberdeen Ladies' Union. Well-known supporters of emigration were invited to address these meetings, as in 1888, when both Ellen Joyce and the Rev R. Mackay, the secretary of the Self-Help Emigration Society, delivered speeches at a Conference of Women Workers held in the Music Hall, Aberdeen. Mackay declared that the Ladies' Union would render a splendid service to the country if, through this conference, public attention were directed more clearly to the value of wisely-conducted emigration. He pledged his support for their emigration campaign, outlined the principles, methods and achievements of his own society and dismissed the opposition to emigration which was being mounted by Socialists in Britain and labour agents in the colonies. Mrs Joyce discussed the practical need for emigration, in view of unemployment and underemployment at home, the good openings and prosperity in the colonies and the ease and safety with which women could now emigrate. She particularly commended the facilities for the emigration of members of the Girls' Friendly Society, and suggested that Canada was the most suitable destination. But both she and Mackay reiterated Lady Aberdeen's opinion that any emigration should be selective, and that those who were not willing to adapt to colonial ways should stay at home. This theme was continued in a paper by Emily Faithfull of the Colonial Emigration Society, which was read to the conference by Lady Aberdeen. Although she favoured state-aided colonisation, Miss Faithfull stressed the importance of stringent selection of emigrants in order to send out only those who were well-trained, well-provided and prepared to work hard.[111]

In establishing its emigration scheme, the Ladies' Union made it clear from the outset that it intended to utilise the services of a number of philanthropic societies and individuals at home and in the colonies. Girls going to Canada were not only sent out in 'protected parties', initially under the Quarrier scheme and later under the BWEA, but they were also received by the Women's Protective Immigration Society at Quebec and Montreal, whose representatives generally secured immediate employment for them.[112] In her report for 1892 Anne Macdonald noted that 'the bad old days when girls arrived and did not know where to go, and risked landing in very undesirable places, are of the past. No girl need, and no girl should, go alone, but through some organisation.'[113] The Canadian government was willing to work with any accredited society to ensure the protection of female settlers, and she expressed amazement at the foolishness of some girls who still preferred to emigrate on their own account.[114] The emigration committee also established contacts with a number of societies and individuals who had a known interest in emigration and who would advise and assist emigrants—including the Women's Christian Association in Quebec, W. C. Van Horne, Vice-President of the Canadian Pacific Railway, W. C. Fowler, agent for that railway in Regina, and a land commissioner in Winnipeg, L. A. Hamilton. If the emigrants did not already belong to the Girls' Friendly Society or the YWCA, they were given a candidate's card for the former society, and urged to become associated with a church.[115]

In 1897 the committee drew attention to the establishment of the Girls' Home of Welcome in Winnipeg, opened the previous year by Octavia Fowler, daughter of a former Lord Mayor of London who had gone to Canada after taking a course at Leaton College. Her committee particularly wished to attract Scottish emigrants, to the extent that they were willing to prepay part of the fare of suitable girls.[116] In the same year a committee had been formed in Montreal in connection with the Canadian National Council of Women, which intended to send an agent to Orkney and Shetland to offer assisted passages to suitable women and to accompany them back to the Dominion.[117] The thirteen girls from North-East Scotland who went to Vancouver in 1898 were met by the YWCA representative there, Mrs Mackinnon, an Aberdonian. She was responsible for welcoming and advising immigrants of all nationalities, and the Aberdeen emigration committee noted with regret her claim that English girls sought her advice far more readily than did Scottish settlers.[118] Individual committee members also made arrangements with personal acquaintances in the colonies for girls to be met on arrival, found employment and sent on to their destinations under proper supervision.

In using the services of existing societies and charitable individuals the emigration committee was concerned both with the well-being of the emigrants and also with financial practicalities. At home, gifts of clothing from individuals and churches in Aberdeen,[119] supplemented by monetary donations, helped to provide outfits for the emigrants, and further financial contributions from benefactors and from the emigrants themselves were expected to cover the costs of passage. The success of the emigration committee's work indeed hinged to a large extent on the amount of financial support it received and it periodically expressed disappointment at the lack of response to its needs. In her appeal for funds in 1884 Lady Aberdeen expressed the hope that sufficient funds would be forthcoming to send out twenty girls to Canada under the Quarrier scheme, at a cost of up to £8 each. She confidently expected that as the benefits of assisted emigration became better known increased subscriptions would allow the scheme to be extended to other needy girls in the area. In fact, by the end of 1884 £119 6s. had been received and only nine girls had been sent abroad at a cost of £86 10s. The emigration committee had not been able to make full use of Quarrier's facilities, as originally intended, since only four girls had gone to Canada and five to New South Wales.[120] All these emigrants, whose ages ranged from sixteen to twenty-three, had found immediate employment as domestic servants, indicating a healthy labour market in both colonies. Yet insufficient funds had prevented the committee from extending its facilities to younger girls who were not quite ready for employment but who could still benefit from emigration. In her first annual report Anne Macdonald stressed that 'the demand for domestic servants is great and always increasing, and the Scheme can be enlarged to any extent, provided funds are forthcoming.'[121] The plea for funds was to be reiterated many times in the next twenty years. In 1886, for example, it was again reported that the committee had been unable to send any young neglected children to Canada using Quarrier's facilities, since the financial requirement of £10 per child would have put too severe a strain on the committee's meagre resources. Although in the annual report for 1887 it was admitted that more people were coming to regard emigration as a viable means of improving the prospects of needy young women, ladies had to be reminded two years later that 'there are very few things that can be done without some money, but emigration cannot be done at all without a good deal of it'.[122] In 1892 Anne Macdonald declared that the public had little knowledge of emigration and even less interest in it and still had to be convinced of its viability and necessity.[123] Four years later, in making an appeal for increased subscriptions in order to maintain its work, the committee claimed 'that Emigration was not in Aberdeen a popular form of philanthropy' and emphasised that emigrants must repay all the money advanced to them if the scheme were to continue.[124]

Financial pressure was largely responsible for the decision to send twenty-seven girls to Western Australia in 1886. At that time Western Australia was the only colony which operated any scheme of assisted emigration, and through the influence of Miss Barlee, the sister of a former governor of the colony, girls could be sent out from London at a cost of only £1 per head. The Western Australian government even paid the emigrants' fares to London if they were recommended as particularly suitable settlers, and in 1886 the Aberdeen Ladies' Union took advantage of these facilities to send abroad a much larger number of girls than its funds would have permitted it to send to Canada. Even more girls could have been sent out if resources had permitted, both as the colony was willing to accept a larger influx and as there were several eligible and eager candidates in Aberdeen. The emigration committee regretted its inability to take full advantage of these favourable conditions in Western Australia, particularly since it was aware that the facility might be suspended at any moment.[125] In 1889 the committee made use of the Queensland government's provision of a free passage to women under thirty-five to send eight girls to that colony, while in the same year and in 1900 a total of three more emigrants went to Western Australia under its free passage regulations.

By far the majority of emigrants went to Canada, however. In 1887 the average travelling expenses of each girl landed at Montreal were reckoned to be £3.18s.6d., consisting of an assisted passage of £3 and a rail fare of 18s.6d.[126] To that sum had to be added the cost of outfit and of further rail travel if the girl's destination lay west of Montreal. From the very beginning it was stipulated that girls should repay a proportion of the cost of their outfit and the whole of their fare, and an engagement to this effect was made before they left.[127] It was hoped that repayments made by one year's emigrants would help to finance the following year's exodus, but despite the committee's efforts this regulation proved very difficult to enforce, and repayments were sporadic and generally inadequate.[128] In 1889 the committee therefore introduced a new requirement whereby girls going to Canada paid the sum of £1 before leaving Aberdeen. If they remained in Montreal no further payment was demanded, but those going further west had to promise to repay the rail fare expended on them. The result, according to the annual report for 1891, was that in that year all six girls who had gone to Winnipeg had repaid their advances in full, the first occasion on which complete repayment had been achieved.

From then on it seems that repayments were made more regularly, often in full. In her report to the Conference of Women Workers in Aberdeen in 1892 Anne Macdonald indicated that this may have owed something to the Union's affiliation to the United British Women's Emigration Association, whose agents in Canada were strict about the repayment of loans and regularly reminded emigrants of their responsibilities.[129] From 1897 they also had the assistance of Octavia Fowler at the Girls' Home of Welcome in Winnipeg, who looked up emigrants, sent on their repayments, and 'does every kind of thing that we have long wished for, and counsels them in every way'.[130] In addition to extracting repayments, the BWEA, through its honorary secretary, Grace Lefroy, also secured grants and loans for a number of Aberdeen emigrants to Canada in the early twentieth century. In 1903 she told the Aberdeen committee that

> We have some good places to fill at London, Ontario. There is a good home there and a Club for the girls. The employers at London pay the expenses on from Montreal, the girls do not pay it back, unless they do not stay a year in their situations, then they have to pay back a proportion, 3s. 4d. for every month unfulfilled.[131]

In June 1904 the BWEA itself gave eight poor Aberdeen girls a free grant of £3 each towards their passage, while in summer 1905 fifteen emigrants were given a similar grant. In 1905 Miss Lefroy secured a loan from the London Factory Fund[132] of the full fare from Liverpool to Montreal for ten Aberdeen emigrants, this loan to be repaid by instalments. In 1906 twelve of the thirty-seven emigrants from Aberdeen to Canada were sent out with the assistance of a loan of £5 per person from this fund, while one of those who left in 1907 was also given a loan from the London fund. The benefits of co-operation with the BWEA apparently convinced the Aberdeen committee in 1900 that it should not alter the arrangement whereby its emigrants were sent to Canada in 'protected parties' in ships of the Dominion Line. Although it had been brought to the committee's notice that other shipping lines offered slightly cheaper rates for actually transporting emigrants, this one consideration was outweighed by the many social—and financial—advantages of affiliation to the BWEA.[133] Pressure on the Aberdeen committee's resources was relieved not only by more regular repayments[134] and the loans or grants secured through the offices of Miss Lefroy, but also by the increasing tendency of emigrants to pay the full fare before leaving home.[135] Others had their fare paid by individuals. For instance, Mrs Sanford, the matron of the Girls' Home of Welcome at Winnipeg, advanced the passage money of a girl whom she took back to Canada with her in 1903, while another Aberdeen girl who emigrated under the auspices of the Ladies' Union in 1905 had her fare paid by her future employer in Ontario.[136]

Between 1884 and 1913 379 women and girls emigrated from North-East Scotland under the auspices of the Aberdeen Ladies' Union. The average annual exodus was less than thirteen, but individual totals ranged from only one emigrant in 1889 to thirty-nine in 1905. While the vast majority (296) went to Canada, girls were also sent to New South Wales in 1884, to Western Australia in 1886, 1889 and 1900, to Queensland in 1889 and to the USA and Natal in 1893. While financial factors sometimes governed the choice of destination, particularly in respect of those sent to Australia, it is evident that economic conditions at home and abroad sometimes governed the extent of the total exodus. In 1891, for example, the emigration committee's funds were relatively healthy, thanks to a legacy of £100, but as the employment market in Aberdeen at that time was also healthy, no urgent demands were being made on these funds.[137] Three years later the committee again reported little emigration activity, since plentiful employment all over Britain had greatly reduced the demand for emigration.[138] On the other hand in 1886, 1904 and 1905 it believed that the increase in applications was attributable to commercial recession in Aberdeen. Particularly in 1904 and 1905, short-time working and low wages in local factories led an unusually large number of girls to apply for emigration and in 1905 the committee sent the largest single contingent in its history, thirty-nine girls, to positions of domestic service in Canada. The BWEA annual reports for 1904, 1905 and 1906 state that respectively thirty-six, ten and twelve Aberdeen girls had emigrated to Canada thanks to loans of £5 each from the Factory Fund. The report of 1905 added that 'Emigration has been one of our most advantageous outlets for girls during the great depression in Factory trade and continued 'Short Time'. Small earnings make 'Hard Times' very definite in many homes.'[139]

By 1908, although many young women were still applying to leave, in most cases their parents withheld consent owing to the onset of depression in Canada. Yet the committee admitted in 1894 and 1899 that increased interest in emigration did not always correspond with economic problems, and contrasted the steady demand of the colonies for suitable emigrants with the fitful desire of eligible women in Britain to meet this need. In many instances there seemed to be no good reason for the fluctuating popularity of emigration, which the committee in 1899 suggested might owe more to the actions of a few enthusiastic applicants in persuading their friends to apply as well, than to economic factors on either side of the Atlantic.[140]

To some extent the emigration committee itself was responsible for fluctuations in the numbers of women who went abroad. Owing to its rigorous selection procedure, the actual annual exodus never matched the number of applications. In all its reports the committee was at pains to stress its adherence to the principle of selection and its abhorrence of indiscriminate emigration. It never deliberately sought out emigrants, but relied largely on a system of personal referral. Candidates were chosen only from those who presented themselves to Anne Macdonald for interview, and the committee's reports regularly spoke of the rejection of unsuitable applicants. In 1890, for instance, forty-three girls applied, but only twelve were sent, and the following year only six of the seventeen applicants were accepted.[141]

The basic criterion for selection was that the girls should be capable of benefitting both themselves and the countries to which they went. Britain had no right, declared the committee's report in 1888, to send out any but the best possible settlers, particularly to those colonies (only Queensland at that time) which paid the whole cost of passage. Girls who had displayed no moral fibre at home were unlikely to profit by emigrating, but might rather help to create a pauper society in the colonies. Others might be of good character, but physically unfitted for emigration, lacking initiative or ambition, or unwilling to adapt to a different culture. The emigration committee had to reconcile the need to thin an excessive female population at home with the danger of allowing girls too much help without demanding a corresponding effort on their part. It became more aware each year of the importance of sending out only those to whom the assisted emigration would be a genuine boon, those who understood the conditions of their future life and were prepared to face and overcome difficulties through hard work and self-denial. The need for careful selection had arisen because too many applicants in North-East Scotland were seen to lack these qualities. They often had little idea of where they wanted to go and what they would encounter when they arrived, but were concerned only with getting away from a hard life in Aberdeen to a new location where they expected conditions and prospects to be brighter. On entering societies where women were a scarce and valuable commodity, they would probably respond by becoming unreliable and impertinent in their work. As Anne Macdonald wrote in her report in 1893:

> One finds out, more and more, that emigrating a girl is only of use to her if she has principle of some kind to start with; if she has that, she learns as she goes on, and is sure to do well; but if she has not, the greater plenty and the feeling that she is more thought of and valued, more or less turns her head and makes her often miss exactly what would be best for her.[142]

But the major issue facing the emigration committee was the conflict between demand and supply, the dilemma shared by contemporary emigration societies all over Britain. The Aberdeen Ladies' Union recognised the difficulty of meeting the colonies' needs without alienating those groups in North-East Scotland on which it most relied for financial and moral support. It was in an attempt to refute criticism from anxious employers of servants that the emigration committee went to such lengths to emphasise its careful selection of assisted emigrants. Its policy of weeding out unsuitable applicants was geared primarily to ensuring that no domestic servants who were required at home should qualify for assistance to emigrate. In 1891, for instance, the emigration committee declared that selection procedures had been particularly rigidly enforced in the previous two years in response to the loud outcry about the shortage of domestic servants. While admitting the existence of such a shortage, they blamed it, like many other female emigration societies, on the tendency of girls to seek alternative employment at home, particularly in shops, rather than on emigration; and in their annual reports they repeatedly stressed that, contrary to popular belief, they did not send away domestic servants.[143]

So who were the 'friendless girls' whom Lady Aberdeen announced in 1883 that her Ladies' Union wished to send abroad? Particularly in the early years of the movement they were drawn primarily from that class which members encountered in other branches of the Union's work—in the 'Lily Band', the clubs for working girls and in the lodging house. They were employed in factories, fish curing establishments and other public works, and even if they had registered their names for domestic service, few employers would have accepted them in view of their poor backgrounds. Most of them would not have been able to emigrate without financial assistance from the Ladies' Union,[144] whereas the emigration committee felt that most trained servants who exercised a little self-denial could afford to emigrate unassisted. Anne Macdonald believed that a major function of her committee was to rescue deserving and capable girls who had gone to the mills for lack of other employment, but who despaired of their poor prospects and would greatly benefit from the new opportunity presented by emigration. Though poor, the candidates selected were often said to be of 'superior intelligence and moral character',[145] possessing initiative and looking forward to the day when they would be able to help their friends and relations:

> [They] were perhaps the eldest of very large families, and were desirous of going out as pioneers, hoping in time to be able to take out the others, parents and all, which is a thing we always encourage, believing it to be one of the very best ways of helping a struggling family.[146]

Although not drawn from the domestic servant class at home, it was primarily to fill positions of domestic service in private houses and hospitals that these girls went abroad, like their counterparts from all over Britain. In 1886 a correspondent in Montreal told the Aberdeen emigration committee that less than half the several hundred applications for general servants in that city were being met. While she would not encourage women who were doing well at home to come to Canada, many untrained poor girls could be instructed in the duties of general service and placed in good employment.[147] Yet while the colonies were willing to accept this 'raw material', they were anxious that the emigrants should be given some preliminary training in the required skills. While the Aberdeen emigration committee believed that its factory girls were often more adaptable and intelligent than trained servants, it recognised the colonies' concern that only emigrants who were immediately employable should be sent out. In order to compensate for the inexperience of its emigrants in household service, it pressed for and in 1888 obtained the Training Home in Aberdeen. Here it believed that girls would not only be instructed in useful skills, but potential emigrants who only wanted a change without being willing to work would be weeded out, while those who were determined to face hardships and persevere would have their horizons widened and be strengthened in their resolve.[148] Some girls secured situations before leaving home, including the two who went to New York and Natal in 1893 and one who emigrated to Ontario in 1905.[149] The committee regularly encouraged girls to learn housework before they went to Canada, where those who were efficient in these marketable skills could earn much higher wages than the incompetent.

The emigration committee particularly encouraged girls to go to Winnipeg, where owing to keen demand, emigrants of all classes most easily found work at high wages. Although the annual reports do not always indicate the destinations of the emigrants, it is evident that many girls did indeed settle in Western Canada. In 1896, for example, only three of the nine emigrants remained in Montreal, where two became wardmaids in the Victoria Hospital and one found a situation at Sault St Marie. Three others followed the example of some of their predecessors by becoming wardmaids in the hospital at Winnipeg[150] while the remaining two travelled two hundred miles further west on the CPR to take up good positions in service. All eighteen emigrants the following year went to Western Canada, four to Winnipeg and fourteen to British Columbia. In 1904 thirteen girls went to Canada, ten to positions of domestic service, two to work in a factory and one to join her sister in Calgary.[151] Thirty-nine candidates for domestic service were sent out in 1905, ten of these going to hospitals in Montreal, Toronto and Winnipeg, where they could earn from $10-$16 a month as wardmaids and kitchenmaids. All but two of the thirty-seven emigrants in 1906 found good positions in private domestic and hospital service, at wages of up to $18 a month, and twenty-nine girls went out to similar positions in 1907.[152] The two remaining emigrants in 1906 were going to join their husbands, as were a further two in 1907, along with four married couples emigrating to join their daughters who had found employment as domestic servants in Canada some time earlier. The three girls who left in 1908 went to Montreal, Toronto and Winnipeg, while all nine who left in 1909 found posts in hospitals and private houses in Toronto. The following year twenty-seven women went to Montreal, Toronto, St Catherine's, Winnipeg and Moosejaw, all to good situations in private families or institutions, and they were followed to similar locations by eight emigrants in 1911.

From time to time emigrants left Aberdeen under the auspices of the Ladies' Union but without making use of its funds. This was first seen in 1885, when in addition to the six girls to whom the emigration committee gave financial assistance, a further five girls from the North Lodge Industrial School were sent out under its protection. This action involved the Ladies' Union in a small way in the policy of removing pauper children which was commended by the Central Emigration Committee, but there is no evidence that any more girls were sent out from the Industrial School in this manner. In the early twentieth century a growing number of women emigrated under the supervision of the Aberdeen Ladies' Union without calling on its funds, but, in accordance with national trends, these were better-off emigrants who paid the full cost of passage themselves before leaving home. Twelve of the thirty-seven emigrants in 1906, for instance, paid their full fare before leaving Aberdeen. The women who fell into this category only wanted to make use of the Ladies' Union's administrative and protective facilities in making their arrangements for travel and reception in Canada. Some were married women who were going to join their husbands[153] but others came into the 'prohibited' class of trained domestic servants. One of the four emigrants in 1902 had been a farm servant near Aberdeen, an orphan girl who had saved £30 from her wages and paid all her passage money before she left for Winnipeg, where she was found a situation by the matron of the Girls' Home of Welcome. One emigrant the following year was a domestic servant who also paid all her expenses prior to leaving and only asked the emigration committee for help in filling up the necessary forms and in making arrangements for her to join a protected party. In such cases, where no financial assistance was requested, the emigration committee relaxed its rule that no trained domestic servants should be sent abroad, and extended its protective and advisory services to otherwise ineligible women.

Emigration under the Aberdeen Ladies' Union: successes and failures

By comparison with the activities of many other emigration societies, the contribution of the Aberdeen Ladies' Union to the national movement was on a relatively small scale, and it failed to extend its influence to other parts of Scotland. In 1892 several Highland girls who visited Aberdeen during the herring season expressed interest in joining protected parties of girls going to Canada and the following year the Aberdeen emigration committee announced that it was to co-operate with the BWEA in trying to encourage emigration from the Western Highlands and Islands. It was to have leaflets printed and circulated to Highland ministers in early Spring 1894, in the hope that the Highlanders would take more account of the minister's encouragement than that of outsiders. But they were sceptical of success, recognising the opposition that those who wished to emigrate would probably encounter from family and friends. (They assumed that such opposition was the reason that they had heard no more from those girls who had expressed the wish to emigrate in 1892). By 1897 the emigration committee had evidently had no success in persuading Hebridean girls to emigrate, despite contrasting the good prospects open to them in Canada with the poverty and bleak future they faced at home.[154]

Some of the Aberdeen emigration committee's problems were attributable to insufficient funds. A guest speaker at the second annual meeting of the Ladies' Union in 1885, a Mr Wilson, contrasted the small exodus from Aberdeen with a much bigger emigration scheme which he conducted in Bristol, and concluded that there was no great demand in North-East Scotland for emigration either to Canada or Australia. He did admit, however, that inadequate funds might be to blame both for the small scale of the movement and the fact that the scheme was not widely known in the area.[155] This was a complaint frequently voiced by the emigration committee itself, which always stressed that its success depended on the amount of financial support it received, both in initial donations and in repayments from assisted emigrants. A reluctance on the part of emigrants to make repayments was a problem shared by many similar societies, and the Aberdeen committee often complained about the ingratitude and lack of conscience shown by some emigrants. In 1893, for instance, Anne Macdonald declared that too many girls lacked self-control, entertaining vague ideas of the existence of unlimited funds which they could claim as a right, and five years later she claimed that all emigrants were capable of repaying their loans within a year of their removal.[156] The increasing extent and rapidity of repayments in later years often owed more to the help of individuals in Canada in securing these funds than to any success of the Aberdeen committee in inculcating a more responsible attitude into its emigrants. Furthermore, we have seen that by the early twentieth century many emigrants were no longer poor girls but better-off women who could either afford to pay their entire fare before leaving, or repay any loans within a very short time.

Yet despite the small-scale nature of its work, and its frequent financial problems, the evidence suggests that the Aberdeen Ladies' Union's emigration committee had considerable success in meeting the needs both of the emigrants themselves and the countries to which they were sent. While it encountered little public criticism at home for the kind of emigrants it sent out, the calibre of these emigrants still satisfied colonists in Australia and Canada, which is perhaps a tribute to the committee's policy of careful selection. In its annual reports the BWEA invariably spoke highly of the work being done in Aberdeen, with reference to the selection of emigrants, the prompt repayment of loans and the way in which successful emigrants encouraged others to follow their example.[157] Evidence of the satisfaction both of colonial employers and of the emigrants themselves was often contained in letters to the emigration committee, some of which were quoted in their annual reports. For instance, all six girls sent out to Canada in 1891 not only repaid their fares as instructed but also sent home unusually detailed letters describing their new lives.[158] Many emigrants praised the travelling and reception arrangements made for them. Those sent out in 'protected parties' were under the care of the BWEA from the time they reached Liverpool until they were found situations in Canada, and in 1895 all those sent out under this scheme thoroughly recommended the arrangements.[159] Two girls who went to London, Ontario in 1903 wrote home enthusiastically of the kindness of the matron who had been in charge of their party and also said how much they had enjoyed staying in three emigrant homes en route to their final destination.[160] Several girls recommended their situations. In 1896 one girl who had spent five years in Winnipeg and then paid a visit home before returning to Montreal wrote to the committee expressing the hope that all Aberdeen girls would be sent on to Winnipeg. Another letter which commended both the travelling arrangements and the opportunities in Winnipeg was quoted in the same report:

> Many girls in Aberdeen believe that when they emigrate they are ill-used, but that is false; everything is very well carried out by the ladies, and if a girl has good intentions she will succeed in Canada ... I would advise every young girl to come to Winnipeg; the country is very favourable; everything is so different. You must explain to the girls in Aberdeen that everything was much better than we expected. Send out as many girls to Winnipeg as you can, for there is a great demand for Scotch girls, specially 'generals and cooks'.[161]

In 1899 an emigrant in British Columbia wrote to her parents that she had not only regained her health but had found a home rather than just a situation on a farm near Vancouver. In 1903 another girl who had been sent to British Columbia several years earlier wrote home from Victoria to say that girls who were determined to persevere need not fear to emigrate, as they would always find work and friends, and only those who were unwilling to work should stay at home. The writer of another letter quoted in the same report announced that she had done far better than she had expected, her wages having risen from $10 to $20 a month. She had put $60 into the bank, was enjoying good health and had all the 'amusement and freedom' she could desire.[162]

In 1901 the secretary of the emigration committee measured the success of the scheme by the fact that none of the emigrants had ever expressed a desire to return home, except on temporary visits.[163] Indeed, the only recorded case of one of the committee's emigrants returning to Aberdeen occurred in 1906, when a girl who had gone to Canada in March came home later the same year on medical advice.[164] Many girls were made so welcome and were so well-treated by their first employers that they often remained permanently in these posts. Several emigrants encouraged their friends and relations to join them in Canada, a trend which was favoured by the emigration committee. An emigrant of 1887 was joined in Canada the following year by her two sisters, all three having previously been employed in factories and workshops in Aberdeen. In 1889 the first emigrant came home on a visit to her parents, having had her fare advanced by her employer, and on that occasion she declared emphatically that all the trouble taken by the emigration committee in sending girls to Canada was well worth-while.[165] One young girl wrote to the committee from Ottawa in 1890, not only to express her own thanks but to say that her widowed mother, a trained laundress who had also been sent out under the committee's auspices, was doing well in her new situation. The girl's younger sister was about to join them to complete the family in Canada. The 1894 annual report commented approvingly that some girls had begun to send for their friends to join them, an indication not only of their prosperity but of their concern for those at home. In 1895 a group of girls actually came back to Aberdeen to tell their friends how much they had profited by emigrating under the care of the Ladies' Union and to encourage these friends to accompany them on their return to Canada the following Spring. The girls all worked as wardmaids in the hospital at Winnipeg, and the committee noted that their enthusiasm was shared by their employers, who hoped that they would lead out a large party of new emigrants from Aberdeen.[166] Girls who did not persuade their families to emigrate sometimes seem to have sent home money for their support; in reporting the high wages and success enjoyed by a number of girls employed in Canadian hospitals in 1905, the committee noted approvingly that their dependents at home were in many cases also participating in these 'good times'.[167]

While much of the credit for the girls' success was undoubtedly due to careful initial selection, the emigration committee's interest did not end with their departure from Aberdeen. The continuing personal interest shown by ladies in Aberdeen and by their counterparts in Canada and Australia must have considerably eased the emigrants' transition to their new lands and helped them to settle more quickly into their new employment. At regular valedictory meetings held for parties of emigrants before they left Aberdeen, the girls were addressed by local ministers and by members of the Ladies' Union and were presented with Bibles, copies of *The Pilgrim's Progress* and lighter reading material for the voyage.[168] They were exhorted not only to repay their loans as soon as possible but to write home regularly with news of their progress. On 2 June 1886 the *Aberdeen Journal* reported a recent valedictory meeting for emigrants, including five girls who had since sailed from Liverpool for Montreal, where arrangements had been made for their reception and in one or two cases for their immediate employment.[169] Formal arrangements made prior to their departure for the reception or employment of new emigrants not only helped to ensure their rapid assimilation but perhaps even stimulated the initial desire to emigrate. In 1886 a Montreal correspondent of the emigration committee expressed the hope that 'you may meet with respectable girls whose parents would not so much object to their emigrating if they knew there is a home for them to come to, and people ready to look after them.'[170]

Such facilities were provided in many parts of Canada. In 1885, for instance, Anne Macdonald reported that the committee had lost sight of none of the girls sent abroad the previous year, several of them being under the personal care of people known to committee members.[171] Individuals such as Jane Evans of the Women's Protective Immigration Society in Montreal, Octavia Fowler of the Girls' Home of Welcome in Winnipeg and Mrs Mackinnon of the YWCA in Vancouver were on hand to counsel and direct new settlers. Their work was complemented by the way in which Lady Aberdeen herself sought out female emigrants from North-East Scotland. Following her first visit to Canada in 1890, she told the annual meeting of the Ladies' Union that she had met all the girls they had sent out to Winnipeg, all but one of whom had previously worked in fish-curing establishments in Aberdeen. All were doing splendidly in their new situations and were regarded by employers in Winnipeg as the best emigrants obtainable from any quarter.[172] When visiting the USA the following year Lord and Lady Aberdeen spent a few days in New York in order to trace some girls who had emigrated under the auspices of the Aberdeen Ladies' Union.[173] During her five-year residence in Canada from 1893 Lady Aberdeen frequently asked the emigration committee to pass on to her the names and addresses of girls whom they had sent to the Dominion and whenever possible she visited these settlers in their new locations. In October 1894, for instance, she and Lord Aberdeen braved a severe snowstorm to visit some farms in the Treherne district of Manitoba, where they had installed some Scottish girls in service, and a Canadian reporter noted on this occasion that 'Lady Aberdeen's encouraging words to the girls and pleasantries to their masters and mistresses endeared her name to many lonely homes.'[174] Further testimony of Lady Aberdeen's personal part in welcoming emigrants to Canada was given in 1895 when a member of the Ladies' Union, Mrs Duff of Hatton, visited the Dominion as a delegate to the International Conference of Women Workers in Toronto. She later told the emigration committee of how the girls whom Lady Aberdeen had sought out in their isolated homes had been greatly encouraged by the personal attention and concern thus shown to them.[175] Then in 1903 Agnes Fiddes, honorary secretary of the emigration committee, followed Lady Aberdeen's example when on a tour of Canada she met several Aberdeenshire emigrants and also visited a number of immigration depots and receiving homes.[176]

Not all the girls wrote home as requested and in some cases the emigration committee had to rely on reports from members who visited Canada, such as Miss Fiddes, or even on Lady Aberdeen herself, for news of their progress. Similar information was provided by colonial acquaintances and the representatives of immigration societies with which the Aberdeen Ladies' Union co-operated.[177] These people also supplied the emigration committee with most evidence of the satisfaction of colonial employers with their recruits from North-East Scotland. Octavia Fowler was always anxious to attract good Scottish girls to Winnipeg, to the extent, as has been seen, of partly pre-paying the passages of suitable candidates;[178] but the most frequent commendations of emigrants sent out by the Aberdeen Ladies' Union seem to have come from Jane Evans, secretary of the Women's Protective Immigration Society in Montreal. Some emigrants in their letters mentioned the service she rendered in meeting girls off the boats and finding them situations immediately.[179] Perhaps she was deliberately seeking out girls from Aberdeenshire, for in 1886 she contrasted the incapable, sickly and wilful settlers sent out by many British emigration societies with the 'nice healthy sensible girls' from Aberdeen who had arrived at Montreal in June. She would welcome more of the same calibre, a sentiment echoed the following year by a number of mistresses in Canada who wrote to the emigration committee expressing approval of the Aberdeen emigrants they had employed. One of these women, a clergyman's wife, wished for more girls to be sent out, provided that such a good batch of recruits could be obtained again. None of the emigrants had remained unemployed for long, often being engaged within an hour or two of arrival. In 1888 and 1889 Jane Evans reiterated her claim that girls from Aberdeen were much sought-after by employers, a claim which, it has been noted, was later made by Lady Aberdeen in respect of Aberdeenshire settlers in Winnipeg. Miss Evans' observation that the girls sent out by the Aberdeen Ladies' Union were popular because they were quiet, steady and willing to learn was supported by the Rev Robert Acton, the immigration chaplain for the port of Montreal. In August 1889 he was in charge of a large emigrant party sailing from Britain on the SS *Lake Ontario*, a party which included seven girls sent out by the Aberdeen Ladies' Union. After arriving in Montreal he wrote to the emigration committee secretary in glowing praise of the Aberdeen contingent:

> In the first place you are to be congratulated on your selection, as they were without doubt the best behaved and most suitable party of girls I have met with this season. Some of the girls I was enabled to provide with excellent situations before they left the ship. They are all now unusually well placed, and will, I believe, give every satisfaction, and we could readily place 500 more of the same kind, and I shall be most happy to co-operate with and forward your very commendable work in any way.[180]

The emigration committee's careful selection of girls perhaps owed something to the influence of Lady Aberdeen, particularly in the 1890s. On her first visit to Canada in 1890 she saw the folly of encouraging indiscriminate female emigration and during her residence in the Dominion later in the decade she became more convinced that Britain should send out only girls who were physically and mentally resilient and likely to be an asset to their new country. While she voiced her opinions in her writings and speeches, and tried to improve the lot of existing settlers by the formation of the Aberdeen Association, it was through the emigration department of the Aberdeen Ladies' Union that she put her principles into practice most directly.

It is difficult to estimate the extent of Lady Aberdeen's personal influence on this body during the thirty years in which it despatched female emigrants from North-East Scotland. Although the Ladies' Union emigration scheme was conducted by a special committee of up to ten members, it was essentially the creation of Lady Aberdeen herself and reflected many of her own interests and priorities. In its choice of candidates the emigration committee acted on its patron's warnings about the difficulties of pioneering in the colonies and her advice that middle-class women who would not undertake hard physical work should stay at home. Furthermore, at least seventy-six per cent of the 379 girls who emigrated under the auspices of the Aberdeen Ladies' Union were sent to Canada. This of course was the country with which Lady

Aberdeen was most familiar, where in the 1890s she both encountered accidentally and sought out deliberately a number of Scots who had emigrated from Aberdeenshire. The success of most of these settlers, including some former members of her own household, helped to convince her of the claims of Canada as an emigrant destination, and her enthusiasm was consistently reflected by the emigration committee. Although there was a similar demand for female labour in Australia, Lady Aberdeen was less familiar with the Antipodean colonies, and the evidence suggests that the emigration committee sent girls there less from choice than for reasons of financial expediency. Perhaps it is also significant that except for a single emigrant to Natal, girls were not sent out to South Africa by the Aberdeen Ladies' Union. This was an area of which Lady Aberdeen had no personal experience and in any case, a considerable number of North-East women went to South Africa under the auspices of the Scottish Women's Emigration Committee, and in particular its Aberdeen representative, Caroline Phillips.

So it is evident that the Aberdeen Ladies' Union had no monopoly on female emigration from North-East Scotland. It played no real part in sending emigrants to South Africa and had a relatively small rôle in Australia. Even in Canada, the destination to which the Ladies' Union devoted most attention, it did not play an exclusive part in promoting female emigration, since many women also went there under the auspices of employment agencies and shipping companies, or without any aid or supervision at all. The Aberdeen Ladies' Union was just one of several societies which responded to the well-advertised demand for female settlers in Canada.

The demise of the Emigration Department

With the outbreak of war in 1914 the emigration department of the Aberdeen Ladies' Union ceased to function, although the range of its activities had in fact been declining for some time. At the time of the conference of the National Union of Women Workers in Aberdeen in 1908 emigration work still featured among the thirty associations represented on the Aberdeen branch of the NUWW, but only three women were sent abroad that year, and emigration was not debated at the conference. This was in contrast to previous national conferences held in Aberdeen, particularly that of 1888, at which emigration had been a major topic of discussion, involving well-known speakers such as Ellen Joyce. It was not that interest in female emigration had evaporated—the evidence of the Aberdeen press proves otherwise. But this same evidence, and more particularly the later reports of the emigration committee itself, indicate some of the reasons behind the demise of the emigration work of the Aberdeen Ladies' Union.

Lady Aberdeen had instituted the scheme in 1884 to offer a new start in life to 'friendless girls', those who lacked the means or the initiative to organise their own emigration. Assistance was to be limited to deserving cases, mainly factory workers from Aberdeen who were prepared to work hard as domestic servants in the colonies, and like many of her contemporaries, Lady Aberdeen had discouraged the removal of middle-class women who were unused to physical labour. Yet by the early twentieth century most of the emigrants who left under the auspices of the Ladies' Union were no longer 'friendless girls' but belonged to the very category which was supposed to be excluded from her assisted emigration scheme—middle-class women who often required no financial aid, but were merely using the facilities of the emigration committee to make their arrangements, particularly so that they could travel abroad in 'protected parties'. Although this was partly indicative of the increasing popularity of emigration with middle-class women since 1884, it was a trend which had eroded the Aberdeen committee's original raison d'être. Instead of assisting and organising the emigration of impecunious females, it was now merely supervising the departure of women who were generally capable of paying their own way and making their own arrangements. And while the emigration committee could no longer justify its existence on the grounds of helping needy girls, it was even unable to sustain its new supervisory function after bodies like the Colonial Intelligence League were created to organise the removal of middle-class women. Thus by 1914 it would seem that the emigration department of the Aberdeen Ladies' Union had simply outlived its usefulness. It was redundant, since the class of girls which it had been created to help either no longer required such assistance or no longer wished to emigrate. Meanwhile their successors were increasingly catered for by a number of other agencies. National emigration societies, concerned to populate all Britain's colonies with educated, middle-class women, absorbed smaller provincial associations, while employment registries and shipping companies played an ever more comprehensive part in organising the emigration of working women from their own localities.

So how should one assess the contribution of the Aberdeen Ladies' Union to female emigration from Britain in the period 1884 to 1914? While the emigration work certainly awakened considerable interest in North-East Scotland, it owed much of its success to the personal inspiration and leadership of Lady Aberdeen. Perhaps it is significant that by the time the emigration department ceased to function Lady Aberdeen had for some time been deeply involved in the organisation of the Women's National Health Association of Ireland and had little time to devote to the affairs of the Union of Women Workers in Aberdeen.[181] Yet the demise of the Union's emigration activities by 1914 does not signify failure; on the contrary, its longevity was a major achievement in an age which saw a proliferation of local emigration societies in Britain but the rapid disappearance of many of them. For more than a quarter of a century the Aberdeen Ladies' Union assisted or supervised the removal of nearly 400 women from North-East Scotland. Although it was not infallible,[182] its careful selection procedures not only placated those who opposed emigration on the grounds that it was taking away much-needed domestic servants but ensured that only the needy and those who were likely to benefit from a new opportunity were assisted. Its select recruits therefore compared favourably with the large consignments of domestic servants recruited, often indiscriminately, by booking agents whose main concern was to claim the commission payable on this category of emigrant. The Aberdeen Ladies' Union recruits seem to have been highly prized in Canada, and by the time new trends in female emigration had made the committee's work virtually redundant, it had made a significant and lasting contribution to the late Victorian and Edwardian exodus from North-East Scotland.

NOTES

1) See vol. I, pp. 129-30. Herbert, for instance (MP for Wiltshire, Secretary at War in 1852 and 1859 and briefly Colonial Secretary in 1855) was involved in a number of philanthropic schemes, and from 1850 to 1852 he ran a society for promoting the removal of unemployed females from London to Australia. Similar organisations sprang up in other parts of the country, including bodies such as the Shetland Female Emigration Fund, established in 1850 to reduce the excess of women in those islands by removing a number of them to Australia. (For details see *AJ*, 25 June 1851).

2) See Helen Cowan, *British Emigration to British North America: the first hundred years* (Toronto, 1961) pp. 223-4. This society paid the women's passages and arranged for their reception in Canada. It seems that the settlers were well received and found good positions. By 1862 two matrons accompanied the emigrant ships, and the women were now expected to repay half the cost of their removal.

3) Her Society for Promoting the Employment of Women was besieged by applicants chasing far too few jobs. In 1861 Rye made her first public appeal for financial assistance in advancing loans to suitable female emigrants in the course of a paper delivered at a congress in Dublin. (See M. S. Rye, *Emigration of educated women* (London, 1861)—paper delivered at the Social Science Congress in Dublin, 1861.

4) See table I, p. 286. See also A. James Hammerton, *Emigrant gentlewomen: genteel poverty and female emigration 1830-1914* (London, 1979), p. 176. The figure of 22,482 refers to the number of female emigrants assisted by two of the main national female emigration societies between 1884 and 1916. This figure probably underestimates the total extent of the movement, since it does not take account of those assisted by the Colonial Intelligence League from 1910 (a total of 260 between 1911 and 1914) or by independent provincial emigration societies. In fact, however, many of the smaller provincial societies —including the Aberdeen Ladies' Union—sent their recruits abroad under the care of these larger organsations, which probably included most of these emigrants in their overall returns.

5) Grace Lefroy, secretary of the British Women's Emigration Association, to Sir Charles Tupper, Canadian High Commissioner, letter dated 25 May 1894. (PAC, RG 76, C-53, vol. 44, file 1378: immigration and colonisation, BWEA). Despite its preference for Canada, the BWEA had to send most of its applicants to Western Australia at that time, since this was the only colony granting free passages to domestic servants.

6) In 1902 and 1903 more women went out to South Africa under the auspices of the South Africa Expansion Committee and the South Africa Colonisation Society than went to Canada. (See table I).

THE FEMALE EMIGRANT 277

7) First known as the United Englishwomen's Emigration Association, it changed its name to the United British Women's Emigration Association in 1888, after representations from the Scottish Girls' Friendly Society and the YWCA in Scotland regarding future co-operation. From 1890 it was known simply as the British Women's Emigration Association (BWEA).

8) South African work was first funded separately in 1901 through the South Africa Expansion Committee of the BWEA (SAX). In 1903 the SAX Committee was reformed into the independent South Africa Colonisation Society (SACS). These bodies liaised with the Women's Immigration Department (a government department created by Lord Milner) in South Africa to organise the removal and resettlement of female emigrants from Britain. See Hammerton, *Emigrant gentlewomen*, p. 162.

9) The British government regarded the SOSBW as the women's department of the post-war Overseas Settlement Committee and allocated it an annual grant of £5,000.

10) Although the FMCES became largely an employment bureau for governesses, it was initially concerned with both middle class and working class emigrants, as were its successors in the field of female emigration. See Una Monk, *New Horizons: a hundred years of women's migration* (London, 1963), ch. 1.

11) *AJ*, 22 Feb. 1888.

12) Ella C. Sykes, *A Home-Help in Canada* (London, 1912), pp. 222-42.

13) See, for instance, 'Who should emigrate?' in *Chambers'*, vol. III, no. 155 (15 Nov. 1913), pp. 799-800, which declared: 'How can we expect the children of these marriages ... to be endued with the religion, the loyalty, and the love of the Empire which are necessary to maintain 'British ideals'?' See also 'The call of the colonies to educated women' in *ibid*, vol. I, no. 49 (4 Nov. 1911), pp. 783-4; Adelaide Ross, *Emigration for Women* (London, 1886); Arthur Brice, 'Emigration for gentlewomen' in *Nineteenth Century*, vol. 49 (Apr. 1901), pp. 601-10; Jessie Saxby, *West Nor' West* (London, 1890); and Elizabeth Lewthwaite, 'Women's work in Western Canada' in the *Fortnightly Review*, vol. 70 (Oct. 1901), pp. 709-19.

14) Sykes, *A Home-Help in Canada*, p. 304.

15) Ellen Joyce, 'On openings for educated women in Canada' in *The Imperial Colonist*, vol. V, no. 55 (July 1906), pp. 100-1.

16) Alicia Cecil, 'The needs of South Africa' in *Nineteenth Century*, vol. 51 (Apr. 1902), pp. 671-92.

17) PAC, RG 76, C-53, vol. 44, file 1378: immigration and colonisation, BWEA.

18) PP 1906 (Cd. 2978), LXXVI, 533: *Report of the departmental committee appointed to consider Mr Rider Haggard's report on agricultural settlements in British Colonies*, vol. 1, pp. 79-85: evidence of Ellen Joyce and Grace Lefroy. From 1888 to 1905 approximately 386 single men had been sent out, compared with 5,267 single women and 1,008 families.

19) Georgina Binnie-Clark first came to Canada in 1905 with her sister, to visit their brother who was homesteading at Lipton, Saskatchewan. She remained in the province until 1914 and lived there again from 1921 until just before the Second World War. She and her sister ran a prairie wheat farm, the story of this enterprise being told in her two books, *A summer on the Canadian prairie* (1910) and *Wheat and women* (1914). The latter dealt at length with opportunities for educated middle class women in wheat farming in Canada. See also Susan Jackel (ed.), *A Flannel Shirt and Liberty: British emigrant gentlewomen in the Canadian West, 1880-1914* (Vancouver, 1982).

20) Two were married to ranchers and the third had visited her son's homestead

in 1909. See 'Real experiences on colonial farms' in *Chambers'*, vol. II, no. 63 (10 Feb. 1912), pp. 172-6.

21) See CIL annual reports, 1912-13, 1913-14 and 1918-19 (Fawcett Collection, City of London Polytechnic). The development of the Princess Patricia Ranch as a training centre was disrupted by the First World War and in 1915 the land was let rent-free to two women on condition that they kept it in cultivation.

22) See, for instance, *Imperial Colonist*, vol. IV, no. 41 (May 1905), p. 58; vol. V, no. 54 (June 1906); *AJ*, 3 July 1902, 21 Mar. 1911, 27 June 1912; and *AFP*, 1 Mar. 1910 (Special Canada issue).

23) *Imperial Colonist*, vol. VI, no. 62 (Feb. 1907), p. 6.

24) Ellen Joyce had first become involved with emigration while working for the Girls' Friendly Society. In 1882 she formed an emigration department within this organisation and two years later paid her first visit to Canada under its auspices. In later years she enlisted the help of colonial branches of the GFS to appoint immigration agents who would meet girls sent out by the BWEA. For further details on the GFS, see Mary Heath Stubbs, *Friendship's Highway: being the history of the Girls' Friendly Society 1875-1925* (London, 1926).

25) Sidney Herbert's Female Emigration Society, for instance, failed partly because the colonists objected to the inability of urban immigrants from London to adapt to domestic and farm service, and there were also complaints of immorality among the women. When two single women were found to be pregnant on arrival in 1852 Australian opposition was such that Herbert's society was forced to disband. See W. S. Shepperson, *British emigration to North America*, p. 125.

26) Ellice Hopkins, 'The industrial training of pauper and neglected girls' in *Contemporary Review*, vol. XLII (July 1882), pp. 140-54.

27) See, for instance, Mary Hutchison, 'Female emigration to South Africa' in *Nineteenth Century*, vol. 51 (Jan. 1902), pp. 71-87.

28) See PAC, RG 76, C-10627, vol. 538, file 803839, part 1: correspondence between H.W.J. Paton and the Dept of the Interior, regarding assistance in sending farm hands and domestic servants to Canada, 1908-14, letters dated 1 Nov. 1910, 7 July 1911.

29) *Ibid*, letters dated 1, 5 Sept. 1910. Margaret Owan (40) found work in an office in Toronto and Margaret Banks (29) went to the United States.

30) PAC, RG 76, C-10644, vol. 564, file 809010: correspondence between Mackay Brothers, Aberdeen and the Dept of the Interior, regarding booking agency, 1910-19, 1921, letter dated 2 May 1913. See also letter dated 9 May 1913 from W. D. Scott, immigration agent at the Dept of the Interior to Herrington, Warner and Grange, solicitors, Napanee, in which he explained that Rait had been deported on the grounds of insanity a year after coming to Canada. He exonerated his agent in Perth from all blame, as he had acted in good faith in response to applications from prospective employers, the actual selection having been made by Mackay Brothers.

31) *Ibid*, letter dated 22 Sept. 1914.

32) PAC, RG 76, C-10627, vol. 538, file 803839, part 2: correspondence between Paton and Dept of the Interior, letter dated 15 Feb. 1917 from J. Mitchell, Inspector Employment Agents, Toronto to W. D. Scott, Immigration Agent at the Dept of the Interior.

33) *Ibid*, letters from Mitchell to Scott dated 12 Apr. and 9 May 1917.

34) PAC, RG 25 (Dept of External Affairs), A2, vol. 146, file C5/86: alleged ill-treatment of Scottish girls who have been induced to emigrate to Canada (1910): John Croll to J. Parker, MP, Secretary of the Labour Party, London,

11 June 1910; and W. L. Barnstead, Nova Scotia govt immigration agency to Dept of the Interior, 4 Aug. 1910. Parker had passed Croll's original complaint to the Canadian High Commission in London, which then ordered the Department of the Interior in Ottawa to mount an investigation.

35)   *EG*, 28 May 1913. Miller's account was confirmed by another Aberdeen emigrant whose experiences were quoted in this same issue of the newspaper. She had gone to Canada in December 1912 with a party from the North of Scotland and claimed they had been 'treated like a herd of swine, and sold like pigs'.

36)   PAC, RG 76, C-10627, vol. 538, file 803839, part 1: undated letter from Etta Brown to Mrs Stewart, Union Grove, Aberdeen, enclosed in a letter from Paton to W. D. Scott dated 8 Aug. 1913. Brown had found work as a cook-general with a doctor's wife in Toronto, along with a fellow emigrant from Aberdeen. On an earlier occasion we find Mrs Stewart liaising with a Miss Turner of Toronto, a former matron of the YWCA in Aberdeen, when she advertised on Miss Turner's behalf for twenty cooks and general servants. (*AJ*, 29 Mar. 1909).

37)   *Ibid*, part 2: letter dated 14 Jan. 1914, from Paton to the Canadian government emigration agent, Aberdeen; enclosed in a letter of 21 Jan. 1914 from J. Obed Smith, Canadian Emigration Dept, London to W. D. Scott, Ottawa. This defence arose in the context of Paton's claim to be allowed, like other bureaux, to charge a fee of up to $7, in addition to the passage money, for services rendered to clients. These services included the advance of the fare, a protected passage and reception facilities on arrival and help in finding employment.

38)   *AJ*, 14 Aug. 1913. Subsequent correspondence on 15 and 16 August pointed out that the exodus of domestic servants would decrease if employers lightened their duties, paid them higher wages and generally treated them more thoughtfully.

39)   Viz: Reid's Registry of Elgin, Alex Longmuir's agency in Stonehaven, and nineteen agencies in Aberdeen—Mrs Shaw of Netherkirkgate, Chivas Brothers, the Imperial Hotel, the Bon Accord Registry, Adam's Registry, the Aberdeen Registry, Miss Horne of George Street, Mrs McRitchie of King Street and A. Collie and Co. of Union Street, the Women's Domestic Guild, King Street, Mrs Stewart's Registry, Union Grove, Miss Minty, Canal Terrace, Miss Grant, Bon Accord Street, Rodger's Emigration Offices, Marischal Street, W. Todd Moffatt, Trinity Quay, Chivas Brothers, Union Street, and Mackay Brothers, Paton's and Davidson's booking agencies. (See, for instance, *AJ*, 4 Mar., 24 Sept. 1887; 11 July 1888; 4 June 1889; 11 Mar. 1890; 15 Apr., 6 May, 12 June, 12, 30 Sept. 1891; 6 Feb. 1895, 23 June 1898; 1, 5 Jan. 1910; 10, 11 Mar., 1 Apr. 1911; 12 Mar., 27, 30 Apr., 10, 21 June 1912; 4 Jan., 15 Feb., 6, 9 June, 1 Sept. 1913; 2, 17 Jan., 6 Feb., 16 Sept., 21 Oct. 1914).

40)   PAC, RG 76, C-10306, vol. 422-3, file 616279, parts 1-7: Jane Radford, Women's Canadian Employment Bureau, Montreal, lists of settlers received. See also *AJ*, 19 Mar. 1909.

41)   *AJ*, 4, 6 Feb., 28 Mar. 1913.

42)   PAC, RG 76, C-10627, vol. 538, file 803839, part 1: Paton to Scott, letter dated 27 Nov. 1913.

43)   *AJ*, 22 Apr., 20 June, 1 July 1913.

44)   See, for instance, *EE*, 5 May 1886, when a correspondent praised the Aberdeen Ladies' Union for selecting only emigrants of 'unimpeachable' character.

45)   Formed in 1907, it undertook pioneer work in the field of mother and child welfare.

46)   In 1888 the World Council of Women was formed in Washington, and at its

first quinquennial meeting in that city in 1893 Lady Aberdeen was elected president of the International Council. A number of Canadians who were present at this meeting approached her later the same year with the request that she take the lead in forming a National Council of Women in Canada.

47) In 1896 the Halifax branch of the Canadian NCW suggested the establishment of a district nursing scheme in commemmoration of Queen Victoria's Jubilee. Lady Aberdeen, who had expressed disquiet at the lack of medical facilities all over Canada, thus became president of a board to establish the Victorian Order of Nurses in the Dominion. Despite opposition from the Conservative press and from the medical profession, the Order came into being in 1898 with the two-fold aim of providing trained nurses and establishing cottage hospitals. A town or district which applied for a nurse would usually undertake to contribute part of the cost, to supplement a grant from the VON central office. A training school was establishd in Ottawa and nurses were sent all over Canada, including a detachment which was sent to the Klondyke goldfields. (See 'The Victorian Order of Nurses in Canada' in *The Nursing Times*, 6 May 1905, pp. 6-7; this article is included in the pamphlet collection in Haddo House MSS, NRA, survey no. 0055).

48) He alleged that several women had turned to prostitution in the wake of a commercial recession which had seen several factories in Aberdeen closed down and large numbers of women thrown out of work. See William Watson, *Pauperism, vagrancy, crime and industrial education in Aberdeenshire, 1840-1875* (Aberd., 1877), p. 3. Watson was Sheriff-Substitute of Aberdeenshire from 1829 to 1866.

49) *AFP*, 22 Mar. 1883; and Ishbel, Marchioness of Aberdeen & Temair, *The Musings of a Scottish Granny* (London, 1936), p. 106.

50) The Haddo House Association was run on the lines of a mutual improvement society and consisted of three orders, members, associates and helpers. The members established and maintained branches for the benefit of the associates, who were mainly domestic and farm servants. Lady Aberdeen chose to form this independent association rather than work through existing bodies such as the Girls' Friendly Society or the YWCA because she wanted to reach girls who were not necessarily of unblemished character (required for membership of the GFS) and those who might be put off by the religious emphasis of the YWCA.

51) See Ishbel Aberdeen, 'Household Clubs: An Experiment' in *Nineteenth Century* (1892), pp. 391-8. (Haddo House MSS, pamphlet collection).

52) By 1897 two more branches had been formed in Canada and in 1909 a branch was formed in Jamaica. See *Onward and Upward: extracts (1891-1896) from the magazine of the Onward and Upward Association*, selected and introduced by James Drummond (Aberd., 1983), int., p. 6; and Alexander Gammie, 'The Countess of Aberdeen's Work for Women' in *Sunday Strand*, Aug. 1906. (Haddo House MSS, pamphlet collection).

53) *Onward and Upward* (vol. 23, May 1909) includes a letter from an associate in Seattle, Washington, Bella Andrews, thanking the secretary for sending the magazine to her sister and enclosing a dollar so that she herself might also receive it. She had gone out to Seattle in the Spring to be married and wrote that 'I like to stay here very well, and do my best to get into the ways, which are quite different from the old country ways'. (*O & U*, vol. 23, May 1909, p. 2).

54) Aberdeen Ladies' Union, annual report (1886), p. 4.

55) Pamphlet dated Dec. 1883 (Haddo House MSS, volumes of news cuttings

relating to Lord and Lady Aberdeen's political and social activities, late 19th
and early 20th centuries: volume marked 'May 1883—May 1885', pamphlet
inserted opposite p. 30).

56) ALU, first annual report, in *ibid* (pamphlet opposite p. 20). See also *The Young
Woman*, Oct. 1892 (Haddo House MSS, volumes of news cuttings).
57) The Bleachfield Girls' Club and the Victoria Club were added to the Girls'
Club and the Lily Band. By 1890 the Lily Band had a weekly attendance of
about 300.
58) An appeal in the press by Lady Aberdeen raised £163 12*s.* for this Training
Home, and a five-year lease was obtained on premises at 39 Marischal Street,
with accommodation for eighteen girls. When the lease expired the Home
moved to smaller premises.
59) ALU, annual report, 1903, pp. 6-7. It was intended that these district unions
should draw together workers in the towns and country districts.
60) The Travellers' Aid Society was established in 1885 to protect young, inexperienced women who were travelling alone and unsupervised. Placards and
handbills were displayed in railway stations and steamship company offices,
giving the names and addresses of women who would meet and look after the
travellers.
61) In 1906, for instance, two girls, bound for Lawrence (USA) and Johannesburg,
were met at New York and Cape Town respectively and directed on the next
stage of their journeys; the following year another local girl was met at New
York and seen off on the next stage of her journey to join her brother in the
USA, and in 1908 an emigrant who was going to Alberta to join her parents
came under the care of the Travellers' Aid Society at Liverpool, St John and
Calgary. (See ALU, annual reports, 1906 (pp. 15-16), 1907 (pp. 16-17) and
1908 (pp. 17-18).
62) See *AJ*, 2 Sept. 1886, 8 Feb. 1889, 12 Sept. 1891.
63) Haddo House MSS, news cuttings, volume marked 'May 1883—May 1885',
pamphlet opposite p. 30.
64) *The Musings of a Scottish Granny*, pp. 52-3.
65) See *The Canadian Journal of Lady Aberdeen*, int., p. xxii; also Marjorie
Pentland, *A Bonnie Fechter: the life of Ishbel Marjoribanks, Marchioness of
Aberdeen and Temair* (London, 1952), p. 88. For discussion of the fate of the
emigrants, see Ishbel, Marchioness of Aberdeen, *Through Canada with a
Kodak*, p. 58 and *Canadian Gazette*, 7 Sept. 1893 (Haddo House MSS, news
cuttings, volume marked 'August 1893—June 1894', p. 41).
66) *Through Canada with a Kodak*, p. 28.
67) The Journal of Lady Aberdeen, 1890-1899 (unpublished): entry for 1 Sept.
1890.
68) *Ibid*, entries for 1 & 9 Oct. 1890.
69) *Through Canada with a Kodak*, p. 123. See also *Canadian Journal*, 30 Oct.
1894.
70) *Through Canada with a Kodak*, p. 137.
71) *A Bonnie Fechter*, p. 91. Lord Aberdeen had given £2,000 towards the fund
started by the Secretary of State for Scotland for the settlement of fifty Highland
crofters in Western Canada.
72) *Through Canada with a Kodak*, p. 156.
73) *Canadian Journal*, 1 Oct. 1893 (pp. 15-16).
74) *AJ*, 30 Jan. 1896.
75) *AFP*, 13 Sept. 1893 (Haddo House MSS, news cuttings, volume marked 'Canada and Chicago March 1892—July 1893', p. 50).

76) See *Canadian Journal*, 17 Feb. 1894 (Guelph); 15 May 1894 (Ottawa); 5 Oct. 1894 (Brandon); 11 Oct. 1894 (Medicine Hat); Aug. 1896 (British Columbia); 15 July 1898 (Cochrane Ranch, NWT).

77) On 4 October 1894 they visited Dr Barnardo's 10,000-acre farm at Russell, where forty boys were in residence. (See *Canadian Journal*, p. 125).

78) *Ibid.* On 2 October 1894 Lord and Lady Aberdeen visited Treherne, Manitoba, where they met a number of children who had recently been settled as 'helps' under the auspices of the Young Colonists' Aid Society. See also below, p. 272.

79) See *Canadian Journal*, 13 Feb. 1895.

80) *AJ*, 4 July 1899.

81) See also *ibid*, 23 Aug. 1899, 24 Nov. 1899.

82) In *Through Canada with a Kodak* Lady Aberdeen spoke of her fellow-passengers on the SS *Parisian* from Liverpool to Quebec. They included a group of young girls aged from three to seventeen, 'taken from misery and destitution to Miss Rye's Homes, from whence they will be drafted, either as servants or else adopted into colonists' homes'. (p. 5).

83) Lady Gordon Cathcart also owned the estate of Cluny in Aberdeenshire, and according to the *Aberdeen Journal* (23 Nov. 1883) she planned to extend her colonisation schemes to include farmers and labourers from her east coast properties.

84) *Through Canada with a Kodak*, p. 94.

85) Quoted in *A Bonnie Fechter*, p. 90.

86) See, for instance, *ibid*, p. 91; *Through Canada with a Kodak*, p. 96, and *Canadian Journal*, pp. 461-2, where she said of Regina in 1898 that 'no one lives here who is not obliged to'.

87) *Canadian Journal*, 18 Oct. 1894 (pp. 139-40).

88) *AJ*, 19 May 1890. Mrs Gillespie also discouraged upper class and professional women, particularly those who had been trained only as lady's helps or teachers, from coming to Canada.

89) *Canadian Journal*, 22 Nov. 1894 (pp. 153-4).

90) *Ibid*, 3 Aug. 1895 (p. 262). The servant at Qu'Appelle had asked for Lady Aberdeen's help in procuring a new situation, to the latter's embarrassment, since she had gained a reputation in the press for upsetting people's servants, and feared she would be blamed if this girl left her post.

91) See Lord Aberdeen's speech to the International Congress of Women in 1899 (*AJ*, 4 July 1899), in which he poured scorn on the idea that women arriving in Canada were immediately surrounded by a crowd of suitors.

92) *Canadian Journal* (Saywell) 22 Nov. 1894 (p. 154) and (unpublished) 4 Dec. 1896. The newly-arrived bride for whom Lady Aberdeen had such sympathy was a Mrs Dundas: 'It was pathetic to see her looking very much a bride in her little two roomed shack with her pretty wedding presents about ... and guessing what the future would probably be, neither of the pair having a cent ... his 20 acres not giving much prospect of providing sustenance. It is cruel to let these sort of people come out here—it is bad enough for the men but for the women it is terrible, especially when the children come & there is no help to be got.'

93) *AJ*, 3 Dec. 1890.

94) *Canadian Journal*, 22 Nov. 1894 (p. 154).

95) *Through Canada with a Kodak*, pp. 149-50.

96) *Ibid*, p. 28.

97) *Ibid*, pp. 177-8.

98) The *Manitoba Daily Free Press* (n.d.) quoted her letter to Stead: see Haddo

House MSS, news cuttings, volume marked 'October 1890—March 1892', p. 73.
99) See *Through Canada with a Kodak*, pp. 102-3.
100) 5 Jan. 1892.
101) *A Bonnie Fechter*, p. 92.
102) 'The Aberdeen Society' in the *Winnipeg Telegram*, 8 May 1907, p. 53.
103) '*We Twa*', Book II, p. 296.
104) *Canadian Journal*, p. 215.
105) *AJ*, 25 May 1899.
106) *Through Canada with a Kodak*, pp. 12-13.
107) Haddo House MSS, news cuttings, volume marked 'May 1883—May 1885', pamphlet opposite p. 30.
108) *Ibid*.
109) *Ibid*, p. 2.
110) See, for instance, ALU, emigration report, 1899, pp. 14-15, for quotation from Ellen Joyce.
111) For details, see *AJ*, 11, 12 Oct. 1888; Haddo House MSS, news cuttings, volume marked 'September 1886—April 1889', p. 33 (undated cutting from *EG*, and *ibid*, pp. 38-9 (extracts from undated, unmarked newspaper referring to the same conference).
112) ALU, emigration report, 1888, p. 17; 1889, p. 14. See also above, pp. 251, 259 and below, pp. 271, 272.
113) Anne Macdonald's report to the Conference of Women Workers in Aberdeen, Oct. 1892 (ALU, emigration report, 1892, p. 16).
114) She gave the example of one intending emigrant who had made her own arrangements to emigrate to Montreal. When her mistress had discovered she had no friends in that city, and no idea of where she would go or what she would do when she arrived, she had sent her to Miss Macdonald. Anne Macdonald then gave her the card of the Women's Protective Home in Montreal, and also wrote ahead with the request that the girl be met at the steamer. In 1893 she noted with satisfaction that more girls were now seeing the need to travel with a protected party (ALU, emigration report, 1893, p. 13).
115) ALU, emigration report, 1892, p. 16; 1895, p. 12.
116) *Ibid*, 1897, p. 12. See also PAC, RG 76, C-15865, vol. 138, file 33136, parts 1 & 2: Girls' Home of Welcome, Winnipeg, 1897-1911 (lists). The Stonehaven agent, Alexander Longmuir, regularly used the Home to accommodate parties of newly-arrived female settlers.
117) ALU, emigration report, 1897, p. 12.
118) *Ibid*, 1898, p. 16.
119) In 1887 the emigration committee expressed thanks to the Cults Ladies' Working Party, Bon Accord Free Church, Queen's Cross Free Church and the Established East Church, amongst others, for donations of material and clothing. (ALU, emigration report, 1887, p. 14).
120) Details of these emigrants are given in Haddo House MSS, news cuttings, volume marked 'May 1883—May 1885', pamphlet opposite p. 20 (first annual report of the emigration committee). Two of the girls were orphans. Of those sent to New South Wales, two had found work in Sydney and one at a distance of 250 miles from that city. Of those who went to Canada, two remained in Montreal and two were sent on to the 'Essex Centre'. All four found immediate employment.
121) *Ibid*, p. 2.

122) ALU, emigration report, 1886, p. 15; 1889, p. 16.
123) ALU, report to Conference of Women Workers, 1892, p. 13.
124) ALU, emigration report, 1896, p. 14. See also below, p. 269.
125) Western Australia's population was so small that it could assimilate only a few settlers at a time. See *AJ*, 2 June 1886—the committee had apparently been forced to suspend emigration to all destinations until funds had been replenished.
126) ALU, emigration report, 1887, pp. 11-12.
127) First annual report of the emigration committee (Haddo House MSS, news cuttings, volume marked 'May 1883—May 1885', pamphlet opposite p. 20).
128) See, for instance, ALU, emigration report, 1887, p. 12—in which it was said repayments were the exception rather than the rule. Matters had improved by the following year, when £29 was received in repayments from the nineteen girls who had been sent out. (ALU, emigration report, 1888, p. 17).
129) ALU, report to Conference of Women Workers, 1892, p. 17.
130) ALU, emigration report, 1897, p. 12.
131) Miss Lefroy's statement quoted in *ibid*, 1903, p. 22.
132) This fund was created in November 1903 to help unemployed factory girls take advantage of the growing demand for their services in Canadian industries.
133) ALU, emigration report, 1900, pp. 14-15.
134) See, for instance, *ibid*, 1897, 1898, 1904-9.
135) In 1906, for instance, twelve of the thirty-seven emigrants paid their fares in full before leaving. (ALU, emigration report, 1906, p. 15).
136) ALU, emigration report, 1903, p. 21; 1905, p. 11. The girl who emigrated with Mrs Sanford was to repay the advance later.
137) ALU, emigration report, 1891, p. 13.
138) *Ibid*, 1894, p. 10.
139) See also PP 1906 [Cd. 2978], LXXXVI, 533, qu. 2305, p. 85, *Report of the departmental committee appointed to consider Mr Rider Haggard's report on agricultural settlements in the British Colonies*. In her evidence to this committee Ellen Joyce particularly mentioned that many factory girls had left Aberdeen under the BWEA's auspices.
140) ALU, emigration report, 1899, p. 14.
141) See also *ibid*, 1895, 1896, 1898, 1899. Some candidates also changed their minds after being selected, which further reduced numbers (e.g. 1895).
142) ALU, emigration report, 1893, p. 14.
143) See, for instance, *ibid*, 1889, 1890, 1897, 1898.
144) Although in 1886 several had apparently paid their own expenses either in total or in part (ALU, emigration report, 1886, p. 13).
145) ALU, emigration report, 1886, p. 13.
146) *Ibid*, 1889, p. 13.
147) *Ibid*, 1886, p. 15.
148) *Ibid*, 1887, p. 13; 1892 conference report, p. 13.
149) ALU, emigration report, 1893, p. 13; 1905, p. 11.
150) *Ibid*, 1896, p. 13.
151) *Ibid*, 1903, p. 22. By that time Canada was beginning to ask for immigrant factory workers who could be employed in the manufacture of clothing, footwear and boxes.
152) One other emigrant, assisted by the London Factory Fund, went to work in a warehouse (ALU, emigration report, 1907, p. 16).
153) E.g., 1906 (p. 15), 1907 (p. 16).
154) See ALU, emigration report, 1897, p. 12.

155) Haddo House MSS, news cuttings, volume marked '1885-1886', pp. 48-9.
156) ALU, emigration report, 1893, p. 14; 1898, p. 16.
157) See BWEA annual reports, 1890, p. 14; 1891, p. 15; 1906, p. 21.
158) ALU, emigration report, 1891, p. 12.
159) *Ibid*, 1895, p. 11.
160) *Ibid*, 1903, p. 21.
161) *Ibid*, 1896, pp. 14-5.
162) *Ibid*, 1899, p. 15; 1903, p. 22.
163) *Ibid*, 1901, p. 15.
164) *Ibid*, 1906, p. 15. She subsequently took a job in Aberdeen and began to repay her fare out of her wages.
165) *Ibid*, 1890, p. 14.
166) *Ibid*, 1895, p. 12.
167) *Ibid*, 1905, p. 11.
168) 1892 conference report, p. 16.
169) See also *AJ*, 18 May 1887, for report of another valedictory meeting for a party of sixteen girls going to Canada.
170) ALU, emigration report, 1886, p. 15.
171) ALU, emigration report, 1885, in Haddo House MSS, news cuttings, volume marked '1885-1886', pp. 48-9.
172) *AJ*, 3 Dec. 1890.
173) '*We Twa*', Book II, p. 300. See also The Journal of Lady Aberdeen, 1890-1899 (unpublished): entries for 13 & 30 Sept. 1891. On 13 September, writing from Montreal, she recorded that 'Yesterday was chiefly employed in unsuccessfully trying to find some girls emigrated by the Aberdeen Ladies' Union.' On 30 September she drove twenty miles from Calgary to the isolated settlement of Fish Creek to visit Mary Emslie, who had joined the Logie-Coldstone branch of the Onward and Upward Association in 1882. On emigrating to Canada she had first worked in an hotel, before taking up employment as a servant on this farm at $25 a month.
174) Quoted in *A Bonnie Fechter*, p. 115.
175) *AJ*, 30 Jan. 1896.
176) ALU, emigration report, 1903, p. 22.
177) In 1890, for instance, the committee admitted in its annual report that it did not hear from as many girls as it would wish, but had heard from other sources that at least seventeen girls had married abroad since the start of the emigration scheme in 1888 (ALU, emigration report, 1890, pp. 13-4).
178) ALU, emigration report, 1897, p. 12.
179) *Ibid*, 1888, p. 17.
180) ALU, emigration report, 1889, p. 14.
181) In 1906 Lord Aberdeen began his second term of office as Lord-Lieutenant of Ireland, remaining in this post for the next nine years.
182) On 5 November 1891 Lady Aberdeen recorded in her journal a meeting in Winnipeg with four girls who had been sent out by the Aberdeen Ladies' Union. Three had settled down well as general servants, but the fourth, a Baptist minister's daughter who had come out with the idea of being a 'lady's help', was unwilling to work, had already changed her employment several times, and wanted to return home. She was a clear example of the kind of settler whom Lady Aberdeen repeatedly said should be discouraged from emigrating, and whom the Aberdeen Ladies' Union would have been expected to weed out during the initial selection procedure.

TABLE I
FEMALE EMIGRANTS FROM BRITAIN, 1887–1916
(under the auspices of the BWEA, SAX Committee[1] and SACS)

YEAR	BWEA EMIGRANTS	EMIGRANTS TO SOUTH AFRICA	TOTAL
1887	154	*	154
1888	155	*	155
1889	402	*	402
1890	547	*	547
1891	406	*	406
1892	443	*	443
1893	225	*	225
1894	532	*	532
1895	433	*	433
1896	450	*	450
1897	417	*	417
1898	353	*	353
1899	298	*	298
1900	439	*	439
1901	458	*	458
1902	321	818[1]	1,139
1903	408	1,218	1,626
1904	528	339	867
1905	603	346	949
1906	774	341	1,115
1907	910	299	1,209
1908	505	266	771
1909	600	308	908
1910	1,057	365	1,422
1911	1,196	401	1,597
1912	1,381	482	1,863
1913	1,201	469	1,670
1914	622	313	935
1915	267	219	486
1916	213	no figure available	213
TOTAL	16,298	6,184	22,482

Source: British Women's Emigration Association: Annual Reports 1887–1916; and *South Africa Colonisation Society: Annual Reports 1903–1915* (in Fawcett Library Collection, City of London Polytechnic).

[1] In 1902 818 women were sent to South Africa under the auspices of the South Africa Expansion Committee (SAX), which was superseded by the South Africa Colonisation Society (SACS) in 1903.

* The emigrants to South Africa were not differentiated until 1902.

TABLE II
ABERDEEN LADIES' UNION—EMIGRATION BRANCH
EMIGRANTS TO VARIOUS DESTINATIONS 1884–1913

Year	Canada	Western Australia	New South Wales	Queensland	Natal	U.S.A.	Unspecified	Total
1884	4		5					9
1885							11	11
1886	6	27						33
1887*	18							18
1888							19	19
1889	12	1		8				21
1890	12							12
1891							6	6
1892	4							4
1893	10				1	1		12
1894*							2	2
1895	6							6
1896	9							9
1897	4							4
1898	18							18
1899	1							1
1900	8	2						10
1901	3							3
1902	4?							4
1903	4							4
1904	13							13
1905	39							39
1906	37							37
1907	30							30
1908	3							3
1909	9							9
1910	27							27
1911	8							8
1912	2							2
1913	5							5
Total	296	30	5	8	1	1	38	379

Sources:
1. First annual report of the Aberdeen Ladies' Union (1884). (Haddo House MSS, newspaper cuttings, volume marked 'May 1883–May 1885', pamphlet opposite p. 20.
2. Second annual report of the Aberdeen Ladies' Union (1885). (Haddo House MSS, newspaper cuttings, volume marked '1885–1886', pp. 48–9).
3. Annual reports of the Aberdeen Ladies' Union, 1886–1909. (Bound volume in Aberdeen Public Library, Local Collection).
4. British Women's Emigration Association, annual reports, 1910–1913. (Fawcett Library Collection, City of London Polytechnic).
* A statement in the 1887 annual report declared that seventy-four people had been sent abroad since the Union was formed. As thirty-three of these left in 1886, and eighteen in 1887, the implication is that twenty-three women emigrated during the first two years of the Union's operations, three less than the total derived from the 1884 and 1885 reports themselves. There is a similar discrepancy in a sub-total given in the annual report for 1894. This report claimed that 127 girls had been sent abroad since the start of the Union's operations. Yet if the numbers in each preceding annual report are added together, a total figure of 147 emigrants is reached for the period 1884–1894.

Epilogue

Several categories of emigrants left North-East Scotland for Canada in the late nineteenth and early twentieth centuries—women, children, tradesmen, a few fishermen and professional and business people, as well as the farmers and farm labourers who had constituted the bulk of the area's exodus since it began. With the exception of some destitute children and also the fishermen, whose sporadic emigration seems to have been provoked almost entirely by economic problems, these emigrants were generally responding to various combinations of the positive and negative influences which have always been a characteristic feature of human migration whenever and wherever it has occurred.

The emigrants clearly had differing needs and preferences. Most of the agriculturists continued to crave personal independence and improved prospects for their families through the ownership of their own farms; businessmen and entrepreneurs sought better outlets for their capital and energies; many female emigrants welcomed the Canadian demand for domestic servants as an ideal opportunity to escape from an over-supplied labour market at home; tradesmen too often emigrated in response to unemployment or financial problems, sometimes as temporary contract workers; and those individuals and societies which sponsored juvenile emigration generally aimed to offer children the chance of a new life across the Atlantic, away from a corrupting environment and bleak future at home.

But whatever the origins, background and priorities of the emigrants, almost all were influenced to some degree by one or more of a few recurring catalysts. As in the earlier nineteenth century, the promise of land continued to attract large numbers to Canada, and most promotional publicity was still targeted at this particularly desirable class of settler. The effects of general precedent and personal persuasion in stimulating a secondary exodus—also evident in the earlier period—assumed even more significance as the nucleus of emigrants from North-East Scotland became bigger and settlement expanded. But probably most vital of all stimuli in this pre-war period was the rôle of the ubiquitous agent in convincing those who, for various reasons, were dissatisfied with life in Scotland that they could improve their situation and prospects by removing to Canada.

The Canadians knew what kind of settlers they wanted and the Department of Immigration waged a positive and extensive campaign in Britain and

Europe to attract these recruits, in particular agriculturists and domestic servants. But the Canadian recruitment campaign was not conducted only by visiting and resident Dominion government representatives. The different provinces and the transcontinental railway companies also competed for settlers, using their own resident and itinerant agents; and all these Canadian representatives liaised closely with the army of booking agents scattered across the country. The booking agents were the linchpins of the whole agency network; they not only made the emigrants' practical travelling arrangements, but also ensured that promotional literature was distributed in their areas and organised the itineraries of visiting professional recruitment agents, as well as encouraging emigration on their own account. The various agents were generally competing for the same types of (mainly agricultural) settler; indeed G. G. Archibald once confessed that he had been unable to supply enquiring granite tradesmen and fishermen with information about opportunities in Canada because these occupations were outside the remit of his office.[1] But openings were no longer confined exclusively to agriculturists and suitable females; some Canadian firms sent representatives to Britain to engage emigrants for industrial employment, and from time to time local booking agents recruited tradesmen for specific (and sometimes short-term) contracts with Canadian employers who had engaged the local agents to act on their behalf. But it was not always the Canadians who took the initiative in recruiting settlers. Many of the women, children and unemployed workmen who emigrated under the auspices of charitable societies never had dealings with Canadian agents; for the philanthropists who devised and implemented schemes of assisted emigration were concerned primarily to alleviate problems of unemployment or social distress in Britain and simply took advantage of the simultaneous Canadian cry for settlers to mount their own individual schemes.

Potential emigrants were therefore exposed to the blandishments of numerous agents, who appeared in different guises and espoused a variety of causes. Most of those who were persuaded to settle in Canada seem to have been satisfied with their move; working farmers at least made few public complaints and rarely returned to North-East Scotland as failed emigrants. Non-agricultural emigration was more controversial. A number of disappointed fishermen returned from Canada within a few months of leaving their Banffshire homes in 1888, and several temporary emigrants expressed dissatisfaction with the terms and conditions of their contracts. Perhaps their disappointment is not entirely surprising. Those who felt they had been forced to emigrate because of economic hardship or who went to Canada with the sole intention of making money and then returning home would be less likely to persevere in the face of difficulties than the agriculturists, most of whom were positively committed to their new way of life and prepared to endure hardships for the sake of ultimate independence and security on their own land. The difference in attitude did not go unnoticed by the Canadian employers and immigration authorities. They were generally satisfied with the farmers and farm labourers, who were often recruited personally by their own agents; but they sometimes complained about the calibre of certain tradesmen and also the recruits sent out by certain charitable emigration societies. Yet with a few exceptions (mainly tradesmen and the occasional incapable domestic servant sent out by a booking agent) North-East Scotland seems to have maintained the good reputation it had established with the Canadian immigration authorities in the early nineteenth century. Not only did the Canadians continue to welcome hard-working farmers and ambitious farm labourers; they were equally pleased to receive recruits from the Aberdeen Ladies' Union and other well-ordered emigration societies; and businessmen and investors, of course, made particularly attractive settlers.

.Does a detailed study of emigration from North-East Scotland serve any further purpose than simply to provide the theme for an exercise in one particular aspect of local history? There was probably nothing unique about the movement from this area. Indeed, the North-East was not a region that was particularly noted for the size of its contribution to the national exodus, for it supplied only a small fraction of the total number of Scottish emigrants. Yet even small regional contributions to the national tide of emigration merit attention and analysis, for throughout and beyond the nineteenth century emigration was a topical feature of regional life, to a greater or lesser degree, in almost every corner of the British Isles. The 'national exodus' was the result of millions of individual decisions made by millions of people across the country, who were provoked to emigrate by many different combinations of grievances and incentives. And regional studies, compiled from local sources, perhaps reflect these multifarious and complex combinations of influences more accurately than do general interpretations of 'British' or 'Scottish' emigration derived primarily from official government records.

In the quarter-century before the First World War Canada—which had always been the preferred destination of emigrants from North-East Scotland—occupied an even more central place in the history of emigration from the region. That is not to say emigrants did not settle elsewhere, or that their settlement does not deserve study. But the sheer volume and consistency of local source material on Canada from the 1880s overshadowed the attention paid to any other country, and seemed to justify a detailed analysis of different aspects of emigration from North-East Scotland to this one particular destination.

The story does not end in 1914, although the outbreak of the First World War certainly imposed a severe check and reduced the exodus to a mere trickle. But even during the war the British government was considering how emigration should be conducted after the return of peace. A Royal Commission of Enquiry into the Self-Governing Dominions, appointed in 1912,[2] spent six years amassing and analysing evidence. But although its final report, issued in 1918, recommended the creation of a central authority to control all aspects of British emigration, including the dissemination of information and the supervision of ticket agents and voluntary societies, opposition from vested interests prevented the passage of legislation to put these recommendations into effect. In December 1918, however, the committee of the Emigrants' Information Office resigned, on the grounds that a voluntary organisation would be unable to cope with post-war problems of emigration, and shortly afterwards the government appointed the Overseas Settlement Committee, 'to deal effectively with the problems which are likely to arise during the period of reconstruction after the war'.[3] The committee's policies were implemented by the Overseas Settlement Office, a newly-created department of the Colonial Office, which also took over the staff and duties of the Emigrants' Information Office, and generally assumed responsibility for the conduct of emigration in the post-war period.

Meanwhile the Empire Settlement Committee, which had been formed in 1917 to investigate opportunities for the settlement of ex-soldiers within the Empire, urged that state aid be offered to all ex-service personnel who wished to emigrate. The result of this recommendation was the short-lived Free Passage Scheme, which between 1919 and 1922 gave free third-class passages to assist around 86,000 ex-servicemen and their families to settle in the Dominions, provided they were approved by the receiving countries and either took up land or were assured of employment. In offering this assistance to a special class of settler, the government had not altered its stance on state-aided emigration, which it continued to regard as unnecessary. But in 1922, in response to signs of post-war depression and pressure exerted by a Conference of Prime Ministers of the Empire the previous year, the Empire Settlement Act was passed, committing the government to a much more active involvement in emigration schemes than it had hitherto been willing to accept.

The Empire Settlement Act was to remain in force for fifteen years. Under its terms the British government agreed to spend up to £3,000,000 a year on state-aided emigration, provided that at least half the cost of any scheme was met by some other interested party; and in the nine years up to 1932 400,000 emigrants were assisted under the Act, through land settlement schemes, assisted passages and government co-operation with voluntary emigration agencies. Initial experiments in large-scale land settlement in Western Australia, Victoria and New South Wales proved to be costly failures,[4] mainly because the emigrants were not of pioneering calibre and refused to work on the land, preferring to congregate in the towns. Canada made a much smaller contribution to group settlement through the '3000 Families Scheme' of 1924, a co-operative venture under which the Dominion government supplied prepared farms to experienced agricultural families while the British government gave the settlers loans to purchase stock and equipment. A much more popular incentive to emigrate to Canada was an assisted passage scheme which operated from 1929 to 1931, when it was withdrawn in response to the Depression. In those three years a total of 58,000 emigrants took advantage of the opportunity to travel to Canada for only £10, on the one condition that they submitted to a medical examination. The balance of the fare was shared between the shipping companies and the British government.

On the whole, however, the Empire Settlement Act did not live up to the expectations of its promoters. Most emigrants continued to leave independently and schemes formulated under the Act accounted for less than forty per cent of the total movement. These schemes were generally directed at Australasia, where the group land settlement experiments failed (predictably) to fulfil their promise of recasting redundant urbanised British emigrants as successful Antipodean farmers. The onset of the worldwide depression then led to the withdrawal of assisted passages to Canada, while aid to Australian emigrants was confined to the families of established settlers. During the 1930s the advocates of assisted emigration remained hamstrung both by these restrictions and by the continuing effects of the Depression; and although the Empire Settlement Act was renewed for a further fifteen-year term in 1937, the outbreak of the Second World War two years later finally killed off all hopes of an extensive redistribution of population within the Empire under its terms.

Clearly much research remains to be done into emigration, not only in connection with the inter-war experiments and the new policies and attitudes that emerged after 1945, but also with reference to the movement during the Victorian and Edwardian eras. The two parts of this study have sought to examine emigration from one particular region of Scotland over the period 1830-1914; they have highlighted the impact of the movement both on the homeland and on the emigrants' destinations (particularly Canada) as it was perceived by contemporary observers and by the emigrants themselves. It is therefore intended to serve not only as a narrow exercise in local history but also as a contribution to the broader history of emigration, and as a stimulus to further regional studies into a phenomenon about which much still remains to be discovered.

NOTES

1) G. G. Archibald's report in Dept of the Interior, *annual report on immigration, 1913-14*.
2) The Commission was appointed following recommendations from the Imperial Conference of 1911 that enquiries should be made into the possibilities of developing further the natural resources of self-governing dominions. See Carrothers, *Emigration from the British Isles*, p. 257 and N. H. Carrier & J. R. Jeffery, *External migration: a study of the available statistics, 1815-1950* (London, 1953) p. 34. [Studies on medical and population subjects, General Register Office: 6].
3) Carrothers, *Emigration from the British Isles*, p. 258.
4) Carrier & Jeffrey, *External migration*, pp. 35-6. By 1932 £9 million had been spent in establishing only 1,000 settlers and their families on land in Western Australia.

Bibliography

MANUSCRIPT SOURCES

1) *Aberdeen School of Industry*
Admission minute books: 1867-74; 1886-98; 1898-1916.

2) *Aberdeen University Archives*
MSS 2655/2/1/1-9 *Operative Masons' and Granite Cutters' Journal*, vols. 1-9, (1901-10).
MS 3184 Correspondence donated by John McBean, October 1984.

3) *Grampian Region Archives*
MS 6/1/9 Aberdour Parochial Board, Record of Applications for Poor Relief, 1891-1915;
MS 6/27/22 Fraserburgh Parochial Board, Record of Applications, 1894-1907;
MS 6/27/23 Fraserburgh Parochial Board, Record of Applications, 1907-11;
MS 6/50/5 Lonmay Parochial Board, General Register of Poor, 1845-1930;
MS 6/50/7 Lonmay Parochial Board, Record of Applications, 1855-1902;
MS 6/64/14 Peterhead Parochial Board, General Register of Poor, 1853-92;
MS 6/64/15 Peterhead Parochial Board, General Register of Poor, 1857-1903;
MS 6/64/17 Peterhead Parochial Board, General Register of Poor, 1869-1931;
MS 6/64/25 Peterhead Parochial Board, Visiting Book of Registered Poor, 1884-90.

4) *Kelowna Museum, British Columbia*
Daily Journal of the Rose Brothers, 1893-5.

5) *Liverpool University Archives*
D2/1/a1—D2/1/a31 and D2/1/a79—D2/1/a87: Dr Barnardo's Homes: chronological listing of boys sent to Canada, 1882-94 and 1910-12.
D6 (iii) (C) 1-20: Marchmont Homes History Books, lists of boys and girls sent to Canada.

6) *National Register of Archives*

Survey No. 0055: Haddo House Papers—contents of 'cupboard three' consisting of various volumes of news cuttings relating to Lord and Lady Aberdeen's political and social activities in the late nineteenth and early twentieth centuries, and extracts from a box of pamphlets covering the same period.

7) *Oakbank Industrial School, Aberdeen*

Visiting Directors' Report Book, 1875-1947.

8) *Provincial Archives of British Columbia*

A-1277: Lord Aberdeen Papers pertaining to British Columbia; E D A63: Earl of Aberdeen, correspondence.

9) *Provincial Archives of Manitoba*

File 28735: Lady Aberdeen enquiry regarding juvenile immigration, 1895-1901; letter from A. M. Burgess to Lady Aberdeen, 2 May 1896.

10) *Public Archives of Canada*

MG 27, C-1352 1L 1B5: The journal of Lady Aberdeen (unpublished).

11) *Quarrier's Homes*

Record books of children sent abroad, vols 1-36 (1879-1915).

12) *The Salvation Army*

The Salvation Army (Canada and Bermuda): George Scott Railton Heritage Centre, Toronto, Archives and Museum: immigration cards, Scottish immigrants, 1913-22.

PRINTED SOURCES

1) *British Parliamentary Papers*

Emigration and Immigration: *Statistical tables relating to emigration and immigration from and into the United Kingdom, and reports to Board of Trade thereon, 1881-1913;*
Emigration and Immigration: *Reports on the Emigrants' Information Office, 1888-1914;*
PP 1890-91 (152) XI, 571: *Report from the Select Committee on Colonisation, 1889-91;*
PP 1894 [C. 7400] XVI, Pts I-III: *Royal Commission on agricultural depression, first general report, 1894;*
PP 1900 Cd. 408 XLIII, 1: *Forty-third report of H. M. Inspector of reformatory and industrial schools of Great Britain, for the year 1899;*

PP 1905 (306) V, 507: *The Unemployed Workmen Act*;
PP 1906 Cd. 2978 LXXXVI, 533: *Report of the departmental committee appointed to consider Mr Rider Haggard's report on agricultural settlements in the British colonies*;
PP 1906 Cd. 3273 XCVI, 583: *Board of Agriculture, report on the decline of the agricultural population of Britain, 1881-1906*;
PP 1913 Cd. 6838 XXXIX: *Report of the departmental committee on reformatory and industrial schools*; PP 1913 Cd. 6839 XXXIX, 117: *minutes of evidence*;
PP 1914 Cd. 7221 XXXI, 533: *Report of the Scottish departmental committee on the North Sea fishing industry*; PP 1914 Cd. 7462 XXXI, 773: *evidence and index*;
PP 1914-16 Cd. 7886 XXXIV, 491: *Report of the departmental committee on reformatory and industrial schools in Scotland*; PP 1914-16 Cd. 7887 XXXIV, 609: *evidence and appendices*;
Hansard: Official Reports, first series, vol. XXVI, 22 May—16 June 1911.

2) *Canadian Government Publications*

National Library of Canada, Official Publications Division: *Annual reports of the Department of Agriculture, 1881-1892*; *annual reports of the Department of the Interior, 1893-1914*.
Public Archives of Canada, microfilm reel no. C-4660, vol. 5, file 41, part 1: emigration from Britain, 1892-1914;
PAC, C-4728, vol. 60, file 26/4, part 5: bonus to booking agents;
PAC, C-4763, vol. 99, file 12681-C: counties from which British emigrants came, 1902-8;
PAC, C-4768, vol. 105, file 17480: Salvation Army immigration records, general file;
PAC, C-7303, vol. 147, file 34873: H. M. Murray's report to Clifford Sifton, Minister of the Interior, 29 Apr. 1897;
PAC, C-7312, vol. 155, file 39501, part 1: arrangements made that Scottish and Welsh farm labourers and farmers wishing to settle in Manitoba and the North-West Territories will be given work on the railway, 1897;
PAC, RG 25, A2, vol. 146, file C5/86: alleged ill-treatment of Scottish girls who have been induced to emigrate to Canada, 1910;
PAC, RG 76, C-53, vol. 44, file 1378: British Women's Immigration Association;
PAC, RG 76, C-10291-2, vol. 401, file 572933: J. Fraser, Auditor-General, Ottawa, re. advertising in the *Aberdeen Free Press*, 1906, 1909-14;
PAC, RG 76, C-10294-5, vol. 405, file 590687: correspondence and weekly reports of John MacLennan, immigration agent in Scotland;
PAC, RG 76, C-10296, vol. 406, file 593269: Hugh McIntosh nominated as a farm delegate to the Old Country;
PAC, RG 76, C-10306, vol. 422-3, file 616279, parts 1-7: Jane Radford, Women's Canadian Employment Bureau, Montreal, lists of settlers received;
PAC, RG 76, C-10315, vol. 435, file 652801: correspondence of John Sinclair, booking agent, Elgin;
PAC, RG 76, C-10318, vol. 440, file 662655: Hugh McKerracher to take charge of an exhibition wagon in Scotland, 1907-21;
PAC, RG 76, C-10414, vol. 479, file 742357: Samuel Jackson, MP, Stonewall, Man., recommending A. R. Bredin, Louise Bridge, Man., as farmer delegate to Old Country, 1908;
PAC, RG 76, C-10421, vol. 487, file 752538, part 1: philanthropic societies which assist immigrants to Canada, 1907-29;

PAC, RG 76, C-10425, vol. 491, file 760771: Donald Grant, Souris, Man., appointed immigration agent in GB (Scotland) farm delegate, 1908-9;
PAC, RG 76, C-10621, vol. 530, file 803485: correspondence of W. G. Maitland, booking agent, Longside, Aberdeenshire;
PAC, RG 76, C-10627, vol. 538, file 803839, parts 1 & 2: correspondence of H. W. J. Paton, booking agent, Aberdeen;
PAC, RG 76, C-10638, vol. 556, file 806656: re. special issue of the *Canada Scotsman*, 15 Mar. 1909;
PAC, RG 76, C-10644, vol. 564, file 809010: correspondence of MacKay Brothers, booking agents, Aberdeen;
PAC, RG 76, C-10680, vol. 679, file 41, part 1: emigration staff, GB, 1893-6.

3) *US Government Records*

United States Statutes at Large, 48th Congress, 1883-5, vol. 23, p. 332: *an act to prohibit the importation and migration of foreigners and aliens under contract or agreement to perform labour in the United States, its territories and the District of Columbia.*

4) *Reports of societies and institutions*

Aberdeen Ladies' Union, *annual reports, 1886-1909* (Aberd. Public Library, local collection);
British Women's Emigration Association, *annual reports, 1888-1914* (Fawcett Library, City of London Polytechnic);
Colonial Intelligence League, *annual reports, 1910-19* (Fawcett Library);
North of Scotland College of Agriculture, *minutes and proceedings, 1917-18*;
Quarrier's Homes, *A Narrative of Facts relative to work done for Christ in connection with the Orphan and destitute children's emigration homes, Glasgow, 1872-1903*;
South Africa Colonisation Society, *annual reports, 1903-16* (Fawcett Library).

5) *Directories, journals and newspapers*

The Aberdeen Directory (Aberd., 1880-1914);
The Aberdeen Free Press;
The Aberdeen Journal;
The Evening Express (1913);
The Evening Gazette (1913);
The Farmers' Advocate and Home Magazine (Winnipeg, Man.) vol. XXXVIII, no. 570 (20 Mar. 1903), pp. 247-9;
The Fraserburgh Herald (1888-9, 1911);
The Imperial Colonist: the official organ of the British Women's Emigration Association and the South Africa Colonisation Society, vol. IV, no. 37 (Jan. 1905) to vol. VI, no. 72 (Dec. 1907);
In Memoriam, 1892-1912 (APL, local collection);
Onward and Upward: the journal of the Haddo House Association, vol. I (1891), vol. 23 (1909);
The Vernon News (1891-5) (Greater Vernon Museum and Archives, Vernon, BC);
The War Cry, 1887, 28 Nov. 1891.

6)   *Pamphlets*

Canada, Dept of Agriculture, *The agricultural resources of Canada. Reports of tenant farmers' delegates and other informations on Manitoba, the North-West Territories and other parts of the Dominion of Canada as a field for the settlement of agriculturists etc* (1881);

Canada, Dept of Agriculture, *Report of the tenant farmers' delegates on the Dominion of Canada as a field for settlement* (1880);

Canada, Dept of Agriculture, *The visit of the tenant farmer delegates to Canada in 1890. The report of Arthur Daniel etc* (1891);

Canada, Dept of Agriculture, *What farmers say of their personal experience in the Canadian North-West* (1881, 1883, 1884);

Canada, Dept of the Interior, *Canada as it appeared to Scotch agriculturists, 1909-1910* (PAC, RG 76, C-10639, vol. 558, file 807176);

Canada, Dept of the Interior, *Canada as seen through Scottish eyes* (PAC, RG 76, C-10638, vol. 557, file 807080, part 1);

Canada, Dept of the Interior, *Canada's Western Heritage. British Columbia. Its farms, forests, fisheries and fruit* (1909) (PAC, RG 76, C-10621, vol. 530, file 803463);

Canada, Dept of the Interior, *Emigration to North-Western Canada: information for intending settlers* (1893);

Canada, Dept of the Interior, *A guide to homesteaders in Manitoba and the territories of Western Canada* (1900);

Canada, Dept of the Interior, *Homes for millions in Canada's vast agricultural domain of virgin opportunity and infinite resources* (1904);

Canada, Dept of the Interior, *Letters from successful Scottish ploughmen* (1909) (PAC, RG 76, C-10633, vol. 548, file 805711);

Canada, Dept of the Interior, *Prosperity follows settlement* (1911) (PAC, RG 76, C-10638, vol. 556, file 806960);

Canada, Dept of the Interior, *The province of Manitoba and N. West Territory. Information for intending emigrants* (1881);

Canada, Dept of the Interior, *Western Canada and its great resources: the testimony of settlers, farm delegates and high authorities* (1893);

Canada, Dept of the Interior, *What Canada produces. Information for intending emigrants* (1874);

Canadian Pacific Railway Company, *Everyday questions answered in regard to the Canadian West and its opportunities and rewards for farmers* (Montreal, 1889);

Canadian Pacific Railway Company, *Practical hints from farmers in the Canadian North-West* (London, 188-?);

Canadian Pacific Railway Company, *Successful farming in Manitoba. 100 farmers testify* (Winnipeg, 1889);

Canadian Pacific Railway Company, *Western Canada: Manitoba, Assiniboia, Alberta, Saskatchewan and Northern Ontario. How to get there, how to select lands, how to make a home* (Montreal?, 1896);

Fifth annual report of the Oldmill Reformatory School, 1862 (AUL Special Collections, King pamphlet collection, K380/5);

'Justitia', *Emigration and the Malthusian craze in relation to the labourers' position* (1886) (British Library Tracts, 1867-87, 8282. de. 24. 1-18) 5)).

7)   *Theses*

M. D. Harper, 'Emigration from the North-East of Scotland, 1830-1880' (unpublished PhD, Univ. of Aberd., 1984);

M. A. Ormsby, 'A study of the Okanagan Valley of British Columbia' (unpublished MA, Univ. of British Columbia, 1931).

8) *Books*

Aberdeen, Countess of (ed.), *Our Lady of the Sunshine and her international visitors*, (London, 1909); *The musings of a Scottish granny* (London, 1936); *Through Canada with a Kodak* (Edin., 1893);

Aberdeen and Temair, The Marquis and Marchioness of, '*We Twa*': *reminiscences of Lord and Lady Aberdeen* (London, 1926); *More cracks with 'We Twa'* (London, 1929);

Aspdin, J., *Our boys: what shall we do with them? Or emigration the real solution of the problem, showing how youths and young men can be put into the way of obtaining a profitable living for the present and a competence for the future* (Manchester, 1890);

Bagnell, K., *The little immigrants: the orphans who came to Canada* (Toronto, 1980);

Barman, J., *Growing up British in British Columbia: boys in private school* (Vancouver, 1984);

Batt, J. H., *Dr Barnardo: the foster father of 'Nobody's Children'. A record and an interpretation* (London, 1904);

Bealby, J. T., *Fruit farming in British Columbia* (London, 1909);

Begbie, H., *William Booth, founder of the Salvation Army* (London, 1920);

Binnie-Clark, G., *A summer on the Canadian prairie* (London, 1910); *Wheat and women* (London, 1914);

Booth, W. *Emigration and the Salvation Army* (London, 1906); *In Darkest England and the way out* (London, 1890); *The recurring problem of the unemployed. One permanent remedy. Emigration—colonisation* (London, 1906);

Bradley, A. G., *Canada in the twentieth century* (London, 1905);

Brayley, A., *History of the granite industry of New England* (Boston, 1913);

Carrier, N. H. & J. R. Jeffery, *External migration: a study of the available statistics, 1815-1950* (London, 1953: Studies on medical and population subjects, General Register Office, 6);

Carrothers, W. A., *Emigration from the British Isles, with special reference to the development of the overseas dominions* (London, 1965);

Carter, I., *Farm life in Northeast Scotland, 1840-1914: the poor man's country* (Edin., 1979);

Cowan, H., *British emigration to British North America: the first hundred years* (Toronto, 1961);

Dictionary of National Biography (1901-11);

Donaldson, G., *The Scots overseas* (London, 1966);

Drummond, J., (introducer), *Onward and Upward: extracts* (1891-96) *from the magazine of the Onward and Upward Association founded by Lady Aberdeen for the material, mental and moral elevation of women* (Aberd., 1983);

Dunae, P. A., *Gentlemen emigrants: from the British public schools to the Canadian frontier* (Vancouver, 1981);

Fairbank, J., *Booth's boots: social service beginnings in the Salvation Army* (London, 1983);

Galton, F., *Inquiries into human faculty and its development* (London, 1883);

Gammie, A., *A romance of faith: the story of the Orphan Homes of Scotland and the founder William Quarrier* (London, 1936);

Gibbon, J. M., *The Scot in Canada: a run through the Dominion* (Aberd., 1907);
Gray, M., *The fishing industries of Scotland, 1790-1914: a study in regional adaptation* (Oxford, 1978);
Hall, A. D., *A pilgrimage of British farming 1910-12* (London, 1913);
Hammerton, A. J., *Emigrant gentlewomen: genteel poverty and female emigration 1830-1914* (London, 1979);
Harris, R. C. & E. Phillips (eds), *Letters from Windermere 1912-1914* (Vancouver, 1984);
Hedges, J., *Building the Canadian West: the land and colonisation policies of the Canadian Pacific Railway* (New York, 1939);
Holliday, C. W., *The valley of youth* (Caldwell, Idaho, 1948);
Jackel, S. (ed.), *A flannel shirt and liberty: British emigrant gentlewomen in the Canadian West, 1880-1914* (Vancouver, 1982);
Johnston, W. (compiler), *Roll of the graduates of the University of Aberdeen 1860-1900* (Aberd. 1906);
Lamb, D. (Salvation Army), *Notice to passengers* [n.p., n.d.];
Lamb, W. K., *History of the Canadian Pacific Railway* (New York, 1977);
MacDonald, N., *Canada, immigration and colonization 1841-1903* (Aberd., 1966);
McKenzie, F. A., *Waste humanity: being a review of part of the social operations of the Salvation Army in Great Britain* (London, 1909);
Mackintosh, W. A., *Prairie settlement, the geographical setting* (Toronto, 1934);
Malchow, H., *Population pressures: emigration and government in late nineteenth-century Britain* (Palo Alto, Calif., 1979);
Middleton, R. M. (ed.), *The journal of Lady Aberdeen: the Okanagan Valley in the nineties* (Victoria, BC, 1986);
Mitchell, D. & D. Duffy (eds), *Bright sunshine and a brand new country: recollections of the Okanagan Valley 1890-1914* (Victoria, 1979);
Monk, U., *New horizons: a hundred years of women's migration* (London, 1963);
Moyles, R. G., *The blood and fire in Canada: a history of the Salvation Army in the Dominion, 1882-1976* (Toronto, 1977);
Ormsby, M. A., *British Columbia: a history* (Vancouver, 1958);
Pearson, A., *An early history of Coldstream and Lavington* (privately published, 1986);
Pentland, M., *A Bonnie Fechter: the life of Ishbel Marjoribanks, Marchioness of Aberdeen and Temair* (London, 1952);
Records of the Arts Class, 1864-1868 (ed. W. S. Bruce, Aberd., 1912); *1870-1874* (ed. J. Smith & J. F. Cruickshank, 1896); *1878-1882* (ed. R. S. Kemp, R. A. Lendrum & J. S. Shewan, 1927); *1880-1884* (ed. H. Cowie, 1923); *1881-1885* (ed. J. Minto & W. G. Tulloch, 1908); *1884-1888* (ed. H. Gray & J. M. Bulloch, 1938); *1888-1892* (ed. W. Garden, 1902); *1901-1905* (ed. T. Watt & J. M. Robertson, 1951); *1909-1912/13* (ed. J. Dunbar & W. Taylor, 1959);
Redmayne, J. S., *Fruit farming on the 'dry belt' of British Columbia* (London, 1912);
Robinson, J. L. (ed.), *British Columbia* (Toronto, 1972);
Ross, A. *Emigration for women* (London, 1886);
Ross, J., *The power I pledge: being a centenary study of the life of William Quarrier and the work he pioneered* (Glasgow, 1971);
Rye, M. S., *Emigration of educated women* (London, 1861);
Salvation Army, *The new settler: a review of the Salvation Army immigration work for 1906* (Toronto, 1907); *Organised empire migration and settlement* (London, 1930); *Statistics of emigration work, Oct. 1903—31 July 1908* (London, 1908); *The surplus: being a restatement of the emigration policy and methods of the Salvation Army, together with a report on last year's work, and introductory note by General*

Booth and prefatory remarks by representative men on the subject of emigration and colonisation (London, 1909); Salvation Army Year Book (1975);

Saxby, J.. West Nor' West (London, 1890);

Saywell, J. T. (ed.). The Canadian journal of Lady Aberdeen, 1893-1898 (Toronto, 1960);

Shepperson, W. S., British emigration to North America: projects and opinions in the early Victorian period (Oxford, 1957);

Skilling, H. G., Canadian representation abroad: from agency to embassy (Toronto, 1945);

Stubbs, M. H., Friendship's highway: being the history of the Girls' Friendly Society 1875-1925 (London, 1926);

Surtees, U., Sunshine and butterflies: a short history of early fruit ranching in Kelowna (Kelowna, BC, 1979);

Sykes, E. C., A home-help in Canada (London, 1912);

Urquhart, J., The life story of William Quarrier: a romance of faith (Glasgow, 1900);

Wagner, G., Barnardo (London, 1979); Children of the Empire (London, 1982);

Watson, W., Pauperism, vagrancy, crime and industrial education in Aberdeenshire, 1840-1875 (Aberd., 1877);

Watt, T. (compiler), Roll of the graduates of the University of Aberdeen 1901-1925 (Aberd., 1935);

Williams, A. E., Barnardo of Stepney: the father of nobody's children (London, 1943);

Wood, S., The shaping of nineteenth-century Aberdeenshire (Stevenage, 1975);

Woodcock, G., Canada and the Canadians (London, 1970).

9) Articles

Anon., 'The Aberdeen Society' in The Winnipeg Telegram, 8 May 1907, p. 53;

Anon., 'The call of the colonies to educated women' in Chambers' Edinburgh Journal, vol. I, no. 49 (4 Nov. 1911), pp. 783-4;

Anon., 'Canada as a home' in the Westminster Review, vol. 63 (July 1882), pp. 1-28;

Anon., 'Colonial farm pupils' in Chambers', vol. III, no. 112 (20 Feb. 1886), pp. 118-9;

Anon., 'Colonial training for gentlemen's sons' in Chambers', vol. II, no. 95 (24 Oct. 1885), pp. 683-6;

Anon., 'Colonies and colonisation' in West. Rev., vol. 131 (Jan. 1889), pp. 13-25;

Anon., 'Cultured colonisation' in West. Rev., vol. 142, (Dec 1894) pp. 673-80;

Anon., 'Daily life on colonial farms' in Chambers', vol. I, no. 37 (12 Aug. 1911), pp. 591-2;

Anon., 'The economy of emigration' in West. Rev., vol. 125 (Apr. 1886), pp. 515-27;

Anon., 'Farm-pupils in the colonies' in MacMillan's Magazine, vol. LXII (July 1890), pp. 193-8;

Anon., 'Life in Canada' in Chambers', nos 888, 905 & 928 (1 Jan., 30 Apr., 8 Oct. 1881) pp. 9-11, 288, 649-50;

Anon., 'Ready-made Canadian farms by easy payment' in Chambers', vol. XIII, no. 652 (28 May 1910), p. 412;

Anon., 'Real experiences on colonial farms' in Chambers', vol. II, no. 63 (10 Feb. 1912), pp. 172-6;

Anon., 'State-directed colonisation' in West. Rev., vol. 128 (Apr. 1887), pp. 71-82;

Anon., 'Upper class emigration' in Chambers', vol XIII, no. 643 (25 Apr. 1896), pp. 257-9;

Anon., 'The Victorian Order of Nurses in Canada' in The Nursing Times, 6 May 1905, pp. 6-7;

Anon., 'Who should emigrate?' in *Chambers*', vol. III, no. 155 (15 Nov. 1913), pp. 799-800);

Anon., 'Work for willing hands: a practical plan for state-aided emigration' in *Blackwood's Edinburgh Magazine*, vol. 143 (Feb. 1888), pp. 273-8;

Aberdeen, Countess of, 'Household Clubs: an experiment' in *Nineteenth Century*, vol. 31 (Mar. 1892), pp. 391-8;

Barber, M., 'The women Ontario welcomed: immigrant domestics for Ontario homes, 1870-1930' in *Ontario History*, vol. 72, no. 3 (1980), pp. 148-72;

Barman, J., 'British Columbia's gentlemen farmers' in *History Today*, vol. 34 (Apr. 1984), pp. 9-15;

Lord Brabazon, 'State-directed emigration: its necessity' in *Nineteenth Century*, vol. 16 (Nov. 1884), pp. 764-87;

Brice, A., 'Emigration for gentlewomen' in *Nineteenth Century*, vol. 49 (Apr. 1901), pp. 601-10;

Cecil, A., 'The needs of South Africa' in *Nineteenth Century*, vol. 51 (Apr. 1902), pp. 671-92;

Crackenthorpe, M., 'Eugenics as a social force' in *Nineteenth Century*, vol. 63 (June 1908), pp. 962-72;

Feilding, W., 'What shall I do with my son?' in *Nineteenth Century*, vol. 13 (Apr. 1883), pp. 578-86; 'Whither shall I send my son?' in *Nineteenth Century*, vol. 14 (July 1883), pp. 65-77;

Gammie, A., 'The Countess of Aberdeen's work for women' in *Sunday Strand*, Aug. 1906;

Gray, A. W., 'Arthur Booth Knox—pioneer rancher' in *Okanagan Historical Society Reports*, vol. 28 (1964), pp. 74-84;

Gray, M., 'Organisation and growth in the east-coast herring fishing, 1800-1885' in P. L. Payne (ed.), *Studies in Scottish business history* (London, 1967), pp. 187-216;

Gregson, P. B., 'Farming in Alberta' in *Chambers*', vol. XII, no. 618 (2 Oct. 1909), pp. 702-3;

Harris, R. C., 'The simplification of Europe overseas' in *Annals of the Association of American geographers*, vol. 67 no. 4 (Dec. 1977), pp. 469-83;

Hopkins, E., 'The industrial training of pauper and neglected girls' in *Contemporary Review*, vol. XLII (July 1882), pp. 140-54;

Hutchison, M., 'Female emigration to South Africa' in *Nineteenth Century*, vol. 51 (Jan. 1902), pp. 71-87;

Koroscil, P. M., 'A Canadian California' in *Horizon Canada*, vol. 3, no. 30 (Sept. 1985). pp. 710-15; 'Boosterism and the settlement process in the Okanagan Valley, British Columbia, 1890-1914' in D. H. Akenson (ed.), *Canadian papers in rural history*, vol. V (Gananoque, Ont., 1986), pp. 73-103;

Lewthwaite, E., 'Women's work in Western Canada' in *Fortnightly Review*, vol. 70 (Oct. 1901), pp. 709-19;

Lindsay, J. A., 'The case for and against eugenics' in *Nineteenth Century*, vol. 72 (Sept. 1912), pp. 546-57;

Lyttleton, E., 'Eugenics, ethics and religion' in *Nineteenth Century*, vol. 74 (July 1913), pp. 155-63;

MacDonald, S., 'Crofter colonisation in Canada, 1886-1902: the Scottish political background' in *Northern Scotland*, vol. 7, no. 1 (1986), pp. 47-59;

Macgregor, J., 'Canada and the North West as an emigration field' in *Contemporary Review*, vol. XLII (Aug. 1882), pp. 218-36;

Martineau, J., 'Natural emigration' in *Blackwood's*, vol. 146 (July 1889), pp. 36-48;

Ormsby, M. A., 'Agricultural developments in British Columbia' in *Agricultural*

History, vol. 19 (Jan. 1945), pp. 11-20; 'Fruit marketing in the Okanagan Valley of British Columbia' in *Agricultural History*, vol. 9 (1935), pp. 80-97;

Osborn, D., 'The Coldstream Ranch' in *Okanagan Historical Society Reports* (1958), pp. 118-21;

Riis, N., 'The Walhachin myth: a study of settlement abandonment' in *British Columbian Studies*, vol. 17 (Spring 1973), pp. 3-25;

Shackleton, D., 'Lord and Lady Aberdeen: Their Okanagan Ranches' in *The Beaver* (Autumn 1981), pp. 10-18;

Shelton, H. S., 'Eugenics' in *Contemporary Review*, vol. 101 (Jan. 1912), pp. 84-95; 'The political aspects of eugenics' in *Contemporary Review*, vol. 107 (Jan. 1915), pp. 105-12;

Staples, S., 'The emigration of gentlewomen. A woman's word from Natal' in *Nineteenth Century*, vol. 50 (Aug. 1901), pp. 214-21;

Tuke, J. H., 'State aid to emigrants, a reply to Lord Brabazon' in *Nineteenth Century*, vol. 17 (Feb. 1885), pp. 280-96;

Wade, J. 'The "Gigantic Scheme": crofter immigration and deep-sea fisheries development for British Columbia, 1887-1893' in *BC Studies*, no. 53 (Spring 1982), pp. 28-44;

Webber, J. 'Coldstream Municipality' in *Okanagan Historical Society Reports* (1951), pp. 77-85;

Webster, G. J., 'Ranching in the Canadian North-West' in *Chambers'*, vol. VIII, no. 394 (17 June 1905), pp. 453-7;

Whiteley, A. S. 'The peopling of the prairie provinces of Canada' in *The American Journal of Sociology*, vol. 38 (1932), pp. 240-52.

Index

Aberchirder, 29, 70, 204
Aberdeen:
  Australasian agents, 9, 10
  booking agents, 18
  Canadian government agency,
    28–37, 70
  churches:
    Crown Terrace Baptist, 16, 40
    Skene Street Congregational, 73
    Woodside Congregational, 17
  departure of emigrants, 10, 19, 32,
    34, 35, 38, 39–40
  economic depression, 166–9
  feeing markets, 54–5
  fishing industry, 150–1
  granite industry, 161–6
  industrial schools, 188, 206–9, 253,
    268
    Female School of Industry, King
      Street, 207
    Nazareth House, 208
    North Lodge Industrial School,
      204, 268
    Oakbank Industrial School,
      208–9
    Whitehall Industrial School,
      207–8
  Salvation Army agents, 214, 218, 219
  Servants' Training Home, 247, 250,
    256, 267
  tradesmen-emigrants, 161–6, 169–79
  visiting agents, 17, 26, 27, 67, 72, 73,
    120, 164, 233
Aberdeen, Countess (later
  Marchioness) of, 60, 108–9, 184,
  187, 188–9, 244–76
  and female emigration, 231, 250–6
  in Okanagan Valley, 113–17, 118,
    132, 138
Aberdeen, Earl (later Marquess) of, 17,
  52, 53, 86, 108–9, 245, 247, 250–1
  charitable emigration schemes,
    188–9, 252–3, 255
  in Okanagan Valley, 102, 112–35,
    137–9
Aberdeen Association (Winnipeg),
  256–9, 273
Aberdeen Association for Improving
  the Condition of the Poor, 6, 247
Aberdeen City Police Force, 167
Aberdeen Distress Committee, 168–9,
  178, 209
Aberdeen Granite Cutters' Union, 163,
  165–6
Aberdeen Joint Station, 19, 37–8, 167,
  172
Aberdeen Journal, see newspapers
Aberdeen Ladies' Union, 189, 207, 231,
  237, 240, 244, 245, 246–50, 290
  promotes emigration, 250, 253, 255,
    259–76
Aberdeen Music Hall, 17, 69, 260
Aberdeen Poorhouse and
  Reformatory, Oldmill, 196, 206–7
Aberdeen Public Library, 6
Aberdeen Savings Bank, 40, 178
Aberdeen Trades Council, 166, 177
Aberdeen University, 66, 110–11
Aberdeenshire, 13, 26, 34, 35–6, 39,
  52–3, 55–6, 58
Aberdeenshire, Banffshire and
  Kincardineshire Association, 39
Aberdeenshire County Constabulary,
  167
Aberdour, 152
Aboyne, 70, 199, 200

Acton, Rev Robert, 273
Adair, Edward, 218
advertisements, 8, 10, 27
  agricultural, 59, 60–2, 64–74
  for females, 237, 243–4
  fishing, 161
  fraudulent, 11, 75–6, 77, 158, 170–1,
    177
  for 'gentlemen' emigrants, 103,
    106–7, 111–12, 120–1
  Salvation Army, 212, 214, 218–19
  for tradesmen, 162–3, 166, 169–70
agents, 1, 8–10, 12–36, 41, 72–4,
    104–5, 164 (see also booking agents,
    farm delegates)
  and agriculture, 60–74
  criticism of, 13, 14–15, 77, 134–5,
    147, 170–8
  Dominion govt, 12–15, 19–36, 56–7,
    68–71, 160, 208, 288–9
  and female emigrants, 239–41,
    242–4
  offer employment, 18, 19, 27, 73–4,
    162–4, 169–70, 215–16
  provincial, 17–18, 20, 30, 41, 71
  railway company, 70–2
  Salvation Army, 215–16, 218–19
  temporary, 20, 21, 30
agriculture: (see also Board of
    Agriculture)
  depression, 2, 52–6
  emigration, 9–10, 14, 15, 26–7,
    51–101, 86–93, 110, 216, 217, 288,
    289
  fairs, 26, 29, 31, 69–70, 71
  labourers, 14, 15, 18, 34–5, 53–4,
    81–3, 86, 186
agriculturists, 23, 52–76, 177 (see also
    agents, and agriculture, farm
    delegates)
  oppose emigration, 12–13, 75
Alberta, 17, 60, 71, 80, 108–9, 110, 217
  drawbacks, 75, 76, 107
  ranching in, 62, 76, 236
Albertson, Mr, 74
Alford, 17, 39, 54, 56, 72, 73, 108, 111
Alford, Vale of, 119
Allinson, Mr (missionary), 201–2
America, see United States
American Granite Cutters'
  [Inter]national Union, 163

Anderson, C. H. (M.P.), 153
Anderson, Mrs, 199, 200
Anglesey, Marquis of, 136
Anglo-Canadian Farm Pupil
  Association, 104
Arbroath, 19, 35, 109
Archibald, G. G., 32, 35, 36, 69, 161,
    289
  relations with booking agents, 15,
    18, 177–8
Ardclach, 77, 78, 86
Argo, Mr and Mrs, 74
Arthur, R. B., 172, 173, 175, 176–7
artisans, see tradesmen
Aspdin, James, 104, 105, 106
Assiniboia, 63, 80, 110, 195
assisted emigration, 2–4, 8–10, 52, 108,
    291
  charitable schemes, 167–9, 178–9,
    183–230, 231–3, 235, 259–76
assisted passages, 8–10, 18, 73, 161,
    169, 172
  females, 261, 262, 291
  Salvation Army, 219
Auchenblae, 62, 66
Australasia, 5, 8–12, 16, 39, 232,
    291–2
Australia, 5, 40, 53, 208, 212, 274
  and Dr Barnardo, 185, 187
  drawbacks, 11
  female emigrants, 231, 239, 250, 269

Bailey, Colonel, 17
Bain, George, 84
Baldour (Man), 66
Ballater, 17, 69
Banchory, 29, 62, 69
Banff (Scotland), 39, 69, 70, 151, 155,
    200
Banff (Alta), 251
Bannermill, Aberdeen, 166, 247
Barclay, William, 162
Barker, A. C., 199, 200
Barlee, Miss, 262
Barnardo, Stuart, 187
Barnardo, Dr Thomas, 183, 184,
    185–9, 192, 252
  and N.E. Scotland, 188–9
Barnardo's Homes, 185, 188, 206
Barr Colony, 55, 79
Barre (Vt), 162

Barrie, James, 152
Bass, Sir William, 121
Bealby, J. T., 135
Beebe Plain (PQ), 163–5, 166
Begg, Alexander (BC agent), 153–7
Begg, Alexander (fur trader), 72
Belleville (Ont), 185, 189, 192, 205
Bennachie Ranch (Vernon), 119
Bible women, 195, 197, 199
Bilborough, Ellen, 185, 192, 205
Binnie-Clark, Georgina, 235
Birse, Frank, 65–6
Birt, Louisa, 186
Black, George, 88
Black, M. H., 9
Board of Agriculture, *Report on the
  decline of the agricultural population
  of Britain, 1881–1906*, 52 & 95 n.2,
  55
Board of Trade, 5, 15
Boer War, 7, 232, 234
Bonar Bridge, 67
bonus payments, 9, 29, 35, 36
  disputed claims, 14–15, 57–8
  female claimants, 231, 240–1, 243
  Salvation Army, 214
booking agents, 13, 56, 57–8, 166, 169
  criticised, 13, 14–15, 172–7, 239–42,
    275–6
  and female emigrants, 231, 232,
    242–4
  liaise with Canadian agents, 17–19,
    23, 28–9, 30, 31, 34–6, 67–8, 70–1, 72
  and non-Canadian destinations, 9,
    10
  offer employment, 73–4
Booth, William, 184, 185, 209–10, 213,
  218, 219, 253
Botriphnie, 196
Bowie family (Elgin), 84–6
Bowman, Thomas, 151
Boys' Farmer League of Canada, 74
Brabazon, Lord (John Moore-
  Brabazon), 2
Bradley, A. G., 104–5, 106, 111
Braemar Highland Gathering, 29
Brandon (Man), 66, 74, 80, 84
Bredin, A. R., 14, 30
Bricklayers' and Stonemasons' Union
  (America), 163
Bristol, 21, 269

British Columbia, 39, 59, 74, 76, 80
  female emigration, 237, 253, 256,
    267, 270
  fisheries scheme, 152–8
  'gentlemen' emigrants, 102, 103,
    109–39
  Salvation Army emigrants, 215, 217,
    218, 219
British Columbia Development
  Association, 121, 136
British Public Schools Association of
  Canada, 106
British Women's Domestic Guild, 244
British Women's Emigration
  Association, 232, 234, 235, 236, 237,
  239
  and Aberdeen Ladies' Union, 259,
    261, 263, 264, 269, 270
British Women's Temperance
  Association, 250
Broadford Works, Aberdeen, 166
Brockville (Ont), 192
Brown, Alex, 109
Brown, R., 162
Brown, R. G., 65–6
Brown, William, 162
Bruce, George (Aberdeen), 73
Bruce, George (Oldmeldrum), 110
Bruce, J., Collithie, Gartly, 52
Bruce, James, 203
Bruce, John (*AFP*), 16
Bruce, Robert Randolph, 120, 136
Bruce, William, 65
Bruce County (Ont), 205
Buchan, Barbara, 151
Buchan, John, 160
Buchan, Mary, 152
Buchan, William, 57
Buchanhaven, 159
Buckie, 9, 67, 148, 152, 155, 156, 159,
  196
Burges, Agnes, 192
Burgess, A. M., 187
Burgess, James, 72–3
Burghead, 160
Burnett, John, 109

Cairnie, 203
Calan, Rev John, 197
Calgary, 30, 62, 66, 75, 109, 171, 267
California, 7, 128

Campbell, Frederick, 32
Campbell, J. N., 9
Campbell, John, 18
Canada: (*see also* agents, agriculture,
emigrants, emigration, fruit
growing, prairies, unemployment)
agency activity, 15–32, 60–74
agricultural settlement, 51–101
assisted emigration, 167–9, 183–230,
231–3, 235, 259–76
criticism of, 12–13, 74–6, 155–6, 158,
170–8, 242
Department of Agriculture, 20, 21,
27, 66, 96 n.31, 169
Department of Interior, 20, 21, 28,
35, 36, 57, 59, 64–5, 67, 240
Department of Marine and
Fisheries, 160
economic depression, 34, 60, 187,
264
government immigration policies,
19–21
investment in, 102, 108–9, 111,
112–39
restricts immigration, 186, 193
rival destinations, 8–12
Canada North West Land Company,
72
Canada West Land Agency, 107
Canadian Agriculture, Coal and
Colonisation Company, 108
Canadian Colonisation Society, 16
Canadian Council of Women, 245
Canadian Granite Cutters' Union, 165
Canadian High Commission, 20–1, 105
Canadian Land and Ranch Company,
73
Canadian Manufacturers' Association,
237
Canadian National Council of
Women, 261
Canadian National Railway, 90
Canadian Pacific Railway, 60, 64, 90,
108, 243, 251, 261
and Aberdeen Association, 258
advertisements, 61, 71–2
in British Columbia, 112–13, 120–1,
134, 138
promoted by agents, 17, 30, 77, 94
Canterbury (New Zealand), 11
Cape Colony, 7

Cariboo, 112, 131
Carmichael, Mary, 241, 242–3
Carnegie, Andrew, 258
Carnoustie, 9, 27, 109
Cartwright (Man), 91–2
Cascade (BC), 110
Cathcart, Lady Gordon, 2, 253
Catholic Emigration Society, 206
Cawdor, 29, 70
Estate, 77
census, 12–13
Cessnock House, Govan, 189
Ceylon, 110
Chalmers, Margaret, 152
charitable emigration societies, 167–9,
183–206, 209–20, 231–2, 244–87,
290
Chicago World Fair, 127
children, emigration of, see emigrants,
children
Children's Aid Society, 206, 208, 209
Chisholm, Caroline, 231
Christie, George, 73
Christie, Joseph, 241–2
churches, oppose emigration, 13
Church of England Emigration
Society, 232
Clark, W. D., 159
Clarke City (PQ), 172–7
Clayden, Arthur, 10
Cock, James, 177
Coldstream Ranch, 108, 112, 117, 118,
137–8
and BWEA, 236
problems, 121–34, 135
Collie, James, 204
Colonial Emigration Society, 232, 260
Colonial Intelligence League, 232, 234,
236, 275
Colonial Office, 2, 3, 210, 231, 291
Colonial Secretary, 4
Columbia Valley Irrigated Fruit Lands
Company, 120, 136
conducted parties, see protected parties
Conference of Prime Ministers of the
Empire (1921), 291
contractors, 172–9
Cook, Hennessey, 17
Cook, John, 67, 162
coopers, 150, 152, 155, 160, 161
Corbett, Thomas, 189

Courtney, William, 10
Coutts, James, 170
Cowie, Alexander, 159
Cowie, John, 160–1
Cracknell, J. E., 17, 72
Craig, Mr and Mrs, 121
Craik, Dr, 86
crofters, 3, 153, 157, 160, 251, 256
Croll, John, 168, 241
Crossfields (Alta), 109
Crowly, R. W., 159–60
Crown Terrace Baptist Church,
    Aberdeen, 16, 40
Cruden, William, 11
Cruickshank, D. C., 17
Cullen, 55
Culsalmond, 12
Cumming, Alex (pamphleteer), 65–6
Cumming, Alexander (graduate), 110
Cumming, William B., 15, 31–2
Cumming family (Cairnie), 203–4
Cummings, Arthur, 58
Cunningham, Thomas, 128–32, 134,
    135

Dalgety, Andrew and Thomas, 208
Dauphin (Man), 84
Davidson, Alexander, 57
Davidson, James, 88–9
Davidson, Mr (Cairnie), 204
Davidson, R. and J., 18, 19, 40, 55, 71,
    74, 162, 166, 169
Davies, Mrs, 251
defrauding of emigrants, 15, 75, 105–6,
    134–5, 172–7, 241–2
delinquents, 187, 201, 204–5, 206–9,
    240, 241
Denoon, James, 196
Dent, Miss, 254
depopulation, 12–13, 36, 40
deportations, 240
depression, 2–4, 14, 184
    agricultural, 51, 52–6
    Canadian, 34, 60, 187, 264
    commercial, 166–9
    and female emigration, 233–4, 264
    fishing, 149–50, 151–60
    inter-war, 291, 292
    in USA, 165
destitution, see emigrants, destitute
Dickson, Rev Andrew, 198

Dingwall, 29, 70, 108
distributing homes, see receiving
    homes
Dixon, William, 20, 21
Dollar, Mrs W. J., 240
domestic servants, 34, 177
    Australasia, 9, 208
    bonus payments, 14
    charitable emigration schemes, 184,
        232, 233, 242, 243–4
    criticism of, 187, 239, 240–1
    and Lady Aberdeen, 250, 254–5, 256,
        262, 264, 266–7, 268, 272, 275
    and Salvation Army, 212, 216, 217,
        219–20
Dominion Lands Act (1872), 60
Donald, John, 162
Donald, William, 58
Donaldson, Miss, 199
Drummond, Henry, 246
Duff, Mrs (Hatton), 252, 272
Dufferin, Marchioness of, 258
Dufftown, 9, 57, 69
Duffus, 69, 200
Dumfries, 27
Duncan, James, 164
Duncan, Thomas, 9, 27
Dundee, 9, 19
Durris, 73
Duthie, Robert, 196

East End Juvenile Mission, 185
Echt, 15, 118
Edmond, Mrs, 197
Edmonton (Alta), 75, 251
Edwards, Mrs, 241
Elgin, 31, 39, 199, 201, 204, 217
    agency work, 18, 23, 29, 58, 69, 70,
        109
Ellon, 200
    emigration from, 39, 63, 167, 217,
        251
    lectures in, 70, 72, 73
emigrant correspondence, 6, 51–2
    agricultural, 62–6, 119
    Australasian, 11–12
    critical, 13, 74–6, 107–8, 158, 171–2,
        174–6, 177–8, 242
    female, 242, 270–1
    unpublished, 77–94

emigrants:
affluent, 4, 102, 108–12, 120–1, 218, 268, 275
agricultural, 51–101 (*see also* agriculture, emigration)
children, 184, 185–209, 216, 288
illegitimate, 198–202, 204, 207
orphan, 192, 193–6, 283 n.120
complain of deception, 15, 75, 134–5, 172–7, 241–2
criminal, 187, 240
destitute, 151, 152–3, 158–60, 167–9, 184, 185–206, 210–12
disappointed, 13, 74–5, 107–8, 121–37, 147, 155–7, 158, 165, 170–8, 241–2, 289
female, *see* domestic servants, female emigrants
temporary, 7, 155, 160–1, 161–5, 172–7, 178, 288, 289
undesirable, 123, 135–6, 187, 240–1
unemployed, 34, 158, 165, 170, 171, 177–8
Emigrants' Information Office, 4–6, 7, 61, 105, 184, 290, 291
emigration:
and fishing, 151–61
indiscriminate, 104, 170, 231, 265, 273, 275
opposed, 2, 3–4, 12–14, 34, 74–5, 155–8, 162–4, 170, 187, 237–43, 254–5
secondary, 19, 32, 62, 111, 138, 265, 270–1, 288
state-aided, 2–4, 52, 108, 183, 184, 291
statistics, 1, 32–40, 41 n.1 & 2, 49–50, 213, 227–30, 286–7
Emigration Aid Union, 209
Empire Settlement Act, 291, 292
Enzie, 64
Esslemong, P. (M.P.), 153, 155, 156
Esson, Alexander, 119
eugenics, 184–5, 234
Evans, Jane, 271, 272, 273
Ewen, Donald, 58

factory workers, 166, 198, 239, 244, 247, 266
Fairknowe Home, 192
Faithfull, Emily, 260

Fane, Colonel, 107
farm delegates, 13–14, 23, 27, 30, 32, 41, 66–8, 70, 111–12
farmers, *see* agriculturists
farm pupils, 103–6, 107
Farquhar, Bella, 244
Farquhar, William, 65
feeing markets, 29, 31, 54, 56, 69, 70
female emigration, 7–8, 76, 184, 231–87, 288 (*see also* domestic servants)
opposed, 231, 237–43
and Salvation Army, 216, 217, 218, 219–20
female emigration societies, 231–87
Female Middle Class Emigration Society, 232, 233
Female School of Industry, King Street, Aberdeen, *see* Aberdeen, industrial schools
Ferguson, George A., 66
Ferguson, W. S., 76
Fiddes, Agnes, 272
Fife, James, 108
Findlater, Sylvester, 110
Findochty, 152
fish curers, 109, 148–50, 155, 217, 266
fishing industry, 148–51, 268
and emigration, 147, 151–61, 217, 288
Fitzpatrick, Rev Hugh, 199
Fleming, J., 208
Fleming, Peter, 9, 23, 26–7, 68–9
Florence, Peter, 162
Fochabers, 9, 69, 73, 201, 217
Forbes, Bill, 88
Fordyce, 72, 204
Forres, 65, 196, 201
Fort Qu'Appelle (Sask), 110, 254
Fortrose, 29
Fowler, Octavia, 261, 263, 271, 272
Fowler, W. C., 261
Fraser, Alexander, 66
Fraser, Margaret, 151
Fraser, Mrs (Aberdeen), 199
Fraserburgh, 38–9, 55, 167, 197
agents, 35, 109
fishing industry, 148, 152, 153–5, 156, 157, 158, 159
lectures, 29, 69
Fraserburgh Society of Winnipeg, 39

free land grants, *see* homesteads
Friockheim, 213
fruit growing, 105, 109, 110, 218
  and Lord Aberdeen, 102, 112–13,
    117–39
Fuller, W. H., 188
fur traders, 59, 72
Fyvie, 39, 70, 167

Galt, Sir Alexander, 20
Galt (Ont), 186, 189
Garioch, Presbytery of, 12
Garmouth, 55, 69, 111
Gartly, 52, 202–3
Gautier, Madame, 257
gentlemen emigrants, 102–46
  problems of, 103–8, 121–38
Gerrard, A., 171
Gerrard, William, 65–6
Gibb, Dr R. S., 66
Gibbon, John Murray, 61, 138
Gillespie, Mrs, 254
Girls' Friendly Society, 237, 246, 255,
    260, 261
Girls' Home of Welcome (Winnipeg),
    261, 263, 264, 268, 271
Gladstone, William Ewart, 153, 245
Glasgow, 189, 193, 217, 258
  agencies, 6, 21, 23, 27, 28
  emigration via, 19, 37, 38, 215
Godsman, Francis, 55, 72
gold fields, 5, 7, 8, 112, 134
Gordon, Captain, 72
Gordon, Carry, 258
Gordon, John Campbell, *see*
    Aberdeen, Earl of
Gordon, Marjorie (Lady Pentland), 116
Gordon's College, Aberdeen, 64
Graham, Thomas (pamphleteer), 65–6
Grahame, Thomas (agent), 23, 26
Grand Trunk Railway, 170, 171
Granite Cutters' Journal (Aberdeen), 8,
    162, 163, 164, 165
granite tradesmen, 147, 161–6, 289
  South Africa, 7, 8
Grant, Donald, 30
Grant, J. F., 55
Grant, John (agent, Dumfries), 27
Grant, John (Alford and BC), 111
Grantown, 29, 70
Gray, William, 152

Green, George, 187
Gregg, Mrs, 241
Greig, R. B., 66, 73
Grey, Lord, 138
Grieve, Andrew, 67
guidebooks, 5, 60–2, 121, 254 (*see also*
    pamphlets, periodicals)
  *Fruit farming on the 'dry belt' of
    British Columbia*, 121
  The Scot in Canada, 61–2
  Through Canada at harvest time, 61
Guisachan Ranch, 113–17, 118, 122–3,
    127–8, 132, 133–4, 252

Hadden, W., 17
Haddo House Association, 245, 246
Haddo House Club, 246
Haddo House Estate, 251, 252
Hadleigh (Essex), 210, 212, 213
Haggard, W. Rider, 184, 210–12
Halifax (NS), 155, 241, 258
Hall, A. D., 56
Hamilton, L. A., 261
Hardie, James, 65
Harper, Annie, 202–3
Harris, Isle of, 84
Hartney (Man), 65
Hazelbrae Home, 186
Herbert, Sidney, 231
Hickman, W. A., 17
Highland and Agricultural Society, 23,
    26, 66
Highlanders, 149, 153, 268
  in Canada, 3, 251, 253
Highlands and Islands, 1, 3, 23, 31, 84,
    268–9
Hollesley Bay Colonial Training
    College, 106
Holliday, C. W., 134–5
home helps, 236, 237
homesickness, 81, 89, 242
homesteads, 9, 58, 64, 66, 186, 212
  for Highlanders, 3
  problems, 60, 63, 75, 104, 257
  recommended, 68, 88
Hope, James, 52
hop growing, 118, 127, 132
Horseshoe Ranch (North Dakota), 116
Howell, Lieut-Colonel T., 218
Hudson's Bay Company, 59, 86, 112,
    254

Hunter, David, 65
Hunter, Joseph, 111
Hunter, Rev, 198
Huntly, 7, 9, 39
  agents, 18, 29, 67, 70, 72
  Quarrier emigrants, 203, 204, 205
  Salvation Army activities, 217, 219

imperialism, 2, 5–6, 103, 184–5, 209,
  219, 234
Indian Head (Sask), 62, 67
indiscriminate emigration, see
  emigration, indiscriminate
industrial schools, 188, 193, 206–9, 246,
  253, 268
Ingram, Mr (Gartly), 203
Insch, 29, 107
International Congress of Women
  (1899), 253
International Council of Women, 245
Inverallochy, 159, 195
Invergordon, 67, 70
Inverness, 23, 29, 39, 54, 69, 70, 217
Inverness-shire, 34
Inverurie, 9, 39, 67, 69, 73
Iowa Agricultural College, 80
Ireland, 3, 13, 21, 245
Irish, 84, 107, 112, 117
Irish Land Act, 52
irrigation, 118, 119–20, 121, 132, 134,
  136, 137–8

'J.P.', 53
Jackson, Charles, 208
Jamieson, G. A., 121–3
Jamieson, George, 110
Jamieson, Mrs, 173
Johannesburg, 7, 8
Johnson, Archibald, 110
Johnstone, John, 202–3
Joss, Mrs, 243–4
Joss, T., 74
Journeymen Stonecutters' Union of
  North America, 163
Joyce, Ellen, 183, 184
  and BWEA, 232, 235
  and Lady Aberdeen, 251, 254, 255,
    259, 260, 274
Joyce Hostel, Kelowna, 237

Kaiser (Sask), 65

Kalamalka Lake (Long Lake), 116,
  117, 118, 130
  Estate, 130
Kamloops (BC), 121, 216
Kanso (NS), 160
Keith, 9, 29, 39, 69, 70, 199
Keith, James, 66
Kelly, Edward, 127, 128, 130, 134
Kelowna (BC), 105, 112, 113, 119, 237
Kemnay, 52
Kempen, Joseph, 171
Keppernach (Ardclach), 77, 78, 80,
  89–90, 91, 93
Ketchen, A. P., 93
Kibble Reformatory, Paisley, 206
Killarney (Man), 3, 80, 90–1, 93, 184,
  251, 253
Kincardine O'Neil, 73
Kinellar, 200
King, A. S., 158
King Edward, 72
Kingston (Ont), 251
Kintore, 9
Klondyke, 134
Knockando, 84
Knowlton (PQ), 186, 189
Knox, Arthur, 112, 117
Kootenay (BC), 120, 135
Krauss, W. F., 127

Lacombe (Alta), 110
Lamb, David, 169, 213, 215, 216, 218
land development companies, 108, 113,
  117, 119–21, 132, 136–7
landing charge, 34, 57
Lang, Rev Gavin, 72
lantern slides, 16, 26
Laurier, Sir Wilfrid, 216
Lavington (BC), 132
Lawrence, Elspet, 152
Lawrence, G. S., 208
Lawrie family (Elgin), 58
Leal, Winifred, 219
Leaton Training Home, 236, 237, 261
lectures, 16–18, 21, 26–7, 233
  Canadian Pacific Railway, 71, 72–3
  Dominion agents', 12, 26–7, 29–30,
    31–2, 69, 70, 208
  Quarrier, 192
  Queensland, 9
  Salvation Army, 214, 218–19

Lefroy, Grace, 263, 264
Levack, Daniel, 208
Ligertwood, Arthur, 110–11
Lindsay, J. G., 66–7
Lintrathen (Man), 78, 81, 84, 88, 89, 91
Lister-Kaye, Sir John, 108–9, 251
Liverpool, 31, 69, 258
  Canadian Information Office, 20
  emigration via, 27, 37, 63, 215, 250
  receiving hostels, 186, 237
Liverpool Education Authority, 206
Lloydminster (Sask), 55
loans, 9, 71, 168–9, 213–14
  females, 235, 239, 263–4, 269, 292
  Highlanders, 2, 3
London (England), 20, 27, 28, 186, 188,
  237, 258
London (Ont), 263, 270
London Factory Fund, 263–4
London Female Emigration Society,
  232
Longmuir, Alexander, 18–19, 74, 121
Longside, 15, 18, 57, 58
Lonmay, 55, 73, 107, 151, 152, 196
Lorne, Lord, 111, 116
Lorne Park (Ont), 74
Lossiemouth, 148, 159, 160, 195, 196
Lothian, Lord, 153
Low, James, 58
Lucas, Charles, 4
Lumb, Agnes, 80, 91
Lumb, Mrs, 91–2, 93
Lumphanan, 119
Lumsden, James, 61
Lute, George, 65

Macarthur, Duncan, 73
McBean, Andrew, 77, 78, 87, 88, 89–94
McBean, John, 51–2, 77–94
McBean, Margaret, 89, 90, 91, 92–3
McDiarmid, James, 64
McDonald, Anne, 259–63, 265–6, 269,
  271
McDonald, John, 208
McDonald, W. A., 107
McDonald, William, 61
Macduff, 9, 151, 198
MacGillivray, Major John, 219
McIntosh, Agnes, 152
McIntosh, Hugh, 67–8
McIntyre, Malcolm, 17, 72

McIntyre, Rose, 241
MacKay, George G., 113–16, 117–18,
  122–3, 127, 134, 252
MacKay, Rev R., 260
MacKay Bros, 17–18, 71, 72, 121
  conducted party, 19
  criticised, 15
  disputed bonus claims, 58, 240
  offer employment, 74, 161, 162, 166,
    169
McKenzie, Hector, 72
McKerracher, Hugh, 30–1, 32, 70
MacKinnon, Mrs, 261, 271
McLean, Henry, 205
MacLennan, John, 28–31, 172, 173,
  175–6
  and agriculturists, 56–7, 67, 69–70
  and capitalist emigrants, 108, 109
  opposed, 12, 13–14
McLeod (Alta), 67
MacMillan, A. J., 73, 233
MacMillan, Charles, 162
Macnamara, Ella, 219
McOwan, Alexander, 67
MacPherson, Annie, 183, 185–6, 189,
  192, 195, 251
MacPherson, Rev R., 201
MacQueen, Alick and John, 84
McRobb, Alex, 65
Main, Mrs, 173
Maitland, William, 15, 18, 57, 58
Mallandaine, E., 120
Manitoba, 59, 60, 252
  emigrant correspondence, 15, 53, 62,
    64, 65, 77–94
  emigration to, 18–19, 39, 54, 110, 217
  employment, 74
  female settlers, 76, 236, 267, 272
  investment, 106, 107
  lectures, 17, 73
Manitou (Man), 66
Marchmont Home, Brockville (Ont),
  192
Marjoribanks family:
  Archie, 116, 251
  Coutts, 116, 117, 122, 123, 127, 251
  Edward, Lord Tweedmouth, 116
  Ishbel, *see* Aberdeen, Countess of
Marr, Charles, 39
Marshall, Henry, 155
Massie, Henry, 171

Masson, Maggie, 242
Masson, Mr (SPCC, Forres), 201
Maud, 31, 39, 54, 70
May, John, 159
Melbourne, 11
Merry, Rachel, 186
Methlick, 53, 118, 189, 245, 251
Métis, 60
Michie, Mr, 73
middle class emigration, 102–12
  females, 232, 233–7, 239, 254, 275
Middleton, William and Catherine,
  118–19
Midmar Ranch (Vernon), 119
Miller, Mrs F. F., 240
Miller, William, 242
Milne, Rev G. C., 17
Milne, Dr George L., 111
Milne, Isabella, 158
Mintlaw, 70
Minty, Miss, 243
Mitchell, Isabella, 240
Mitchell, John, 63
Moffatt, W. T., 9, 17, 18, 71, 74
Monquhitter, 29
Montana, 7
Montreal, 13, 34, 78, 162–3
  Female Emigrants' Home, 256
  female emigration, 242, 244, 251,
    263, 266, 270, 271, 273
  Victoria Hospital, 267
  Women's Protective Immigration
    Society, 254, 271, 272
Moore, A., 30
Moosejaw (Sask), 19, 267
Morden (Man), 57
Morris (Man), 62
Morrison, George, 65
Mortlach, 110
Murray, H. M., 23, 27, 111, 160
Murray, James, 32
Music Hall, Aberdeen, 17, 69, 260
Mutch, A. E. G., 57
mutual improvement associations, 17
Myles, T. A., 47

Nairn, 29, 51, 67, 69, 70, 73
  Academy, 78
  Mutual Improvement Association,
    78
Nanaimo (Vancouver Island), 109

Napanee (Ont), 240
Napier Commission, 3
Napinka (Man), 84
Natal, 8, 264, 267, 274
National Association for Promoting
  State-Directed Emigration and
  Colonisation, 2–3, 183–4, 253
National Emigration League, 2
National Union of Women Workers,
  245, 247, 274
Nazareth House, Aberdeen, see
  Aberdeen, industrial schools
Nebraska, 152
Nethy Bridge, 23
New Brunswick, 18, 74, 161
Newburgh, 55, 110
New Deer, 39, 54
Newfoundland, 152, 161
New Pitsligo, 162, 200, 202
New South Wales, 8–9, 11, 206, 262,
  264, 292
newspapers, 6, 16, 21, 61, 257
  oppose emigration, 12, 13, 14, 34,
    105, 155–8
  record emigration, 37–40, 152–3
  Aberdeen Free Press, 16, 75, 151
  Aberdeen Journal, 6, 7–8, 9–11
    Aberdeen Association, 257, 258
    agents, 16, 17, 18, 19, 28, 29, 31
    agricultural depression, 52–5
    agricultural emigration, 61, 62–3,
      66, 67, 71–2, 106
    agricultural employment, 73–4
    British Columbia, 111, 120–1
    child emigration, 188, 207, 209
    comments on economic
      depression, 166, 167, 168, 169
    emigrant correspondence, 62–3
    evidence of emigration, 36–40
    farm pupils, 107
    female emigrants, 243, 244, 250,
      271
    fishing industry, 151, 152, 155,
      157, 158, 160
    granite industry, 162, 166
    negative comments, 12–14, 74–5,
      167, 170, 171, 172–7, 178
    Salvation Army, 217, 218, 219
  Banffshire Journal, 78
  Canada Scotsman, 62
  Daily Mail, 13, 167

Evening Express, 166, 173, 241
Evening Gazette, 166, 173, 174, 177,
  242
Fraserburgh Herald, 155–6
Highland News, 78, 86
Inverness Courier, 77
Kelowna Clarion, 110
North Star & Farmers' Chronicle, 29
The Scotsman, 78
Social Gazette, 214
The Times, 56
War Cry, 212, 214
New York, 250, 267, 272
New Zealand, 8, 10, 11–12, 109, 185,
  207–8
Niblett, Mrs H., 17, 32, 244
North British Society, 241
Northern Ocean Ticket Office, 74
North Lodge Industrial School,
  Aberdeen, *see* Aberdeen, industrial
  schools
North of Scotland Bank, 149
North Shore Power Railway and
  Navigation Company, 172
North West Territories, 55, 60, 252, 256
  criticised, 108
  farming, 53, 62, 64, 72, 79
Nova Scotia, 32, 155, 156–7, 241, 258

Oakbank Industrial School, *see*
  Aberdeen, industrial schools
Oak Lake (Man), 84
Okanagan Land and Development
  Company, 113, 117
Okanagan United Growers Ltd, 134
Okanagan Valley, 103, 104, 105, 110
  and female emigrants, 236, 237, 255
  and Lord Aberdeen, 102, 111–39,
  252
Oldmeldrum, 39, 54, 72, 110
Oldmill Poor House and Reformatory,
  Aberdeen, 196, 206–7
Ontario, 107, 110
  agents, 15, 17, 18, 20, 30, 71, 73
  child emigration, 193
  farming, 53, 61, 64, 74
  female emigrants, 240, 267
  and Salvation Army, 216, 217
Ontario Agricultural College (Guelph),
  106

Onward and Upward Association, 245,
  246, 256, 257
Oregon, 7, 119, 128, 134, 208
Orkney, 68, 261
Ottawa, 162, 258, 271
Overseas Settlement Committee, 291

Paisley (Ont), 30
Paisley (Scotland), 206, 217
Palmer, James, 164
pamphlets, 23, 26, 29, 60–1 & 96 n.31
  & n.32, 69, 70, 75, 103, 207, 214,
  235 (*see also* guidebooks,
  periodicals)
  Canada, the land of opportunity, 29
  Canada in a Nutshell, 29
  *Letters from successful Scottish
  ploughmen*, 64–5
  Prosperity follows settlement, 65
Pandosy, Fr Charles, 112
parish assistance, 151–2, 158
Park, John, 55
Parliament, 3, 13
Paton, H. W. J., 17, 36
  advertises employment, 18, 19, 74,
  166
  disputed bonus claims, 57–8
  female emigration, 239–40, 241,
  242–3, 244
  organises lectures, 71, 72
Patterson, Captain William, 218
Paul, E. B., 110
Peace, Walter, 8
Pennie, James, 158
Penticton (BC), 119
periodicals, 61, 76, 77, 103, 234, 235–6,
  257 (*see also* guidebooks,
  pamphlets)
  Chambers' Edinburgh Journal, 61, 76,
  103, 236
  Farmers' Advocate, 79–80, 84, 86–8,
  94
  The Field, 120
  Imperial Colonist, 235–6, 237
  Nineteenth Century, 103
  Nor' West Farmer, 80, 84, 91, 93
  Onward and Upward, 246, 251, 255,
  259
  Review of Reviews, 257
Perrie, James, 64
Peterborough (Ont), 186

Peterhead, 39, 54, 69, 217, 218
  child emigrants, 197, 202, 209
  fishing industry, 148, 150, 151, 152,
    159
Peterhead and Fraserburgh
  Fishermen's Association, 159
Phillips, Caroline, 8, 274
Phillips, Jack and Daisy, 136
pioneering, problems of, 72, 75, 76,
  133, 273
Pittendreigh, James, 74
Poplar Lake (NWT), 64
Portage-La-Prairie (Man), 86, 88, 171
Portessie, 155, 156
Potts, John, 62
prairies, 59–64, 71–2, 77–94, 108, 111,
  134, 158
  market for fruit, 120, 134
  problems of living on, 254, 256–7
Pratt, W. F., 162
Prefontaine, R., 160
premiums, 103–6, 107
Preston, W. T. R., 20–1, 28, 64, 170,
  216
Priddis (Alta), 110
Prince Albert (Sask), 177
Princess Patricia Ranch, 236
protected parties, 18–19, 63, 74
  female 237, 243, 259, 261, 264,
    269–70, 275
  Salvation Army, 214–15, 218
Provincial School of Agriculture,
  Truro, NS, 106
public schoolboys, 102–3, 104, 107, 121
Public Schools Emigration League, 106

Quarrier, Mary, 196
Quarrier, William, 184, 185, 189–206,
  259, 261, 262
Quarrier's Orphan Homes of Scotland,
  189–206
Quebec, 78, 161, 217
  Clarke City, 174, 175
  female emigrants, 251, 252, 259
Queensland, 9–10, 16, 23, 262–3, 264
Queen's Unemployed Fund, 168

Radford, Jane, 243
Rae, John, 66
Raglan County, New Zealand, 10

railway companies, 17, 19, 41, 59, 70–2,
  289 (see also Canadian Pacific
    Railway)
railway workers, 8, 64, 167, 169–70
Rait, Mary, 240
ranching, 76, 104, 106, 108–9, 112, 236
Ranford, H. S., 10
Rathen, 69, 195
Rayne, 12
receiving homes, 185–6, 187, 189, 192,
  193, 209, 272
Red Deer (Alta), 75, 119
Redmayne, J. S., 112, 121
reformatories, 206–9
Regina (Sask), 19, 79, 261
Reid, Ben and Co., 73
Reid, James, 155, 156
Reid family (Alford and BC), 119
Reid Station (PQ), 169
remittance men, 105
rent remissions, 52
rents, 68, 72, 89
Ricardo, W. Crawley, 108, 117, 127,
  134, 138
Riddell, Rev, 195
Riel Rebellion, 60
Ritchie, Charles, 68
Ritchie, M. A., 151
Robbins, Rev Dr John, 219
Robertson, Alexander, 163–4
Robertson, George, 176–7
Robertson, John, 209
Rocking Chair Ranch (Texas), 116, 251
Rocky Mountains, 17, 71
Roman Catholics, 196, 208
Rominisky, Mrs, 241
Rose, George and Hugh, 110
Ross, Adelaide, 232
Rothes, 9, 69, 110, 217
Rothiemay, 69, 73
Rothienorman, 17
Royal Agricultural College,
  Cirencester, 106
Royal Commission on Agricultural
  Depression (1894), 52 & 95 n.3
Royal Commission on the Crofters and
  Cottars of Scotland, see Napier
  Commission
Royal Commission of Enquiry into the
  Self-Governing Dominions (1912),
  290

Royal Scottish Geographical Society,
  17
Rupert's Land Act, 59
Russell, George, 9
Russell (Man), 186
Rye, Maria, 183, 186, 192, 232, 239,
  253

St Andrew's Association, Quebec, 175
St Catherine's (Ont), 267
St Combs, 159
St John (NB), 155
St John's Collegiate Farm, Assiniboia,
  106
Saltcoats (Sask), 3, 68, 184
Salvation Army, 168–9, 175
  agents, 17, 218–19
  assisted emigration schemes, 184,
    185, 206, 209–19, 253
  Migration and Settlement Dept, 213
  Rescue Home, Glasgow, 200
Sandison, Alexander, 171
Sanford, Mrs, 264
Sangster, George, 58
Santa Barbara (Ca), 7
Saskatchewan, 59, 80, 110, 118, 217
  farming, 57, 58, 66, 107
  Saskatoon, 57
Sault St Marie (Ont), 267
Saunders, Professor, 132
Scorgie, Charles, 208
Scott, W. D., 16, 31
Scott, Winifred, 244
Scottish Agricultural Commission, 66,
  73
Scottish Farmers' Alliance, 53
Scottish Mothers' Union, 250
Scottish Women's Emigration
  Committee, 8, 274
Seabank Rescue Home, Aberdeen, 247
Select Committee Enquiry into
  Colonisation (1889), 3, 184
Self Help Emigration Society, 253, 260
Shaftesbury, Lord (Anthony Ashley
  Cooper), 185, 231, 232
share farming, 104
Shaw, Captain, 160
Sheed, John, 67
Shetland, 261
shipping companies:
  Allan Line, 78, 243, 258

Beaver Line, 258
Dominion Line, 258
Donaldson Line, 19, 243
Henderson Line, 23
Shuswap and Okanagan Railway, 113,
  116, 252
Sicamous (BC), 112, 116
Sifton, Clifford, 142 n.42
Sim, Alex, 58
Sim, James, 159
Simpson, Peter, 15
Sinclair, John, 18, 29, 58
Sinclair, Miss, 198
Skene Street Congregational Church,
  Aberdeen, 73
Slains, 73
Slater, James, 159
Small, William, 62
Smart, Miss (Elgin), 201
Smart, Jas A. and Co., 34, 171
Smith, A. G., 110
Smith, Alex and William, 57
Smith, Beecher, 17
Smith, Donald Alexander, see
  Strathcona, Lord
Smith, Duncan, 62
Smith, J. Obed, 16, 29, 31, 34, 36
Smith, John, 152
Smith, Samuel, 186
Smith, William, 258
Smyth, Captain, 215
Snellgrove, Rev Maurice, 188
Society for the Overseas Settlement of
  British Women, 233
soldier-settlers, 7, 234, 291
Somers, George, 175, 176
Souris (Man), 30
South Africa, 5, 7–8, 12, 78, 206
  and Dr Barnardo, 185, 187
  female emigrants, 232, 234, 246, 274
South Africa Colonisation Society,
  232, 234, 245
SPCC, 195, 201, 202, 203, 241
Spence, James, 66
Spottiswoode, Farquhar and Mrs, 207
Sprattsville (Sask), 63
Stanstead Granite Quarry Company,
  163–5
Stark, W., 16
state-aided emigration, see emigration,
  state-aided

statistics, *see* emigration, statistics
Stead, W. T., 246, 257
Stearle, J. W., 163
Stephen, Robert (Peterhead), 159
Stephen, Robert (Fraserburgh), 197
Steven, John, 66
Stewart, Duncan, 111
Stewart, Isabella, 18, 74, 242, 244
Stonehaven, 18, 19, 29, 55, 74, 158, 202, 217
Strachan, James (Aberdeen), 10, 53
Strachan, James (BC), 111
Strachan, Margaret, 152
Strathcona, Lord (Donald Smith), 20, 63, 77
Strichen, 73
strike-breaking, 164–5
Stuart, Alexander, 155, 156
Stuart, Baillie (Inverness), 73
Stuart, W. G., 23, 26–7
Swansons (booking agents), 74
Swift Current (Sask), 73
Sydney, New South Wales, 11
Sykes, Ella, 236

Tain, 29, 67, 70
Tait, John, 58
Tantallon (Sask), 57
Taranaki (New Zealand), 10
Tarland, 18, 73
Tarves, 65, 112, 245
Taylor, Captain, 218
Taylor, Mr, 73
Taylor, Mrs (Napanee), 240
temporary emigration, *see* emigrants, temporary
Texas, 116, 251
Thain, James, 155
Thompson, Alex, 65–6
Thompson, J. C., 166
Thompson Mrs (Toronto), 219
Thompson River, 121
Thomson, Captain, 17, 30, 71
Thomson, C. J., 67
Thomson, Stewart, 63
Thomson, Messrs William and Sons, 258
Three Thousand Families Scheme, 291
ticket agents, *see* booking agents
Tindall, Rev J. J., 200
Tisdale (Sask), 212

Toronto, 63, 75, 155, 168, 209
agriculturists, 55, 58
coopers, 152, 158
female emigrants, 18, 232, 241, 242, 244, 267
Stanstead Company, 163–4
unemployment, 34, 170, 171–2
Townsend, E. R., 107
tradesmen, 7, 147, 148, 166–79, 288, 289
complaints, 13, 170–8
granite, 7, 161–6
and Salvation Army, 217
South Africa, 7–8
trades unions, 162–6
Transvaal, 5, 7
Travellers' Aid Society, 250
Treherne (Man), 64, 272
Troup, George, 173
Troup, James, 173, 174–5, 176
Truro (NS), 106
Tupper, Sir Charles, 20
Turriff, 9, 29, 39, 67, 70, 73, 74

Udny, 55, 197
Unemployed Workmen Act, 168
unemployment, 165, 288
Canadian, 34, 170, 171, 177–8
female, 231, 233, 264
fishermen and, 148–60
'gentlemen', 103
United States, 5, 20, 169, 170, 264
emigration to, 1, 3, 6–7, 40, 54, 208
granite industry, 161–2
and Salvation Army, 210, 217, 218
University of British Columbia, 110
Urquhart, Elgin, 199

Vancouver, 107–8, 109, 110, 113, 162, 215, 251
farming, 55
female emigrants, 261, 270
fishing, 158, 159
unemployment, 34
YWCA, 261
Vancouver Island, 103, 112, 153, 212
Van Horne, W. C., 261
Vernon (BC), 113, 116, 118, 119, 135, 237
jam factory, 118, 123, 127, 131
Vernon, Forbes, 117, 118, 122–3

vessels:
  SS *Cassandra*, 172
  SS *Empress of Ireland*, 37
  SS *Ionian*, 218
  SS *Kensington*, 215, 216
  SS *Lake Ontario*, 273
  SS *Letitia*, 19
  SS *Parisian*, 58, 252, 254
  SS *Sardinian*, 78
  SS *Vancouver*, 215
Victoria (Australia), 291
Victoria (Vancouver Island), 258, 270
Victoria League, 258–9
Victoria Stonecutters' Union, 163
Victorian Order of Nurses, 245
Vining, Rev A. J., 16
Virden (Man), 61, 67

Wadena (Sask), 65
Walhachin, 121, 136–7
Walker, Alex, 107
Walker, Dorothea, 103
Walker, J. Bruce, 23, 28, 31
Walker, Thomas, 74
Walker, William, 15
Wallace, Andrew, 208
warnings, 13, 147
  agriculturists, 74–5, 86–7
  females, 239, 241–2, 254–5
  fishermen, 155–7, 158
  fruit growers, 121–37
  granite workers, 162–5
  public schoolboys, 103–6, 107–8
  unemployment, 170, 171, 177–8
Washington State, 118, 119, 134
Watson, Sheriff William, 245
Watt, Dr (Aberdeen County Medical
  Officer), 36
Webster, G. J., 76
Western Australia, 10, 23, 262, 264, 291
Whitehall Industrial School,
  Aberdeen, *see* Aberdeen, industrial
  schools
Whitehills, 242
White Valley Irrigation and Power
  Company, 132
Whitney, J. P., 216
Whittle, Peter, 208
Wick, 29, 148
Will, Isabella, 152
Will, John, 251

Wilson, Alex, 65–6
Wilson, Jane, 152
Wilson, Mr (Bristol), 269
Windermere Valley (BC), 120–1, 136,
  145 n.103
Wingate, Mr, 70
Winnipeg, 60, 71, 216
  Aberdeen Association, 256–8
  child emigrants, 208, 209
  farming, 11, 66, 78, 84, 110
  female emigrants, 17, 251, 254, 267,
    268, 270, 271, 272
  Girls' Home of Welcome, 261
  lectures, 16, 17, 32
  opportunities for tradesmen, 169
  protected parties, 18–19
  unemployment, 34, 172
Winnipeg Trades and Labour Council,
  170
Witwatersrand, Transvaal, 7
women, *see* female emigrants
Women's Canadian Employment
  Bureau, 243
Women's Christian Association,
  Quebec, 261
Women's Domestic Guild of Canada,
  243–4
Women's Emigration Society, 232
Women's National Health Association
  of Ireland, 245, 275
Women's Protective Immigration
  Society, 251, 259, 261
Woodside, Aberdeen, 167, 198
Woodside Congregational Church,
  Aberdeen, 17
Woolavington, Lord, James
  Buchanan, 132–3
Wooler (Ont), 17
World War I, 3, 11, 32, 136–7, 213, 256,
  274, 290–1
World War II, 292
Wyllie, H. H., 107

YMCA, Aberdeen, 10, 40, 188
YMCA, Lancashire, 17
Young Colonists' Aid Society, 252
YWCA, 237, 246, 261
  Aberdeen, 17, 21
  Toronto, 242
  Vancouver, 261, 271

Zealandia (Sask), 62, 67